STO

ACPL IT[...]

DISCARDED

SO-ATF-969

3 1833 00407

Non-Fic.

AUG 27 '64

INTERNATIONAL
OPERATIONS SIMULATION

with comments on

DESIGN AND USE
OF MANAGEMENT GAMES

INTERNATIONAL OPERATIONS SIMULATION

WITH COMMENTS ON

DESIGN AND USE

OF MANAGEMENT GAMES

by HANS B. THORELLI

Professor of Business Administration, University of Chicago

and ROBERT L. GRAVES

Associate Professor of Applied Mathematics, University of Chicago

Assisted by LLOYD T. HOWELLS

GRADUATE SCHOOL OF BUSINESS
THE UNIVERSITY OF CHICAGO

The Free Press of Glencoe

COLLIER-MACMILLAN LTD., LONDON

Copyright © 1964 by The Free Press of Glencoe
A Division of The Macmillan Company

Printed in the United States of America

All rights in this book are reserved. No part of this book may be used or reproduced in any manner whatsoever without written permission except in the case of materials contained in Appendix IV-VI.

For information, address:

The Free Press of Glencoe

A Division of The Macmillan Company
The Crowell-Collier Publishing Company
60 Fifth Avenue, New York, N.Y., 10011

Collier-Macmillan Canada, Ltd., Toronto, Ontario

DESIGNED BY ANDOR BRAUN

Library of Congress Catalog Card Number: 64-16969

Foreword

1285446

THE CREATION OF NEW KNOWLEDGE is one of the high purposes of a university. The discovery of new truths is generally the product of long and painstaking thought and inquiry, which universities are uniquely equipped to support. Such discoveries are of vital concern to business as to all of our institutions; and research about problems related to business operations is a major function of the Graduate School of Business of the University of Chicago.

At the School, scholars drawn from a variety of disciplines bring their varied talents and methods to bear on special problems and methods of business. Research is of both a basic and applied character; the truth is sought assiduously, wherever the search may lead; and results are available to all who have the capacity and the need to employ them.

Beyond the *discovery of knowledge* lies its *dissemination*. To be effective, knowledge and ideas must move outward from the University to the business community. Results of work at the School must be published and made available.

Almost half a century ago the School inaugurated a significant publications program, with the present volume as its most recent expression.

In *Materials for the Study of Business*, initiated in 1916 under the editorship of Dean Leon Carroll Marshall, and continued by Dean William Homer Spencer, 50 titles were published; many became classics in their fields. In 1938 the series was renamed *Business and Economic Publications;* under the editorship of Dean Spencer, 13 volumes were published. Additionally, in the two decades prior to 1948, the School published some 70 monographs under the general title, *Studies in Business Administration*. The current *Studies in Business* series was initiated under Dean W. Allen Wallis, who edited the first six volumes.

The present volume – eighth in the current series – is devoted to the International Operations Simulation (INTOP) of the University of Chicago. It is the result of a truly interdisciplinary effort – indeed, it may be stated that the mobilization of interdisciplinary forces is a prerequisite to success in this type of project. We hope that this simulation in the management game form will find important applications in research and business planning as well as in management education.

The development of advanced simulations involves considerable cost in skilled manpower and computer time. We are happy, therefore, to be able to present a detailed account to the public, particularly in view of the fact that so few reports of similar depth about progress in this field exist at the present time. The Graduate School of Business will do what it can to facilitate the application of the INTOP simulation by other users.

GEORGE P. SHULTZ, *Dean*
Graduate School of Business
University of Chicago

Preface

TWO FRONTIER AREAS OF BUSINESS ADMINISTRATION are visited in this work. International business operations is one, and management simulation by gaming is the other. The International Operations Simulation (INTOP), around which the book is structured, represents the first application of a sophisticated game design to management problems in overseas operations and in coping with overseas-based competitors in domestic markets. An elementary presentation of the simulation is given in the companion publication, *International Operations Simulation Player's Manual* (The Free Press of Glencoe, 1963). The flexible model around which the simulation is built also permits its ready adaptation to purely domestic business situations without any loss in depth.

The needs of several categories of readers have governed the preparation of this volume. Its prime purpose is to provide all information necessary for anyone interested in the use of the INTOP simulation or in evaluating its varied possibilities. Ample experience from the Executive Program as well as standard MBA courses in the Graduate School of Business at the University of Chicago indicates that the simulation has considerable potential as an instrument of *management development* at the level of overall policy and organization as well as in such functional areas as marketing, finance and production. Participation seems to stimulate business executives as much as graduate students. But in addition INTOP was deliberately designed to serve as an instrument of *research*. We had particularly in mind the simulation of internationally and otherwise dispersed (not necessarily decentralized) business operations and markets. However, the relative complexity of the model, which effectively forces a division of labor among decision-makers, also makes the game eminently suitable for research on leadership and task-oriented groups. The uses of simulation by gaming for *business planning* purposes remain relatively unexplored, although work is in progress in this area at several institutions. As suggested in an appendix to the present volume we feel that a simulation of the INTOP variety might prove useful both in trying out different types of organization in diversified concerns and as an educational instrument in the implementation of organizational change.

A major deficiency of existing literature on management simulations is its scant attention to the varied problems of game administration and to the integration of games in the broad context of educational programs or particular academic courses. An important aim of this book is to make a pioneer effort in these areas. We have been stimulated in this work by our conviction that to derive maximum benefit from a management simulation one must use it in an integrated fashion with other educational techniques, such as lectures and independent study, the aim being to achieve a degree of closure between theory, simulation and business practice. The book should be of some value to educators interested in making such use of simulation exercises whether or not these readers expect to become personally engaged in the routine of game administration. As most of the problems of administration are not unique to INTOP, the book should interest administrators of other games as well.

A secondary purpose is to furnish some guideposts and a source of inspiration for designers of other management simulations. While a considerable number of manual as well as computerized games are already in existence, this rapidly developing field is still in its infancy. Judging by our own jagged learning experience, future creators in this field should stand to gain by all attempts at systematic exposition of present efforts. Unfortunately, most literature in the past has been either completely detached from any particular construct and limited in its practical usefulness on this ground, or on the other hand directed only to an enumeration of player's rules with or without cryptic admonitions to the administrator. Due to the flexibility and modular design of INTOP it is our hope that some game builders will find it useful to make direct application of some of its features. Other designers, by contrast, may find here points of departure or pitfalls to be avoided. Even so, our labor will not be in vain.

As the book is written with a variety of readers in mind, a few words of guidance may be in order. The general reader – be he an executive or an educator – will find a broad discussion of the purpose and uses of management games and the claims made by their proponents in the introductory chapter. If he is interested in the problems involved in the design and administration of complex simulations he will also address himself to the treatment of Economic Models and Programming Approaches (Chapter 3) and at least summarily to the chapter on Game Administration (Chapter 4). If he is not versed in mathematics he may prefer the overall presentation of the INTOP simulation in Chapters 2 and 5.

The prospective *user* of the International Operations Simulation in its standard version may confine himself to Chapters 2 (presentation) and 4 (administration) and those parts of the appendix to which reference is made in these chapters. The administrator – or his assistant – should also have some understanding of computer operations and the methods of changing program parameters or individual company outputs (the first two sections of Chapter 5). There is no need for a user or business planner to go through the detailed mathematical treatment in Chapter 3.

Literally scores of different games may be staged by using the basic INTOP model: international and domestic, aimed at general management and functional management, with few teams and with dozens of teams. Readers having other applications in mind than those which may be accommodated by the standard version of the simulation will probably wish to consult Chapter 6, A Modular, Multi-Purpose Simulation.

It is more difficult to advise *the game designer, the researcher* and *the business planner*. Beyond Chapters 1 and 3 (or 2, if a non-mathematical treatment is preferred) the choice will presumably be dependent on a variety of considerations about which it is difficult to generalize. The simple outline of the book should prove helpful here. As we are aware that different people are likely to read different parts of the work, a certain amount of overlap between parts was found desirable.

The reader with some background experience of management games will recognize that INTOP possesses some unusual features in addition to being the first simulation oriented to international business problems. The simulation forces participants into a stream of truly entrepreneurial decisions of business philosophy and objectives, as distinct from the strategy-tactics routine to which most other games quickly settle down. It is sufficiently complex to make good internal organization most desirable, and the data furnished the teams are presented in such a form as to make possible deliberate experimentation with different types of organization structures and decision-making processes. In addition, the simulation permits inter-company negotiations covering a variety of transactions (sales, loans, patent licenses). The presence of this feature also means that there is literally no limit (other than that of practicality) on the number of decisions which a team may make during a given session. The complexity of the basic model notwithstanding, the full-blown exercise may accommodate as many as 25 teams with a total of 125 participants or more. On the other hand, a viable game may be staged with as few as three or four teams with a total of ten or twelve participants. Some variants of the simulation permit up to 72 teams.

One of the major characteristics of INTOP is its modular design and the extraordinary degree of flexibility within each programmed section of the model. This feature literally permits each administrator to write his own bill of particulars. As demonstrated in Chapter 5, any administrator by merely filling out a form — requiring no familiarity with computers — can change any parameters of the standard model, such as size of markets, manufacturing costs, corporate tax rates, demand elasticities, etc. Whatever changes are to be made will depend on the purpose which the simulation is intended to serve in each instance.

The INTOP *Player's Manual* is published separately. While Chapter 2 of the present volume contains much of the same information, the reader is likely to find it convenient to have a copy of the manual at hand. This book has been written in such a manner that reading it will not give a participant in the simulation an undue advantage. What minor advantage he may gain may be a reasonable reward for the effort. Program tapes are freely available at cost, as are decision forms and other supplementary materials. Further information about the simulation may be obtained by writing the Graduate School of Business of the University of Chicago, Chicago 37, Illinois. (The *Player's Manual* should be ordered through a bookstore.)

The standard INTOP program is written in the FORTRAN computer language. Past runs of this program have made use of IBM 7090 machines in Europe and the United States. In principle any computer which will take FORTRAN programs and is equipped with large-scale memory should be able to accommodate the simulation. The program also exists in a version dovetailed to Remington Rand Univac computers. Due to the "bilingual" character of the program we have avoided tying the main discussion to any specific computer. Certain appendices are FORTRAN-oriented. Mimeographed instructions are available on technical details differing in the Univac version.

The International Operations Simulation is a product of research at the Graduate School of Business of the University of Chicago. It was developed by a group consisting of the undersigned and Lloyd T. Howells. Hans B. Thorelli initiated the project and served as the coordinator of our efforts. Robert L. Graves assisted by Howells is primarily responsible for the design of underlying mathematical models, although teamwork of all members of the group was clearly required. As regards the authorship of the present volume it is to be noted that Thorelli wrote Chapters 1, 2, 4 and 6 and, assisted by Howells, Chapter 5. Graves wrote Chapter 3. For the project as a whole the members of the group naturally accept joint responsibility.

Several faculty members of the School have contributed valuable ideas; we especially wish to thank Professors Franklin B. Evans, Lawrence Fisher, Charles T. Horngren, John E. Jeuck and George H. Sorter. Mr. Barry Brown elegantly handled a myriad of programming problems on the main model on the Univac, and Mr. Ken Orr capably handled the programming of the marketing research part. Of the several programming contributions in the FORTRAN translation work we wish to mention especially those of Mr. David C. Kleinman and Mr. Glen Buckles. Sarah Thorelli has handled professionally the editing and proofreading work, and also assisted in many ways during the three years of research and development.

We are grateful to the Graduate School of Business for encouragement as well as for funds from General Electric Company research grants for programmers and computer operations. Special thanks are due to Professor Alex Orden for unstinting moral support and high-priority service on the Univac equipment on which the model was originally developed, as well as to the University of Chicago Computation Center for similar IBM 7090 service during the FORTRAN program translation phase. A good part of the 7090 time was made available under a general grant from the National Science Foundation to the University.

Hans B. Thorelli
Robert L. Graves

Haskell Hall
University of Chicago
May 1964

Contents

Diagrams, Forms, Graphs, Lists and Tables

CONTENTS

INTERNATIONAL OPERATIONS SIMULATION

with comments on

DESIGN AND USE
OF MANAGEMENT GAMES

Chapter **1**

Of Games and Game Design

LIKE so many prior arrivals on the educational scene – lectures, seminars and case discussions among them – management games are here to stay. This statement can now be made without any doubt; yet there continues to linger in the minds of many much doubt and many questions concerning the functions, construction and effects of games and their proper place in various curricula as well as in research. The present work makes no pretense at answering all questions or trying to allay all doubts. However, in this introductory chapter we shall discuss basic problems of application and design in a manner which may assist the reader with less practical experience of gaming to form his own reasoned views.

Later chapters are devoted to the International Operations Simulation (INTOP), representative of a small but growing class of fairly complex general management games which we consider particularly suited to executive development in corporations (particularly but not exclusively those engaged in international business), to business school training at functional as well as general business policy and organization levels and to a variety of research and business planning uses.

Games as simulation and training devices originated with the military, who for several decades were the only interested party. The last fifteen years have witnessed the emergence of business games as well as diplomacy and international relations games,[1] and simulation by gaming is rapidly finding many other applications,[2] ranging from

[1] Cf. Harold Guetzkow, ed., *Simulation in International Relations* (1963).

[2] Cf., e.g., the bibliography of some recent games *infra*, 396ff.

the planning of state university systems via city governmental affairs to the determinants of public opinion. No particular degree of familiarity with these developments is required here; neither shall we attempt a systematic analysis of an already oft-surveyed and rapidly burgeoning literature.[3] Pointers from our own experience as participants in and administrators and designers of management games will, however, be used to highlight the discussion.[4]

1. Simulation by Gaming: Purposes of Games

GAMES REPRESENT a form of simulation.[5] The concept of simulation is not without its ambiguities in either popular or scientific parlance.[6] We find it natural and useful to think of simulation as "a technique for studying the behavior of complex systems."[7] Thus, it involves the use of a model of reality comprising a bundle of interrelated variables, and the manipulation and/or observation of the behavior of this system over time. More often than not it is impossible to represent in the simulation *all* variables at play in reality and to assign them their proper relative weights. The proximate test of the value of simulation is whether by such means we increase our general understanding of the real system; the ultimate test is whether simula-

---

3 Cf. for general background American Management Association, *Simulation and Gaming: A Symposium* (AMA Management Report No. 55, 1961, hereafter cited as AMA), especially the contribution by Lois Stewart, "A Survey of Business Games," 16–26; Joel M. Kibbee, Clifford J. Craft and Burt Nanus, *Management Games — A New Technique for Executive Development* (1961, hereafter cited as Kibbee-Craft-Nanus); *Proceedings of the Conference on Business Games as Teaching Devices Sponsored by the Ford Foundation and School of Business Administration, Tulane University*, edited by William R. Dill, James R. Jackson and James W. Sweeney (1961); and Kalman J. Cohen and Eric Rhenman, "The Role of Management Games in Education and Research," 7 *Management Science* (Jan. 1961), 131–66. Note also Paul S. Greenlaw, Lowell W. Herron and Richard H. Rawdon, *Business Simulation* (1962, hereafter cited as Greenlaw-Herron-Rawdon).

4 The collective experience of the authors involves participation in a dozen different manual and computerized games, and administration of six or seven of these. In addition before

the development of INTOP was undertaken, Graves had designed a stock-market addition to the UCLA Game II. Thorelli completely revised the well-known McKinsey game, published by G. R. Andlinger, "Business Games — Play One," 36 *Harvard Business Review* (Mar.-Apr. 1958), 115–25. In its original form this manually administered game failed to include price as a variable, surely a crucial limitation in an ostensibly marketing-oriented game.

5 "A business simulation or game may be defined as a *sequential decision-making exercise structured around a model of a business operation, in which participants assume the role of managing the simulated operation.*" Greenlaw-Herron-Rawdon, 5. Italics in the original.

6 It is interesting to note that Webster's Unabridged Dictionary as late as the 1956 printing of the Second Edition speaks of simulation as an "act of simulating, or assuming an appearance which is feigned, or not true; pretense or profession meant to deceive."

7 Kalman J. Cohen, "Two Approaches to Computer Simulation" in Academy of Management, *Proceedings of Annual Meeting, Dec. 28, 1960* (Tempe, Ariz., 1961), 36–41, 36.

tion permits us to predict developments in the realistic situation with greater accuracy.

Games are generally designed to meet only the more modest of these tests; that is, they purport to portray reality only in a broad and general way. In this one respect management games resemble the classical economic theory of the firm, although the more complex game simulations at least incorporate a great many more variables, economic as well as institutional, than one would expect to find in any model based on that theory. Game designers usually have not been interested in building a "computerized copy" of reality in any given industry,[8] and we think for good reason. At least at the present stage of the art, the number of variables and the complexity of interaction involved generally speak in favor of highly specialized, non-game models for this more sophisticated but typically also more narrowly applicable species of simulation.[9]

For a more detailed discussion of the purposes of business management games — and we shall focus on such games — it is convenient to distinguish three somewhat separate areas of application, namely, education, research and business planning.

A. *Education*

In the area of education three major types of purposes may be distinguished: to increase the student's understanding of business problems at the functional level (marketing, production, etc.), of the inescapable interrelatedness of the functions and parts of a business and of the various firms in an industry, and to broaden the grasp of, and provide some practical training in, the problems of organization, policy and decision-making processes in general. Many games are designed to provide exclusive or special emphasis on a certain business function, such as marketing or finance. In these simulation exercises students get an opportunity to grapple with such functional and sub-functional problems as market research and forecasting, sales management, pricing, physical distribution, advertising, or investment policy, procurement of financial resources, budgeting and financial control. While the details of these problems will differ from any specific situation facing the students in real life, the principal elements, their *general* linkage and their *dynamics* will be sufficiently similar to offer the students a taste closer to "the real thing" than that of almost

[8] We say "computerized" as it is felt that the inherent limitations of manual game models in the area of information processing effectively preclude their use for predictive purposes.

[9] A most interesting notion applied by George J. Feeney, then of the General Electric Company, is that of simulating a marketing management game as an assist to decision-making by the players. In this experiment one of the teams is provided with a subsidiary computer, which on the basis of no more than data about the history of the game apparently is capable of predicting the results of proposed future strategies better than the average team. Cf. Martin Shubik, "Simulation of the Industry and the Firm," 50 *American Economic Review* (Dec. 1960), 908–19.

any other potion educators are in a position to offer.

Even quite simple game models do show up the inevitable inter-connectedness between various parts of business. The risks of narrow-minded specialization, "localism," and suboptimization[10] are usually demonstrated quite forcefully and in surprisingly realistic ways. Judging by our experience in the Executive Program of the Graduate School of Business at Chicago and by information from several corporate development programs, this facet of business games seems especially pertinent in training at the middle management level.

The more complex games will do what the simpler games do in the functional and inter-functional areas. In addition, they are generally vastly superior instruments for top management and leadership training in general, due to their automatic emphasis on problems of organization, policy and decision-making processes. The number of decisions to be made, and the amount of information processing required for reasonably intelligent decisions, is so great as to confront the teams with the urgency of a sensible division of labor, the desirability of long-range planning and the merits of applying a variety of techniques of management analysis such as cash-flow budgeting and rate-of-return analysis. The team leader is given an excellent opportunity for sensitivity training, and for all members an experience in group decision-making and action is provided in which they get a chance to observe and improve their own "style" in an informal, if rarely relaxed, organized interaction context.[11] An incidental payoff of participation in a complex game is that it forces players to learn how to live with computers. Whatever the effects of computerization in business will be, we will see more of it. Team members will learn, usually the hard way, that generally speaking computers are characterized by inexorable logic paired with complete lack of judgment.[12] It turns out to be quite a strain on untrained minds to write computer instructions and decision rules under these highly realistic constraints.

B. *Research*

There can be no doubt that management games hold a vast potential as instruments and settings for research. This is especially

[10] Cf. Hans B. Thorelli, "The Tantalizing Concept of Productivity," 4 *American Behavioral Scientist* (Nov. 1960), 6–11, and *Productivity Measurement Review* (Aug.-Nov. 1960), 1–8.

[11] To the extent that creativity is a characteristic which may be acquired it also seems likely that complex yet flexible games may be highly useful in creativity training. This is especially true in a simulation exercise such as INTOP where the number of truly entrepreneurial alternatives available at any given time is considerable – indeed, knows no definite limit. If a simulation is run for such a purpose the administrator should be prepared to lend his assistance toward the implementation of even fairly wild schemes going beyond the standard framework of the game, such as loans between the teams with profit-sharing clauses attached, factory leases, certain types of tax-dodging behavior, etc.

[12] Progress in computer simulation of human learning and judgmental processes has not yet proceeded far enough to permit more than experimental application in the gaming area.

true in two fields, economics and marketing constituting one and organization theory and behavioral sciences the other. As to economics and marketing, the discussion about the most efficacious research applications seems to have swung like a pendulum between two extremes. Some persons seem to think that designing game models resembling as closely as possible the constructs of classical economics is highly desirable, presumably with a view to "check out" these as a prelude to their ultimate application to real-life situations. Apart from the nagging question of whether we can ever hope to transplant an essentially static theory into something practically applicable even in a highly structured game environment, there is the challenge of using a new instrument of research inductively rather than deductively. In other words, by incorporating institutional and behavioral features of real-life markets into our game models, we may begin to learn things about the relationships between market structure and market strategy that in a new light, which is sorely needed.
we never knew before. At least we may begin to view these relationships

Several other avenues of economic research suggest themselves. One might try to gauge the impact of changes in public policy – especially with regard to antitrust and tax legislation and international trade policy – in terms of both aggregate effect on behavior and reaction times. It is further most likely that our understanding of decision-making under conditions of uncertainty and risk will be increased by experimentation with varying degrees of such conditions in controlled game situations.[13] Certainly such endeavors would represent a marked step forward from most highly artificial and simple experiments in gambling and choice behavior of the past. There are also the great new vistas opened by the emerging *behavioral* theory of the firm, which focuses on the impact of institutional and organizational factors on business decision-making within firms.[14] There is already enough empirical evidence at hand to assert with sublime confidence that the organization structure and information-handling processes of the firm greatly influence its specific decisions in such vital areas as price, output, equipment acquisitions, advertising and so on. Here we find the vital cross-link from economic theory to organization theory and behavioral science.

Simulations may also find applications in research aimed at the industry rather than the firm. Thus, some of the more sophisticated

[13] The degree of risk may be systematically varied by introducing environmental events which participants have been warned may occur as well as by differentiating the resource allocation to teams. Uncertainty may be studied by systematically varying the amount, reliability and timeliness of information feedback to the teams from zero to well beyond the limit of data digestible within a given time constraint.

[14] Cf. R. M. Alt, "The Internal Organization of the Firm and Price Formation: An Illustrative Case," 63 *Quarterly Journal of Economics* (Feb. 1949), 92–110. See also E. T. Penrose, *The Theory of the Growth of the Firm* (1959) and R. M. Cyert, E. A. Feigenbaum and J. G. March, "Models in a Behavioral Theory of the Firm," 2 *Behavioral Science* (Apr. 1959), 81–95.

games could well be used in elementary simulations of market structures of widely different characteristics as regards production and demand functions, degree of competition and number of participating companies.

The research opportunities presented by management games in the area of organization structure and behavior seem almost unlimited. Again it must be kept in mind, however, that only games with a certain minimum level of complexity will meet the criterion of reasonable realism, both in terms of portraying real-life institutional and economic conditions and being conducive to realistic division of labor among team members. If these conditions are fulfilled, a myriad of research projects which have been carried out under the common label of "small-group research" may be replicated in an environment which in many instances would represent a clear-cut advance in degree of realism. If the results achieved under small-group laboratory conditions stand up in experiments repeated in complex games, this would seem to support at least a preliminary rebuttal to the argument that what we learn in the small-group laboratory may not be at all transferable into the realm of reality. Game simulation may also be used heuristically to generate new hypotheses for research on actual organizations.

Some of the most interesting research perspectives are now opening as regards formal organization and the interaction of formal and informal in organization. Under what circumstances in terms of personnel, objectives and environmental conditions should structural elements emphasize purpose (product), clientele, function and/or geographical area? What environmental circumstances favor delegation of decision-making authority? How are structure and behavior influenced by variations in accounting systems?[15] What are the characteristics of those groups which will stand up better under time pressure than others? What is the effect of a new member on an on-going organization? How will various restrictions on information flow affect team performance? These are only some of the many questions which we may hope to shed new light on.[16]

The psychologist, the sociologist and the organization theorist alike will be interested in exploring the emergence and exercise of leadership in initially unstructured but heavily task-oriented groups. By changing parameters in terms of the game task environment, number and composition of team members and their assignments, we may also

[15] Preliminary experience with IN-TOP indicates that the way decisions and accounts are grouped on input and output data sheets in the simulation has a noticeable effect on the structuring propensities of teams free to choose their own organizational arrangements.

[16] For further examples see Cohen-Rhenman, *op. cit.*, 164. See also John L. Kennedy, James E. Durkin and Fred-erick R. Kling, "Growing Synthetic Organisms in Synthetic Environments" (mimeographed address at the 1960 Meeting of the Eastern Psychological Association), accounting for fascinating, if as yet highly preliminary, work in the Department of Psychology at Princeton University, and excellent, if highly critical, comments by Morton Deutsch on the same paper. The Princeton experiments make use of a stock-market game, "SOBIG."

gain new insight into what is really meant by the assertion that leadership is largely situationally conditioned. While it is certainly premature to make definite statements in this regard it is also likely that certain types of personality tests based on performance in management games will be developed.[17]

Bargaining and game theory constitute another research area of multi-disciplinary interest in which simulations permitting meaningful inter-team transactions hold great promise. Simulation-based research may, for example, help test the hypothesis once propounded by Harold Guetzkow that the more adequately the members of a group envision the techniques of inter-group collaboration as means to their ends, the greater the tendency to move toward collaboration.

Clearly, our brief survey has suggested only a few of the great many research opportunities presented by management games. It is also clear that most or all projects suggested could be carried out by alternate means. Some can, and undoubtedly will, be executed on real-life businesses, in which case the question of realism, at least, need no longer bother the researcher. But research on real-life organizations, especially if it involves experimentation, is generally extremely costly – costly in terms of time, in terms of direct expense involved and frequently also in terms of upset or disturbed human relations. In all these respects working in the game environment represents a distinct advantage. On the other hand, a sophisticated management game has the advantage of much greater realism (subjective if not objective) than the simplified situations employed in much small-group research in the past.

Considering the vast potential use of management games for research purposes, one may legitimately ask why the accomplishments to date (even including the respectable work at Carnegie Institute of Technology) are but quite modest. A number of reasons explain this situation. The most powerful one is probably that these games are so new. The main effort of researchers in the past has been to conceive of game models and then to try to make them work. The latter part of the effort is not to be underestimated, as making a complex game of the type needed for much economic and organizational research really "fly" will often involve several man-years of work by highly qualified people. Neither can we lose sight of the fact that the *prime* motivation behind the development of new games in the past has been their use for educational purposes. An often heard observation on the campus is that the exigencies of educational application will tend to hold back

---

[17] Note that "performance" here should probably not be taken as synonymous with "winning the game" in terms of either "objective" criteria (profitability, asset growth, etc.) or perhaps even subjective ones (i.e., each team will have its own levels of aspiration). We would rather think that indications of quality of play, cre- ativity, risk-willingness, consistency, etc. would be of greater interest.

The MATRIX game developed by the Procter and Gamble Company is used as a self-service aptitude test in production management by executive trainees. This game will be described in an American Management Association monograph.

the use of games for research in the absence of a clear-cut policy to the contrary.

c. *Business Planning*

The third major area of application of management games is business planning. For present purposes it seems natural to look upon this as an area of applied research, as opposed to research of a more fundamental nature just discussed. Again, a distinction seems useful (even if in the end artificial) between simulation of markets and economic systems on the one hand and administrative systems on the other. Simulation of the former kind typically aims at the examination of alternate specific production, finance, marketing, etc., policies of the firm under game environmental circumstances which in *some* important respects portray real markets. An excellent example is the Pitt-Amstan Simulator, a game patterned on the distribution of plumbing and hardware supplies. Participants seek to achieve an "optimal" allocation of their resources in vying for the trade of several hundred individually designated customers with different needs, trade status and buying criteria. While the variations between various customer groups in the game has always reflected the diversity found in actual markets in a general way, we understand that the "Simulator" is now being modified to incorporate all "relevant" characteristics of all individual Amstan customers.[18]

For the near future at least management games as instruments of business planning are likely to find even greater use in the simulation of administrative systems. A number of production scheduling and inventory management games already illustrate this. However, we are also thinking of such major problem areas as overall organization structure, information processing and communications procedures.[19] This point is discussed at some length in A Note on Organization Simulation by Gaming in Appendix VII.

The beginning made in utilizing management games in business planning is even more modest than in the area of more fundamental research. The two areas may be expected to feed into each other in a

[18] Whether the Pitt-Amstan Simulator will actually be usable as a *game* – or "only" as a specialized, non-game planning instrument – after these modifications remains to be seen. We still have some way to go before we can justifiably use Greenlaw-Herron-Rawdon's term "high-fidelity simulation" about a management game.

[19] The writer a few years ago served as a consultant to a Chicago area steel company having problems in the management of innovation, which showed an unpleasant tendency to "fall between the chairs" of R & D, marketing and production. Confronted by this problem today he might well suggest that an excellent means of clarifying the issues involved for the executives concerned – including the company president – would be to let them participate as a team in a run of the International Operations Simulation, each man preferably in a job occupied by one of the other three in their daily work. Of course not *all* kinds of organization problems would lend themselves to this kind of demonstration; it so happens that INTOP does incorporate the management of innovation.

cumulative process in the future. Meanwhile, the greatest and prob-ably most lasting value of simulation by gaming in business planning is that it affords management a fast and relatively low-cost opportunity to try out new ideas on a preliminary basis in a non-committal setting, and in doing so to uncover a number of unforeseen factors and ancil-lary ideas which should be taken into consideration in making the original proposal a more viable one when ultimately translated into practice.

2.   Types of Games

A GREAT MANY TYPES of management games may be distin-guished by purpose, manner of play and mode of administration.

A. Specific Purpose

We have just discussed the fact that from a general point of view business games may serve educational, research or business planning purposes. Most games in the past have been restricted to serve educational ends; presently an increasing number are designed for research and business planning as well. Although the emphasis will differ from one game to another, few if any games are confined to research or business planning alone. It seems legitimate to expect a growing specialization in this regard in the future although there will always be a market for multi-purpose games, if nothing else for economic reasons.

Another useful way of distinguishing among the purposes of games is based on the subject matter vs. the process of decision-mak-ing. A majority of games focus on subject matter exclusively; none neglect it completely. General management games incorporate a more or less well-balanced mix of the major functions of the business, such as marketing, research and development, finance and production (less often: procurement, employee relations). A vital purpose of these games is to provide an overall perspective and to improve the "feel" of the players for the interrelatedness of the various functions.

On the other hand, functional games, of which marketing games are perhaps most typical, are confined largely to problems within a relatively narrow area. The game designers make some effort to relate the function in question to other aspects of the business; often this part of such games seems rather artificial. The inherent advantage of functional games is that they can pry far deeper into the particular function than is possible in general games of corresponding com-plexity. With reference to subject matter there are also a number of highly specialized games at the subfunctional level, devoted to such problems as production scheduling, inventory control or the logistics of the firm. Frequently the purpose here is to train the students in a specific problem-solving technique, such as the application of a given inventory control formula.

As far as we know, no management game as yet has been designed to concentrate on the process of decision-making to the extent of making the contents of decisions a secondary matter. While such an emphasis can certainly be achieved in non-competitive simulations, and has been characteristic of group-dynamics research involving competition between somewhat task-oriented small groups, we frankly doubt the feasibility of building a reasonably realistic management game involving the simulation of competitive interaction between firms where the decisions as such become a marginal matter.[20] Nevertheless, a few highly complex management games – Carnegie Institute's revised detergent industry game and INTOP primarily come to mind – do give considerable emphasis to organizational, human relations, information-handling and decision-processing factors. The two games mentioned permit the game administrator, by various devices and incentives, to shift the relative emphasis between contents and process from one play to another. The very nature of these games ensures, however, that teams will give more than nominal attention to both of these matters at all times. We do not doubt that this attention to organizational factors heralds a trend in management games of the future.

B. *Level of Management*

Games may also be distinguished by the level or levels of management where decisions are being simulated. By and large it is true that general games are also top-management games, while functional games aim at middle management and the more specialized subfunctional games at the middle and junior management levels. *Ceteris paribus*, most complex games may encompass a broader sample of the management group horizontally and/or hierarchically. In some of these games, such as INTOP, each team may be given freedom to decide exactly what parts of the management structure of the firm the team should include, when such discretion is in line with the purpose of play.

C. *Individual vs. Group Decision-making*

Many games, notably at the functional and subfunctional levels, are designed for each participant to represent an individual decision-making unit. In what is probably a majority of games, however, group decision-making is the rule. Very often the internal organization of the group is prescribed; in other instances the structure of decision sheets and output data itself is deliberately or inadvertently

[20]   For a seemingly contrary view, see
Stewart in AMA, 21ff.

geared to result in a given internal organization. As was suggested in the discussion of the specific purposes of games, instances where organization problems have been made a principal element of the game are as yet fairly rare.

D. *Interactive vs. Non-interactive Simulations*

Management simulations in the form of gaming by definition are competitive.[21] Games that attempt to reproduce the dynamics of an industry or a market are almost always interactive. Games about scheduling problems or specific administrative techniques often are non-interactive, that is, the players vie for the best score independently of each other as in bowling.[22] Like the golfer, a player of such a game can also compete against his own best prior score, or struggle to achieve or exceed some standard set by the game designer.

E. *Manual vs. Computerized Simulations*

Most everyone seems to feel that the game designer should strive for the highest degree of realism possible within the confines of his resources. At the risk of provoking protest we submit that in the matter of realism there is nothing the best manually administered game can do that the best computerized game cannot do, but that there are many things a computerized game can do that a manual game cannot do (at least if we wish the play to take less than a lifetime). A customary representation by proponents of manual games is that these games can be made to incorporate a certain sensitivity, a degree of personal judgment and an adaptation to the particular circumstances of a given game play, something which they say computerized games can never aspire to.[23] To the extent that this is an invocation of romanticism rather than realism the argument is irrelevant here. What counts is that a good computerized game allows for the feeding-in of as many judgmental factors, acts of God and changes in the overall environment as it pleases any individual administrator of the game to introduce. To take but one example, the MIT Marketing Management Game as well as INTOP have built-in optional provision for the judgments of experts of such matters as the quality of advertising text and layout, the efficacy of product improvements, etc. Bank-loan applications may be passed on in a personal way rather than by the computer, if desired. Strikes, slowdowns, currency revaluations, tax and tariff rate changes and the emergence of competition from substitute commodities are additional examples of major change in environmental parameters

21 If there is no element of competition there can be no game, *ibid.,* 18, to the contrary notwithstanding.
22 The fact that the INTOP simulation may be transformed into a non-interactive exercise where such an exercise best meets the purposes at hand is illustrated in Chapter 6.

23 This is a claim made for MATRIX, the plant manager game developed by the Procter and Gamble Company.

which have found use in INTOP. Within the area of reasonable relation to realism, sophisticated computer games can make fully as much use of the initiative and personal judgment of the administrator as any manually administered game conceived thus far.

In addition, the degree of realism in simulating complex situations can be made appreciably higher in computerized games. These can incorporate scores of variables where the manual game has to stop at a few or a dozen. And what is more, these variables may be represented by functions which very often are manifestly superior to those used in manual games. Manual games are confined largely to linear functions or random number tables and *ad hoc* judgments due to the considerable effort involved in figuring out the results of dynamic interaction among even a limited number of variables. In some respects the difference is analogous to that between chess and ticktacktoe.

What has just been said is in no way intended to disparage manually administered games. Such games do possess a very great advantage in that the cost of running them typically is quite modest, while computerized games – if machine time is calculated on a commercial basis – usually involve hundreds of dollars in machine expense. The latter type of game also requires access to a computer, which may be a physical constraint, although not so when play is intermittent rather than continuous as is increasingly the case. For many specialized purposes manual games will be superior, for the excellent reason that the type of interaction simulated is quite simple. In many cases the purposes of game play can also be achieved with but modest degrees of realism, making the use of a manual game natural.

3.   Pointers on Design and Selection of Simulations

THE FREQUENTLY VOICED CLAIM that in order to become a good user or administrator of management games one must first *build* one makes as much sense as the notion that the good driver is the one who built his own car. The arguments advanced in favor of this view are that "game design itself is an extremely valuable educational experience for the instructor or trainer,"[24] that feedback between cohorts of players may render a game useless after a number of runs at a given institution and that only by designing his own game will the instructor be certain that it will actually suit his purpose. The emergence of the do-it-yourself gospel in this area should also be seen against the background of the fact that few really usable game-administration manuals have been published in the past (none for a computerized game at the time of writing) and from the lack of availability of good games until very recently.

It *is* a stimulating experience to design games. But the costs in-

[24] Greenlaw-Herron-Rawdon, 69.

volved almost surely outweigh the personal educational benefits accruing to the designers. True, a simple manual game may be designed and broken in within a few months, but its educational value to the designer is also limited. We doubt very much whether a sophisticated computerized game on the scale of the Carnegie or Chicago simulations can be built and brought under control for less than $30,000–50,000, including at least one man-year each of senior manpower and programming assistance and considerable computer "debugging" time – this despite the fact that future designers will have the benefit of the publication of both of these games.

The problem of feedback between different cohorts of players is of practical significance with regard to quite simple games in which the most successful strategies may be easily deduced. Such feedback is also a problem in complex simulations with a rigid model, or in which the resetting of parameter numbers is troublesome. On the basis of personal experience we may say that a simulation which is both complex and flexible – such as INTOP – literally presents no such problem.[25]

In the past most management games have been single-purpose in character. Even so, there are scores of marketing simulations, dozens of general management games, etc. Unless the prospective administrator wants a simulation which actually attempts to replicate a *specific* real-life situation with "high fidelity" (likely to be a very costly proposition) there is at this time quite a broad range of choice. Furthermore, a game like INTOP, which was conceived as a modular multi-purpose simulation from the beginning of the design effort, allows each user to restructure the simulation to serve any given purpose within very broad limits, as demonstrated in Chapter 6 of this work.

Even if it seems quite unwarranted to encourage each potential user of management games to design his own model a discussion of certain aspects of game construction may still serve a useful purpose in suggesting to a potential user the criteria which he may apply in the selection of a simulation and to the designer *in spe* some basic questions he will encounter in his venture. The present section has been written with these considerations in mind.[26]

A. *Bias of Designers*

Management simulations never give a perfect portrait of reality. No matter how intricate the computer equipment used, the picture is always impressionistic, both as regards the traits of reality incorporated and their relative emphasis. In effect, simulations tend to reflect the biases of their designers. This is of little concern if all the

---

25 Cf. *infra*, 180f.

26 The technology of game design is discussed at some length in the Kibbee-

Craft-Nanus and Greenlaw-Herron-Rawdon volumes. The models incorporated in INTOP are discussed extensively in Chapter 3 below.

designer wants to do is to teach the players how to apply a narrowly specified technique, such as a formula for inventory control in a given situation. Often the problem of bias will also tend to become smaller the more complex the game: the more the number of variables increases, the less the likelihood that undue emphasis (or de-emphasis) of any one of them will unduly affect the game or the players.

Judging by our own experience (which of course also may be biased), the problem is apt to be especially serious at the intermediate level, i.e., in games purporting to represent the whole or at least a major part of a management function, such as marketing or production. Most designers of marketing games seem bent on teaching players the lesson that in the modern economy price variation, and notably price cutting, is (or should be?) a secondary competitive instrument. A given investment in advertising, selling effort or R & D almost invariably yields greater returns than a corresponding price cut.[27]

The problem of bias is one which we shall probably never be able to eliminate completely as long as it is possible to interpret reality in different ways. Honesty, and ultimately the faith of the game users in the value of games, requires that designers drop their false pride or pretense of knowing-it-all and openly state their biases. Where this cannot be done without furnishing players with too many "leads," the simulation should probably be redesigned. The next best thing is to present game materials against a background discussion of the assumed underlying "realities" rich enough to enable thoughtful players at least to derive the biases involved by indirection.

B. *Realism*

It is usually assumed that game designers should aim at incorporating the greatest degree of realism possible in their models. But what is meant by realism is far from clear. Objective realism is one thing, verisimilitude or subjective realism another. The degree of objective realism need be no greater than called for by the purpose of the game. If the aim is to simulate the distribution of plumbing supplies for groups of executives in the plumbing industry a very high degree of realism is called for, or the game will presumably not teach participants very much. If the aim is to display the fact that the different managerial functions are interrelated in *any* firm, or to provide a view of problems in international business operations, the criterion of objective realism demands no more than that the variables and problems selected are interrelated in a meaningful manner and that they represent the *types* of functions, data and situations encountered in real life. Indeed, when the purpose is general, undue anchorage of the model

---

27   When UCLA Game I was played experimentally by a score of members of the faculty of the Graduate School of Business at Chicago, two teachers who based their strategy on the premo-nition that this was the case came out on top. The Andlinger industrial marketing game even refuses to recognize price as a variable, cf. *supra*, 2, note 4.

in the details of a specific industry, or specific parts of the world, may cause disputes about institutional facts and relationships of no real consequence to the objectives of the game and very well may divert the attention of the participants to peripheral matters. In other words, objective realism may be too great as well as too small.[28]

Before leaving objective realism, we should emphasize the importance of avoiding what is clearly unrealistic. Any game designer knows that this is easier said than done. An example of what we are referring to apparently occurred when an IBM marketing management game was demonstrated to Midwestern universities in Chicago in the winter of 1961. It turned out that this version of the IBM game did not have a redistribution function, i.e., when a firm ran out of inventory no customer was ever assumed to turn to another supplier. Having found this out during a series of unfortunate decision periods, a team decided to "spoil the game." It proceeded to cut prices to the bone, thereby attracting most of the customers in the market. The team was unable to supply their trade, but every other team was stuck with giant inventories. As one might expect, a downward spiraling of prices set in, but the sabotaging team always cut deeper. When the session was called off, all teams were on the road to bankruptcy.[29]

To be an effective learning device, games must stimulate *involvement* among participants. Experience as players and administrators of games prompts us to say that a *sine qua non* for involvement is verisimilitude. If the players are not subjectively convinced that the simulation is reasonably realistic, they are apt to believe – rightly or wrongly – that nothing good can come out of it. Thus, in a conflict between objective and subjective realism, the game designer faces a delicate choice, especially where an aim of the game is to impart a new image of reality. Reality is frequently more "fantastic" than the average person's perception of it.[30] *Minor* elements of subjective unreality are not likely to bother participants. Indeed, they may give rise to discussions about the nature of the corresponding reality which in themselves may be quite rewarding.

---

[28] War games among the military have apparently achieved high degrees of both objective and subjective realism. In part this is doubtless due to the considerable resource commitments with which defense projects are blessed. Generally speaking, however, it seems to be the case that realism and credibility are more difficult to achieve the less closely the subject matter is related to economic activity. See, e.g., Bernard C. Cohen, "Political Gaming in the Classroom," 24 *Journal of Politics* (May 1962), 367–81, especially 374.

[29] An early version of INTOP had a minor but nevertheless irritating design weakness. The computer had been instructed to read "0" in any empty decision box. When a couple of teams forgot to record a price decision, the computer assumed the price was zero, and in effect gave their inventory away. The present model holds the goods in inventory for another quarter when no price is given.

[30] "Sometimes it may even be necessary to make certain parts of a model intentionally *unrealistic* in order for the whole to seem realistic to players." Joel M. Kibbee in AMA, 9. Italics in the original.

c. *Simplicity Not Necessarily a Virtue*

A popular notion about management games is that simplicity is a virtue per se. We are far from convinced that this is true. If the simplicity is too great dysfunctional behavior on the part of students may be generated. An attitude of "beat the game" may easily become rampant. And while we love to speak of the simplicity of nature, the realities of modern business are indeed far from simple. We should avoid conveying the impression that most of its problems can be reduced to a few equations. Simplicity, then, is worth striving for only as long as it does not conflict too sharply with realism and other design criteria.

Simplicity as such is most clearly out of place in simulations which aspire to make participating groups grapple with the problems of internal organization in a reasonably realistic fashion. Unless there is sufficient complexity to really warrant internal specialization and division of labor among the teams, game designers should avoid any pretense that their creations are suitable for organization simulation.

d. *Complexity vs. Playability*

The objective reality intended to be simulated in a game frequently calls for great degrees of complexity.[31] Sooner or later the designer will run into diminishing returns along the complexity axis, however. Funds may become a bottleneck (and complex games *are* expensive to design). Available computer equipment will often impose constraints. Scarcity of knowledge concerning the nature of interaction in a system is apt to grow with its complexity. Not least is the limitation of playability.

Playability is a relative concept. Over-complexity (or other negative influences on playability) may initially only manifest itself in a deterioration of the quality of play. When the quality of play is poor enough to warrant ruling the game as not playable is a matter of judgment. The prior background knowledge of participants and, importantly, the time allowed for decision-making, are other important determinants.

Complexity may evidence itself in game rules, in the structure of decision forms, in the simulation model itself, in the number of decisions to be made and in other ways. Interestingly, if the number of decisions normally made each decision period is taken as a criterion we find that complexity, too, is a highly relative matter. It is true that in some well-known games players are held to half a dozen or some similar given (and fairly small) number of decisions. In the Carnegie game, on the other hand, a team *may* make as many as 300 decisions in a given period – although a viable operation may frequently be

31 Cf. Cohen-Rhenman's hypothesis: "As the complexity of the game increases, the subjective realism will also increase, *ceteris paribus*," *op. cit.*, 145.

conducted on the basis of a third (or less) as many. The INTOP simulation goes one step further, in that there is actually *no limit* on the number of decisions a company may make in any one period.[32] Again, a team may survive by making *one* decision every quarter: that of reinvesting its capital and earnings in government bonds. In the Carnegie and Chicago simulations each team may actually settle for the degree of complexity in its operations which seems most suitable or challenging to it.

The relationship between complexity and playability is a multi-faceted one. For instance, it is frequently possible to simplify the rules of the game, or the forms on which teams record their decisions – and hence increase playability – by using more complex computations. Conversely, features of the game model as well as the amount of computation may sometimes be simplified by using more elaborate rules and forms thereby tending to decrease playability.

E. *Degree of Determinism*

The existence of risk in an objective sense and the prevalence of uncertainty in a subjective sense in business is well known. The incorporation of risk and uncertainty in management games is highly desirable. In some games this is done by the introduction of random or stochastic terms. Sometimes game administrators will add in such major changes in the "givens" of the game as strikes, tax increases, etc. with varying degrees of advance warning. All this is probably to the good. It must be remembered, however, that even games which are in fact strictly deterministic may "still present an apparently uncertain situation to the players, since the consequences of identical decisions by one firm may differ from period to period"[33] due to competitive actions, the progress of business cycles, etc. In practice, the game designer has to walk a tightrope between the legitimate demand of the players that they be able to see some cause-effect relationships emerging from their decision-making endeavors and the realities of risk and uncertainty.

Whatever the balance struck, any good game should point up the value – and cost – of obtaining information reducing critical uncertainties. Typically, this is done by providing teams with the opportunity of buying different types of market research data or consulting services, by allowing subscription to a periodically appearing trade journal and by furnishing annual reports of competitive companies.

F. *Qualitative vs. Quantitative Factors*

"The decisions generated in gaming are based entirely on quantitative criteria, and this, of course, is very unreal. In gaming,

32 Beyond scores or hundreds of intra-company decision points lie the virtually limitless opportunities for sales, patents and loan transactions between participating companies.
33 Cohen-Rhenman, *op. cit.*, 148.

each company's marketing dollar is just as effective as every other company's marketing dollar, and each employee is as good as every other."[34] Being typical of much criticism of management games, this half-truth leaves much to be desired. First of all, it overlooks the deliberate inclusion of uncertainty in virtually all games. Further, the second part of the statement overlooks the fact that several modern games include an "effectiveness factor," which may vary the return on a marketing dollar, for instance, according to the relative judgment of a set of advertisements or sales-promotion plans by an outside panel. To assume that each employee is as good as every other is probably not unrealistic when the average skill of thousands of lower-echelon employees is considered. As far as participants in the games themselves are concerned — whether they play individually or in teams — the statement is plainly *not* true. There are really no other limits on the introduction of qualitative elements in *good* game models than the imaginativeness of game administrators, the reasonable demand that some semblance of cause-effect relationships be preserved and the ability of participants to react to the changes introduced. It is a different matter that these possibilities have not been used nearly enough in the past in most games.

G. *Dynamics*

Simulation involves interaction of the variables in a system over time. This dynamic aspect of management games is their unique asset in relation to most other educational instruments. In order to provide feedback from the interaction to the teams and afford them an opportunity to make new decisions on the basis of the data received, game play is generally divided into "decision periods" (in some respects corresponding to accounting periods in real life).[35] The determination of a suitable period generally offers no great problem;[36] the most common period simulated by one set of decisions appears to be one quarter. Frequently, of course, the amount of time it takes for a decision to become effective or for a process to be completed is longer. Plant construction may take two or three years, bank loans may be amortized over five or ten years, etc. As games are typically played only for eight to twenty periods, some long-range phenomena often must be shortened, i.e., the plant may be ready two or three quarters after the decision to build it was made. No serious criticism has been launched against game designers taking this type of liberty with Father Time.

---

34 Dr. Carl F. Kossack, IBM Research Center, in AMA, 48.

35 There is, of course, no inherent reason for decision periods and accounting periods to coincide. In future games the emphasis will likely be shifted towards segregation of many decisions from accounting periods, taking into consideration that policy decisions are frequently long range, while tactical decisions may be in need of change several times during a single accounting period.

36 For a contrary view, see Kibbee in AMA, 12.

Certainly, the inclusion of such long-range decisions emphasizes the dynamics of games, and hence the need for planning on the part of the teams.

H. *Forestalling Dysfunctional Behavior*

As every game model represents a compromise between such different criteria as realism, playability, easy administration and easy computation of results, it is inevitable that any game has certain weak spots inviting manipulative behavior on the part of some or all players of a type that would not be possible in reality or otherwise is alien to the purpose of the simulation. The existence of major deficiencies of this type often will generate an attitude of "beat the computer" or "blow up the game" among some teams. The emergence of the former attitude is guarded against most effectively by designing models complex enough not to place a premium on the raw mathematical skills of some players. Propensities to try to blow up the game usually emerge when a team suffers from what they consider an "unfair" impact of a design weakness. While the designer cannot prevent self-destructive behavior on the part of one team, it is imperative that models be designed so as to prevent that team from spoiling the game for others.[37]

Of special importance is an incessant drive to minimize the probability of results being affected by clerical errors, whether they originate with the players or with administrative personnel. While the average participant will take such tribulations in his stride, personal experience and observation prompts us to emphasize that even a fairly modest error may completely demoralize a team which for some reason or other lacks spirit. The elimination of sources of error is one of the reasons why a new game should never be played in public until it has been subjected to several experimental runs.[38]

4. Pointers on Play

A. *Number of Teams and Members per Team*

The number of teams in a game is largely predetermined by its purpose and the model itself. Manual games are generally restricted to a dozen teams or less, due to the computational problems encountered with great numbers of teams. Computer games using relatively simple models have been known to accommodate upwards of one

---

[37] Note, for instance, the importance of incorporating a redistribution function, cf. *supra*, 15.

[38] An example of an error-generating design weakness: in an early version of INTOP, production decisions were to be recorded on the decision forms in terms of hundreds of products to be manufactured. As all monetary decisions (except price) were in terms of thousands of dollars, this proved to be a source of unnecessary confusion in the experimental runs. The production decision is now recorded in thousands of units.

hundred teams.[39] With growing model complexity the maximal number of teams even in computerized games tends to be fairly limited. The original Carnegie Tech model as well as the MIT game, for instance, permit only three teams, and are thus necessarily confined to an oligopolistic market. The current version of the Carnegie game will accommodate six teams. In spite of its high degree of complexity INTOP may be used with up to 25 teams.

The maximal number of members per team depends largely on the complexity of the game and the time available for an effective organizing effort and intra-team communication in decision-making. The AMA game is known to have been run with up to 15 members per team, which seems to constitute the upper limit so far. Four to seven members is quite common in computerized games, and up to half a dozen members have been used to advantage in manual games. INTOP has been run with a standard complement of four to seven members per team, but experimental runs will be made with two or three times that number; the INTOP model would seem to lend itself to perhaps greater division of labor than the AMA game.[40]

B. *Emphasis on the Long Range*

Herbert A. Simon pointedly speaks about a "Gresham's Law of Administration." In the absence of concerted effort to the contrary, routine matters tend to steal the attention from major policy problems, and short-range planning tends to push out long-range. Valid in real life, this observation is also quite relevant in the game situation. If there is any merit in the general notion of "professional management" (and we are assuming there is), management games should certainly emphasize the importance of long-range planning. At least two important implications would seem to follow. First, the number of decision periods in a game run should be great enough to permit the teams to establish a working organization (a few periods of shakedown may be desirable), to get their teeth into long-range planning and to see the fruits of it. This requirement speaks in favor of at least eight to ten decision periods.[41] If available time is at a great premium, there are various possibilities of "telescoping" some periods. This need not necessarily be a loss in learning experience, as telescoping deci-

---

[39] Professor Robert L. Graves at the Graduate School of Business at Chicago has adapted the UCLA Game II for play with 90 teams (each "team" in this case consisting of one student).

[40] At Chicago some experiments have been made running towards the opposite extreme, i.e., minimizing the number of team members even in such a complex game as INTOP. When students in a marketing management course participated in that exercise in single-member teams some complaints were voiced concerning the amount of out-of-class work required for effective participation.

[41] A fairly great number of decision periods is also indicated by the fact that the principal types of problems encountered may change over time. In a typical general management game, for instance, the major bottleneck situations are apt to be found in production, finance and marketing in temporal sequence.

sions without intermediary feedback of results effectively forces teams to think in terms of *policy* decisions. At the other end, no serious effort has been made to our knowledge to establish at what number of decision periods diminishing returns set in. As far as we know, no complex game has been played with an identical complement of teams for more than twenty distinct decision periods. Presumably, the optimal number of periods will vary with the characteristics of both the individual participants and the game being played.[42]

Second, we feel it quite vital (in apparent contradistinction to most game users) to emphasize that the game play actually simulates but a brief span of time in the life of modern, presumably perpetuate corporations. When action potential for the future at the termination of the game is held out as an important criterion of performance, it is our experience that players will not sacrifice long-range objectives for short-range advantage.[43]

c. *Time Available for Decision-making.*
Continuous vs. Intermittent Play

Broadly speaking, the time available for making decisions during each period of play during a game run should be related to the complexity of the game. In practice, one finds in use periods ranging from a few minutes to two hours or more. Other circumstances being equal, formal decision periods may be shortened if participants are given the opportunity to prepare the groundwork for decision in the time between game meetings. This presupposes intermittent rather than continuous play.

A popular notion among game administrators, notably those who propound the virtues of continuous play, is that decision periods should be made short enough to subject the players to considerable time pressure. In our view, this is a highly dangerous generalization. It should be clear, for instance, that where groups rather than individuals play the game, there should be ample time in the early part of the game for the teams to solve their organizational problems. If long-range planning is going to be more than a pipe dream, teams must be allowed at least periodically to set aside some considerable time for this purpose. Also, we are really averse to the idea that decision periods should "normally" be short enough to put the teams under duress — the notion that most real-life business decisions are made under such conditions is far from convincing in the absence of

---

42 There is a trend in game design toward lessening the dependence on formal accounting and decision periods; at some stage it may become necessary to discuss optimal length of play in terms of some other general criteria.

43 If this point is made unequivocally clear to participants we have found there is no need to keep the total number of decision periods "secret," a device practiced with only moderate success by some game administrators.

more tangible evidence than we now have.[44] And even if this were so, it is far from self-evident that normal training conditions should be made to simulate this particular aspect of such a reality. It is an entirely different matter that occasional drastic restrictions in available time for decision-making may serve a very worthwhile purpose. Clearly, *some* business decisions are made under duress. Also, such abbreviated decision periods, especially if introduced without prior notice and comparatively late in the game, may serve a purpose as one type of test of the viability and efficacy of the internal organization among the teams.

By this time the reader should be able to perceive that we are somewhat skeptical about game sessions involving continuous play. We feel strongly that the value of complex games is reduced rather severely if there is no time intermediary between decision meetings. This is not merely because a serious application of analytical techniques to intricate data requires more time than a formal decision period is likely to afford. Even more important, in order to digest voluminous data, gain an overall perspective and acquire a sense of the interrelationships between the whole and its parts the average participant needs time for personal and unhurried reflection. We are convinced that much of the learning experience is lost if this process is frustrated.

There is less objection to continuous play in quite simple games. However, many such sessions witness the emergence of an artificial supercompetitive spirit and a steamed-up emotional atmosphere which may actually hamper the educational process. Limited time and other constraints may occasionally force the use of even some of the most complex games in continuous play. This *may* be better than playing no game at all, but it must be understood that continuous play has serious shortcomings. We confidently predict a gradual shift in the field in favor of relatively greater use of intermittent play in the future.

How long should the period between decision meetings be? Experience to date suggests no hard-and-fast answer. Even in highly complex games teams are certainly capable of formal decision meetings once or twice a week without strain, provided that the administrator can furnish output data a day or two in advance of each session.[45] Furthermore, it is quite feasible to accelerate the dynamics of play by requiring decisions for two (or at times more) periods at each meeting without any intermediary feedback. Finally, it should be pointed out that intermittent play makes it perfectly feasible to arrange gaming by mail. This has already been amply demonstrated in INTOP as well as the UCLA and Pitt-Amstan games. To facilitate mail play,

---

[44] Lately even the prior claim to ulcer fame of business executives has been questioned by medical authorities.

[45] Manifestly, teams which do have an opportunity to meet informally *in corpore* out of "class" do enjoy a differential advantage. In a residential executive development course where all teams have this opportunity, the intermission between the feedback of output and the subsequent formal decision session may well be cut down to an hour or two in even most complex simulations.

game administrators frequently resort to a technique known as leap-frogging. This simply means that teams in period t make decisions on the basis of output data from period $t - 2$, while decisions for period $t - 1$ are being processed. There is nothing extraordinary in this process, as businessmen in reality often have to make decisions on the basis of uncomfortably dated information. Indeed, the use of leap-frogging frequently seems to provide an extra spur to long-range planning.

This, at least, was the reaction of a team of executives in Stockholm, Sweden, participating in a regular INTOP class run of the Graduate School of Business at Chicago. The Chicago teams were making their decisions on the basis of current output, but due to the limitations of the transatlantic mail system the Swedish team had to practice leap-frogging. Nevertheless, in terms of profitability and other conventional criteria of success the overseas company wound up in fourth place among fourteen teams.

It may be observed that leap-frogging has also been used in continuous play (for example by George J. Feeney in administering the General Electric Marketing Game) as a means of providing for flexibility in what in such play may otherwise become a very hectic processing schedule.

Rapid feedback of data in cases where processing and play take place in different localities will be promoted by the Dataphone System and even more advanced techniques for high-speed data transmission over great distances presently under development.[46] These devices are likely to promote more widespread utilization of computerized games of a sophisticated nature.

D. *Evaluation Sessions and Continuous Feedback*

That half of the value of the game lies in the post-mortem evaluation session is still a widely held notion among practitioners.[47] Again, our experience prompts us to differ. Many evaluation sessions – notably after games with one or two days of continuous play – are in fact no more than supercharged exercises in the post-rationalization of team behavior.[48] This especially tends to be the case where most or all participants are employees of the same company in real life. We are certainly not arguing against postgame critique sessions as such. But we are suggesting that these sessions, if they are to be really re-

---

[46] Use of conventional telephone hookups for the oral transmission of complex game data is usually not as fast, or as satisfactory in terms of minimizing errors, as physical conveyance by automobile, as long as play and processing take place in the same city.

[47] "The critique is the most important part of the gaming session because it is here that the lessons are driven home." Kibbee-Craft-Nanus, 19. And again on 85: "In many ways, the most important part of a game program is the critique session."

[48] For similar observations, see Paul S. Greenlaw and Stanford S. Kight, "The *Human Factor* in Business Games," 3 *Business Horizons* (Fall 1960), 55–61, and AMA, 58ff.

warding, place great demands on teacher as well as students, and that even a well-run review session plays a relatively modest role in a well-balanced game. The prime learning in a dynamic educational situation is − or should be − "in the doing," that is, in the making of decisions, the observation of their results and the immediate analysis of cause-effect relationships. Thus *continuous review* should be emphasized as an indispensable part of the system, as indeed it is in well-organized real-life decision-making. In addition, provision may be made for periodical longer-term reviews, preferably involving comparison with other teams. Such discussion may be stimulated, e.g., by distributing to each team "annual reports" of all other teams and setting aside special time for their analysis. The administrator or outside experts may assist further by auditing and counseling activity.

E. *Enriching the Game Experience*

The learning experience in management games may be enriched very considerably by a great array of activities which go beyond the straight play of the game but are closely integrated with it. Many such activities which have been tried out with INTOP are discussed in Chapter 4. Here we shall only give a few illustrations.

An important exercise stimulating policy thinking and long-range planning is the formulation of decision rules for several periods at one and the same time. These policies may pertain to all decision areas in the simulation, or only to certain aspects (such as marketing in general or advertising in particular in an overall management game). The teams may be permitted to make tentative policies or obliged to define rules which in effect bind them for a certain number of periods; the rules may be made unconditional or conditional upon the attainment of certain intermediary results, etc. This is a highly promising frontier area in game development.[49]

Games offer a wide field of application of analytical techniques. Students may be asked to apply various types of rate-of-return, direct costing, break-even and cost-of-capital analyses. They may be required to submit sales forecasts and cash budgets and explain how these were derived. Often statistical and mathematical methods and marginal economic reasoning may be useful. Cash flow, sources-and-uses-of-funds and other worksheets and statements may be prepared and so on.

The importance of flexibility and creativity can be stressed, and player sensitivity to changes in the institutional environment may be

[49] One might even contemplate on occasion to give the teams a chance to remake their decisions for a given period and then rerun the data. *One of the things teams will learn from such an experience is that in a competitive business it is literally true that "history never repeats itself."* Cf. Kalman J. Cohen and Merton H. Miller, "Some Thoughts on the Management Game of the Future" (mimeographed, Carnegie Institute of Technology, Feb. 1961), D8–D11 and by the same authors, "Management Games, Information Processing and Control" (mimeographed CIT, June 1961), 12ff.

increased, by the introduction of special incidents manifesting them-selves in terms of change in basic game parameters. We are thinking, for instance, of new legislation, evidencing itself to the players in such forms as lower taxes, credit restrictions, tariff increases, etc. Strikes may be declared, certain plants destroyed by acts of God, mergers be-tween teams permitted, substitute products may emerge and severely restrict the market available for the product(s) involved in the game, or conversely, that market may suddenly expand violently as new uses for its product(s) are found. There are few practical limits to the amount and types of change which may be incorporated into a well-built model of the more ambitious variety.

The feeling of realism as well as the quality of the learning ex-perience may be increased further by calling in experts for review and counsel. For instance, auditors may undertake a management audit; a banker may pass on loan applications; and outside executives or faculty members may be invited to serve as members of the board of company teams.

5. Effectiveness of Games in Education

A. *Problems of Measurement*

We know little about the effectiveness of management games as an instrument of education. Indeed, we do not even know for sure how to distinguish a good game from a bad one, although it is believed that the discussion in earlier sections of this chapter pro-vides certain bearings in this regard. All this is certainly disturbing, especially in view of the appreciable costs involved in the design and use of at least more complex games.[50] Yet our high degree of ignorance is hardly surprising in view of the fact that such simulations have been around for less than a decade. It is really a good deal more dis-concerting that we know so singularly little about the effectiveness of the case method, of group discussions, of role playing, of the in-basket test and of other educational techniques which have been around for quite some time. Indeed, we know precious little even about the efficacy of the classical lecture, beyond the fact that students can be made to feed back selected parts of it on tests.

We shall not here go into a detailed discussion of the vexing prob-lems of gauging the effectiveness of educational instruments. Clearly, the measurement effort in business education has to proceed on two levels: the effectiveness of instruments in contributing on one hand to the standards established by educators as regards student knowl-edge and abilities and on the other to student performance in real-life business positions. The problems on the first level are bad enough, on the second they are truly exasperating. To begin with, we have not even cleared up the basic question as to how much native character-

[50] Cf. Cohen-Rhenman, *op. cit.,* 151.

istics count in relation to acquired talents and environmental influences in conditioning a successful business leader, although psychol-
ogists and other students of leadership with each new volume seem to
be placing increasing emphasis on the latter groups of factors. Even
if we have a firm idea about the role of inculcated know-how, the
pivotal question remains how we go about ferreting out the significance
of any one educational (or practical) experience from the aggregate.
And many relationships are bound to be of such a long-range and in-
direct nature that they will be very hard to establish in practice.

With regard to the effects of games specifically what spurious
evidence we have at this time emanates largely from preliminary
studies undertaken by Dean William R. Dill and his colleagues at
Carnegie Tech.[51] It seems to suggest that there is little or no correlation
between success in the CIT game *measured in terms of accumulated
profits* (*not* in terms of quality, consistency, creativity of play or many
other alternate criteria of superior performance which might be applied) and success in business (for which again a host of alternate
criteria might be used). Also, there is no correlation between team
averages in the Admission Test for Graduate Study in Business and
team success in the game. But then, of course, we have no clear indication that high scores on the ATGSB predestines one to a successful
career in management either. What seems to be reasonably clear is that
what students get out of management simulations differs in nature
from what they get out of other means of learning.

B.   *Games Compared to Cases,* ETC.

In a nutshell, a business game is *a dynamic and live case.*
While a case of the traditional type provides an essentially static snap-
shot of a business problem situation, the game yields a moving, multi-
dimensional picture. Even more significant, perhaps, is the fact that in
games the students have to *live* with their own decisions; they are
personally forced to take the consequences of their recommendations.
Feedback and re-enforcement as means of supporting the learning experience are relatively minor elements of the case method,[52] but are
indispensable, built-in concepts in a game.

51   Cf., e.g., William R. Dill, "Educational Effects of Management Games —
Some   Experience   and   Questions"
(mimeographed, CIT, Feb. 1961) and
W. R. Dill, William Hoffman, H. J.
Leavitt and T. O'Mara, "Some Educational and Research Results of A Complex   Management   Game"   (mimeographed, CIT, Oct. 1960). Note also
James L. McKenney, "An Evaluation
of Business Gaming as a Learning Experience" in *Conference on Business
Games at Tulane University, op. cit.,*
116–22.
52   Recognizing that this is a weakness of the method, case writers are increasingly turning to sequential case
situations in the same firm. Another
interesting departure followed at close
range by the author of this chapter as
the then Director of the Industrial
Council for Social and Economic Studies in Stockholm (SNS) is based on
providing the students with a relatively
unstructured situation from which they
have to build up the case themselves
in a series of meetings under the guidance of a body of experts. For a discussion of later work at SNS in this
area, see Cohen-Rhenman, *op. cit.,*
153ff.

Another fruitful comparison in attempting to display the characteristics of a management game as a vehicle of learning involves the theater:[53]

In a play, the author and the actors are not trying to extend the experience of the audience by presenting useful *facts* about the world. Indeed, many of the most forceful and effective dramas involve events and surroundings that are totally unrelated to the day-to-day reality of the audience. A good play alters, not our experience, but the manner in which we interpret our experience. Old facts take on new meanings and future experience is seen with improved understanding. An effective play provokes *insight*. This is precisely the purpose of the strategy simulation exercise (a General Electric marketing game). In effect, the exercise is a play in which the participants are simultaneously the audience, the actors and, to a large extent, the playwright.

This quotation in effect also brings out a basic similarity between gaming and role-playing. A main difference between the two lies in the fact that games involve role-playing over an extended period of time and, again, to a greater degree than customary in role-playing, force participants to accept personal responsibility for their behavior.

A characteristic feature of games is that they almost invariably stimulate considerable excitement and personal involvement on the part of participants. As educators have sadly learned, this is not always the case with most other means of communication at our disposal. The question has even been raised that perhaps "*too much* involvement takes place in management games, and that, consequently, the individual cannot lower his defenses sufficiently to accept feedback from others in the group on the adequacy of his behavior, beliefs, feelings, or attitudes."[54] Or, conversely, any teaching tool generating such a high degree of involvement "could be a very good way of getting the wrong things across."[55] Our own observation — not scientifically validated — is that in a complex game extended over a considerable period of intermittent play a skilled administrator will usually not have too much trouble guiding involvement into constructive channels. To us it seems premature in *that* situation at least to start complaining about too much frosting before we know a good deal more about the cake, *i.e.*, what *other* characteristics and effects of gaming are.

Of course, games *do* have some limitations as compared to other items in the tool-kit of management development. As suggested, they tend to be costly. To be really rewarding it is probably always going to be true that they will have to be rather time-consuming. Even the more advanced games can only cope with one basic set of market or other institutional characteristics in the course of a given run, even if it may be changed relatively freely. It is true that in some game models — including our own — even drastic change in basic parameters is possible.

[53] George J. Feeney, "Marketing Strategy Simulation Exercise III" (mimeographed, Marketing Services Research Service, General Electric Company, Feb. 1960), 2. Parentheses supplied.

[54] Greenlaw-Kight, *op. cit.*, 58. Italics in the original.

[55] John F. Lubin in AMA, 42.

But if the changes are *too* radical there is no longer any continuity, and cause-effect relationships in decision-making become too tenuous to provide for effective re-enforcement. The case method practiced over an equal amount of time offers the opportunity of greater variety in problem settings.

c. *Functional Insights*

Among other things, the effectiveness of a management simulation as a teaching tool depends on what the administrator is trying to teach with it and on the level of education or experience of participants. In the Pitt-Amstan Simulator game the intention appears to be to teach junior and middle executives how to make better management decisions within an environment which is held in a great many respects to resemble closely American-Standard operating conditions. Top management of the firm apparently feel that this is being accomplished, and somewhat similar experiences are reported concerning the A T & T Financial Management Game and Boeing's Operation Interlock. Doubtless it is also true that highly specialized games can make participants become better production schedulers, sales forecasters, etc., within the specific framework simulated.

Nevertheless, we venture the opinion that in the area of functional knowledge and ability games will continue to contribute mainly by "dramatizing the concepts of management and making them more graphic and concrete and, thus, more understandable."[56] In a majority of games the problems of the general area of management portrayed and their broad interrelations will be emphasized, rather than specific institutional facts. Ample opportunities of finding applications for analytical techniques of a general nature (marginal reasoning, cost-of-capital analysis, etc.), rather than specific formulas, will be increasingly emphasized in these games, and we may fairly expect greater proficiency in the practical use of such techniques as a result.

d. *A Holistic View*

There is no doubt that a good management simulation *can* present a holistic view of many seemingly disparate functions in a business. Evidence also exists to indicate that many participants for the first time get a real feel for "the Big Picture" in a firm's operations by playing an advanced game.[57] A good simulation does not fail to demonstrate the ever-present problem of suboptimization in all organizations. In an increasingly specialized and complex economy this effect

[56] Richard Rawdon, "Learning Management Skills from Stimulation [*sic*] Gaming," (Address in *Industrial Relations*, Bureau of Industrial Relations, University of Michigan, Dec. 1960), 14.
[57] Cf., e.g., comments by participants in the Boeing game reprinted in *ibid.*, 9. Many statements to the same effect appear on questionnaires anonymously submitted by middle-management executives as well as campus graduate students participating in INTOP.

of games would seem to be welcome. There is similarly evidence to support the view that if executives are deliberately given assignments in the simulation *not* corresponding to their real-life positions, this may indeed help them to acquire a better understanding of the problems of people working in other functions or at other levels of management. They may also acquire a better view of how their own job meshes with the contribution of others — and vice versa. This effect of games is worthy of further exploitation as well as exploration, as the main emphasis in many executive development programs is to bring about a change in attitudes rather than to impart new knowledge.

E. *Insight into Decision-making Processes*

Complex games which really require an effective *group* decision-making effort for successful participation by necessity subject participants to an organizational and human relations experience which in some cases may be quite substantial. In considering alternate means of organizing the team effort — whether to emphasize customer categories, geographical areas, products or functions and what degree of delegation to authorize, etc. — executives participating in INTOP have frequently stated that they recognize very real problem situations from their own experience. Game participation apparently does sharpen diagnostic ability in identifying problems in the organizational area as well as regards the subject matter of decisions to be made. The opportunity of making a diagnosis of his own style of decision-making in a team and of upgrading his capacity to empathize, i.e., to understand the problems and attitudes of others, also seems to be seized upon by many players. This is also true with regard to the opportunity to practice bargaining skills built into INTOP and a few other games.

Some games at least also seem quite effective in teaching participants the value of planning — and notably *long-range* planning, an area in which many real-life businesses still seem to have a hard time going from sounds to things. That intelligent planning requires a well-organized flow of data is also made clear. Complex games further teach the necessity of being selective, of focusing not on all data but on data *relevant* to given decisions. Almost all games worthy of the name point up the importance of competitive intelligence of a systematic nature. In view of the great deficiencies in this area existing in business today, many a game may be worth its salt merely by bringing out this particular point.

Computerized games provide an experience of participating in man-machine systems in general and living with computers in particular. They manifestly serve to stimulate the interest of participants in simulation as a general technique of attacking management problems.[58]

58   W. R. Dill, "Educational Effects of Management Games," *op. cit.,* A3. Cf. *supra,* 27.

Today we are confined to speaking largely in terms of the initial effect rather than the ultimate effectiveness of simulations as means of preparing people for management jobs or improving their performance in present positions. What we already know about initial effects should definitely encourage their further use, especially in combination with other educational techniques. Meanwhile, research efforts directed toward establishing the effectiveness, as well as the possible dysfunctional aspects of management games, should certainly be accelerated.

6.   Role of Games in Education

WE SHALL CONCLUDE the chapter with some remarks on the role of simulations in management education, whether in industry or at schools of business. Games should be viewed as representing one of many educational tools, each of which have properties which are in part unique and in part overlapping with the characteristics of other tools. Many individual educators, and indeed entire business schools, will associate themselves with a particular tool almost to the point of exclusion of all others. Witness, for instance, the extraordinary faith placed in the case method at the Harvard School of Business Administration at a time when that School exercised a more dominating influence over American business education than at present.

It is probably true to say that the current is now in the direction of a more relativistic view of all tools, a view forcefully supported by the Pierson and Gordon-Howell reports on the education of businessmen.[59] The trend unmistakably is toward the parallel use of several teaching methods, a balanced portfolio of educational tools. A crucial point of view in this context is the *integrative* one: where several methods are used they should re-enforce each other rather than be permitted to take off in widely divergent directions.

Integration may be achieved in various ways. By way of illustration, teachers at the Graduate School of Business at Chicago have used INTOP as well as revised versions of the Andlinger and the UCLA II games in individual courses in combination with lecture-discussions and written assignments. At the Carnegie Institute of Technology a different route has been chosen in that the CIT game is given as a distinct "course," but with many tie-ins with standard courses in finance, accounting, marketing and so on. At both institutions, as indeed in a number of executive development programs in industry, educators have found that an advanced management game may serve as a convenient and stimulating focal point for broader discussions of theory as well as a source of golden opportunities of applying specific

[59]   Cf., e.g., G. Leland Bach's essay in Frank C. Pierson and others, *The Education of American Businessmen — A* *Study of University-College Programs in Business Administration* (1959), especially 336ff.

analytic techniques. Management game situations have also proved singularly well suited to the application of role-playing and in-basket exercises.[60] How integration is brought about is probably less important than that some substantial degree of closure is in fact achieved.

Evaluation of performance in any management simulation depends, of course, on the purpose of that game and the circumstances under which it is being used. Generally speaking, it is true that the more complex the simulation the greater the problem of evaluation. Criteria of "success" become increasingly numerous, and the importance to be assigned to any one of them increasingly controversial. The fact that this is also a problem of real life is a source of some consolation. Our own feeling is that relatively little emphasis should be given to the general type of criteria which Wall Street analysts might apply in evaluating a concern. Such caution seems especially warranted in view of the fact that we know too little as yet about the determinants of success in these terms. "Winning the game," in other words, should not be a prime criterion.

Greater emphasis may be given to the *quality* of play in terms of purposiveness of the team in striving for the goals established by itself, in terms of the internal and sequential consistency of its plans and decisions and in terms of the imaginativeness of its actions. This theme is further developed in Chapter 4, which also discusses the evaluation of individual participants in team play.[61] Given this approach to evaluation it would seem entirely justified to make a certain part of the grade in a course or program of which the game is an element dependent on performance in the simulation (and any specific assignments relating to it) provided that this is clear to the students from the outset.[62] In this way potential recalcitrants (of which there may be some even in management games) are also given an incentive to take an active part.

[60]   This point is illustrated in Chapter 4 on game administration.
[61]   See *infra,* 195ff.

[62]   This is already being done at several institutions, Carnegie, Chicago and Princeton among them.

Chapter 2

INTOP:

An Overall Presentation*

1. Purpose

THE UNIVERSITY OF CHICAGO International Operations Simulation is the first major business simulation exercise oriented toward the specific problems of international trade and overseas operations. It derives special significance from the fact that international operations — and competition from abroad in domestic markets — will become an increasingly vital element in the evolving enterprise system of the 1960s. The rather high degree of realism in the game also brings out the fact that effective solution of international business problems often requires diagnostic ability and conceptual thinking to a greater degree than most other management situations — and whatever other merits business games may have they *do* stimulate these qualities.

The simulation is intended to illustrate with some considerable degree of realism the types of problems encountered in overseas operations and international competition at home and their *general* significance to management. We are interested not only in external issues but also in problems of internal organization and cooperation which tend to beset international concerns more than others. Personal observation in the General Electric Company and interviews with presidents of several other large American and European companies in international business furnished the base for the selection of parameters and variables believed to be both relevant and representative in a broad sense. In a general and selective way the game also portrays

---

* In this chapter a vertical line in the margin indicates passages also incorporated in identical or closely similar form in the *International Operations Simulation Player's Manual* (1963).

Users of INTOP may find this arrangement practical in deciding what materials to include from this chapter in the oral briefing of players.

various institutional characteristics of the international economic environment, such as the fact that during the postwar period business cycles have differed between nations in *timing* as well as in amplitude, and that the European Economic Community (EEC) countries have had a more rapid rate of economic growth than our own.[1]

While a prime purpose of the simulation is to increase understanding of the problems of international operations in general, and those of the multi-national corporation in particular, INTOP is so designed as to yield substantial payoff in *general management training as well*. This is achieved by a balanced representation of such classical functional areas of real-life companies as finance, marketing, production, and research and development. The companies will also face major problems of personnel, executive teamwork and internal organization: the number and complexity of decisions make survival depend on effective division of labor *within* company teams. The relative complexity of a management game of this nature makes the use of a computer indispensable. The exercise is programmed in FORTRAN for IBM and other types of equipment and for Remington Rand Univac.

Among the particular advantages of INTOP is that this simulation forces participants into *a stream of truly entrepreneurial (top management) decisions* of business philosophy and objectives (as opposed to the heavy strategy-tactics emphasis of most other games). This is accomplished by continually facing the teams with the choice of representing national or international companies, and, if the latter, whether by exporting, licensing, or selling to overseas distributors, or overseas-based manufacturing. In addition, there is the choice between a single-line and a diversified producer.

A principal aim of the simulation is to focus the attention of participants on the challenging idea "that changing a business — finding it new roles, new customers, new markets — is even more important than operating it efficiently."[2] Whatever the stance adopted, participants are necessarily faced with groping for logic in the business objectives-strategy-tactics sequence.

The emphasis on entrepreneurial decisions makes it imperative that the *top-management* level be represented in the organization of participating teams. However, the purpose is also to make ample room for *middle management* simulation whenever desirable. If we assume, for instance, that a given company elects to organize geographically, top management may be represented by a president (in Liechtenstein) and two area vice presidents in the U.S. and the EEC. Each vice president may have functional managers reporting to him, and, indeed, in

1 When and if the United Kingdom and/or other countries join the EEC INTOP Standard parameters governing that part of the simulation ("Area 2") will be redimensioned accordingly.

2 John B. McKitterick, "Profitable Growth–The Challenge to Marketing Management," an address given at the 45th National Conference of the American Marketing Association, June 20, 1962 (mimeographed), 22.

many areas of the game there is ample room for subfunctional management as well. The marketing manager in, say, the U.S. may well make effective use of a sales manager and a marketing research manager. The level or levels emphasized should primarily depend on the specific purpose for which the game is being run. It is flexible enough to allow wide variety in this regard.[3]

INTOP is a fast-moving exercise. This is assured by a model providing for vigorous competitive interaction in consumer markets in combination with opportunity for inter-company selling, borrowing and licensing. The dynamics are further emphasized by a number of time-lag and scheduling functions. Yet a wealth of data is provided, enabling skillful management to bring operations under reasonable control. A major purpose of the game is to stress *the role of long-range planning* as an indispensable instrument in this context. Subsidiary aims in this area are to encourage the *selective and efficient use of data* and to draw the attention to the value of systematic collection and analysis of *competitive intelligence*. One of the biases of the design group is that a majority of business firms fail to make systematic use of competitive information or provide adequate facilities for its orderly collection.

An important consideration in the design of INTOP was its future use as a *business planning* and *research instrument*.[4] In particular, it has been built with simulation of multi-national corporate organizations in mind. However, the game by analogy – or by simple change of parameters, if desired – is equally applicable to the internal cooperation problems of any dispersed and diversified concern operating exclusively in domestic markets. Basic environmental characteristics may be held constant or varied within unusually broad ranges. It is also possible to introduce drastic simplification in the game if the research or business planning aims at hand so permit or require. Conversely, the modular design of the model facilitates its amendment or expansion when desired.

The foregoing is a condensed restatement of the specific purposes which were uppermost in the minds of the INTOP design group. In addition, the group had a broader aim in mind: to design a modular, *multi-purpose* game. That is, we wanted *to give every administrator of the game a chance to write his own ticket as to the purpose, complexity and functional content of the exercise*. The result is a game which without undue effort can be restructured to meet almost any of the purposes for which games are being used (as discussed in the first part of Chapter 1). Detailed suggestions as to how the standard model may be simplified or further enriched for various purposes are given in Chapters 4 and 5. Some variations going beyond the standard framework are discussed in Chapter 6.

---

3 Some suggestive organization patterns are displayed on the back cover of the *Player's Manual*.

4 Cf. Appendix VII and *supra*, 4ff for illustrative applications in these areas.

2. Fitting INTOP into Educational Programs

INTOP is built for use in industry as well as schools of business. The richness of the model ensures that playing the game in itself is a stimulating experience. It may also be a rewarding one if the emphasis is on group decision-making[5] and on pointing up the interrelational aspects of the various parts of a business rather than on the decisions as such.[6] There is no doubt in our minds, however, that the full potential of the simulation as an educational tool can be realized only when it is used in combination with other tools, such as lectures, and when students are encouraged to view the simulation as a focal point for the application of analytical techniques learned outside the game.[7]

Management development programs in international business operations is the most obvious field of INTOP application. The emphasis of the game on general management, entrepreneurial decisions and problems of organization also makes it eminently suitable for any integrative general management course. To illustrate, in the last four years INTOP in conjunction with lectures and written assignments and/or case discussions has formed the backbone of the Business Policy and Organization course, the capstone course in the two-year Executive Program of the Graduate School of Business at Chicago.[8] The simulation is also being used in Advanced Marketing Management courses with regular graduate students, and it provides the integrative theme in an Industrial Marketing course at the School.[9] Naturally, in the latter types of courses the marketing functional aspects of management are given more emphasis than overall policy and organization which are highlighted in the Executive Program course. As suggested in Chapter 6, it should also be possible to use INTOP in courses in production, accounting and, notably, finance management to great advantage.

1265446

3. General Model and Designer Biases

A. *General Models*

A basic assumption in the building of our model was that a business may be described with a fairly high degree of specificity in terms of four major dimensions, viz., geographical area, mode of operation, output (products or services) and clientele.[10] The definition,

5   This does not exclude participation on an individual basis in certain instances, cf. *supra*, 10.

6   Testimony by US Steel executives after one-day continuous play, May 1961.

7   Cf. *supra*, 24, 28, 30.

8   Cf. *infra*, 186ff.

9   In the last-named course, the INTOP-INDUSTRIAL version of the game is used; cf. Chapter 6, Section 6.

10   Or, in the vernacular, the "where," "how," "what" and "whom" of the business.

and redefinition, of the business in these terms is a prime entrepreneurial responsibility. INTOP provides the teams with several alternatives along each dimension as indicated by Fig. 1. The number of options explicitly listed is vastly increased by the fact that in principle

FIG. I *Entrepreneurial Opportunity in INTOP*

Business Dimensions	*INTOP Options*
Area	U.S., EEC, Brazil, Liechtenstein
Mode of Operations	Financier, research institution, distributor, producer-marketer, subcontractor
Product	X (portable radio), Y (vacuum cleaner), each product in five variants
Clientele	End consumers representing three different cultures, industrial distributors

any kind of combination is possible. A company may carry on financing and patent licensing operations from its home base (always in Liechtenstein), while being a full-fledged producer-marketer in the U.S., a subcontractor in the EEC and a distributor in Brazil — just as it may be any one of these things. But resources are limited enough to drive home the important lesson that no single company can be all things in all areas. Specialization is necessary under the cold star of scarcity in the world of INTOPIA as well as in real life.

More graphically, we are postulating that each firm represents an input-output system operating in from one to four external (national)

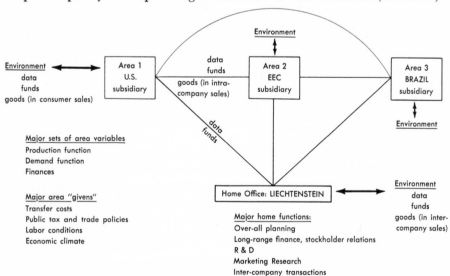

FIG. 2   *A Multi-National Corporation in its INTOP Environment*

environments. The complexity of data and decisions will vary appreciably depending on what stance a team chooses to take, but even when
the stance is a fairly simple one the group will face substantial problems of internal cooperation. This is suggested by Fig. 2, which represents a system of a multi-national corporation and its environment in
the game.

While all corporations are assumed to have their home office in
Liechtenstein (well-known international tax haven), they may elect
to operate in only one or two of the three areas. Indeed, a company is
perfectly free to confine itself to Liechtenstein, carrying on the functions of a commercial finance institution and research and development institute by means of securities investments, inter-company loans
and patent licensing transactions.

The diagram in Fig. 2 is mildly suggestive of a geographically
oriented internal organization. However, this is merely for convenience in presentation. The internal organization of each company may
be oriented to product, to function or to geographical area. While it
is up to the companies to decide on suitable degrees of delegation and
decentralization, operating statements are arranged in such a way
that far-reaching decentralization based on profit responsibility by
area or by product is possible. As many successful businesses have a
functional organization, such a structure has other, compensating
advantages. These may be most clearly apparent in a fairly centralized operation based on division of labor according to professional
specialties of the management group. Various combinations of structuring principles are, of course, also possible.

To contemplate the interaction between various parts of the company and their environment (inside as well as outside), it is fruitful
to think in terms of *flows* of data, funds and products. Looking at the
internal environment first, we find that the Home Office may engage
in an exchange of funds and data with the subsidiaries. The flow of
funds from home to the areas and, in due course, increasingly in the
reverse direction is quite analogous to what is found in real life. The
intensity and directional emphasis of data flows is in large part conditioned by the amount of delegation and decentralization practiced.
What marketing research studies are undertaken by the Home Office
may, for instance, be determined by area requests in one company and
by central initiative in another. In either case, the actual procurement
of such data from the outside is undertaken by the Home Office.[11]
Whenever a firm engages in inter-company sales, information about
such transactions constitutes an important part of the data flow between home and the area(s) affected. While no goods flow through
the Home Office, and while authority to conduct negotiations leading

11 For purposes of the game it may be assumed that the Home Office has found it efficient to represent all the parts of the company in dealing with one of the several market research agencies which in fact are active in all three areas simulated in the game.

to inter-company sales may be delegated to the areas, INTOP Standard rules require the president's signature on *all* inter-company transactions. This is to protect the administrator, who might otherwise soon devote a considerable part of his time trying to resolve intra-company jurisdictional disputes. Other data from home to areas may pertain to product improvements acquired by R & D or license from other companies. Areas may submit capital appropriations requests, long-term plans for area development, etc.

While an interchange of data and funds between home and areas is indispensable, intercourse between subsidiaries in different areas is a matter of company discretion. Typically, such intercourse takes the form of intra-company transfers of products from one area to another, accompanied by requisite flows of data and funds.[12]

As Fig. 2 indicates the interchange of data, funds and products[13] between the firm and its environment is considerable. As in real life, the firm informs the market about its products and the conditions on which they are for sale, and gets a continuous feedback of environmental reaction in the form of sales data and competitive information. Through the *Gazette* (organ of the World Federation of Appliance Manufacturers) and the administrator the company is also kept informed about other relevant developments in the environment, notably as regards government-business relations, labor relations, the stock market and business climate. The company may further enrich the data flow by engaging in R & D and marketing research or by negotiating special consulting services from the administrator or other experts.

Each company is provided with starting capital (usually ten million dollars). In the course of the game the flow of working capital may be increased by ploughing back profits, by short-term borrowing for current needs in the different areas of operation, and by long-term borrowing (within sound banking limits) by the Home Office for long-range expansion or general consolidation of a shaky company. In addition, stock market confidence is reflected by an addition to the working capital of well-run companies each quarter. Companies are also free to arrange loans between themselves. A final safety valve in cases of outright distress is credit extended by suppliers on stiff terms.[14] When the patience of both banks and suppliers is exhausted the company involved is forced into bankruptcy.[15]

---

[12] Transfer of funds between areas not connected with intra-company sales can only take place via the Home Office. Such transfers may still be accomplished within any given decision period.

[13] The only case when there is no outside disposal of products (to consumer markets or other companies) occurs when a company restricts its activities to being a financier and/or research institute. To simplify Fig. 2 we have chosen not to represent flows of services.

[14] The extension and repayment of supplier credit is an automatic function in the game; cf. *infra*, 58, 60, 267f.

[15] To avoid forcing a team out of the game the administrator (representing the creditors) may require that the ailing company merge with another firm, or that it dispose of some of its plants to increase liquidity; cf. *infra*, 372ff.

Surplus liquidity may be absorbed in the areas by the purchase of short-term, low-interest bonds, and at the Home Office by investing in higher-yielding securities.

Each company may manufacture and/or market either or both of *two different products*. As an assist to the imagination it may be instructive to think of these as a portable, battery-operated transistor radio and a household vacuum cleaner, respectively. As the purpose of the exercise is to tackle *general* business problems, however, and to emphasize the necessity of learning about an industry by experience and research, we have deliberately avoided any attempt to "reproduce" any one specific real-life market in detail. As in real life, the *management of innovation* poses crucial problems in the INTOP simulation. By *research and development* (R & D) patented improvements may be achieved. Each of the two products may have up to four improvements (or "grades") in the course of the simulation. Patents may be licensed, globally or nationally, selectively or exclusively, and with provision as to the maintenance of minimum prices, etc.[16]

To avoid unrealistic and exasperating complication, it is possible to manufacture only two grades of each of the two basic products in any given area during any given quarter. Furthermore, a company may *market* only two grades of each of the two products in any given area in any given quarter (whether it manufactured these goods, bought them from another company or did both). For convenience reasons these two grades are called the *standard* and the *deluxe* models.

B. *International Variables*

Figure 2 is also instructive in pointing to the major sets of givens and variables[17] which lend INTOP its distinct international character. Among international differences beyond control of the teams are transfer costs (representing shipping, insurance, customs, paperwork, etc.) incurred in the shipment of goods from one area to another, capital transfer taxes which may be imposed by countries in balance-of-payments difficulties, local economic climates and growth rates, corporation tax rates and tax carryover provisions and interest rates on government bonds and area bank loans.[18] These factors are all directly represented by parameters in the standard model. In ad-

---

16 In the event that markets get too highly organized, the U.S. Department of Justice may bring an antitrust suit resulting in a court decree for compulsory licensing or dedication to the public of any patent controlled by violating concerns manufacturing or marketing in the United States.

17 The words "givens" and "variables" are used loosely in the text about phenomena as viewed from the horizon of *players*. As pointed out in Chapters 4–6 almost any features and parameters in INTOP may be changed by the administrator.

18 The administrator, representing the major commercial bank in Liechtenstein, may either set a flat interest rate for bank loans in that country or set individual rates on the merits of each loan application. Cf. *infra*, 194.

dition, other constraints with international implications may easily be incorporated, such as import quotas, strikes, rising materials costs, currency revaluation, antitrust laws, government purchasing, bank failures, subsidies, price control, dismantling of trade barriers or even earthquakes.[19]

The three clusters of variables subject to appreciable degrees of control by team companies all present major international differences. These sets of variables focus on the production function (manufacturing management), the demand function (marketing management) and on problems of financial management. In the field of manufacturing management maximum capacity and optimal level of operations of plants vary by area (as well as by product), reflecting differences in the technology employed. Fixed and variable manufacturing costs are different in the different areas, as is the "mix" of these cost elements. Common economies stemming from the joint administration of several plants making the same product also evidence geographical variation.[20]

The demand functions of the American, European and Brazilian markets present a number of variations. In area consumer markets price elasticities vary with products as well as grades (as determined by the number of patented improvements). The effectiveness of advertising at both the company and total industry level fluctuates from one area to the other, as does aggregate market potential and rate of growth of demand for the two products. The relative merit of agents vs. a captive sales organization as channels of distribution is not the same in the EEC as in the U.S. or Brazil. Inventory carrying charges (for warehousing, etc.) also are internationally variable.

The considerable diversity among the areas with regard to financial management is conditioned to a great extent by variations in such givens as tax and interest rates and by the differentiated patterns of resource allocation generated by the divergent production and demand functions. The relative tightness of financial markets is further reflected by differential rates of turnover of accounts receivable and payable and by maximal amounts of supplier credit available at less than extortionate interest charges.

c. *Common Economies and Specialization*[21]

We have already emphasized the need for every entrepreneur to put scarce resources to effective use by specialization. In most management games the room for each team to carve out its own distinct niche of the market, partially secluded from direct inroads of com-

[19] Cf. Chapters 4 and 5.
[20] In addition, the model permits the administrator to introduce local variations in rates of depreciation and obsolescence as well as in the effectiveness of money spent on production methods improvement.

[21] For the benefit of participants common economies are summarized in INTOP Memo 2, reproduced on the inside of the back cover of the *Player's Manual* as well as in Appendix VI of this volume.

petition, is extremely limited. Due to the flexibility offered by INTOP along each of the four major business dimensions discussed under Subsection A above, each team throughout the simulation is presented with new opportunities of selecting, enlarging or relocating its individual niche. As in real life, the art of nichemanship largely lies in combining a degree of specialization imposed by resource limitations with the utilization of a bundle of common economies and opportunities to prevail on increasing returns to scale. In this way a differential advantage in relation to actual and potential competitors may be secured.

Major common economies in INTOP may be derived on a functional, product or area basis. In production major economies may be derived by operating several plants for one product in a given area, as methods improvements are immediately applicable to all such plants and as fixed costs per unit of output decline as the number of such plants grows. In financial management it will generally pay to consolidate all loans in Liechtenstein. In marketing common economies are available in advertising and in channels of distribution. A given advertising expense promotes the standard and the deluxe models of a given product each with the same effectiveness as the same amount would have in furthering the sales of only one quality of that product. Both agents and captive sales organizations derive common economies from handling both products in a given area rather than only one of them.

Product-oriented common economies are mainly to be derived by concentrating production of a given product to as many plants in a given area as possible in order to enjoy lower fixed manufacturing costs per unit of output. Despite international transfer costs it is often possible to concentrate production in the U.S. (or the EEC) of a product, and market it in that area as well as Brazil and, occasionally, the EEC (or the U.S.).

Area-oriented economies may be derived by concentrating on *one* product in manufacturing and advertising (if both standard and deluxe models of the product are being marketed) and by marketing *both* products, to derive the common economies in commercial and administrative (C & A) expense (whether incurred by agents or captive distribution). In marketing two products, minor common economies will also be obtained indirectly as a result of modest degrees of cross-product brand loyalty.

At the home office level marketing research represents a source of common economies. Many of the services available provide worldwide data for both products, thus favoring concerns diversified both geographically and product-wise. R & D provides another example of global economies in that any given patent obtained by a company may be exploited in all areas.[22]

[22] The only exception to this rule would occur if the patent were obtained by a license with territorial restrictions. Even so, the U.S. Department of Justice may invalidate some restraints of this type.

Specialization is further promoted by certain returns to scale independent of common economies. Prime example in the production area is the fact that variable manufacturing cost at any given level of output is always lower if only one grade of a product is produced in a given plant than if standard and deluxe models are made in the same plant. In marketing returns to scale are found in advertising for a given product in a given area in that the full effectiveness of a given amount of advertising is obtainable only if a certain number of units of the product are available for sale. In each area there are also sizable returns to scale associated with captive sales organizations, as a major element of cost for this form of distribution is fixed.

Finally, there are modest and rapidly diminishing returns to scale with regard to R & D for each product separately.

D. *Dynamics of the Exercise*

The dynamic aspect is perhaps the single most important characteristic of management games distinguishing this educational instrument from most others. The dynamics of INTOP is derived from four major sources:

1.   the sequential nature of decision-making
2.   the presence of several important time lags
3.   the interaction with competing companies
4.   environmental changes in the course of the game

Each decision period corresponds to *three months* of real-life operations. To get full benefit from the dynamics of sequential decision-making with continuous interplay of decision inputs and result outputs, it is our belief that the game should be run for at least twelve decision periods ("quarters"). In practice this may mean as few as eight decision-making sessions, as the first three quarters of operation may be conveniently "telescoped" into one session,[23] and as it seems to constitute a challenging experience to the students to require them in one or two of the later sessions in the game to make decisions for two or more quarters per session. In effect, this is one of several means of forcing the importance of planning to the surface. Moreover this procedure stimulates participants to separate areas of decision amenable to policy-making from areas in which continuous temporizing may be necessary.

A considerable number of significant time lags are involved in the game. Most important perhaps are those involving plant construction and production. Plant construction takes two quarters (decision

---

[23] The set of decisions for quarter 1 are vital in that they involve such commitments as the first round of plant construction, whether and to what extent to engage in R & D, etc. On the other hand, quarters 2 and 3 (in which sales are not yet possible) largely involve routine follow-up of quarter 1 decisions.

periods) to complete.[24] In addition, special restraints placed on plant construction in Brazil during the first three quarters of the game effectively serve to hold back the arrival of the industrial revolution in that country, in line with real-life experience. Production in INTOP *always* goes into inventory at the end of the quarter in which a decision to manufacture a given quantity was made. Only in the following quarter may the products be sold or transshipped. Further, all transfers of goods from one company to another or from one area subsidiary to another take an extra quarter. Straightforward time lags of up to half a year also occur with regard to accounts receivable and payable, making flow-of-funds planning a necessary and relatively complex task in the standard version of the game.

Of a slightly different character are a host of delayed cause-effect relationships. In the areas of R & D, advertising and methods improvement the effects of a given expenditure will be only partially visible in the period in which the expense-decision was made, the remaining benefits emerging in later quarters. Stock market confidence based on a company's earnings and dividend record, and manifested in additions to working capital, also builds up only gradually.[25]

At this stage it may be appropriate to point out that there are also a few offsetting factors in the simulation placing a premium on stability of operations. Foremost of these are the costs of change in the rate of manufacturing output and in the number of offices in a captive sales organization. In both cases the costs of change accelerate with the magnitude of the change.

While sequential decision-making and differential timing of cause-effect relationships are sufficient to make any business game a dynamic experience, it is possible to simulate *market dynamics* only by competitive interaction among the participating teams. As in most general-management games competition among the companies in the various end markets represented in the model is a cardinal feature of INTOP. In addition, the dynamic of this particular exercise is vastly enhanced by the built-in opportunities for *direct interaction* between the companies. Inter-company transactions may involve buying and selling, giving and taking of patent licenses as well as borrowing and lending. We have had ample experience on which to base our contention that each of these types of direct interaction literally adds an entire dimension to the dynamic of games.

To appreciate fully the fact that change is perennial and to learn not only to live with change but also to capitalize on it, participating companies should be faced with long-range transformation as well as short-term disturbances in the basic operating environment. In many

24 Admittedly, this period is short. Yet it is long enough to make investment in plant a truly long-range consideration for participating teams. An administrator who feels a longer period is called for can achieve this simply by filling out a "Wonder Card" for the computer; cf. *infra*, 219ff.

25 Cf. *infra*, 107f. The relatively complex R & D function is discussed on 109ff and 241.

rigidly programmed games (notably several well-known computerized models) the only type of environmental change provided for is a long term growth trend in aggregate demand in combination with short-term market fluctuations simulating business cycles.[26] As we have had reason to indicate in various contexts, properly programmed games can easily be made to accommodate almost any changes in environmental circumstances (strikes, currency revaluations, etc.) which an imaginative administrator may wish to introduce. Some of these tribulations may be introduced without prior warning, in the manner of acts of God. To stimulate orderly adjustment to changing environmental constraints and opportunities, however, it is important that teams in most cases are given ample advance notice of such developments or at least of the possibility of their occurrence.

E. *Designer Biases*

It was pointed out in Chapter 1 that all games by design or inadvertence reflect the biases of their makers with regard to what variables and features that are important enough to warrant incorporation in the models as well as what types and magnitudes of impact which might reasonably result from given sets and magnitudes of decisions. Unfortunately, it is a great deal easier to identify one's neighbor's prejudices than one's own. We are not able to give an adequate representation of our particular set of predilections here. A few illustrations will have to suffice. It is our sincere hope, however, that a critical reader will become rather fully aware of our value dispositions in the course of this work, as pain has been taken to be highly explicit and quite detailed in the presentation of all features of the simulation, and in the way we attempt to rationalize different aspects of the model. Indeed, even participants in the exercise are better forewarned about designer propensities than the players of most other games: the INTOP *Player's Manual* is more articulate than any other management-game instructions with which we are familiar.

By and large, we probably feel more strongly about the "proper" administration of games than about particular features or cause-effect relationships in the model itself. Our views concerning continuous vs. intermittent play, the desirability of integrating games with other learning instruments, the amount of time which should be allowed for decision-making, and similar matters of administrative concern were set forth in the first chapter. Other administrative predilections—more specifically INTOP-oriented—are ventilated in Chapter 4.

Let us, then, try to illustrate a few of our biases in model design. In the area of marketing we are old-fashioned enough to believe that price is an important variable in electrical appliance markets—even in

---

[26] Occasionally — as in INTOP — the collective behavior of the industry as regards price, R & D and advertising policies may itself modulate such aggregate changes in demand.

affluent societies. Conversely, we have given advertising less play than one finds, say, in the IBM Marketing and UCLA I and II games. We feel that inventory management should play a *relatively* modest role in a general international business operations game, and that when a company is out-of-stock our provision for redistributing most of its unsold potential during the out-of-stock period among companies capable of supplying the market is punishment enough.[27] In contrast to many other game designers we also believe that it is possible to spend too much money on R & D even in this innovation-minded era. In production management we have embraced the notion of a substantially parabola-shaped variable manufacturing cost curve with a single optimum for individual plants. Influenced by some of our Chicago colleagues, we have tried to give some heed to direct-costing type of accounting in production.[28] Mindful of the fact that this type of costing system is far from universally accepted, we have left the door open for other game administrators to switch to a more traditional system, however.[29]

In the area of executive organization for decision-making in international operations we have systematically tried to *avoid* any given bias. Decision forms and output sheets are oriented in such a way as to permit organization by product, by area or by function or by any given mix of these structuring approaches found suitable by individual teams.[30] Similarly, we have tried to make it feasible for participating companies to adopt whatever degree of centralization or delegation of decision-making which may seem appropriate to them.

The INTOP model possesses a number of significant characteristics not commonly found in other management games. These features are summarized in Subsection F below. The incorporation of each of them is based on a strongly held conviction that their presence is highly desirable in a general-management game. We leave it to the reader to pass his own judgment as to their desirability. The model is flexible enough to permit the easy elimination of any one of them he may find superfluous or undesirable in any given context.

In conclusion, it must be re-emphasized that at almost any juncture it is possible for the INTOP administrator to substitute his own notions as to reasonable cause-effect relationships and patterns of interaction for the particular set of biases which beset the designers. It is true that the general structure of equation systems is given, but

27   In some games there is also a lost good-will effect extending over one or two later periods. The administrator who feels that this is a desirable feature may introduce it in INTOP by manipulating the marketing effectiveness index of individual companies; cf. *infra*, 195.

28   Cf., e.g., David Green, Jr., "A Moral to the Direct Costing Controversy?" 33 *Journal of Business* (July 1960), 218–

26, and Charles T. Horngren and George H. Sorter, "Direct Costing for External Reporting," 36 *Accounting Review* (Jan. 1961), 84–93. See also *infra*, 281.

29   Cf. *infra*, 101f.

30   Perhaps in this way the merits of a global rather than a national (American, Brazilian, etc.) view of international operations is injected into the model.

most changes which others may wish to introduce can probably be effectuated by re-dimensioning of selected parameters—a simple matter in INTOP. Thus, for instance, if it is felt that too little heed is given to advertising as a marketing variable, its impact may be changed at the administrator's pleasure. Indeed, it is possible to differentiate the effectiveness of a given decision at the individual company level, thus making allowance for qualitative as well as quantitative aspects of the decisions, if so desired.[31]

F. *Summary: Highlights of INTOP*

This section has given a highly condensed and somewhat abstract description of the International Operations Simulation. Five cardinal features of the game should stand out above all others. First, INTOP is specifically focused on *international* business problems. It is the first major management game oriented toward simulating the environment and operations of multi-national corporations and the impact of international competition in domestic markets. At the same time this game represents a well-balanced *general* top-management simulation exercise, giving broad representation to such classical business functions as production, marketing, finance and accounting in addition to overall corporate planning. Secondly, the game has sufficient complexity to make a fairly elaborate division of labor and good *organization* most desirable. Decision forms and output sheets—together constituting the nucleus of operating data—are arranged in such a form as to make possible deliberate experimentation with different types of organization patterns and decision-making processes. Thus the game affords the splendid opportunity of simulating organization structure and process problems as much as the subject matter of business management. Depending on the purpose of running the game in each case the emphasis may be placed on subject matter, on organization or on both.

Thirdly, INTOP permits a variety of *transactions between participating companies* (sales, loans, patent licenses), in addition to conventional selling in end consumer markets. This feature adds a new dimension of realism to the game. It also adds a new dimension of management training in games: negotiation. This is not merely to provide exercise in bargaining, although the value of self-observation in informal bargaining relationships in itself may well be considerable. At least as important is the fact that the discussions preceding an inter-company transaction provide an effective role-playing experience in grappling with basic management problems. Furthermore, only by this means is it really possible to provide a reasonable facsimile of reality with regard to patterns of specialization, integration and diversification among participating companies.

Fourthly, each team throughout the play of INTOP is faced with

[31] Cf. *infra,* 195.

an ubiquity of *entrepreneurial* opportunities and decision situations. There is really no practical limit to the number of alternate stances a participating company may adopt,[32] as indicated by our introductory discussion of the possible variations along such basic business dimensions as area, product, mode of operations and clientele. Most other games, after an initial set of basic choices have been made, fairly quickly settle down to a routine characterized by marginal variations of price, advertising and production (or some corresponding variables). In INTOP there is the constant possibility – and often strong competitive pressure – to re-evaluate and redefine the fundamental objectives and *modus vivendi* of an enterprise.

The fifth major characteristic of INTOP is its modular design and the *extraordinary degree of flexibility* within each programmed segment of the game model. This feature literally permits each administrator to write his own bill of generalities as well as particulars. Several examples of what may be accomplished by way of major redesign as well as minor variation by quite simple means will be given in later chapters. Meanwhile, one illustration as good as any is provided by the fact that any or all of the four just highlighted aspects of the model may be reduced in scope or eliminated entirely and yet leave a perfectly viable management game of a more conventional type, i.e., a game focused on a single (or regionalized) domestic market simple enough to play by individual participants rather than organized teams, an exercise where the dimensions of each company are determined at the outset, and where no inter-company transactions are permitted. For certain purposes, and especially when time is a great constraint, simplifications of this type may be highly desirable. It should be added that in no other major game do the cardinal features of INTOP just discussed figure concurrently at the present time – indeed surprisingly few simulation exercises incorporate any one of them.

4. The Game Structure Detailed. Decisions To Be Made by Participants

THIS DETAILED presentation of the International Operations Simulation follows closely the main part of the *Player's Manual*, as indicated by vertical lines in the margin.

The information is based on the INTOP Standard version for which program tapes, printed manuals and all other accessories are available.[33] Almost no single statement made is sacred in terms of what may be done with the game model. We wish to re-emphasize this here rather than do

---

32 Taken in conjunction the third and fourth points bring out the fact that there is also no limit on the number of decisions that may be made in any given period of a run.

33 Working materials are also available in slightly less streamlined form for INTOP-INDUSTRIAL, a version of the game focusing on industrial marketing problems. Cf. *infra*, Chapter 6, Section 6.

so at every step of the presentation. A great number of suggestions for variations on the standard theme are given in Chapter 4. That chapter also contains a wealth of practical suggestions for day-to-day management of the game.

The reader interested in more basic changes of the entire INTOP structure is referred to Chapter 6. Such a reader should also benefit from the discussion of the simulation oriented to economic theory and mathematical models in Chapter 3.

A. *Company Organization and Home Office*

Each company decides upon its own internal organization and division of labor. However, the president must have ultimate authority and he is responsible for on-time delivery of company decisions to the administrator.

When the exercise begins only the Home Office located in Liechtenstein is in existence, administering the starting capital. As investments are undertaken in Brazil, the EEC or the U.S., the Home Office transfers the requisite funds. When the initial capital is exhausted, the Home Office may engage in long-term borrowing. In general, it is responsible for the overall financial function (including dividend policy, etc.), as are most corporate headquarters in real life.

If the company decides to engage in R & D, this function is handled in the home office laboratories. Any product improvement patents obtained may be applied in any or all of the territories in which the company is operating.

Company relations with market research agencies and trade association membership are also handled by the Home Office.

B. *Products and Improvements, R & D*

Companies may produce and/or market either or both of two basic products, X and Y. In some respects it may be helpful to think of X as a portable transistor radio for battery operation, and of Y as a vacuum cleaner. Typical prices for economy-model radios and cleaners in the various areas as the simulation begins are listed in the Schedule of Costs, Charges, Time Lags and Marketing Research Services, reproduced at the end of this chapter. While the cleaner and radio markets are clearly *largely* independent of each other, a minor amount of interaction may realistically take place (cf. Background Data on Brazil, the EEC and the U.S. at the end of this section).

The probability of success of an R & D program is related to the consistency, size and durability of the program. Initial investments in an R & D program are applied to hiring and organizing an effective staff. As the program continues the probability that the staff will develop product improvements increases. Each product may have up to four improvements, every improvement representing a patent. The unimproved economy models of the products are called X_0 and Y_0, respectively. Improvements X_1, X_2, X_3 and X_4 (or Y_1 to Y_4) can only be reached in chronological order by R & D. (However, a company is free to negotiate for *any* improvement by patent license from another company.) Later improvements incorporate earlier ones (X_3 includes X_2 and X_1, and Y_2 includes Y_1, etc.). As in real life some improvements will be more successful than others; *occasionally a technological improvement may prove to be an outright failure from a marketing point of view*. There are no common economies in R & D for X and Y.

A particular level of improvement, such as X_2, may be reached by several alternate routes (an increasingly characteristic feature of modern technology), each of which is patentable. Each different patent for X_2 has cost and demand effects identical with every other X_2 patent.

A company may hoard any number of improvements by R & D and/or by taking licenses from other companies. But the company can only produce and/or market two grades of X and two grades of Y in a given area during a given quarter. The maximum degree of product improvements obtained by R & D or patent licenses appears on the last line of the ancillary data sheet.[34]

Contrary to some popular notions it is indeed possible to waste money in R & D. Beyond a certain point the incremental yield of R & D expense in any laboratory becomes nominal. If a company wants to specialize heavily on R & D it can speed up its own research by taking licenses on lower grades from other firms or contract to use their research facilities.[35]

c. *The Management of Innovation*

For the first time, INTOP brings the vexing problems of innovation management to the fore in a business simulation. The patented improvements – each with different production and demand characteristics – furnish the nucleus in this area. Companies must decide on a stance vis-à-vis product innovation; if they embrace such a policy they are faced with the issue of whether to embark on their own R & D program, or to take licenses from others, or both. They may well prefer to obtain improved products from outside suppliers. In either case, they must decide whether it is worthwhile to incur the costs of marketing research and consulting services to obtain estimates of market potential and production costs before they "plunge." When patents are obtained conflicts may arise between executives who would like to see the company make exclusive use of the improvements and those who would rather exploit innovation by licensing others. Due to time lags and the two-grades-per-area-at-any-given-

---

[34] This is one of the output sheets, samples of which are reproduced in Appendix II as well as in the *Player's Manual.*
[35] One means by which such R & D contract work may be arranged is the Specialization Agreement-Research, reproduced in Appendix IV. This type of contract has not been extensively used in past runs.

time limitation optimal utilization of innovation calls for synchroniza-
tion of R & D, production and marketing at all times.

It must be remembered that entrepreneurial innovation is not
limited to the introduction of new or improved products. Any combination of resource utilization and services performed resulting in
the capture of a new niche in the several domestic and international
markets depicted in the simulation represents pioneering in the
broader and proper sense of economic innovation. As in real life, the
number of such combinations in INTOP is virtually legion — no company is ever in the position of tapping all opportunities available.

D. *Area Operations*

Production and demand functions, local tax and interest
rates vary from one area to another. For these and other international
differences see Background Data on Brazil, EEC, and U.S. and the
Schedule of Costs, Charges, Time Lags and Marketing Research
Services.

One of the first decisions a company has to make is to select the
area or areas in which it wants to be active. In this context it must
also make an initial choice regarding mode of operations, that is,
whether it wants to produce and/or market and/or license in the
area (or areas). (It is, of course, possible to start out modestly in an
area by selling through local agents, for instance, with a view toward
later manufacturing there if prospects are promising.) Some companies may prefer to restrict their operations to Liechtenstein, serving
as R & D and licensing institutes and/or financiers.

The *capital* needed to initiate operations in an area must be
transferred from the Home Office. Short-term operating funds may be
borrowed or invested locally.

E. *Production Management*

1] SCHEDULING OF PLANTS AND PRODUCTION

Plant construction takes two quarters. Production may begin in the
third quarter. Production *always* goes into inventory at the end of
the quarter in which manufacture takes place. Hence, consumer selling — as well as inter-company and intra-company (between areas)
transfers of goods — may begin in the fourth quarter. As shown in
the table below the sequence is:

QUARTER	1	Construction
	2	Construction
	3	Production (to inventory)
	4	Selling

It is, of course, well known that the electrical manufacturing
industry generally got started a good deal later, and on a much

smaller scale, in *Brazil* than in the U.S. and the EEC. There is also a chronic shortage of investment capital in that South American country. To reflect these facts adequately the rule has been made that *for each new plant (X or Y) for which construction has begun in Brazil during quarters 1-3 a minimum of $1,500,000 of Brazilian Government securities must be held until the end of quarter 3.* There will be no such stipulation in quarter 4, and, barring unforeseen economic and political events, no similar regulation will be reintroduced later.

2] PLANT CHARACTERISTICS

For cost of acquisition and capacity of plants in the various areas, see Schedule of Costs, Charges, Time Lags and Marketing Research Services. Plants must be fully paid for in the quarter in which construction is begun. Plants depreciate at a linear rate of 5 per cent per quarter. Depreciation, a noncash expense, begins in the first quarter in which the plant is "on stream." A maximum number of three X plants and three Y plants may be built in an area. *Old plants may be disposed of* at a reasonable discount (although *not* to other companies in the game),[36] and new plants may be constructed any time. The X plants in *an area can produce only two grades* of X (such as X_1 and X_4), and the Y plants in a given area only two grades of Y. Maximal efficiency in a single plant is obtained by producing only *one* grade at optimal capacity, as production of two grades in one plant entails certain interference costs. If a company has two or more X (or Y) plants in a given area and wants to manufacture two grades of X (or Y), it will be most economical to manufacture the two grades in separate plants, as long as marketing conditions permit loading of all plants anywhere near optimal capacity. Further production cost reductions may be obtained by investing in *methods improvement*, which tends to take effect gradually. Any degree of methods improvement achieved will be automatically applied to all X (or all Y) plants in an area. (As these improvements relate to the local technology of production they are not transferable internationally. Neither are they negotiable.)

Variable manufacturing costs tend to increase as plants grow *obsolete*. The rapidly changing technology in the transistor radio industry is reflected in a higher rate of obsolescence of X plants than of Y plants. On the other hand, a given amount of funds allocated to methods improvement will tend to have a greater cost-reducing (or at least obsolescence-retarding) effect in a radio than in a cleaner plant. If a company has several plants of different ages and wants to produce only in one factory, it is clearly most prudent to use the one built most recently.

36 Participants are asked to see the administrator when they wish to sell a plant. Cf. *infra*, 160f and INTOP Memo 4, reproduced in Appendix VI.

3] MANUFACTURING COST CHARACTERISTICS

Production cost consists of two elements. One is *fixed cost* (plant maintenance and security, salary overhead, insurance, taxes, etc.), which in accordance with modern principles of accounting (direct costing) are not "inventoried." When a company builds several X plants (or several Y plants) in an area they are assumed to be adjacent to each other, resulting in certain common economies (cf. Schedule of Costs). There are *no* common economies for X and Y plants located in the same area. Fixed costs are not incurred until the first quarter in which the plant is "on stream." They are paid directly out of cash during the quarter in which they are incurred.

The second element of manufacturing costs is *variable cost*. Such costs are at a minimum at the optimal capacity rating of the plant, which varies by product and area. At very low rates of capacity utilization, unit cost is fairly high and constant. (It may be assumed that manual technology is then employed.) After a certain point of capacity utilization has been reached, the unit cost function takes the shape of a parabola (with its minimum at optimal capacity). By accelerated input of the factors of production, output may be increased at growing unit cost until the *maximum* capacity rating of the plant is reached (cf. Schedule of Costs). Variable manufacturing cost per unit for a higher grade of product X or product Y is higher than for lower grades of the same product. Assuming output reasonably close to optimal capacity, variable manufacturing cost will generally be 25–35 per cent of the price of economy models at the beginning of the simulation, as listed in the Schedule of Costs.

As in most modern manufacturing operations there is a premium on *stable rates of production*. Any change in rate of output (up or down) entails certain costs of adjustment (severance pay, etc.) or break-in. Thus, the lowest possible unit cost at any given rate of output is attainable only after at least two quarters of operation at that level.

F. *Limit on Number of Grades*

It is clear that a company having access to all improvements of X could *produce* all these grades, given plant facilities in all areas. However, a company may *market* only two grades of X (and two of Y) in any *one area* in any *one quarter*. Other circumstances equal, there is a clear-cut advantage from a selling point of view in carrying a *full line* of a given product, i.e., having both a standard and a deluxe model in the company's area(s) of operation. (See below under Marketing Management.)

If a company which is already marketing two grades of a product in a given area wishes to introduce a new grade in the area, this may be done in any of four ways:

1. By deferring the introduction of the third grade until inventories of one of the earlier grades have been absorbed by regular market sales;

2. By transferring the inventory of one of the earlier grades to another area;

3. By selling the inventory of one of the earlier grades to another company;

4. By introducing the third grade without first getting rid of one of the earlier grades. In this case the next lowest of the three grades will automatically be reduced to the level of the lowest of the three grades. Realistically, this corresponds to obsolescence costs incurred in cleaning out old inventory. In this way the rule is preserved that a company may only market (or keep in inventory) two grades of a given product in a given area at any given time.

G. *Marketing Management*

1] COMPETITIVE VARIABLES: PRICE, ADVERTISING, GRADE, AND STANDARD-DELUXE MODELS

The crucial determinants of the sales volume of a given company are price, advertising, grade and whether standard only or both standard and deluxe models are marketed.[37] *Prices* may be set only in dollar units; maximum permissible price at any time is $99.00. Customers generally tend to resent steep, sudden price increases. Similarly, consumers are pleasantly surprised by price cuts but their initial delight is tempered by cold-blooded comparative shopping after one quarter. Note that if in a given quarter no price is given (or price is set at 0), goods will be held in inventory during that quarter.

Advertising – which is applicable *only in consumer selling* – may be applied to either product X or product Y. However, as ads may conveniently feature two models of the same product, a given amount of advertising will promote the sales of each of two grades of X (or of Y) approximately as effectively as it would promote only one grade of the product. It is not possible to advertise for individual grades of X or Y. Advertising is only effective in a given area, but its effect extends over several quarters with gradually diminishing strength. There is no goodwill "spill-over" from advertising for X on the sales of Y, or vice versa.

Other circumstances being equal, a high *grade* of a product should reasonably be expected to command a higher price at a certain volume, or a higher volume at a certain price, than a lower grade of the same product (although some improvements may be "duds").

While being the first with a product improvement conveys considerable temporary advantage, every follower – whatever his grade

---

[37] Sales in a given area are also somewhat dependent on the number of companies marketing the same product there; see *infra*, 92ff.

of product – will have certain introduction problems during the first quarter of marketing. As in reality, these problems may be countered by an extra low price in the quarter of introduction or, if the company is willing to forego sales for one period, by a high introductory price which the company is then able to cut "due to the warm reception of our product by the public."[38]

If a company has only one model in *beginning* inventory it is *standard*, regardless of what grade it may happen to be. However, INTOP consumers are sophisticated and hence able to distinguish between an X_0 and an X_1 (or X_2, etc.) just as well as between a Volkswagen and a Rolls Royce – even though these two cars represent the standard offerings of their manufacturers.

Consumers have a certain preference for firms marketing *both standard and deluxe models of a given product.* Assume that firm A is marketing only standard and firm B both standard and deluxe of product X. Assume further that both firms offer their standard models under identical conditions. Aggregate unit sales of X of firm B will be greater than those of firm A, although B's sales of standard units alone will be smaller than A's.

How much greater B's total sales of X will be than A's will depend on the relative prices of B's standard and deluxe models. Generally, a given percentage increase in deluxe price will reduce deluxe unit sales by a greater percentage than the relative gain in standard unit sales, although a certain amount of brand loyalty may be counted on (i.e., some of the deluxe customers will "switch" to the standard model of the same brand). Conversely, a given percentage decrease in deluxe price will increase deluxe unit sales by a greater percentage than the relative loss in standard unit sales (the latter results from brand-loyal standard customers "trading up" to deluxe).

Finally, it may be noted that there is a *modest* degree of *cross-elasticity of demand for products X and Y.* As detailed below in Background Data on Brazil, the EEC and the U.S. this interdependence of demand between X and Y is nowhere very great. It is certainly trivial as compared to the relationship between standard and deluxe models of a single product.

2] CHANNELS

The selection of *channels* is an important marketing management decision. The consumer market in any given area may be approached by three different channels, i.e., by using other companies as distributors (inter-company sales), by manufacturer's agents, or by a captive sales organization. In *principle, these channels are all equally effective in reaching the market,* that is, the channels do not differ in inherent sales promotion ability, but they do differ widely in cost and

---

[38] Similar problems of introduction may occur during the first quarter in which a company is marketing either product in a given geographical area.

degree of commitment by the company. *Inter-company sales* may be used in parallel with agents or with a captive sales organization, but agents and captive sales force cannot be used together. Inter-company selling introduces *no* directly recordable cost, since such sales are negotiated by the top executives of the company in person as part of their general management duties. Such sales may relate to X or to Y or to both. *Agents* work on a fixed-fee-per-unit-sold basis (see Schedule of Costs). They may be used for either or both products. As a full line is of some advantage (and greater sales reduces unit overhead), agency fees are somewhat lower when X and Y are sold concomitantly than when only one of the products is sold this way. The company retains full authority over the conditions of sale in the end consumer market. Agency has the advantage that it involves virtually no long-range risks or commitments by the company, and agents' fees are paid only in proportion to sales. The main disadvantage is fairly high cost per unit sold.

A *captive sales organization* may be created in any area by the establishment of a central sales office plus *1-9 regional sales offices.* The quarterly cost per office in the various areas is indicated in the Schedule of Costs. The cost of the central office is always equal to that of two regional offices. In addition to the fixed office charges each quarter there are certain sales costs connected with each unit of product sold. These charges vary by product and area. In areas where agency fees are low for a given product and the company is only marketing that product, it is generally inadvisable to establish a captive sales organization unless unit sales are quite substantial. A captive sales organization will handle either X or Y or both products. Selling costs will be allocated to each product according to units sold and the relative cost of handling each product.

Any *change in the number of offices* (up or down) involves certain costs (severance pay, costs of moving, etc.). Thus, the lowest possible selling cost at a given sales volume and a given number of offices is attainable only after at least two quarters of operation with that number of offices.

A decision to change the number of regional offices (or to switch from agency to captive sales organization or vice versa) takes effect only at the *end* of the quarter. Thus, if in a given quarter a company decides to go from agents to captive distribution, sales in that quarter will still be handled by the agents. However, the company incurs the cost of change to the new arrangement during the decision quarter. Similarly, if in a given quarter a company decides to go back from captive to agency distribution, selling costs during that quarter will still be based on the captive organization existing immediately before the decision was made. The company again incurs the cost of change to agency during the decision quarter. The moral is clearly that it costs both time and money to change your distribution setup.

As sales volume increases, savings in selling cost may be derived by expanding the number of regional offices in a captive organization (and vice versa). Note that there is a premium on gradual, planned expansion; change costs accelerate briskly as the number of offices opened or closed increases. There is no special charge for the establishment or elimination of the central office (which is added or deleted automatically as a company switches from agency to captive distribution or back).

As sales volume increases (decreases) a captive selling organization will tend to have greater (less) merit from a cost point of view. On the other hand, captive distribution entails heavy commitments extending over several quarters.

It should finally be noted that a company may use itself as distributor in *intra-company sales* by shipping goods from one area to another for resale in the latter area.

3] MARKETING RESEARCH

Marketing research is encouraged by the provision of a wealth of market and company operating data each quarter. Companies may decide to pay for an array of additional market studies available on a contract basis. For a detailed discussion, see Section 5 below.

H. *Shipping and Other Transfer Costs*

It is important to remember that shipping from one area to another requires time equal to one decision period (whether the transfer is made between subsidiaries of one company or between different companies).

If a company buys goods manufactured in a given area by another firm, those goods may be resold in that same area in the following quarter. (They must first be shipped from the seller's to the buyer's inventory.)

All goods are sold "cost, insurance and freight" (*cif*), meaning that transfer costs are charged against the seller. Selling prices should be calculated accordingly.

I. *Inventory*

Inventory is book-valued at average cost (of production, or purchase, as the case may be). Inventory charges vary somewhat by areas (cf. Background Data), and they are generally lower for any given quantity of X than for the same quantity of Y. However, inventory charges are the same for all grades of a product. Due to shortage of conveniently located warehouse space, inventory carrying charges accrue at a rate accelerating as the quantity in inventory increases (and faster for X than for Y). Inventory charges accrue only for goods left unsold at the end of the prior quarter which were also on hand at the beginning of that quarter. (Hence, goods produced – but not saleable – in a given quarter are *not* charged with inventory cost.)

Only two grades of a given product may be in inventory in a given area at a given time. If a company is left with three grades in an area at the end of a quarter, the next to the lowest grade will automatically be reduced to the level of the lowest grade.

If a company's potential sales in the consumer market during a given quarter exceed its available stock (i.e., opening inventory), actual sales will be limited to the amount of stock availability, and the major part of the excess will be sold by competitors who are not similarly stocked out. In other words, in the event of a stock-out a majority of customers caught short simply switch suppliers.

If a company is selling both in the consumer and industrial (inter-company) markets, industrial sales take priority of deliveries from inventory. Intra-company shipments from one area to another are also taken out of inventory before consumer sales. If there is a stock-out in the consumer end of the business, the major part of the excess potential sales will be redistributed among competitors as above.

If a firm engaged in inter-company selling does not have enough goods in stock to satisfy the contracted demand of the buying company, the seller's plant will work overtime to *expedite* his obligations. Thus, a company buyer is always assured of delivery. However, the extra costs incurred by the seller are quite considerable. They will appear under sales expediting on the income statement.[39]

J. *Financial Management*

The starting capital of each company is $10 million. Several aspects of the finance function were outlined in the general overview of the simulation in Section 3 of this chapter.

Generally speaking, in accord with good corporate practice the Home Office may be expected to handle long-term and overall financial management, while financial management in the areas concentrates on short-term and local problems.

The Home Office has to supply an area with a requisite amount of initial working capital when operations have begun in the area. Area working capital may be increased by plowing back local profits, by additional capital injections from the Home Office, by short-term bank borrowing and, in emergency situations, by supplier credits.[40]

---

39 This is one of the output sheets, samples of which are reproduced in Appendix II as well as in the *Player's Manual.*
40 Note that funds may be transferred from one area to another only via the Home Office. The requisite bookkeeping transactions and cash transfers may be accomplished within a quarter.

1] AREA FINANCES

Short-term bank loans and investments in local government paper of surplus funds in the areas are in principle for ninety days. Both loans and investments may be renewed within certain restrictions, although a *formal decision to do this is necessary*. At the beginning of the simulation interest rates *per quarter* are as follows:

	U.S.	*EEC*	*Brazil*
Bank loans	3	3½	4
Government paper	1	1	1½

The quantity limit of area bank loans is a reasonable percentage of the excess of current assets over current liabilities in the area at the beginning of the decision period in which the loan is sought (current assets being cash, Accounts Receivable, inventories, short-term securities then on hand; current liabilities being supplier credit, Accounts Payable and outstanding local short-term bank loans). The loan also must not exceed $9,999,000. If either of these limits is exceeded, and if the company does not have enough cash in the area to meet current obligations, the requisite part of the excess will automatically be regarded as supplier credit (see below).[41]

A company cannot have both short-term bank loans and short-term government securities investments in an area at one and the same time. Thus, if in an earlier quarter the company had invested in short-term securities, but now is deciding to take up a short-term loan in that area, the bank will first arrange for the sale of the securities (automatically). Teams should take this into account in arranging a loan.

Investment in local government paper is a convenient way of putting short-term surplus funds in an area to use. Such investment is limited to $9,999,000 in each area. Reinvestment may be made (by explicit decision) every quarter. It is possible to invest in area securities without conducting any other operations in the area, provided that the requisite funds have first been transferred from the Home Office.

Supplier credits will be automatically provided to the extent needed to meet current obligations in an area. As long as these credits are $300,000 or less in Brazil, or $600,000 or less in the U.S. or EEC (the "switch-over" amount), these credits are obtained at a lower interest rate than when they rise above the switch-over amount. Interest rates for supplier credits in the areas are 6 per cent per quarter below switch-over and 8 per cent above. Interest is charged for the same quarter in which this type of credit is made available. Whenever there is residual cash available at the end of a quarter's transactions in an

---

[41] If no supplier credit is called for, any excessive loan decision will be automatically scaled down to the maximum currently permissible limit.

area it will *automatically* be used to pay off any outstanding supplier credits in the area.

Plant depreciation and *fixed plant expense* are handled automatically. Beginning the quarter when construction is finished, they appear in the joint depreciation and fixed plant expense account on the income statement. Note, however, their essentially different character: while depreciation is a noncash expense, fixed plant charges are taken directly out of cash (without going through Accounts Payable) each quarter. Depreciation is linear and extends over 20 quarters. Plants must be fully paid for in the quarter in which construction is begun.

Accounts Receivable accumulate whenever sales (whether consumer, inter-company or intra-company) are made in (or from) any area, but a certain proportion of these sales are paid for immediately. In the EEC and Brazil a certain percentage of sales are made on the basis of a two-quarter credit, while others demand only one-quarter credit. In the U.S. no sales demand two-quarter credit; however, some do require a one-quarter credit. The *approximate* percentages of sales income going into cash, A/R 1 and A/R 2 on the balance sheet, are respectively:

Area	U.S.	EEC	Brazil
Cash	40	50	30
A/R 1	60	20	30
A/R 2	—	30	40

Delays and advance payments will cause certain variations around these percentages.

Accounts Payable consist in part of variable (*not* fixed) manufacturing costs, and costs of goods in inter-company or intra-company buying. Functionally they are analogous to sales and Accounts Receivable. The schedule of Accounts Payable becoming due for payment immediately, and in A/P 1 and A/P 2, respectively, is identical with that for Accounts Receivable. Note, however, that A/R and A/P are "out-of-phase" by one quarter as goods made in a given quarter cannot be sold until the following.

Corporate income taxes in all areas have a lag of one quarter, and appear in A/P 1 on the balance sheet. Sales expediting costs, being of an emergency character, come directly out of cash. Fixed plant expense and all other current expenses are also cash items.

2] **HOME OFFICE FINANCES**

A *minimum cash requirement* of $50,000 in the home office cash account at the end of every quarter is required by the Bank.

Bank loans of a long-term nature may be obtained for expansion or financial consolidation. The maximum amount obtainable is determined in each case by the Bank (represented by the administrator), as is the duration of the loan. The interest rate is generally 3 per cent per quarter.

Inter-company loans may at any time be negotiated by any company from one or more other companies. The companies may settle on any terms mutually agreeable. The terms *must* be registered with the Court (as represented by the administrator). As long as a borrower does not go bankrupt, he is forced to live up to the agreement, and deficits will be covered by supplier credits. In case of bankruptcy the amount recovered by the lender will be determined by the Court.

Stock market confidence will be reflected by a cash addition to working capital each quarter to well-run companies. It may be assumed that the stock market has access to past quarterly earnings, dividends and asset data, as well as *current* dividends, and that its confidence in well-run firms grows over time. No such additions to capital can be expected until the company has an earnings and dividend record to stand on. (On the other hand, the INTOP stock market is not capable of evaluating a company's future prospects.) While these additions to capital generally will be smaller than dividend payments, it must be remembered that such payments constitute *one* of the important, generally applicable criteria of company performance. Paid-in-capital may also be a criterion used by the Bank in passing on home office loan applications.

Long-term securities investments of surplus funds may at any time be invested in the Home Office. These always yield 1.7 per cent interest per quarter. These investments may be recalled at any time without penalty. It is assumed that the portfolio is re-examined every quarter – hence, a formal decision to reinvest is necessary. Failing this, the investment will be regarded as canceled, and the funds transferred to cash.

Supplier credits will be automatically provided to the extent needed to meet current obligations in the Home Office. As long as these credits are $1,000,000 or less they are obtained at an interest rate of 5 per cent per quarter. Beyond this amount the rate is 7 per cent per quarter. When the patience of suppliers is exhausted (as communicated by the administrator), a company goes bankrupt. The determinants of such a fatal event are size of indebtedness (absolute and relative to assets and sales) and future prospects of the company. Whenever there is residual home office cash available at the end of a quarter's transactions, it will *automatically* be used to pay off any outstanding supplier credits.

K. *Marketing Research, Trade Association Gazette and Consultation*

The (fictional) World Federation of Appliance Manufacturers publishes the quarterly *Gazette*. It contains factual information about the state of the world economy in general and the appliance markets in particular, forecasts, gossip about members of the industry and other news of varying degrees of relevance and reliability. The *Gazette* is only available to members; the annual membership fee is $40,000.

The Home Office also may contract for various marketing research and consulting services; cf. Section 5 of this chapter.

L. *Inter-company and Intra-company Transactions* [42]

Three major types of inter-company transactions may take place: *lending, licensing* and *selling*. Inter-company loans have been described under Financial Management above. An inter-company transaction may be confined to one quarter (except patent licenses, which must be given for at least two quarters). Such transactions may also be made for two or more quarters, at the discretion of the parties. Such *standing contracts* will be officially binding on the parties only if registered with the administrator.

1] PATENT LICENSES

All patent licenses must be given for *at least two quarters* and have to be registered with the Patent Office (as represented by the administrator). Beyond this requirement such licenses may be granted subject to any conditions mutually agreeable (fixed price and/or royalty, with or without territorial restrictions, selectively or exclusively, with or without provisions for minimum prices on the end product, etc.).[43] However, the parties involved share with the Patent Office the responsibility for the fulfillment of licensing contracts; the adherence to such agreements is not an "automatic" feature of the simulation (as indeed it is not in the real world).

Why would a company be interested in taking a license? Some companies prefer this way of capitalizing on innovation to financing their own R & D programs. Even companies running their own R & D may find that they may speed up the stream of innovations in this manner: as grade X_3 incorporates X_2 and X_1 as well, a company only possessing, say, X_1, may find it appropriate to take a license for X_3. It may thereafter elect to drop its own R & D or continue the program directly towards X_4.

Why would a company be interested in giving a license? Some companies may find they have more improvements than they can effectively utilize (due to the two-grades-per-product-per-area-in-any-

---

42   Decision Card No. 3 is used for all of these transactions. Note that even where a standing contract has been entered into it is necessary for the parties to fill out such a card each quarter pertaining to the part of total contract fulfillment scheduled for that quarter. Standard decision forms are reproduced in Appendix IV.

43   Note that a licensee in turn can license others, unless his license agreement explicitly enjoins him from doing so. Such a sublicense may only be granted a quarter after the original license was obtained.

given-quarter limitation). Also, due to the likelihood that other companies sooner or later will make a parallel invention, the pioneer has to weigh the advantages of maximum exploitation of his temporary quasi-monopoly position on his own against sharing the benefits with others willing to pay for the privilege. This can be done very effectively by means of area, time, quantity, and similar types of restrictive clauses, if so desired.

Patent licenses can be granted only a quarter after that in which the licensor obtained the grade licensed. The licensee can exploit the patent only a quarter after that in which it was obtained by him.

2] INTER-COMPANY (INDUSTRIAL) SALES

These sales also may be made on any conditions agreed to by the parties involved, whether distribution or subcontracting is intended. Such sales are apt to be especially beneficial in cases where one of the companies enjoys the economies of specialization on one product, or where the parties are active in different areas, or where a company wants to clean out its inventory of one grade of a product preparatory to introducing another one. They may, of course, be made *within* an area as well as across boundaries. In either case, the transfer operation demands a time of one quarter prior to the product's being resold by the buyer. The sales contract must specify from which area and to which area the transfer is being made, as well as the companies, thousands of units, and the unit price involved. If the grade involved is not one which the buyer already is marketing in the area concerned, he should remember the two-grades-in-any-given-area-at-any-given-time limitation. (Otherwise the next to the lowest grade will be automatically merged with the lowest in his inventory.)

Intra-area transfer of goods between different companies involves certain costs for transportation and insurance, although these are smaller than in international trade. These costs are on a *cif* basis (chargeable to the seller).

3] INTRA-COMPANY TRANSFERS OF GOODS

Each company is free to make intra-company transfers from one area to another. The company must decide for itself at what price per unit such transfers should be made (facing the same vexing problems of intra-corporate economics as real-life concerns). Such intra-company sales naturally are subject to the regular international transfer costs. As in other international transactions these costs will be charged to the selling division of the company.

M. *Background Data on Brazil, the EEC and the U.S.*

I] SIZE OF MARKET, NATURE OF DEMAND

With 190 million Americans and the world's highest standard of living, the *U.S.* market, of course, has the greatest potential of the three areas. The *EEC* has over 160 million consumers, but a combined GNP only about one-half of that of the U.S. Standards of living are, however, unequally distributed in the area. The northern four of the six countries, with a population well in excess of 70 million, have living standards rapidly approaching those of this country. GNP is still growing at a more rapid rate in the EEC than in the U.S. While full freedom of internal mobility of factors inside the EEC is still a few years off, business behavior has shown itself to be strongly anticipatory, hence the treatment of the area as a unified economy in INTOP. *Brazil*, with some 65 million inhabitants, as nearly as we can make out (in view of artificial exchange rates, etc.) has only 1/6 to 1/10 of the gross national product per capita of the U.S. The Brazilian economy is in a hothouse type of expansion, involving rates of inflation as high as 30 per cent in some recent years.[44] The Brazilian market for vacuum cleaners is also somewhat constrained by the fact that electrification is a good deal less than universal in rural areas. On the other hand, this very circumstance makes the battery-operated radio market a good deal greater than might otherwise be the case.

Consumer information and product awareness regarding any one product in any one area at any one time tend to vary somewhat with the number of companies *marketing* in the area. If the number of companies marketing, n, is less than the total number of firms in the simulation, N, the market potential will be below normal,[45] although the relation between actual potential and normal will always be appreciably greater than n/N.

The comparatively late beginnings of the Brazilian electrical manufacturing industry is reflected by the special regulations concerning construction of local plants during the early decision periods referred to above.

2] PRODUCT MARKET DIFFERENCES BY AREA

In all areas the higher-quality *portable transistor radios* enjoy the position of a coveted prestige item. In Brazil cheap and simple, battery-operated portables are also rapidly coming to be regarded as a necessity of life in many outlying territories not yet touched by electrification and by the economically least well-to-do living in the fringe districts of metropolitan areas. These cheaper models are also

44 Cf., *Survey of the Brazilian Economy 1960*, published by the Brazilian Embassy, Washington, D. C., 60ff. The Montevideo treaty of February 17, 1960, provided for a Latin American Free Trade Association (involving initially Brazil, Mexico, Argentina, Uruguay, Paraguay, Chile and Peru). LAFTA was subsequently established in the summer of 1961. As the impact of the treaty as yet is rather uncertain, and as LAFTA in any case provides for a 12-year transition period, it was not felt either desirable or called for to include consideration of its effects in INTOP.

45 Should the number of companies marketing a product in an area temporarily decline — for instance, during a strike — the brand loyalty of many consumers will manifest itself in a similar reduction of total market potential.

popular in the U.S. and the EEC, not least among the teenage set. Nevertheless, in the latter two areas low-quality portables tend to suffer somewhat from the competition from cheap table-model radios.

A characteristic feature of the portable transistor radio market is a *wide price spread* between sets of different quality and, to a considerable extent, even between different brands of approximately equal quality. In Brazil this spread tends to be tempered by the fact that the high-quality market is relatively thin. As in that area the cheaper models are bought primarily by low-income groups, the net effect is fairly high sensitivity to price. Price elasticity is smaller in the EEC and least pronounced in the U.S.[46]

Aggregate demand for portable transistor radios at the beginning of the simulation may be most conveniently expressed in terms of a comparison with aggregate demand for vacuum cleaners at the same time (see p. 74f). In the EEC the initial radio market is around 40 per cent of the initial cleaner market in terms of *units*. In the U.S. the corresponding figure is approximately 60 per cent. In Brazil it is 100 per cent. The rate of growth of the portable radio market is everywhere healthy. The growth rate is highest in Brazil, lowest in the U.S. Yet the U.S. market is likely to remain the largest by a substantial margin even at the termination of the simulation.

What makes it difficult to be narrowly specific in discussing the transistor radio market is its susceptibility to developments in the broader environment. For example, continued expansion of Brazilian radio networks could well open up substantial territories now unsuitable for small portables. Similarly, if manufacturers could effectively lick the problems of portable FM radios a vast potential market in the U.S. (and a smaller one in the EEC) would open up. On the other hand, continued electrification in Brazil, or a lowering of prices on table-model radios in the other areas, at least in the long run would have the effect of moving the demand curve down for the portable radio industry.

Vacuum cleaners are, of course, necessities of life in the U.S. Housewives are appreciative of basic improvements in the product, hence high quality models sell well. Somewhat paradoxically, economy models at the other end of the scale are also popular. They are preferred by low income groups; in addition there has been a trend of late among home-owning suburbanites to buy a second, cheap cleaner for basement (notably playroom) areas.

In the EEC, too, the cleaner is an indispensable part of the household — not least among the well-to-do Dutch and Germans. There is a preference for medium-quality models. Among Brazilians the cleaner suffers from its complete lack of prestige appeal. It also competes with relatively cheap domestic labor. As a result, any cleaner that

[46] Price elasticity at the industry level and at the firm level are covariant, the former, of course, being smaller than the latter. This applies to both X and Y.

will "do the job" tends to be acceptable to most purchasers.

Price sensitivity, by and large, for any given grade of vacuum cleaner is somewhat less in all areas than for portable radios. As between areas, price elasticity for cleaners tends to vary in the same direction as for radios, i.e., it is greatest in Brazil and lowest in the U.S. Note, however, that what was said about consumer preferences for certain grades may modify this rule for individual grades and areas in some cases.

Aggregate demand for vacuum cleaners will normally correspond to at least one and one-half times the optimal capacity of one plant per area per company participating in the simulation. If fewer than all companies are active in the area, market potential will be smaller (see above text at note 45). The vacuum cleaner industry is a mature one in all areas; its growth is substantially parallel to that of the local economies in general.

Interdependence of demand for radios and cleaners in the end consumer market is nowhere very great. In Brazil brand loyalty with regard to cleaners is carried over to radios only to a limited extent. Such cross-product brand loyalty in that nation is somewhat greater — but still miniscule — among consumers who first bought their radio. In the EEC cross-product brand loyalty is somewhat greater than in Brazil. It works stronger from cleaner to radio than in the opposite direction. In the U.S. cross-product loyalty is a bit greater than in the other two areas (although still modest). As in Europe, it is greater from cleaner to radio than vice versa.

3] SENSITIVITY TO ADVERTISING

Speaking very broadly, the portable radio market in all parts of the world tends to be more sensitive to advertising effort by individual firms than the cleaner market. Also, as a rule the U.S. market is least sensitive to advertising (due to the high level of background noise), while the Brazilian market is the most sensitive. The only exception to this rule occurs in vacuum cleaners, where U.S. sensitivity is a fraction higher than in the EEC, due to the current trend toward segmentation into economy and ultra-deluxe sectors of demand in this country.

Sensitivity to aggregate industry advertising expense is close to zero for vacuum cleaners in the U.S. For all other areas (and for the U.S. in the case of radios), it is true that at least a modicum of expansion of aggregate demand follows from an increase of total industry advertising expense. The variations are in the same general direction as at the individual firm level, although the amplitude, of course, is smaller.

4] COMMERCIAL AND ADMINISTRATIVE EXPENSE

C & A expense tends to adjust itself to area market potentials and other local conditions. *Agents* in Brazil, for instance, reflecting at once the strong position of the merchant class and the limited market, require high fees, as indicated in the Schedule of Costs. U.S. agents have the lowest margins on radios anywhere, while EEC representatives almost match them with regard to vacuum cleaners (a necessity of life to the European middle class – hence easy to sell). As regards *captive sales organizations*, the Schedule reflects the fact that overhead costs tend to be highest in the U.S. and lowest in Brazil. On the other hand, unit variable cost of selling is lowest in the States and highest in Brazil (largely due to more efficient communication and transportation systems in the U.S. than anywhere else, and the somewhat time-consuming pleasantries of negotiation in Brazil). In terms of unit costs, radios are everywhere cheaper to distribute than vacuum cleaners (although the difference is very small in captive distribution in the EEC). It may be noted, finally, that the costs of change (moving, severance pay, etc.) in switching from agency to captive distribution (or vice versa) or adding (or eliminating) regional sales offices are the same in all areas.

5] COSTS OF PRODUCTION AND CAPITAL

As may be derived from the Schedule of Costs, *investment in productive capacity* is more expensive per unit of capacity in Brazil than in the other two areas. Construction labor, while cheap, is not very productive; the cost of capital is high; building materials are perhaps on par with other countries; and productive equipment (all imported in the electrical manufacturing industry) is a great deal more expensive than in the EEC or the U.S.

Radio and cleaner plants in the different areas have *different optimal and maximal capacity ratings*. Generally speaking, these differences reflect variations in production technology of the two products and in local economic development. In Brazil, where the degree of mechanization is relatively low, permitting considerable flexibility, maximal capacity of radio plants is more than 50 per cent greater than optimal. The difference is somewhat less in the EEC and least in the U.S. Vacuum cleaner production technology is fairly mature and mechanized and the difference between optimal and maximal capacity is everywhere relatively smaller than for radios. Again, the relative difference is smallest in the States and greatest in Brazil.[47]

The *fixed cost* element of manufacturing cost tends to be somewhat lower in the EEC relative to capacity than in either of the other two areas, as the Schedule indicates. The common economies stemming from joint administration of several X plants (or Y plants) are also slightly greater, again speaking relatively, in the EEC than in the U.S. or Brazil. Presumably the EEC edge in this field stems from

---

[47] On the other hand, for both products it is ordinarily true that at beyond (or below) optimal capacity operation, variable costs increase the least in the U.S. and the most in Brazil.

the lower cost and smaller size of management and staff groups in that area than in the U.S., as well as greater physical proximity of the various installations in multi-plant operations than in the other two areas.

Brazil, being "a generally high-cost producing area"[48] has *direct manufacturing costs* appreciably higher than both the U.S. and the EEC. The high-cost characteristics of Brazil are due to the relatively lower productivity of factory labor as well as greater materials expense (smaller quantities bought of raw materials due to lower output, heavy tariffs on imported components). In addition, Brazil evidences high volatility in labor-management relations. Direct manufacturing costs in the U.S. tend to be somewhat lower on radios and somewhat higher on cleaners than they are in the EEC.[49]

Direct manufacturing costs for higher grades of X and Y tend to increase in all areas due to the additional stylistic and functional features of the high-grade products. Generally, variable costs increase at a higher relative rate for radios than for cleaners.

Inventory charges, while the same for all grades of a product, vary by area as well as product. They are appreciably higher in Brazil for a given quantity of inventory than in the other two areas, as warehouse space tends to be dimensioned to local market potentials. In addition, warehouses in Brazil must be equipped with climate control to protect against excessive humidity. As long as inventories are no more than "normal," however, charges are fairly modest. Inventory charges in the EEC are about the same as in the U.S.

Capital interest rates were accounted for under Financial Management. Generally speaking, the Brazilian capital market is both tighter and smaller than those of the EEC and the U.S. The capital markets of the latter two areas are more nearly similar.

6] GOVERNMENT AND BUSINESS RELATIONS.

INTERNATIONAL TRADE POLICIES

Corporation tax rates are 52 per cent in the U.S., 45 per cent in the EEC and 30 per cent in Brazil. (These rates are fair approximations

48 National Industrial Conference Board, *Production Costs Abroad* (Studies in Business Economics No. 61, 1958), 28. This report states that "the experience of United States Companies in Latin America is mixed, but in general the data placed that area in the high-cost column." With regard to Brazil specifically, "in three of the nine cases, costs are 145% or more of American costs. In four, they are 116% to 145% or more of American costs; in the remaining two they are 106% to 115%." *Ibid.*, 25ff. Cf. Yale Brozen, "The New Competition — International Markets. How Should We Adapt?" 33 *Journal of Business* (Oct. 1960), 322–26.

49 The realism of this particular "given" in the simulation depends on which European country one has in mind. We are assuming somewhat arbitrarily that in a well-integrated EEC the cost structure will tend to approximate relatively high-cost French rather than relatively low-cost German conditions. The underlying rationale is principally that wage rates will rise more rapidly in the EEC than in the U.S., while the productivity of labor will remain lower.

of existing conditions.) The rate in Liechtenstein is 10 per cent, emphasizing the tax haven nature of that country.[50] Generally speaking, taxes are incurred in the same quarter in which taxable income is made; the amount payable goes into A/P 1 in all areas.

In INTOP tax legislation, the U.S. allows only the carrying forward for *one* quarter of *up to 50 per cent* of the net *operating* loss in any given quarter. In the EEC this rate is 30 per cent, and in Liechtenstein 100 per cent. These carry-forward provisions are administered *automatically*. No other carry-forward or carry-back arrangements exist.

Brazilian Government relations to business and international trade policies are in a category somewhat different from those of the other areas. The policies of Brazil are in large part governed by considerations of local industrialization, inflationary pressures and recurring, or even somewhat chronic, balance-of-payments problems. Special incentives may be granted from time to time to foreign concerns establishing local manufacturing subsidiaries. On the other hand, balance-of-payments difficulties may impose restrictions on capital export from Brazil, tariff changes,[51] quota restrictions on imports, etc.

We must remember, however, that complete stability of public policy is nowhere to be found in this world. Sensationally enough, the rather modest "deterioration" in the balance-of-payments situation of the U.S. in 1959-60 brought to the fore such extraordinary proposals as limitations on the investments of U.S. concerns abroad, to pose but one example. Occasional major dislocations in trade conditions within and between even such supposedly "mature" economies as that of the EEC and the U.S. may therefore well be expected. The best hedge against such phenomena would possibly be to be equally heavily engaged in all areas and products. Yet, the limitations of resources, in the world of INTOPIA as in the real world, makes selectivity a necessity — posing a great challenge to management.

7] BUSINESS CYCLES AND ECONOMIC INDEX

The quarterly economic index published in the *Gazette* reflects current market conditions. As sales of portable radios and vacuum cleaners are differentially affected by such factors as changes in the business climate, general economic growth and gradual shifts in consumer styles of life, separate indexes may be published for X and Y from time to time. Amplitude and timing of cycles may vary between the

---

[50] The actual rate is unknown. It may be assumed that the direct profit-making activities at the Home Office will be of limited scope as compared to most area operations in most companies.

[51] At the time of writing, Brazilian tariffs on home appliances are actually 120 per cent of *cif* value (!), but it has been necessary to scale down this enormous disparity appreciably here, in order to make exports to Brazil at all possible. Indeed, in reality many more appliances were actually imported to Brazil than made locally until very recently despite skyscraping tariffs.

areas. No complete correlation with sales volume can be guaranteed, as changing volume of course also reflects changing competitive strategies.

5. Additional Standard Information for Participants

SECTION 4 GIVES a detailed description of the INTOP model substantially identical with the main part of the *Player's Manual*. It is admittedly a considerable amount of structural information. On the other hand, we definitely wanted to avoid the overly cryptic and artificial kind of description which is still an unfortunate characteristic of most management simulations. If game instructions are to be suggestive of the broad range of management problems simulated – as we feel they should be – the manual must needs be different from a set of poker rules. Our experience indicates that the average participant has no more difficulty in obtaining a workable grasp of the INTOP environment than he would have in reading up for the discussion of a complex case of the type one associates with the Harvard Business School.

As a ready source of reference in decision-making sessions, all numerical data in the model with which students should be familiar are published separately in the Schedule of Costs, Charges, Time Lags and Marketing Research Services as Subsection B below. Its publication as a separate part has the additional advantage of facilitating parameter changes by the administrator, who simply can have a new Schedule mimeographed. Alternatively, if the changes are few, they may be inserted on the blank pages provided for the purpose in the Schedule of Costs part of the *Player's Manual*.

Another element of the standard documentation with which participants are supplied is the Marketing Research section of the *Player's Manual* (Subsection A below). It is printed separately due to the richness of marketing research data available in the game. Also, team members not concerned with environmental intelligence activities can perhaps afford to disregard this particular section.

Finally, the *Player's Manual* also contains a guide and commentary to the decision forms and output data sheets used in the simulation. As that commentary pertains to formal rather than to substantive matters it is excluded here. However, sample decision forms are reprinted in Appendix IV and sample output of company financial and marketing research data in Appendix II below. It may be noted that the ancillary data sheet of the FORTRAN output reproduced in Appendix II is somewhat more detailed than the corresponding sheet of Univac output which may be found in the *Player's Manual*. Otherwise input as well as output formats are the same for all practical purposes in the FORTRAN and Univac versions of the International Operations Simulation.

A. *Marketing Research Detailed*

Each company is provided with continuous feedback of a wealth of information about its own operations through the quarterly output sheets. Realistic decision-making also requires considerable information about the task environment in which business operates. Companies receive such data on a *regular* basis, and it is also possible to undertake *special-order* marketing research.

The *regular* flow of environmental intelligence stems from three sources: the quarterly output sheet labeled Market Research 1, the *Gazette* of the World Federation of Appliance Manufacturers (WFAM) and annual financial reports from all companies in the industry. Of these, companies get Market Research 1 and the annual reports of competitors without charge. As the organ of the WFAM the *Gazette* will be hurried to companies quarterly as the principal benefit of membership in the Federation, which costs $40,000 a year.

1] ANNUAL FINANCIAL REPORTS

Each company receives consolidated balance sheets and income statements of all companies in the industry in quarters 4, 8, 12 and so on. The data presented are identical with those appearing in the consolidated column of the more detailed balance sheets and income statements for quarters 4, 8, etc., which every company receives for its own operations. Hence it should be noted that *all* information in the income statement pertains only to *one quarter*.

2] MARKET RESEARCH 1

A specimen copy of the Market Research 1 sheet is reproduced as part of the sample output.[52] The upper half presents price statistics, giving all prices posted during the current quarter broken down by company, area, product and quality (standard-deluxe). Note that some of the prices may have been too high and hence not have yielded any sales; sales in units by company can be obtained by ordering special marketing research. The lower half of Market Research 1 states what *grades* of the two products (by standard and deluxe) are

[52] The reader is referred to Appendix II of this book.

being manufactured[53] by each company in each area in the current quarter. Thus, by going back to prior quarter grade data, it is often possible to determine to what quality (or qualities) of goods current prices are applied. (This is not possible where a company bought or shipped between its own subsidiaries goods of other grades.) Note that a "no production" indication during a given quarter does not necessarily mean the absence of either current sales, inventory or plant facilities.

3] MARKET RESEARCH 2

A number of standard marketing research data obtainable on a commercial basis are listed as Items 1-18 in the catalog of *Marketing Research Services* (cf. the last page of this chapter). The concrete meaning of these services (except numbers 17 and 18) is illustrated in the sample of the Market Research 2 output sheet in Appendix III. A few items deserve special comment:

Item 1. The *Gazette* may be obtained by becoming a member of the World Federation of Appliance Manufacturers. The *annual* fee is $40,000, which entitles you to four quarterly issues. Publication begins in quarter 4. A regular feature of the *Gazette* is a discussion of the business climate, including presentation of the economic index and a forecast for at least two quarters ahead. In addition the journal regularly carries information about changes in tariff rates, materials costs, labor conditions, government regulations of international and domestic trade, etc. of interest to the industry. (Some of this information will be given to all companies, whether subscribers or not.) Especially helpful, and occasionaly amusing, are the gossip columns, which give more or less reliable data about individual members of the industry, such as expansion plans, new product improvements, advertising campaigns, organization changes, dividend policy and so on. Many companies also find the *Gazette* a convenient means for public announcements about their desire to trade, license or enter into financial transactions with other firms. Members of the industry may also let off steam by writing letters to the editor.

Item 2. Consumer sales in units by *company*, product, quality and area. Note that standard and deluxe are accounted for on separate groups of lines. In addition, you will get *industry* totals, as in Item 3.

Item 3. Total *industry* consumer sales in units by product and areas are given separately for standard and deluxe.

Items 5, 6, 8, 9, 13, 14 and 16. These items are all in thousands of dollars.

---

[53] A "0" denotes that grade 0 is being made. In the FORTRAN program, "— 0" denotes "no production," while in the Univac program an asterisk (*) is used for this purpose.

Items 6, 9, 14. Total industry expense, as a *3-quarter average*, for advertising, methods improvement and R & D, respectively. These 3-quarter averages are of interest in that while expense in any one of these areas during a given decision period will have major impact immediately, such appropriations will continue to have a diminishing effect in subsequent periods. Most of the total effect will ordinarily be exhausted at the end of two quarters after that in which the decision was made.

Item 11. In each pair of numbers the first gives the number of companies engaged in *consumer* selling (whether via agents or a captive sales organization) of the *standard* version of the respective product in the respective area. The second number tells you how many companies are correspondingly engaged in consumer selling of the *deluxe* version. Ordinarily, all companies selling deluxe in an area are also selling standard there. Very often, however, the number of companies selling standard will be greater, as any one-quality product offering is presumed to be standard (whether it is X_0 or X_4).

Items 12-16. As these items refer to home office functions they are not broken down by area. The R & D data are classified by product.

Item 17. *Test Marketing* made by your agency under this heading will yield a prediction of how much you could hope to increase unit sales at a constant price (or increase price at constant unit sales) by introducing the grade of X (or Y) which you specify in relation to X_0 (or Y_0), assuming no advertising and no competitive counter-measures. The information will be delivered in a special report.

Item 18. *Manufacturing Cost* estimates will be given by your consultant on the percentage increase in variable manufacturing cost which you may expect by producing the grade of X (or Y) which you specify in relation to producing a similar volume of X_0 (or Y_0). The information will be delivered in a special report.

To order Items 1-18, Decision Card 2 (Home Office) is used. It has a heading "Marketing Research & Gazette." A couple of lines down you will find that you can make a maximum of three selections among Items 1-18 (No. 1 refers to the *Gazette*) in any given quarter. If you want to order one item only, specify its *Item number* in the first box. If you want more than one item specify the second and third items in ascending order in the subsequent boxes. The computer will bill you for the items ordered automatically. *Remember that if you order Item 17 and/or 18 you must specify product and grade for which the information is desired.* Information for a single grade of a single product of either Item 17 or Item 18 constitutes a separate item.

The total cost of marketing research items and consulting services ordered will appear under the item "Market Research" on the income statement for the quarter in which these items and services were ordered. The expense comes out of home office cash with no delay.

4] SPECIAL CONSULTING SERVICES

The management consulting firm of Arthur DeBig (represented by the administrator) is available for special services. You may approach them with any inquiry, although they are known to be fairly choosey as to the assignments they are willing to take on. The fee for any such special consulting service is subject to negotiation. *The fee is always payable in advance,* even though their report may take more than one quarter to complete, depending on the nature and difficulty of the assignment.

To stimulate your imagination, we present some illustrations of services extended by this well-known firm in the past:

Items 3-16 under Marketing Research Services — they are usually able to get these data for *any quarter prior to the current one* for 60 per cent of what you would have to pay for up-to-date information. The cost may be even lower if you are willing to accept reasonable estimates rather than exact data.

Number of patent licenses, who is licensing whom, order of magnitude of royalties per unit.

Who is selling what to whom in inter-company transactions.

Number, size and company affiliation of captive sales organizations in the different areas.

Rank order of firms according to advertising appropriations, by product and area (dollar amounts are hard to get at, however).

Cumulative data for all quarters on total industry advertising or methods improvement by product and area, cumulative R & D expense by product.

Cumulative dividends declared by company.

Optimal plant capacity, i.e., the rate of output for an X-plant or a Y-plant in a given area at which direct variable manufacturing cost is at a minimum.

Sales by companies for one product in one area currently.

Sales advantage from having both standard and deluxe models in an area.[54]

Payment for consulting services must be made in the quarter in which they are negotiated. You will record the decision on Decision Card 2 (Home Office) in the treble box appearing under "Marketing Research and Gazette." *Insert the dollar amount* (in thousands). It will be added to any standard market research items you may order on the same form, and the total cost of consulting and marketing research services will appear under the item "Market Research" on the income statement for the quarter in which these services were ordered. The expense comes out of home office cash that same quarter.

[54] The administrator will be provided with the necessary information to answer this question when obtaining the program tape and related materials.

B. *Schedule of Costs, Charges, Time Lags and Marketing Research Services*

Basic Cost and Resource Data

Starting Capital: $10,000,000. Your bank ordinarily will require a minimum amount of $50,000 in the home office cash account.

MAXIMAL CAPACITY PER PLANT BY PRODUCT AND
AREA PER QUARTER (UNITS)

	U.S. (Area 1)	EEC (Area 2)	BRAZIL (Area 3)
X (radios)	22,000	18,000	12,000
Y (cleaners)	36,000	29,000	10,000

Optimal output rate as a rule differs relatively most from maximal in Brazil and least in the U.S., and relatively more for radios than cleaners.

ACQUISITION COST PER PLANT BY PRODUCT AND AREA, $

	U.S.	EEC	BRAZIL
X	1,200,000	1,000,000	700,000
Y	1,800,000	1,500,000	700,000

Notes: 1. You can have a maximum of 3 X-plants and 3 Y-plants in each area. 2. Plants may be disposed of at a discount (see administrator).

Plants are paid for in cash the first quarter of construction. *Deprecation* is linear and automatic, over a period of 20 quarters, beginning when the plant comes "on stream."

FIXED COST OF PLANT (NOT TO BE CONFUSED WITH DEPRECIATION)
BY PRODUCT, AREA AND NUMBER OF PLANTS, $ PER QUARTER

	UNITED STATES			EUROPEAN ECONOMIC COMMUNITY		
No. of Plants	1	2	3	1	2	3
X	70,000	95,000	105,000	50,000	65,000	70,000
Y	100,000	150,000	180,000	70,000	100,000	110,000

BRAZIL

No. of Plants	1	2	3
X	35,000	55,000	65,000
Y	35,000	50,000	60,000

Direct variable manufacturing cost will generally be 25-35 per cent of the price of economy models at the beginning of the game. At beyond-optimal capacity operation, variable costs increase the least in the U.S. and the most in Brazil.

TYPICAL CONSUMER PRICES OF ECONOMY MODELS AT
BEGINNING OF THE SIMULATION $:

	U.S.	EEC	BRAZIL
X (radios)	24	28	32
Y (cleaners)	45	50	55

Market Potential. It may be safely assumed that normal

long-term potential for Y corresponds at least to 1½ plants optimal capacity per company and area. In the beginning quarters the market for X in the EEC is about 40 per cent, in the U.S. about 60 per cent, and in Brazil about 100 per cent of corresponding Y-markets in units. (In both cases the company is assumed to have both standard and deluxe models.)

Consumer information and product awareness regarding any one product in any one area at any one time tend to vary somewhat with the number of companies *marketing* in the area. If the number of companies marketing, n, is less than the total number of firms in the simulation, N, the market potential will be below normal, although the relation between actual potential and normal will always be appreciably greater than n/N.

INTERNATIONAL TRANSFER COSTS (AT BEGINNING OF GAME), $ PER UNIT

	U.S. to EEC or EEC to U.S.	U.S. or EEC to Brazil and vice versa
X	4	6
Y	10	18

INTRA-AREA TRANSFER COSTS, $ PER UNIT, ALL AREAS

X 1
Y 2

Note: Intra-area transfer costs are incurred only in inter-company sales within an area.

Corporation tax rates: in the U.S. 52 per cent, in the EEC 45 per cent, in Brazil 30 per cent, in Liechtenstein 10 per cent (only on current gross earnings in local operations). Up to 50 per cent of operating loss in a given quarter in the U.S., up to 30 per cent in the EEC, and up to 100 per cent in Liechtenstein, will be carried forward for *one* quarter *automatically*.

INTEREST RATES FOR AREA 90 DAY BANK LOANS, QUARTERLY

Area	U.S.	EEC	Brazil
Percentage	3	3½	4

While renewable in principle, the amount of these loans is limited to a reasonable proportion of the excess of current assets over current liabilities in the area at the beginning of the quarter (and in any case to $9,999,000).

INTEREST RATES FOR AREA GOVERNMENT SECURITIES INVESTMENT, QUARTERLY

Area	U.S.	EEC	Brazil
Percentage	1	1	1½

There is an upper limit on such investments of $9,999,000. They may be renewed.

Standard interest rate for home office long-term bank loans: 3 per cent per quarter. Time and quantity limit of loan subject to negotiation with Bank (administrator).

Interest rate for home office securities investment: 1.7 per cent per quarter. Quantity limit $99,999,000. Company may recall funds any time without penalty (even though this is to be thought of principally as long-term investments).

INTEREST RATES FOR SUPPLIER CREDITS IN
AREAS AND HOME OFFICE, QUARTERLY

	Area	Home Office
Below switch-over	6	5
Above switch-over	8	7

Switch-over amount in Brazil $300,000, in the U.S. and the EEC $600,000, and in Liechtenstein (Home Office) $1,000,000. Ultimate limit of these credits occurs when the patience of suppliers is exhausted, in which case you will be notified by the administrator.

R & D. Minimum cost to keep one scientist with minimal equipment working on improving product X is $30,000 per quarter, and in the case of product Y $40,000 per quarter. Any greater amount may be invested (not necessarily in units of 30,000 or 40,000 dollars). There are no common economies in R & D for X and Y.

COMMERCIAL AND ADMINISTRATIVE EXPENSE IN
CASE OF AGENCY, $ PER UNIT AND AREA

	U.S.	EEC	Brazil
X isolated	3.50	4.50	5.00
X combined	3.30	4.00	4.00
Y isolated	5.50	5.50	7.50
Y combined	4.00	4.50	5.50

X isolated (Y isol.) when you are only selling X (or Y).
X combined and Y comb. when you are selling both X and Y.
Formula for combined charges in an area:
(X comb. × units of X) + (Y comb. × units of Y) = agent's fee.

Basic data re C & A expense in case of captive sales organization, by area and quarter:
Minimum combination is one central office plus one regional office.
Maximum combination is one central office plus nine regional offices.
The central office is equal to two regional offices in cost.

Quarterly cost per regional office (administrative overhead) in the U.S. is $18,000, in the EEC it is $9,000, and in Brazil it is $7,000. Cost incurred by changing number of offices (or by switching from agency to captive or vice versa) are the same in all areas. They accelerate with the magnitude of change. Direct variable selling cost is highest in Brazil, lowest in the U.S., and is everywhere lower for X than Y.

The earliest possible moves with regard to plant construction, production, and marketing are indicated in the schedule below.

QUARTER 1 construction
2 construction
3 production (to inventory)
4 marketing

Note that *each* new plant (X or Y) for which construction is begun in Brazil during quarters 1-3 requires a deposit of $1,500,000 in Brazilian Government securities, which must be held until the end of quarter 3.

Goods produced in a given quarter go into inventory at the end of that quarter. Hence *there is a lag of one quarter between production and selling.*

International *transfer of goods* (inter-company or intra-company), and intra-area shipment of goods in industrial sales (inter-company), takes a period of one quarter. (The goods go into the recipient's inventory at the end of the quarter in which they are transferred.)

There is a certain time lag before investments in R & D have their *full* effectiveness in terms of the probability of reaching a product improvement. A patent may be used immediately after the company has been notified by the Patent Office (on the ancillary output sheet) that the patent has been granted. *Patent licenses* can be granted only a quarter after that in which the licensor obtained the grade licensed. The licensee can exploit the patent only a quarter after that in which it was obtained by him.

Accounts Receivable. Proceeds from all sales (consumer, intra- & inter-company) are available immediately or with a one-quarter (A/R 1) or two-quarter (A/R 2) lag *approximately* in the following proportions (delays and advance payments cause certain variations):

Area	U.S.	EEC	Brazil
Cash	40	50	30
A/R 1	60	20	30
A/R 2	—	30	40

License and interest income goes to cash.

Accounts Payable. The schedule of Accounts Payable (for *variable* manufacturing expense, and intra- & inter-company sales) becoming due immediately, and in A/P 1 and A/P 2, respectively, is identical with that for Accounts Receivable. (Note, however, that A/R and A/P are "out of phase" by one quarter, as goods made in a given quarter cannot be sold until the following.) Taxes in the areas go to A/P 1. All other expense, including fixed plant expense, comes directly out of cash.

Advertising and Methods Improvement. Expenditure on advertising and methods during a given quarter will have its major impact immediately but will continue to have a diminishing effect in subsequent quarters.

Business cycle effects. Note that amplitude as well as timing of business cycle effects have differed noticeably between various areas of the world in postwar years.

Stock market confidence. Improvement (or deterioration) in a company's position is only *fully* reflected in changes in stock market confidence (and hence, in the rate of addition to cash) with a certain lag. There are never any deductions from cash due to lack of confidence.

MARKET RESEARCH SERVICES[55]

Item Number		Cost
0.	Special consulting services by Arthur DeBig.	negotiable
1.	Subscription to the *Gazette* for one year, due in Quarter 3, 7, 11, etc.	$ 40,000
2.	Consumer sales in units by company, product, quality, and area in current quarter. (Also includes Item 3.)	60,000
3.	Total industry consumer sales in units by product, quality, and areas, currently.	12,000
4.	Number of companies advertising by product and area, currently.	2,000
5.	Total industry advertising expense by product and area, currently.	8,000
6.	Total industry advertising expense by product and area, 3-quarter average.	10,000
7.	Number of companies currently engaged in methods improvement by product and area.	1,000
8.	Total industry methods improvement expense by product and area, currently.	3,000
9.	Total industry methods improvement expense by product and area, 3-quarter average.	5,000
10.	Number of currently producing plants by product and area.	2,000
11.	Number of companies currently engaged in consumer selling by product, grade and area.*	2,000
12.	Number of companies currently in R & D by product.	1,000
13.	Total industry R & D expense by product currently.	6,000

* This item refers to companies actually making sales during the quarter. Prices on the Market Research 1 output sheet may not always have resulted in sales.

[55] The differences between prices for individual marketing research items originate in two considerations: the relative value of the items in company decision-making and the relative difficulty of procuring the information in practice.

Item Number		Cost
14.	Total industry R & D expense by product, 3-quarter average.	$ 9,000
15.	Number of companies currently engaged in marketing research.	500
16.	Total industry marketing research expense currently.	1,000
17.	Test marketing of any one product grade (please specify product and grade).	12,000
18.	Consultant's opinion on increase in variable manufacturing cost (in relation to X_0 or Y_0) for any one product grade (please specify product and grade).	3,000

YOU ORDER MARKET RESEARCH ON THE HOME OFFICE FORM
(DECISION CARD NO. 2)

Chapter **3**

Economic Models and

Programming Approaches

Introduction

IT IS CONVENIENT to think of a business simulation as a model of some segment of a general, though abstract, economic reality. Thus, as indicated in the earlier chapters, the game administrator and the participants are to imagine themselves in a real situation and to ignore insofar as possible the fact that all activity takes place in a model. This means that there are a great many ideas of what the reality is like; in fact, even the game designers themselves may not interpret in the same way all of the characteristics of the reality which the model mirrors. On the other hand, there is a unique and well-defined model, and it is necessary to spell out in a precise way exactly what its properties are.

There are two useful points of view from which to look at an economic simulation model. The first of these employs the language and concepts of economics and business. This approach requires us to examine the supply curve and its underlying costs as well as the demand curve and its determinants. On the other hand, the ultimate definition of the model is in the computer program. This chapter discusses the model from this viewpoint by presenting a description of the state variables (generally appearing as accounting data on company output) and the transformations which change the values of the variables. The program articulates this description which in total determines the behavior of the firms in the model. There are, of course, certain important features which can be understood better from one point of view rather than the other. The particular form of the manufacturing cost function is primarily an economic matter and need receive only passing mention in the computer-oriented description. On the other hand, the timing and mechanics of inter-company transactions are of great importance in the computer context but of minor importance economically.

It is important in the descriptions which follow (as well as in the model itself) to be able to isolate manageable portions of the model. From both the economic and computer viewpoints it proves workable to use the natural divisions which are ordinarily used to describe the firm and the economy. Thus for most purposes the firms are separate entities. Moreover, the operating areas within a firm (Area 1, 2 and 3 in INTOP) can be treated as entities which are to a large extent disjointed both from each other and from a firm's Home Office. Within a single area of one firm the two products – denoted X and Y in INTOP – interact explicitly only in the marketing sector and to a small extent in the demand function. Within each product it is possible to distinguish the functional divisions of manufacturing and marketing. For many purposes these divisions can be treated separately. Finally, the functional divisions of finance, research and development, and accounting which exist in the operating areas and/or in the Home Office may also be viewed as modular building blocks.[1]

This separation within the geographic and functional areas is a relative matter. It is part of the essential character of INTOP that interactions among the parts of the model occupy an important place. The significant fact is that the points at which interactions occur can be specifically labeled in the course of the descriptive process. In the dynamics of actual play it is possible for relatively complicated interactions to be constructed from the simpler interactions present in the model. Then, too, many activities within a firm interact implicitly as they all make competing demands on the limited resources, such as cash.

In the exposition of the game in Chapter 2 it was pointed out that the firms may choose to assume different roles in the various product-area combinations. Indeed, budget constraints will force most of them to do this. In the description of the model to be given in this chapter it is not possible to describe all of the variations which might be – or even those that have been – encountered in a play of the game. Rather we shall examine an area where a firm is operating an integrated business including both manufacturing and marketing.

1. An Overview of the Economic Aspects of INTOP

TO VIEW THE FIRMS within INTOP as economic entities it is necessary to describe the components of the supply and demand functions which face the firm in both the short run and the long run.

[1] These building blocks make it possible to design a great many new games on the basis of the original model. Cf. Chapter 6 below.

It would be desirable from an economist's point of view to be able to find equilibrium positions of the firm, but in general this is a very difficult task. A relatively explicit statement of the system of equations it would be necessary to solve in order to do this is given later in this chapter.[2] Here a highly simplified model containing many of the features of the complete system is presented. It enables us to see the important features of the production functions, the supply side of the model, and the consumer market equations, the demand side of the model. Further, the essential steps in finding the equilibrium positions can be described and will lead to the analysis by which appropriate parameters for the model can be selected.

In the simple model, the firm has one factory whose initial cost is F; it manufactures and markets one model of one product. In the equilibrium state, the firm must select the price P and advertising expenditure A. These quantities are the only decisions of the firm which influence sales quantity Q. The firm manufactures a quantity Q consistent with market demand and incurs manufacturing cost MQ and marketing cost S. Note that we here consider the marginal cost of manufacturing to be constant and the total cost of marketing to be fixed, as we want some element of fixed cost. Later in the chapter a fairly detailed description of the actual form of these functions is given.[3] The analysis there is more complicated because M and S are functions of several variables.

One of the simplest forms of the demand equation is $Q = P^{e_p} A^{e_a} K$, where K denotes a combined economic index and scaling factor.[4] One of the main virtues of this functional form is that it yields constant price and advertising elasticities. Further it provides the basis for a simple algebraic treatment for redistributing demand to other firms when a given firm cannot fill its orders. Of course the function has the undesirable property of not being defined when $P = 0$ and $A = 0$. The way in which this difficulty is circumvented is shown later.[5]

In order to create a viable firm it is necessary to select values for the quantities in Fig. 3 in such a manner that the net income Y is some reasonable fraction of investment.

In the selection of values we must also ensure that the equations in Fig. 4 are satisfied. These equations consist of definition identities and the conditions arising from the fact that the derivatives of income Y with respect to price P and advertising A must vanish. If the last three items in Fig. 3 are ignored in this analysis, we must choose thirteen quantities in such a way that six equations are satisfied. This leaves seven choices to be made. In making these choices we will, of course, want all quantities except e_p to be nonnegative, thereby requiring the quantities Q, P, A and K to be positive. The form of the

2   Cf. *infra*, 114.
3   Cf. *infra*, 100.
4   The demand equation in the actual model is given in a form which makes

scaling very easy. Also the constant K can be thought of as embodying the decision variables of the other firms.
5   Cf. *infra*, 90.

FIG. 3   *Variables and Parameters of Simple Economic Model* *

F	factory cost
Q	sales quantity
P	price
M	average (and marginal) manufacturing cost
S	total marketing cost (fixed)
A	advertising expenditure
Y_E	(economic) income
R	revenue
C	total manufacturing cost
K	economic index
e_p	price elasticity
e_a	advertising elasticity
r	rate of return

t	tax rate
d	depreciation rate
Y_A	(accounting) income

* The symbols appearing below the horizontal line apply to accounting entities and do not affect the economic model.

equation defining Y_E arises because working capital needs are explicitly accounted for in the model. We assume that goods manufactured in one period are paid for in that period but are not available for sale until the next period.

FIG. 4   *Equations of Simple Economic Model* *

$$\log Q = e_p \log P + e_a \log A + \log K$$
$$Y_E = R - C - A - S - r\,(F + C)$$
$$e_p = -\,R/(R - C)$$
$$e_a = A/(R - C)$$
$$R = PQ$$
$$C = MQ$$

$$Y_A = (R - C - A - S - dF)\,(1 - t)$$

* The equation appearing below the horizontal line applies to accounting entities and does not affect the economic model.

The *pro forma* balance sheet and income statement are shown in Fig. 5. Taxes are set equal to zero. The age of the plant measured from the time it is able to produce is denoted by i. The balance sheet and income statement, together with the relationships given in Fig. 4 for the profit-maximizing firm, give the model builder or administrator a framework for selecting reasonable values of the parameters in the demand equation and the magnitudes which must appear in the cost functions.

FIG. 5 *Accounting Statements of Simple Economic Model*

BALANCE SHEET (Period i)

Accounts	Symbols	Values
Cash	$(i-1)[R - C - S - A - r(F + C)]$	$(i-1)(46{,}000)$
Inventory	C	80,000
Current Assets	Cash + Inventory	$34{,}000 + i\,46{,}000$
Net Plant	$F(1 - id)$	$920{,}000 - i\,46{,}000$
Total Assets	Net Plant + Current Assets	954,000
Current Liabilities	0	
Retained Earnings	Cash $- idF$	$-46{,}000$
Invested Capital	$F + C$	1,000,000
Total Liability and Equity	$F(1 - id) + $ Cash $+ C$	954,000

INCOME STATEMENT (Period i)

Accounts	Symbols	Values
Sales Revenue	R	250,000
Cost of Goods Sold	C	80,000
Gross Margin	$R - C$	170,000
Marketing Expense	S	40,000
Advertising Expense	A	24,000
Depreciation	dF	46,000
Gross Profit	$R - C - S - A - dF$	60,000
Dividends	$r(F + C)$	60,000
To Retained Earnings	Gross Profit $-$ Dividends	0

In the following, one approach is suggested, but certainly others are possible. The procedure is to select the entries which appear on the balance sheet and income statement and use these to deduce the economic quantities.[6] The price and advertising elasticities are the essential ones. As a specific example, the following quantities can be assigned arbitrary numerical values as shown.[7]

Invested Capital $= F + C$	$=$	1,000,000	
Sales Revenue $= R$	$=$	250,000	
Manufacturing Cost $= C$	$=$	80,000	
Marketing Cost $= S$	$=$	40,000	
Return on investment $= r(F + C) =$		60,000	$r = 6\%$
Economic Income $= Y_E$	$=$	0	
Depreciation $= dF$	$=$	46,000	$d = 5\%$

[6] This approach is further detailed, and ranges of suitable minimal values in the INTOP model discussed, in Chapter 5, Section 3.

[7] The quantity below the horizontal line refers to an accounting entity which appears in the economic model as a fixed cost.

The formula for Y_E in Fig. 4 yields advertising cost $= A = 250{,}000 - 80{,}000 - 40{,}000 - 60{,}000 - 46{,}000 = 24{,}000$. Other formulas given in Fig. 4 yield

$$e_a = 24{,}000/(250{,}000 - 80{,}000 - 40{,}000) = 0.184$$
$$e_p = -(250{,}000/170{,}000) = -1.47$$

Only at this stage need the units be selected. One of P, Q and M may be selected arbitrarily. We may select $P = 25$ and set $Q = 10{,}000$ and $M = 8$ which will yield

$$K = QP^{-e_p} A^{-e_a} = 10{,}000 \ (25)^{1.47} \ (24{,}000)^{-0.184}$$

The numerical quantities at the right of the sample balance sheet and income statement in the table in Fig. 5 show the values of the accounts in period i. Note that the retained earnings are always negative since depreciation is not "inventoried" but is charged during the first period when goods are manufactured but not sold. Matters will be set aright in the period in which the plant has been fully depreciated; however, since no depreciation is charged, no manufacturing is allowed in this simplified model, but the goods manufactured in the previous quarter may be sold.

Alternatively, one can start from the economic side and specify e_p and e_a rather than R and C. The formulas of Fig. 4 permit one to write

$$Y_E = A/e_a - S - r (F - (e_p/e_a) A - A/e_a)$$

This equation may be solved for A and then R and C can be determined.

It is of some interest to examine the situation facing the firm when it chooses between one factory and two factories. The actual model of INTOP may be very grossly approximated by saying that the two factory investment is not twice as large as the one factory investment and that the marginal cost M is smaller for two factories than for one.

If the firm adopts as the rate of return r that which it can earn in alternative investments, such as government securities, it is easy (though somewhat lengthy) to show that for low values of r it is rational to build two plants, while for high values of r it is rational to build one. One of the problems facing firms in the simulation is to decide the cost of the possible errors in choice.

The following sections give a detailed exposition of the important functional areas in the model.

2. The Economic and Mathematical Aspects of the INTOP Simulation

A. The Functional Areas

It is obvious that a gaming model derives much of its essential character from the functions which determine the firm's costs and the equations which express its orders in the consumer market as functions of price, advertising expenditure and other relevant variables.

In a well-designed simulation these functions should be constructed to meet several criteria. First, it is highly desirable that they be expressed in terms of parameters or tabular values in such a way that a wide range of behavior may be obtained by different choices of the parameters. For example, the administrator should be able to specify the fixed and variable portions of manufacturing cost independently. Further, he should be able to say how sensitive consumer sales are to price and advertising. These principles are well recognized, and most recent computer games embody them.[8] It is also desirable that it be possible to change the parameters *during* the course of the play. In most cases this is easy to arrange in INTOP.[9] For instance, no special care need be taken in order to change the parameters in the manufacturing-cost function during the course of a game. Similarly, it is possible to change the acquisition cost of a factory during the play, since both the original cost and the current value of each factory are recorded.

It is also desirable that the form of the function be chosen so that some approximate analysis of rational firm behavior is possible. This means, first, that functions should be expressed as formulas rather than as sets of tabular entries and second, that formulas in which the variables can be separated are preferred. Naturally there are some places in which this cannot be done. Within the sections on the various functional areas the framework of an economic analysis is presented, and the first part of the chapter concludes with a discussion which shows how the entire model fits together.

Most of the sections to follow treat the functional areas within the firm. The accounting area is omitted as it does not contain anything which influences the economic behavior of the model.[10] The first section deals with the general way time and change are dealt with in the model as an attempt is made to use a fairly standard procedure in all of the areas. The consumer market is discussed in the second section.[11]

[8] Joel M. Kibbee, Clifford J. Craft and Burt Nanus, *Management Games, A New Technique for Executive Development* (1961), 121ff, 154ff.

[9] Cf. *infra*, Chapter 5, on use of Wonder Cards in changing parameters.

[10] Accounting could have such content if the firms were allowed to make decisions which directly affected the ways in which income is calculated. Firms might, for example, be allowed to choose from among various ways of calculating depreciation expense or be required to capitalize a certain fraction of research or licensing expenditures.

[11] The firms also interact in markets for goods, licenses and money (loans). In these cases the purpose of the "market" is to insure that the technical arrangements negotiated by the companies themselves are carried out rather than to allocate sales by formula. Thus the model itself contributes nothing to the economic content. The technical discussion is placed in the computer section.

B. *Time and Change*

Time is one of the most elusive concepts in economics and business. An important function of business games is to place the participants in an environment in which time and change are crucial factors. It seems desirable from the design viewpoint to have a unified manner of treating time and change. Certain timing considerations have already been discussed. The basic unit of time within the simulation is a constant which is ordinarily taken as a quarter in real life. The factory construction period is zero or more quarters. It takes one quarter to produce goods and one quarter to ship them to another area or company. Cash transfers occur instantly, but payments and receipts for goods may (and generally do) move more slowly.[12]

To mirror reality it is desirable to provide for delays or lags in the response of parts of the system to current information or decisions. The consumer market will not reach equilibrium directly after a price change. Manufacturing costs may not reach equilibrium immediately following a change in the level of output. The desired qualitative behavior can be achieved rather simply by using essentially the variables themselves and their first differences with respect to time. A reasonable short-run manufacturing-cost curve, reflecting changes in level of output, is gotten by adding a function of the first difference in level of output to a curve which gives the long-run cost. Similarly, short-run fixed marketing costs depend on the sales offices opened or closed, and are added to the long-run fixed costs which depend on the total number of offices. This convention effectively limits the "short-run" to one period.

In certain other functions one may desire to make the effects of change more gradual. To achieve this goal the familiar device of exponential smoothing is used. This requires that "effective values" be introduced for those variables which are treated in this fashion.[13] To illustrate the notion we shall consider the advertising expenditure and its effective value. The effective value of advertising in period t is given by

$$\bar{A}_t = A_t + \alpha\,(\bar{A}_{t-1} - A_t)$$

or

$$\bar{A}_t = \alpha\,\bar{A}_{t-1} + (1 - \alpha)\,A_t$$

where

$\bar{A}_t$ = effective value in period t

$\bar{A}_{t-1}$ = effective value in period $t-1$

A_t = expenditure in period t

α = lag parameter

The effective value is used in all of the functions where the effect of the variable is needed. For advertising this is the demand function. Of course, the actual value is used on the income statement and in

12   Cf. *infra,* Financial Tasks F2 and F6 in Fig. 25.

13   These are noted in the appropriate places in the text. They are price, advertising, research, research probability, methods improvement, dividends and earnings.

calculating the effects on all other accounts. The behavior of the lagging formula as a function of α is well known. The portion effective in period t of an incremental expenditure A in period 1 is $(1 - \alpha)\, \alpha^{t-1}\, A$. If this same expenditure is made in periods 1 through t, the useful effect in period t is $(1 - \alpha^t)\, A$. To achieve an effective value of A in period 1, the expenditure in that period must be $A/(1 - \alpha)$. If an expenditure of size A is made in all subsequent periods, then the effective value will remain at A.

Assume that an expenditure of amount $A/(1 - \alpha)$ is made in period 1. For some purposes it is useful to regard the amount by which this expenditure exceeds A, that is, $\alpha\, A/(1 - \alpha)$, as an "investment." In general, if the effective value of a variable associated with an expenditure is A, then the equivalent "investment" is $\alpha\, \bar{A}/(1 - \alpha)$.

The consequences of selecting different values of α may be

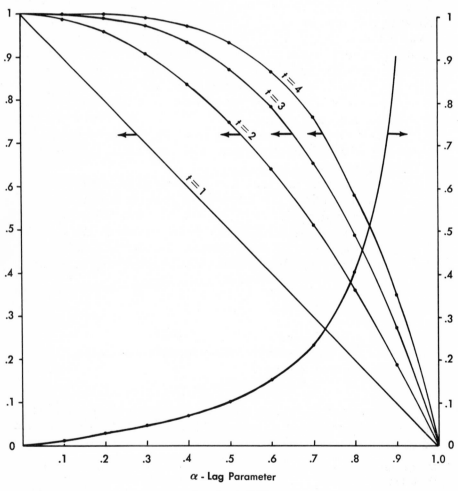

FIG. 6   *Lag Effects*

viewed in two ways. One may specify how long an incremental expenditure must be sustained to make the difference between effective
value and the expenditure small. Or the investment needed to give
the desired effective value instantly may be specified. Both of these
ways of looking at the problem are illustrated in Fig. 6. The curves
starting in the upper left-hand corner give the effective value after
unit expenditures for up to four periods. For $\alpha = 0$ the effect is instantaneous, while for $\alpha = 0.5$, about 94 per cent of the effect will
be felt in the fourth period. The curve starting in the lower left-hand
corner gives the "investment" necessary in period 1 to achieve the
desired effective value. at once. For $\alpha = 0$, no investment is necessary.
If $\alpha = 0.5$, the investment equals the expenditure; and if $\alpha = 0.75$,
the investment is three times the expenditure. Negative values of α
are sometimes useful. Over-reaction (to price changes, for example)
can be achieved by choosing $\alpha = -0.1$ or -0.2. This gives an oscil-
latory behavior which is small and not troublesome as long as α is
small.

Other timing considerations occur within the model. For example, patents acquired within a period either by a license agreement or
a successful research and development effort cannot be exploited by
manufacturing until the next period, and a new model cannot reach
the market until the period after that. These rules are embodied in
the detailed listing of tasks and the arrow diagrams which appear
at the end of the chapter.

c. *The Consumer Market*

The equations which determine sales in the consumer market
have a simple structure but present a rather frightening appearance.
For this reason we shall introduce the variables, parameters and equations a few at a time.

The simple relationship between sales quantity per unit time Q
(the modifier "per unit time" will be omitted but understood hereafter) and effective price $\bar{P}$ is essentially the one used before in the
simplified model,[14] namely,

$$\log Q = e_p \log \bar{P} + e_k \log K$$

where K is a scaling constant and e_p is the price elasticity. That is,
in this relationship

$$(\bar{P}/Q)\,(dQ/d\bar{P}) = e_p$$

This simple conceptual model can be generalized conveniently. It is
computationally more convenient to introduce two scaling parameters
and write

$$\log (Q/Q_0) = e_p \log (\bar{P}/P_0) + e_k \log K$$

[14]   For a definition of symbols used in
this subsection, see Fig. 8.

for then the point $Q = Q_0$, $\bar{P} = P_0$ and $K = 1$ is on the demand curve.

This equation accommodates only one firm. To allow all firms to interact we write

$$\log (Q_i/Q_0) = (e_p - x_p) \log (\bar{P}_i/P_0) + x_p \, \Sigma \log (\bar{P}_j/P_0) + e_k \log K$$

as the demand curve for the ith firm. Here x_p is the cross elasticity which expresses the influence of the other firms' prices on firm i and Σ denotes the sum over all n firms. The equation also permits us to express the industry price elasticity as $E_p = e_p + (n - 1) x_p$. These elasticities have the familiar meaning; if one firm raises its price one per cent, its sales will increase by e_p per cent (since $e_p < 0$, this is actually a decrease in sales) and the sales of each of the other firms will increase by x_p per cent. If every firm in the industry raises prices one per cent then total industry sales will increase by E_p per cent. Again, this last quantity is ordinarily negative.

The equation above has a practical defect which forces us to modify it still further. Firms which have no inventory set a price of zero. This is awkward since then the log function is not defined. To bypass this difficulty we approximate $\log (\bar{P}/P_0)$ by $2 \log [(\bar{P} + P_0)/2P_0]$.

With this new formula the elasticity is no longer a constant. It is easy to show that

$$(\bar{P}/Q) (dQ/d\bar{P}) = e_p [(Q + Q_0)/Q] [\bar{P}/(\bar{P} + P_0)] = e_p f$$

To discuss the formula it is convenient to assume that for all companies, except the one in question, $\bar{P} = P_0$. When $\bar{P} = P_0$, the elasticity is e_p; while for $\bar{P} > P_0$, the elasticity is greater than e_p. Fig. 7 shows

FIG. 7 *Elasticity Adjustment Factor f*

$\bar{P}/P_0$ \ e_p	-1	-1.5	-2	-2.5	-3	-4
0.0	0.0	0.0	0.0	0.0	0.0	0.0
0.4	0.44	0.40	0.38	0.36	0.34	0.32
0.6	0.63	0.58	0.55	0.52	0.50	0.47
0.8	0.81	0.78	0.75	0.72	0.70	0.66
0.9	0.91	0.88	0.87	0.85	0.83	0.80
1.0	1.00	1.00	1.00	1.00	1.00	1.00
1.1	1.10	1.14	1.16	1.21	1.25	1.34
1.2	1.21	1.28	1.38	1.49	1.63	2.02
1.4	1.46	1.72	2.08	2.77	4.32	–
1.6	1.75	2.36	3.96	17.7	–	–
2.0	2.67	8.42	–	–	–	–
$\bar{P}/P_0$ for $Q = 0$	3.00	2.18	1.83	1.64	1.52	1.38
Q/Q_0 for $\bar{P} = 0$	3.00	4.65	7.00	10.2	15.0	31.0

Point Elasticity $= f$ times e_p

the size of the elasticity adjustment factor f for several values of e_p and $\bar{P}/P_0$. This shows that the departure from constant elasticity is not too great when $\bar{P}/P_0$ is near 1. The second from the bottom row shows the price $\bar{P}$ at which $Q = 0$. At this point the price elasticity is infinite. The bottom row gives the maximum quantity which can be sold.

In the discussion so far we have alluded to Q as the quantity sold. Actually if the value of Q determined by the formula exceeds the available inventory then sales are set equal to inventory and part of the excess quantity is distributed to the other companies. The mechanism for doing this may be envisioned as follows. Each company having a shortage (inventory less than orders) in turn artificially raises its effective price to just that level at which orders equal inventory. If several companies have a shortage initially, then additional shortages will develop in the process. Hence the process is repeated several times; five has been a satisfactory number. To avoid tampering with the prices themselves as well as to permit other interpretations of the redistribution mechanism, new "stock-out" variables z_i and new elasticity parameters e_z and x_z are introduced. The new version of the demand equation then becomes

$$q_i = (e_p - x_p)\, p_i + x_p\, \Sigma\, p_j + e_k\, k \\ + (e_z - x_z)\, z_i + x_z\, \Sigma\, z_j$$

Here we have also introduced the new notation

$$q = 2 \log\, [(Q + Q_0)/2Q_0] \\ p = 2 \log\, [(\bar{P} + P_0)/2P_0] \\ k = \log K$$

As mentioned above, the variable z can be thought of as an artificial price variable, with the interpretation that customers respond to a stock-out as they would if the firm raised its prices just to the point at which orders equal inventory. The variable z may equally well stand for less extensive advertising or lower quality — anything that would send customers to another product is a possible interpretation. The sign convention adopted in the mathematical formulation requires that e_z and x_z have the same signs as e_p and x_p. The details for determining the values of z_i will be given later.

Now we introduce advertising and grade (quality) into the demand equation. There are several ways in which advertising might affect the demand equation. It might simply shift the demand curve to the right if its effect were viewed as informing the consumer about the product. Or, if one assumes that everyone in the relevant consumer population knows of the product's existence, advertising might make the consumer less sensitive to price. That is, e_p might be a function of effective advertising $\bar{A}$. Finally, these effects might exist together. To keep the model conceptually simple, only the first effect is included. By letting $a_i = 2 \log\, [(\bar{A} + A_0)/2A_0]$, the term $(e_a - x_a)\, a_i + x_a\, \Sigma\, a_j$ is added to the previous expression for q_i. Again this means that the entire demand curve is shifted and that advertising elasticity is approximately e_a, when $\bar{A}$ is near A_0.

The effect of grade could enter in several ways, too. The simplest model is obtained by treating it in the same manner as price and advertising. If firm i has grade $g(i)$, then we let $r_i = \log R_{g(i)}$ where R_g is a tabular parameter having values which may be arbitrarily assigned for $g = 0, 1, 2, 3, 4$. Ordinarily $R_0 = 1$ and $R_g > 0$ always so that it is not necessary to modify the logarithm function. The term which is added to the expression for q_i is $(e_r - x_r) r_i + x_r \Sigma r_j$. The mnemonic "$r$" stands for research, the ultimate source of grades greater than zero.

At this point the demand function is

$$q_i = (e_p - x_p) p_i + x_p \Sigma p_j + (e_a - x_a) a_i + x_a \Sigma a_j$$
$$+ (e_r - x_r) r_i + x_r \Sigma r_j + (e_z - x_z) z_i + x_z \Sigma z_j + e_k k$$

where the sums are taken over all firms. We call the set of all firms N and henceforth write $N(p)$ rather than Σp_j.

The demand equation does not yet recognize the fact that there are standard and deluxe models. The only distinguishing feature between these models is the grade number g, and the standard model always has the lower grade number. If there is only one grade, it is standard. In order to make the demand function for standard and deluxe models essentially the same and still have them interact (if desired) we introduce additional cross elasticities so that the price and grade variables for the deluxe product will affect the demand of standard, and vice versa. In the following equation the barred parameters are these new cross elasticities and the primed state variables are those of the deluxe product.

$$q_i = (e_p - x_p) p_i + x_p N(p) + (\bar{e}_p - \bar{x}_p) p_i' + \bar{x}_p N(p')$$
$$+ (e_a - x_a) a_i + x_a N(a) + e_k k$$
$$+ (e_r - x_r) r_i + x_r N(r) + (\bar{e}_r - \bar{x}_r) r_i' + \bar{x}_r N(r')$$
$$+ (e_z - x_z) z_i + x_z N(z) + (\bar{e}_z - \bar{x}_z) z_i' + \bar{x}_z N(z')$$

The expression for q_i' is obtained by exchanging the primed and unprimed variables with the exception that a_i, a and k are left alone since advertising and the economic index affect both models in the same way. This equation allows us to identify the elasticities shown in Fig. 8.

FIG. 8 *Definitions and Relations for the Consumer Market Model*†

A. *Parameters*

Q_0 = quantity base point (PS01)
P_0 = price base point (PS02)
A_0 = advertising base point (PS03)
K = economic index (PS24)

† Symbols within parentheses, e.g. (PS01), after the names of parameters and variables refer to the "Dictionary" listing of program parameters and state variables reproduced in Appendix I.

FIG. 8 *Definitions and Relations for the Consumer Market Model* (Continued)

The following quantities have a subscript p, r, z or a, which stand respectively for price, quality, redistribution and advertising.

E^+ = elasticity for the product; industry (PS07, PS11, PS15, PS19)

E = elasticity for the model; industry (PS08, PS12, PS16)

e^+ = elasticity for the product; firm (PS09, PS13, PS17, PS20)

e = elasticity for the model; firm (PS10, PS14, PS18)

In terms of these elasticities and the number of firms, one can express the firm elasticities and cross-elasticities for total product (both qualities) and the corresponding industry elasticities. (The FORTRAN program calculates the starred quantities shown below from those given above; these quantities are used in the actual program.)

$\bar{E} = E^+ - E$ = other model cross elasticity; industry

$\bar{e} = e^+ - e$ = other model cross elasticity; firm ($*$)

$x^+ = (E^+ - e^+)/(n-1)$ = product cross elasticity; interfirm

$x = (E - e)/(n-1)$ = model cross elasticity; interfirm ($*$)

$\bar{x} = x^+ - x$ = other model cross elasticity; interfirm ($*$)

In addition there are

e_k = economic index elasticity (PS23)

E_{pab} = price elasticity of product a on b; industry (PS21)

e_{pab} = price elasticity of product a on b; firm (PS22)

$x_{pab} = (E_{pab} - e_{pab})/(n-1)$ = price cross elasticity of product a on b; interfirm ($*$)

α = exponential weight for calculating effective values (PS04, PS05)

R_g = marketing grade index (PS06)

B. *Variables*

Q = quantity of consumer sales (VS03)

P = price of consumer sales (VS07)

$\bar{P} = \alpha_p \bar{P} + (1 - \alpha_p) P$ = effective price (VS11)

A = advertising expenditure (VS09)

$\bar{A} = \alpha \bar{A} + (1 - \alpha) A$ = effective advertising (VS12)

g = inventory grade (VS18)

I = inventory units (VS17)

M = marketing effectiveness index (VS13)

The formulas which express sales as a function of the other variables are stated in terms of the following quantities:

$q = 2 \log ([1 + (Q/Q_0)]/2)$

$p = 2 \log ([1 + (\bar{P}/P)]/2)$

$a = 2 \log ([1 + (\bar{A}/A_0)]/2)$

$r = \log R_g$

$k = \log K$

$s = 2 \log ([1 + (I/Q_0)]/2) - 2 \log$ (orders); the latter is a function of p, a, r etc.

z = redistribution variable

The quantities q', p' etc. are defined similarly; the prime stands for the other model.

In the absence of shortages, we can say that if all firms change prices of both models by one per cent then industry sales will change by E_p^+ per cent. If one firm changes its prices of both models by one per cent, its sales will change by e_p^+ per cent while industry sales will change by (E_p^+/n) per cent. The situation as regards change in the price of one model is similar. If all firms change the price of one model by one per cent, then industry demand for that model will change by E_p per cent and for the other model by $\bar{E}_p$ per cent. If the initial demands for both models were the same then the total industry demand changes by $(E_p^+/2)$ per cent. An analogous statement is true for the firm.

The expressions for q and q' contain another term as well, namely $(e_{xyp} - x_{xyp}) p_y + x_{xyp} N (p_y) + M_x$ for product X. The corresponding expression for product Y is $(e_{yxp} - x_{yxp}) p_x + x_{yxp} N (p_x) + M_y$. The first two terms in this expression are the means by which an added advantage is given to firms which market both products. It might be preferable to have some other indicator than non-zero price to indicate the presence of the other product in the market, but this device does work. A better signal might be sales of the other product in the previous period. If it is required that $e_{xyp} > 0$ and $x_{xyp} < 0$, one would have $e_{xyp} + (n - 1) x_{xyp} > 0$ if Y sales stimulate X sales on the industry level and $e_{xyp} + (n - 1) x_{xyp} < 0$ if the opposite is true. The last term M_x is the marketing effectiveness index. It may be assigned arbitrarily by the administrator to give extra advantages or penalties to individual firms.

The value of z_i for each company is chosen so that $N (z) + N (z')$ is minimized subject to the constraints that $z_i \geq 0$, $z_i' \geq 0$, $q_i \leq 2 \log [(1 + I_i/Q_0)/2]$ and $q_i' \leq 2 \log [(1 + I_i'/Q_0)/2]$ where I_i and I_i' are the amounts of goods in inventory. These latter inequalities express the requirement that $Q_i \leq I_i$ and $Q_i' \leq I_i'$. Thus if a company does experience a stock-out, the corresponding z_i is positive; and if it does not then $z_i = 0$.

The values of z_i and z_i' which satisfy these conditions are obtained by an adaptation of the Gauss-Seidel method of solving linear equations. Starting with $z_i = z_i' = 0$, we find the actual (logarithms of) orders q_i and q_i' and calculate shortages as $2 \log ([1 + (I_i/Q_0)]/2) - q_i = s_i$ and $2 \log ([1 + (I_i'/Q_0)]/2) - q_i' = s_i'$. These expressions, being the differences of logarithms (approximately), are relative shortages. It is these which will be redistributed to the other firms. Since a quantity is added to the logarithm of the orders of the other firms, those with larger orders will acquire a greater absolute share of the redistributed orders.

It is clear that initially $s_i < 0$ corresponds to a shortage. The "undistributed shortage" at a later stage in the iterative process is

$$\Delta_i = [s_i - (e_z - x_z) z_i - (\bar{e}_z - \bar{x}_z) z_i' - x_z N(z) - \bar{x}_z N(z')]$$

If Δ_i is negative, set $z_i = z_i' + \Delta_i/e_z$. Since $e_z < 0$, this will increase

z_i. It has turned out in practice that five iterations over the whole set of z_i and z_i' give results which are accurate to about one per cent. After the values of z_i' and z_i have been determined, the expressions for q_i are adjusted. Then the values of Q_i are determined and, as a final check, sales are set equal to the smaller of Q_i and I_i.

It is the rule rather than the exception that not all firms are active in a market. This means that some z_i assume positive values. This makes sales larger than they otherwise would be for the active firms and changes the actual elasticities facing the active firms. It is possible to examine explicitly portions of several special cases in which shortages exist and thereby exercise some control over the size of the total market when only some of the firms are active. Here we are interested in three special cases. First is the no shortage case. In the second case all of the firms have standard models and none has deluxe. In the third case some of the firms have both models and others have neither model. We discuss these cases in order to gain insight into the selection of parameters. In all of the cases we shall suppose $a = r = r' = 0$ and examine only the price situation.

Case 1: No shortages exist; this is the "normal" case. We shall assume that $p = p' = p_n$. Then $q = q' = q_n = E_p^+ p_n + k$. Given arbitrary numerical values for q_n, E_p^+ and p_n then k can be selected so that the relationship is satisfied. Ordinarily P_0, Q_0 and K would be selected so that $q_n = 0$, $p_n = 0$, $k = 0$. Note that we have set $e_k = 1$.

Case 2: There are no shortages in standard product. No firm has any inventory of deluxe. We further suppose that $p = p_n$ and $p' = p_0$. Let q_s be the quantity variable for standard product and q_0 be the quantity variable for deluxe product. In this discussion we shall let the corresponding p and z elasticities and cross elasticities be equal. This is done in order that the customers of firms which have stock-outs behave as they would if these firms raised their prices to just that point at which the quantity ordered is equal to the inventory at hand. Thus we can drop the subscripts p and z. Then

$$q_s = E p_n + \bar{E} p_0 + \bar{E} z' + k$$
or
$$q_s = q_n - \bar{E} p_n + \bar{E} p_0 + \bar{E} z'$$
We also have
$$q_0 = \bar{E} p_n + E p_0 + E z' + k$$
$$= q_n - E p_n + E p_0 + E z'$$

Solving this equation for z' and substituting in the expression for q_s yields

$$q_s = q_n + (\bar{E}/E)(q_0 - q_n)$$

This in turn yields

$$\bar{E}/E^+ = 1/[1 + (q_0 - q_n)/(q_s - q_n)]$$

Thus since $q_0 = -\log 4$ one may specify the sales q_s (at the normal price) which one desires when only one model is in the market and thereby determine $\bar{E}$. Then it follows that E is also determined since $E = E^+ - \bar{E}$.

Case 3: Several of the firms (b in number) have both models, and the balance ($n - b$ in number) have neither model. We again specify the behavior of the market when those with a positive inventory set a price of p_n (for both models; we ignore quality effects) and sell a quantity corresponding to q_b, and those without product charge p_0 and sell a quantity corresponding to q_0. The symmetries which are present allow us to write

$$q_b = (e^+ + (b - 1)x^+) \, p_n + (n - b) \, x^+ p_0 + (n - b) \, x^+ z + k$$
$$\text{and } q_0 = (e^+ + (n - b - 1)x^+) \, p_0 + bx^+ p_n + (e^+ + (n - b - 1) \\ x^+) \, z + k$$

These relations can be rewritten as

$$q_b = q_n + (n - b)x^+ \, (p_0 + z - p_n)$$
$$q_0 = q_n + [e^+ + (n - b - 1)x^+] \, [p_0 + z - p_n]$$

By eliminating the term $(p_0 + z - p_n)$ we find that

$$e^+/E^+ = 1 - [(n - 1)/(n - b)] \, [(q_b - q_n)/(q_b + q_0 - 2q_n)]$$

This means that one may specify the sales q (at the normal price) which one desires when b firms are in the market with a full product line and the others have no inventory. This will determine e^+/E^+ and also x^+ since $E^+ = e^+ + (n - 1)x^+$. The formula for e^+/E^+ depends on n and b. When the number of companies n is large, e^+/E^+ is approximately a function of $n/(n - b)$ and thus depends on the relative number of firms actively in the market.

We can now summarize this particular scheme for choosing market parameters.

1. Select one point on the "normal" demand function by choosing P_0, Q_0, A_0 and K.
   It is easiest to set $K = 1$ for then $k = 0$. Similarly choose Q_0 so that $q_n = 0$.
2. Select the industry price elasticity E^+ arbitrarily.
3. Choose the desired sales Q_s in case 2 and set $q_s = 2 \log \, ([1 + (Q_s/Q_0)]/2)$.
   Then determine E and $\bar{E}$. Note that $q_0 = 2 \log ([1 + (0/Q_0)]/2) = - \log 4$.
4. Choose the desired sales Q_b in case 3 and set $q_b = 2 \log \, ([1 + (Q_b/Q_0)]/2)$.
   Determine e^+.
5. Choose e arbitrarily, noting that $e \leqq e^+$ is logically necessary since $e^+ = e + \bar{e}$ and $\bar{e} \geqq 0$.
6. Set $E_z = E_p$, $e_z = e_p$, etc.
7. The simplest choice for the "r" elasticities is to set $e_r = e_p$, etc. This means that when $R_g/R_0 = 1.1$ that a price $P = 1.1 \, P_0$ will yield sales which are approximately the same as the base case. The approximation relies on the fact that for small t, the value of $\log \, (1 + t)$ is approximately $2 \log [1 + t/2]$.

8. The industry advertising elasticity E_a should be a fairly small nonnegative number. It has already been shown that the steady-state optimal advertising expenditure is given approximately by $A = e_a$ times (Revenue − Variable Cost). This would presumably make $0 \leqq e_a \leqq 0.5$ a reasonable range from which to select e_a.

D. *The Marketing Cost Functions*

This section discusses the various cost functions associated with sales. Since the consumer market was discussed in the last section, shipping costs, sales expediting costs, commercial and administrative costs and inventory costs are taken up here.

1] SHIPPING COSTS

Shipping costs depend on the number of industrial and intra-company sales sent to each of the various areas. Since the unit cost parameters subsume not only freight but tariffs (and possibly subsidies), the cost from Area 1 to Area 2 is not necessarily the same as that from Area 2 to Area 1. These costs are designated by PS33, PS34 and PS35.[15] There are no economies or diseconomies of scale nor any fixed cost. The total shipping expense is denoted by VS08.

2] SALES EXPEDITING COSTS

A sales-expediting cost (VS10) is incurred in the event that orders for industrial sales exceed the seller's inventory. This is done to avoid the rationing problem which would occur if only certain orders were filled in the face of a shortage. To make this course of action relatively unattractive, orders filled in excess of inventory incur the sales expediting cost; the unit cost for sales expediting is the unit (average) inventory value (VS19) plus a substantial penalty cost (PS30). At the beginning of each period, if the inventory is zero, the unit inventory value is set to the maximum manufacturing cost (PM02) due to the fact that the program permits sales expediting even if no factories have been built.

When there is insufficient inventory to accommodate intra-company sales, the orders are simply not filled.

3] COMMERCIAL AND ADMINISTRATIVE COSTS

The commercial and administrative cost is the only cost function in which the two products interact directly. Thus economies of scale exist across product lines as well as within a product line.

The notation used in this discussion of the cost function is shown in Fig. 9. If the firm uses a distributor (i.e., $S = 0$), then the cost is

15 For the names of these and similarly designated items in the following discussion see Dictionary of INTOP parameters and variables in Appendix I.

given by

$$C \text{ \& } A \text{ cost} = S_{1x} Q_x + S_{1y} Q_y \text{ if only one product is sold}$$
$$= S_{2x} Q_x + S_{2y} Q_y \text{ if both products are sold}$$

If the firm has S sales offices, then

$$C \text{ \& } A \text{ cost} = (S_{3x} Q_x + S_{3y} Q_y)/(S + 1) + S_4 (S + 2)$$

FIG. 9   *Commercial and Administrative Parameters*
and State Variables *

A.   *Parameters*

S_1 = agency unit selling cost when one product is sold (PS27)

S_2 = agency unit selling cost when both products are sold (PS26)

S_3 = captive distribution unit selling cost (PS25)

S_4 = captive distribution cost per regional office (PS28)

S_5 = cost coefficient in cost function for changing number of offices (PS29)

B.   *Variables*

S = number of regional sales offices (VS14)

ΔS = change in number of regional sales offices (VS15)

Q_x, Q_y = total sales quantity, both models (VS03)

$C \text{ \& } A \text{ cost} =$ commercial and administrative expense (VS16)

---

* Symbols within parentheses after the names of parameters and variables refer to the "Dictionary" listing of program parameters and state variables reproduced in Appendix I.

The commercial and administrative cost is allocated to the two products as shown on the income statement. The only allocation which is not obvious is the term representing the expense of maintaining regional sales offices and a central office $S_4(S + 2)$. This is allocated in the proportions $S_{3x} Q_x$ and $S_{3y} Q_y$ unless both of these quantities are zero in which case the allocation is in proportion to S_{3x} and S_{3y}.

In case sales offices are either opened or closed, another element of cost $S_5 (\Delta S)^2$ is incurred. This too is allocated in proportion to the appropriate variable costs (either the S_1, S_2 or S_3 term). If all of the variable costs are zero, then the allocation is made with respect to the corresponding variable cost coefficients. The optimal number of sales offices is easy to determine. The total cost in the steady state is given by Cost $= (S_{3x} Q_x + S_{3y} Q_y)/(S + 1) + S_4 (S + 2)$. This is a minimum when

$$S + 1 = [(S_{3x} Q_x + S_{3y} Q_y)/S_4]^{0.5}$$

(This formula does not yield an integer; hence the next lower and higher integers must be tried.) Substituting this expression in the cost formula yields

$$\text{Cost} = 2[(S_{3x} Q_x + S_{3y} Q_y) S_4]^{0.5} + S_4$$

which shows that the optimal cost goes up roughly as the square root of number of sales. This analysis assumed that the "investment" $S_5 (\Delta S)^2$ associated with opening offices could be ignored in the long-run analysis. Clearly if either S_5 or the interest rate take on very large values this assumption is incorrect. It is also clear that the stated optimum value must be compared with the appropriate formulas which govern when $S = 0$.

This function was chosen because it gives the desired properties – decreased short-run variable costs and increased short-run fixed costs – in a simple way. A physical realization is to imagine an area as a straight line with consumer sales spread uniformly over the line. If the S sales offices and the central regional office are represented by points uniformly spaced on the line then the average distance of a point on the line to the nearest sales office varies as $1/(S + 1)$ and the variable portion of the sales cost varies as the average distance of a customer from a sales office.

Figure 10 shows the value of $5Q/(S + 1) + 10,000 (S + 2)$ for various values of the number of sales offices S. The cost for agent

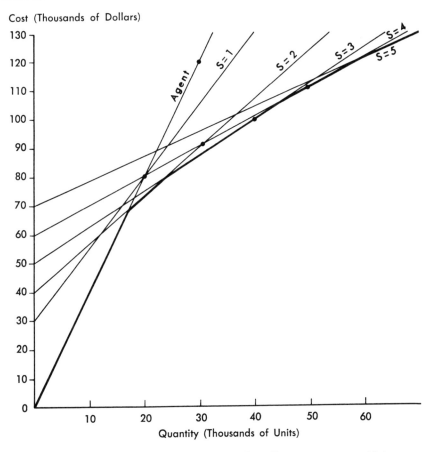

FIG. 10   Plot of Commercial and Administrative Function

distribution is taken as 4Q. The heavy line shows the least cost achievable corresponding to the best choice of number of sales offices. Note that in this example, it is never optimal to have only one sales office.

4] THE INVENTORY COST FUNCTION

The inventory costs of the two products are independent. The cost depends only on the total number of units (both models) on hand after all sales have been made and before purchased and manufactured goods have been placed into inventory. The formula is

$$Cost = LI + SI^2$$

The symbols are defined in Fig. 11. The linear parameter L must be nonnegative. Ordinarily the square parameter S is chosen to be positive so that the marginal cost increases; however, this is not necessary. Fig. 12 shows the total inventory cost, the average inventory cost and the marginal inventory cost for $L = 1$, $S = 10^{-5}$.

FIG. 11   *Inventory Parameters and Variables* *

A. *Parameters*
     $L =$ linear coefficient (PS31)
     $S =$ square coefficient (PS32)

B. *Variables*
     $I =$ total inventory of both models of the product (VS17)

*   The symbols again refer to the Dictionary in Appendix I.

Since floating-point arithmetic is used in the program it is usually the case that a fractional number of units will be in inventory. This would be troublesome only when there is less than one unit in inventory because a firm which wished to change grades might have its new receipts, both production and purchased, downgraded. Thus if the inventory is less than one unit, this fractional unit is added to consumer sales and the other accounts adjusted as appropriate.

E. *The Manufacturing Functions*

The four costs or expenses directly associated with manufacturing are plant depreciation, fixed plant overhead, direct manufacturing cost and methods improvement. The first two costs are combined in the income statement. The formula is

Depreciation and Fixed = Sum of $(dV + F)$

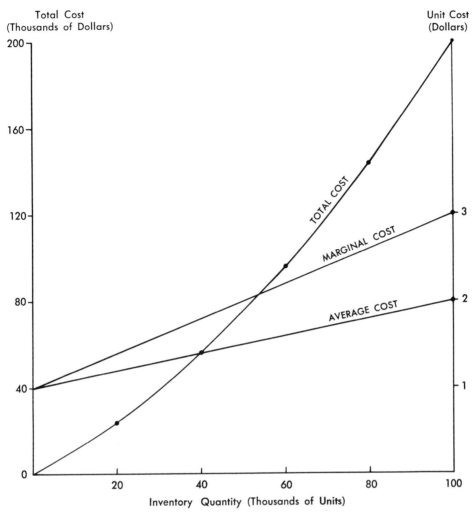

FIG. 12   *Plot of Inventory Cost Function*

These symbols are defined in Fig. 13. The formula applies when a plant is ready to produce. Both the original acquisition cost of the plant V and the fixed overhead F can vary for each plant. For a given product and area, V could vary if the cost of plants (PM17) were changed during the course of a run. The value of the parameter F depends on the number of the plant. To give economies of scale, the costs for plants with higher numbers would have smaller values. It is also possible to have economies of scale with two plants and diseconomies of scale with three plants. We remind the reader that dV is not a cash expense, but F is a cash expense. The cost F is not "inventoried"; the cost M_1 discussed below is "inventoried." (M_1 is 0 in INTOP Standard which uses direct costing in manufacturing.)

Expenditures for methods improvement affect the direct manu-

FIG. 13   *Manufacturing Parameters and*
State Variables *

A.   *Parameters*

d = depreciation rate (PM20)
F = fixed overhead cost (PM19)
M_1 = fixed direct cost (PM01)
M_2 = maximum unit cost (PM02)
M_3 = minimum average cost (PM03)
M_4 = cost multiple – one model (PM04)
M_5 = optimum production level – one model (PM05)
M_6 = cost multiple – total (PM06)
M_7 = optimum production level – total (PM07)
M_8 = cost multiple – one model, level change (PM08)
M_9 = cost multiple – total, level change (PM09)
M_{11} = area grade differential (PM11)
M_{12} = obsolescence cost multiple (PM12)
M_{13} = factory construction time (PM13)
M_{14} = methods improvement – maximum cost reduction (PM14)
M_{15} = methods expense yielding half of maximum cost reduction (PM15)
R_S, R_D = grade cost differentials for higher standard and deluxe grades (PM16)
α_M = exponential weight for methods improvement (PM10)

B.   *Variables*

V = initial value of plant (VM12)
S = standard production (VM06)
D = deluxe production (VM06)
ΔS = current S – previous S if previous $S \neq 0$; otherwise 0 (VM06 – VM07)
ΔD = analogous to ΔS
A = factory age (VM10)
M = methods improvement expense (VM04)
$\bar{M}$ = effective methods improvement expense (VM03)
C = total manufacturing cost (VM09)

* Symbols within parentheses refer to the Dictionary reproduced in Appendix I.

facturing cost so the two items are discussed together. Fig. 13 contains the definition of the symbols which are used in this discussion. The formula for direct manufacturing cost is relatively complicated, and the rest of this subsection is devoted to it. The figure is calculated for each plant and the total amount is allocated to standard and deluxe models.

Total manufacturing cost depends on the amount of standard production and the amount of deluxe production both in the current period and in the previous period. It also depends on the current grades of the standard and deluxe models, the effective value of methods improvement and the plant age.

The total cost is given by

$$
\begin{aligned}
M_1 &+ S \min (M_2, [M_3 + M_4 (S - M_5)^2 + M_6 (S + D - M_7)^2 \\
&+ M_8 (\Delta S)^2 + M_9 (\Delta S + \Delta D)^2] [1 + M_{11} (R_S - 1)] \\
&[1 + M_{12} (A - M_{13})] [1 - M_{14} \bar{M} / (M_{15} + \bar{M})]) \\
&+ D \min (M_2, [M_3 + M_4 (D - M_5)^2 + M_6 (D + S - M_7)^2 \\
&+ M_8 (\Delta D)^2 + M_9 (\Delta D + \Delta S)^2] [1 + M_{11} (R_D - 1)] \\
&[1 + M_{12} (A - M_{13})] [1 - M_{14} \bar{M} / (M_{15} + \bar{M})])
\end{aligned}
$$

The first term M_1 is ignored if both S and D are zero. Otherwise it is allocated to standard and deluxe in proportion to the values of S and D. The second term is allocated entirely to standard and the third entirely to deluxe.

The meaning of the individual terms within the total expression is as follows:

M_1 represents the fixed costs which are present if the plant operates at all. Included are such things as a skeletal maintenance staff, heat, light and other costs incurred when the plant doors are open.

M_2 is the upper bound to the variable unit manufacturing cost. Its basic function is to act as a safety valve, that is, to prevent excessive average costs at very low or very high levels of operation.

The parameters M_3 through M_7 allow several types of long-run cost curves to be represented as parabolas. The "pure" cases require either that $M_4 = 0$ or $M_6 = 0$. (If both are zero, the long-run marginal costs are constant.) If $M_4 > 0$ and $M_6 = 0$, then manufacturing processes for different models are independent, and interactions if any will arise because total factory capacity will not permit $S = D = M_5$. At the other extreme, if $M_4 = 0$ and $M_6 > 0$, then the manufacturing processes for different models are intimately related, and the lowest average cost is obtained when $S + D = M_7$. When both $M_4 > 0$ and $M_6 > 0$, then the process is partly joint and partly independent. When only one model is being produced, $D = 0$, and the long-run average cost curve is still a parabola.

The next parameters M_8 and M_9 are used to represent the short-run average cost functions. The functional form chosen means that the short-run average cost curves are parabolas which are tangent to the long-run average cost curves. When $M_8 > 0$ and $M_9 = 0$, added short-run average costs for a given model depend only on changes in the production level of that model. When $M_8 = 0$ and $M_9 > 0$, then additional short-run costs depend on changes in total production. The particular definition of ΔS in case the production in the previous period was zero was selected so that firms will not face large additional short-run costs when they start production in a new factory. If $M_8 = 0$ and

$M_9 > 0$ and a firm changes from producing standard models to producing deluxe models, then $\Delta S = - S$ and $\Delta D = 0$. Thus an increased short-run cost is incurred in this case. This is true even when the grade number of this period's deluxe is the same as that of last period's standard. This anomaly has not proved to be a difficulty in practice.

The term $1 + M_{11} (R_s - 1)$ determines the increased cost associated with the different grade numbers. The value of the parameter, R_s, depends on the numerical grade of the standard model and is to be thought of as determining the "normal" additional cost associated with a given grade. The same values apply in all areas. M_{11} permits cost variations among areas. R_s may, but need not, be the same as the grade index which appears in the consumer market equations. Often it is desirable to have at least one grade which is more expensive to produce but which does not sell as well as lower grades.

The term involving M_{12} and M_{13} is the factory obsolescence factor. If costs are to rise at the rate of two per cent per quarter and the construction period is two quarters, then one should choose $M_{12} = 0.02$ and $M_{13} = 2$.

The final term involving M_{14}, M_{15} and $\bar{M}$ determines the reduction in cost due to expenditures for methods improvement. The functional form allows one to specify the maximum fraction of cost reduction which can be achieved M_{14} and the level of expenditure M_{15} which will achieve half the maximum benefit. The function was chosen to give diminishing returns in a simple manner.

To aid in the selection of actual values of parameters, it is useful to analyze parts of the manufacturing cost function a little further. We have noted that the central (steady-state) part of the function, M_3 through M_7, allows the average manufacturing cost to be either a constant or one of several parabolas. If for simplicity we examine only $S [M_3 + M_4 (S - M_5)^2]$, the average cost is $M_3 + M_4 (S - M_5)^2$ and the marginal cost is

$$M_3 + M_4 (S - M_5) (3S - M_5)$$

These are both parabolas. Average cost is a minimum when $S = M_5$ and marginal cost is a minimum when $S = M_5/3$. If one chooses $M_4 M_5{}^2 = M_3$ then average costs remain within 1.5 times the minimum average cost over a fairly wide range of operation, but the marginal cost becomes quite high (3.67 times the minimum average cost) for large production rates. The long-run average cost (LRAC) and long-run marginal cost (LRMC) are shown in Fig. 14 for the case $M_3 = M_4 M_5{}^2 = 1$.

If the term $M_8 (\Delta S)^2$ is added to the average cost, then the short-run costs are higher than the long-run costs. Fig. 14 shows the short-run average cost (SRAC) and the short-run marginal cost

Cost (Dollars)

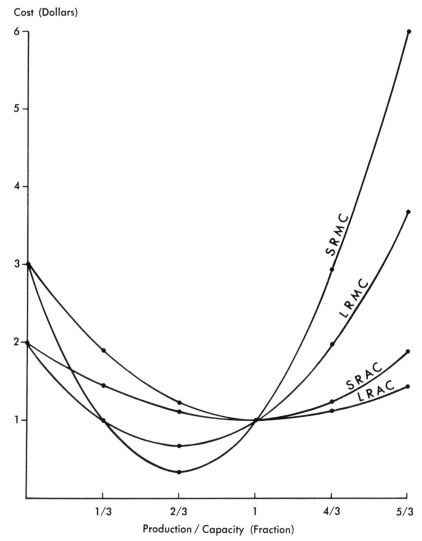

Production / Capacity (Fraction)

FIG. 14   *Plot of Manufacturing Cost Functions*

(SRMC) given that production had been at the point $S = M_5$ and that $M_8 M_5{}^2 = 1$. As indicated before, the various SRAC curves are all tangent to the LRAC curve.

A similar approximate analysis can be made for the other "pure" case by examining the term involving M_6 and M_7. The results can be expressed in terms of $S + D$ if the grade effects in the multiplication term $1 + M_{11} (R - 1)$ are ignored.

Rather than pursue this approach we next turn to another interpretation of the expression

$$S [M_3 + M_4 (S - M_5)^2 + M_6 (S + D - M_7)^2]$$
$$+ D [M_3 + M_4 (D - M_5)^2 + M_6 (S + D - M_7)^2]$$

Again we ignore the term involving the grade. This expression can be rewritten as

$$(S + D) [M_3 + M_4 (S + D - M_5)^2 + M_6 (S + D - M_7)^2]$$
$$+ M_4 SD [4M_5 - 3 (S + D)]$$

The first part of this expression gives average cost in terms of a parabola whose argument is $S + D$, that is, in terms of total production. The second part $M_4 SD [4M_5 - 3 (S + D)]$ may be viewed as an interaction or interference term. If M_4 is less than zero, then as $S + D$ increases the entire term gets larger. When $S + D < 4M_5/3$ it is similarly desirable, other things equal, to have $S = D$. When $S + D > 4M_5/3$ it is desirable to have either S or D small. In the more usual situation $M_4 > 0$, and S or D should be small when $S + D < 4M_5/3$.

To determine marginal cost as a function of S and D is a very involved problem. This is true because, given the production levels S and D and their grades, it is necessary to select the correct number of factories and the optimal value for methods improvement. This will give rise to a number of discrete problems since for some levels of output it may not be clear whether one plant or two plants is preferable.

It is possible, however, to make some rough calculations to determine approximately an optimal value for $\bar{M}$. Let $C(\bar{M})$ be the total variable manufacturing cost (excluding M_1) as a function of $\bar{M}$. Then we have

$$C (\bar{M}) = C (0) [1 - M_{14} \bar{M}/(\bar{M} + M_{15})]$$

In the steady state it is desired to choose $\bar{M}$ so that

$$C (\bar{M}) + \bar{M} [1 + r \alpha_M/(1 - \alpha_M)]$$

is a minimum. Here α_M is the lag factor for M and r is the required quarterly rate of return on capital. Recall that to maintain $\bar{M}$ at a constant level, $\bar{M} \alpha_M/(1 - \alpha_M)$ must be "invested," and the cost of this amount is $\alpha_M r \bar{M}/(1 - \alpha_M)$.

By taking the derivative with respect to $\bar{M}$ we find that

$$\bar{M} + M_{15} = M_{15} [M_{14} C (0)/(M_{15} [1 + \alpha_M r/(1 - \alpha_M)])]^{0.5}$$

Thus $\bar{M} + M_{15}$ varies as the square root of $C (0)$, the total variable cost and as the square root of M_{14}, the maximum fraction of cost reduction possible.

To examine the formula in more detail, let us take $r = 0$. Then $\bar{M} + M_{15} = [M_{14} C(0)/M_{15}]^{0.5}$. The optimal value of $\bar{M}$ is zero when $M_{14} C(0) \leq M_{15}$. To make M_{15} the optimal value for $\bar{M}$ requires that $M_{15} = M_{14} C(0)/4$. The expenditure gives a gross savings of $M_{14} C(0)/2$ and a net savings of $M_{14} C(0)/4$.

F. *The Financial Functions*

The two aspects of the finance portion of the model discussed here are the flow of funds through Accounts Payable (A/P) and Accounts Receivable (A/R) and the function which determines additions to paid-in-capital as a result of stock market confidence. The latter is intended as a crude approximation to the tangible benefits which accrue to a company whose earnings are good and which pursues a "reasonable" dividend policy. No theoretical or empirical justification is claimed for the particular function chosen. The symbols used in this discussion are defined in Fig. 15.

FIG. 15   *Financial Parameters and Variables* *

A. *Parameters*

F_1 = stock market confidence function, minimum $\bar{D}/\bar{E}$ ratio (PF24)
F_2 = stock market confidence function, maximum $\bar{D}/\bar{E}$ ratio (PF25)
F_3 = stock market confidence function, maximum fraction of dividend returned (PF26)
α_1 = fraction A/R 2 to A/R 1 (PF02)
α_2 = fraction A/R 1 to cash (PF03)
α_3 = fraction A/P 2 to A/P 1 (PF04)
α_4 = fraction A/P 1 to cash (PF05)
t = time period

B. *Variables*

C = addition to paid-in-capital
D = dividends (VF31)
$\bar{D}$ = effective dividends (VF29)
E = earnings
$\bar{E}$ = effective earnings (VF30)
r = revenue
d = disbursements
ar_1 = initial value of A/R 1, accounts legally receivable one period hence (VF01)
ar_2 = initial value of A/R 2, accounts legally receivable two periods hence (VF02)
ap_1 = initial value of A/P 1, accounts legally payable one period hence (VF03)
ap_2 = initial value of A/P 2, accounts legally payable two periods hence (VF04)
c = cash (VF05)

* Symbols within parentheses refer to the Dictionary reproduced in Appendix I.

The addition to paid-in-capital for stock market confidence depends on the effective value of dividends $\bar{D}$ and the effective value of earnings $\bar{E}$. The formula is

$$C = 4F_3 \, \bar{D} \, [(\bar{D}/\bar{E}) - F_1] \, [F_2 - (\bar{D}/\bar{E})]/(F_1 - F_2)^2$$

provided that this quantity as well as $\bar{D}$ and $\bar{E}$ are positive. Otherwise no addition is made to paid-in-capital. The parabola represented by the second two factors will ordinarily be chosen so that it is a maximum somewhere in the interval $0.3 \leqq \bar{D}/\bar{E} \leqq 0.7$ and so that it is negative for $\bar{D}/\bar{E} > 1.2$, for example. The new value of $\bar{D}$ is calculated before the function is evaluated, but the new value of $\bar{E}$ is calculated after the function evaluation. This is intended to reflect the fact that investors will be aware of dividends virtually instantly but will not react to changes in earnings as rapidly. If so desired the total amount of paid-in-capital may be used by the administrator as an indicator in determining the amount and terms of the bank loan he will extend to the firm.

There are three rules which might constitute reasonable behavior on the part of a firm which seeks a dividend policy. These are

1. maximize return per unit dividend, $C/\bar{D}$,
2. maximize net return, $C - \bar{D}$, and
3. maximize total return, C.

The first relation is the one in terms of which the parameters are stated; the maximum value which $C/\bar{D}$ can attain is F_3. The third policy is rational when the necessity to obtain outside financing is paramount and the financing obtainable is based on paid-in-capital. The second policy is selected when one wishes to maximize the difference between cash inflow C and cash outflow $\bar{D}$. The behavior of the formula can be illustrated by selecting $F_1 = 0$, $F_2 = 1$, $F_3 = 1.5$. Fig. 16 shows the three cases with the optimal value of $\bar{D}/\bar{E}$ for each case displayed on the diagonal. None of the outcomes are very sensitive to the value of $\bar{D}/\bar{E}$ in this example. To make the decision a more sensitive one, F_1 and F_2 should be given values which are close together.

FIG. 16 *Behavior of the Stock Market Confidence Function*

	Policy		
	1	2	3
$\bar{D}/\bar{E}$	0.50	0.57	0.67
$C/\bar{D}$	1.50	1.47	1.33
$(C - \bar{D})/\bar{E}$	0.25	0.26	0.22
$C/\bar{E}$	0.75	0.83	0.89

Next we turn to the other portion of the financial part of the model where formal analysis is helpful. To compute the working-capital requirements for the firm it is necessary to examine the way in which funds flow through Accounts Payable, Accounts Receivable and cash. It is possible to select the parameters α_1, α_2, α_3, α_4 which govern this flow in such a manner that the actual flow of funds is faster or slower than the "legal" timing in which purchased or manufactured goods are actually paid for two periods after they are acquired and in which cash for goods sold is actually received two periods after the sale. These parameters may be changed during the course of the game, although in actual practice they have not been. If their values are zero, then the funds flow as the names of the accounts suggest. Positive values correspond to faster flow and negative values to slower flow. If all of the parameters are equal to one then the flows are instantaneous.

The discussion given here does not purport to be an exhaustive treatment of a firm's cash budgeting problem but rather to indicate some of the more important features. In particular we consider only the effects of manufacturing costs and sales revenues on the accounts. We shall suppose that the difference between sales revenues r and manufacturing disbursements d is to be removed each period from the cash account to be used for other purposes such as advertising, dividends, etc. The precise effects of these other transactions may be examined independently. For example, the income tax is not actually deducted from cash until the period following the one in which it appears on the income statement.

The sequence of events which transpire within a period is shown in the table in Fig. 17. The value of each of the accounts can be observed only at the end of a period, so it does not matter if any of them become negative during a period.

Let us assume that a firm begins to manufacture in period t and to sell in period $t + 1$. If the difference between receipts r and disbursements d is removed from the cash account beginning with period $t + 1$ (the income in this period will be positive), then the state of the accounts at the end of the periods of change is as shown in Fig. 18.

The amount of working capital needed in the equilibrium state is $(2 - \alpha_1 - \alpha_2) r - (2 - \alpha_3 - \alpha_4) d + d$. If it is required that the industry in which these firms exist be in cash-flow equilibrium with the total economy, then $\alpha_1 = \alpha_3$ and $\alpha_2 = \alpha_4$. In this case, the working capital requirements are $(2 - \alpha_1 - \alpha_2) (r - d) + d$, and we see that as money moves more quickly ($\alpha_1 + \alpha_2 > 0$) the working-capital requirements are smaller.

G. *The Research and Development Function*

Research and development is the only part of the model in which random variation is embedded explicitly.[16] The research parameters and variables are listed in Fig. 19. The functions which

---

[16] Such variation can, of course, enter other parts of the model by adding a random component to coefficients in the various other functions. This is managed simply by use of Wonder Cards. See Chapter 5.

FIG. 17   *Schematic of Cash Flows in Areas*

Event	A/R 2	A/R 1	Cash	A/P 1	A/P 2
End of period $t-1$ First flow	ar_2	ar_1	c	ap_1	ap_2
	0	ar_2	$c + ar_1 - ap_1$	ap_2	0
Receipts Disbursements	r	ar_2	$c + ar_1 - ap_1$	ap_2	d
End of period t	$(1-\alpha_1)\,r$	$(1-\alpha_2)(ar_2 + \alpha_1 r)$	$c + ar_1 - ap_1$ $+ \alpha_2(ar_2 + \alpha_1 r)$ $- \alpha_4(ap_2 + \alpha_3 d)$	$(1-\alpha_4)(ap_2 + \alpha_3 d)$	$(1-\alpha_3)\,d$

FIG. 18   *Development of Cash Flow Equilibrium Position*

End of Period	A/R 2	A/R 1	Cash	A/P 1	A/P 2
$t-1$	0	0	c	0	0
t	0	0	$c - \alpha_3\alpha_4 d$	0	0
$t+1$	$(1-\alpha_1)\,r$	$(1-\alpha_2)\,\alpha_1 r$	$c - (1-\alpha_1\alpha_2)\,r - (\alpha_3+\alpha_4-1)\,d$	$(1-\alpha_4)\,\alpha_3 d$	$(1-\alpha_3)\,d$
$t+2$ and on	$(1-\alpha_1)\,r$	$(1-\alpha_2)\,r$	$c - (2-\alpha_1-\alpha_2)\,r - (\alpha_3+\alpha_4-1)\,d$	$(1-\alpha_4)\,d$	$(1-\alpha_3)\,d$

determine the research effectiveness $\bar{R}_t$ and probability $\bar{p}_t$ of obtaining a patent license are

$$\bar{R}_t = \alpha_1 \bar{R}_{t-1} + (1 - \alpha_1)(R_t - R_1)$$
$$\bar{p}_t = \max [0, \alpha_2 \bar{p}_{t-1} + (1 - \alpha_2) \bar{R}_t / (\bar{R}_t + R_2)]$$

FIG. 19 *Research and Development Parameters and Variables**

A. *Parameters*
  α_1 = exponential weight for research effectiveness (PR01)
  α_2 = exponential weight for research probability (PR02)
  R_1 = minimum useful research expenditure (PR03)
  R_2 = additional research expenditure yielding probability 0.5 (PR04)
  p = random number
  r = quarterly interest rate

B. *Variables*
  R_t = research expenditure (VR05)
  $\bar{R}_t$ = effective research expenditure (VR06)
  $\bar{p}_t$ = probability of receiving a patent (VR04)
  V_t = present value of an optimal research expenditure policy
  Y = expected additional profit per period if a patent is obtained

* Symbols within parentheses refer to the Dictionary reproduced in Appendix I.

A patent for the next improvement is obtained if $\bar{p} \geq p$ where p is a pseudo-random number uniformly distributed between 0 and 1. A new number p is generated for each product and company. In the event that $\bar{p} \geq p$, then $\bar{p}$ is set equal to zero after the patent is granted. The two variables $\bar{R}$ and $\bar{p}$ are used to distinguish the effectiveness of a research organization and the probability that the organization will discover a patentable idea. The notion is that the searching process must start again after a discovery. The chance of success of a good organization as measured by $\bar{R}$ will build up faster than that of a poor organization. In general it is felt that $\bar{R}$ should react rather quickly to changes in R, while $\bar{p}$ should change more slowly. The presence of R_1 will cause $\bar{p}$ to drop fairly rapidly when research expenditures are discontinued even though it rises slowly when R is increased. Further, if research and development expenditures are discontinued for a time, then $\bar{R}$ becomes negative, and an additional expenditure is required to overcome this disability. On the other hand, the program prevents $\bar{p}$ from becoming less than zero.

One possibility in the simulation is for one firm to use another as a research subcontractor. This is appropriate for some levels of total expenditure because the marginal probability is a decreasing function of $\bar{R}$. This alternative is not economical for lower levels of expenditure because each of the organizations must overcome the R_1 threshold.

It is a simple exercise to show that when the total expenditure is greater than $2 [R_1 + (R_1R_2)^{0.5}]$ then the expenditures should be split but not otherwise. Thus if $R_1 = 20,000$ and $R_2 = 45,000$ then the most that one firm should spend is $R = 100,000$ which will yield in the long run a value of $\bar{p} = 0.64$. A constant expenditure of 200,000 in one firm would yield $\bar{p} = 0.8$ while if two firms each spend 100,000 the composite probability is 0.8704.

It is also useful for sizing and analyzing the model to have an approximate value for the optimal value of R. To derive this value we assume that $\alpha_1 = \alpha_2 = 0$. As shown in Fig. 19, let r be the quarterly interest rate and Y be the expected additional profit per period which will result from exploiting a patent optimally. A dynamic programming approach can be used to find the optimal value of R.

Let V_t be the present value in period t of following an optimal policy from period t on. Then $V_t = \max$ (for $R \geqslant 0$) $[\bar{p} (Y/r) + (1 - \bar{p}) V_{t+1}/(1 + r) - R]$ where of course $\bar{p} = (R - R_1)/(R - R_1 + R_2)$. Now $V_t = V_{t+1}$ since the lags have been removed, so we can write

$$V_t = \max \text{ (for } R \geqslant 0) \ [\bar{p} (Y/r) - R (1 + r)/(\bar{p} + r)]$$

The solution is

$$R = R_3 + ([R_2/(1 + r)] [Y + R_3])^{0.5}$$

where $R_3 = R_1 - r R_2/(1 + r)$

To use this formula one must use estimates of r and Y. If the previous values of R_1 and R_2 are used together with $r = 0.05$ and $Y = 100,000$ (after the adjustments to make it compatible with Home Office research expense before taxes) then the optimal value of R is about 93,000. If $Y = 50,000$ the optimal expenditure is about 73,000.

This analysis is very crude since the lag parameters were omitted. Probably a more important omission is the benefit accruing to the first several companies getting a patent. These companies will be in a position to license other companies. Alternatively it is possible for a company to make no expenditures for research but to rely on obtaining a license from another company.

The model can be changed by giving the parameter PR05 a positive value. In this case a patent is granted when $\bar{p}_t \geqslant$ PR05, and research and development will in effect be transformed into a deterministic function.

H.   *The Equilibrium Position of the Firm*

There is now sufficient information on hand concerning both the demand and cost sides of the model to present the system of equations which would confront those firms who choose to maximize net income. The goal is not to solve these equations but to give an approximate statement of how parameters may be chosen in the real model and to show how sensitive a firm's profits are to modest departures from "optimal" decisions.

At the outset it is necessary to make a number of simplifying assumptions. Most of these assumptions arise because calculus is the tool which is used to examine the equilibrium position of the firm, and it is not possible systematically to examine the income differences which arise from different values of discrete variables. Thus in this analysis the number of plants, the numerical grades of standard and deluxe models and the number of area sales offices are regarded as fixed. There would seem to remain the conceptual possibility of carrying out the analysis outlined here for each combination of the discrete variables. The fact that the firms interact in the consumer market raises the number of combinations enormously, so it seems well to ignore the possibility of finding all equilibrium positions.

Some of the other assumptions play a similar role. Product X and Y interactions in the consumer market are ignored. This and the fact that the number of sales offices is regarded as fixed effectively disconnects X and Y. Inter-company and inter-area shipments are ignored. The effect of plant age and methods improvement expenditures on manufacturing cost are also disregarded here in the calculation of marginal cost. Finally, the cash budget constraint which is particularly important in the short run is ignored.

This catalog of simplifications may appear to be quite imposing. Within the choices which face the firm there still remain many items of interest and importance. Then, too, when the sales of standard and deluxe can be determined approximately, it is possible to examine certain of the quantities which have been fixed or ignored to see whether the assigned values are roughly consistent with product sales.

In the discussion here, the notation of the section on the consumer sales function will be retained. The demand equations of that section can be written

$$q = e_p\, p + \bar{e}_p\, p' + e_a\, a + k$$

and
$$q' = e_p\, p' + \bar{e}_p\, p + e_a\, a + k'$$

where here k and k' subsume all of the decision variables of the other firms as well as the economic index and the (fixed) grades of the standard and deluxe models. In this analysis it is convenient to suppose that p is exactly the same as $\log (P/P_0)$ in order that e_p represent the price elasticity. A similar assumption is made for q and $\log (Q/Q_0)$ as well as the other variables.

On the cost side of the model, the assumptions allow the total cost to be expressed as a function of Q and Q' alone, for instance, total cost $= T(Q, Q')$. The marginal costs, denoted by M and M', are the partial derivatives of T with respect to Q and Q'. They are, in general, functions of both Q and Q'. For the purpose of this analysis it is permissible to suppose that the cost function T includes manufacturing cost and marketing cost; the other elements of cost which appear on the income statement can be ignored.

Income in the steady state can be expressed as

$$Y = PQ + P'Q' - T\,(Q, Q') - A$$

In the equilibrium position the partial derivatives of this expression with respect to P, and P' and A must vanish. These partial derivatives are

$$\frac{\partial Y}{\partial P} = (e_p + 1)\, Q + \bar{e}_p\, Q'\, (P'/P) - e_p\, Q\, (M/P) - \bar{e}_p\, Q'\, (M'/P)$$

$$\frac{\partial Y}{\partial P'} = (e_p + 1)\, Q' + \bar{e}_p\, Q\, (P/P') - e_p\, Q'\, (M'/P') - \bar{e}_p\, Q\, (M/P')$$

$$\frac{\partial Y}{\partial A} = e_a\, [(P - M)\, Q + (P' - M')\, Q']/A - 1$$

The problem of the firm in a very simplified sense is to solve five simultaneous equations in five unknowns. The unknowns are P, P', A, Q and Q'. The equations are the two demand equations and the three equations which result from setting the partial derivatives equal to zero. As suggested in an earlier section of this chapter it is conceptually simple for the model builder to choose values for the unknowns listed above which yield a reasonable income statement and balance sheet and then to determine the elasticities. To give the relevant equations for this purpose explicitly, it is helpful to introduce some additional symbols. Let

$$R = PQ$$
$$R' = P'Q'$$
$$J = (P - M)\, Q$$
$$J' = (P' - M')\, Q'$$

The symbol R stands for revenue and J for "pseudo profit." Then the equations for the elasticities are

$$J\, e_p + J'\, \bar{e}_p = -R$$
$$J'\, e_p + J\, \bar{e}_p = -R'$$
$$e_a = A/(J + J')$$

Now if $J \neq J'$ then there is a unique solution for e_p and $\bar{e}_p$. If $J = J'$ then there is a solution only if $R = R'$ and then it is possible to find the value of $e_p + \bar{e}_p$. In either case it is true that

$$e_p + \bar{e}_p = -(R + R')/(J + J')$$

To give $e_p + \bar{e}_p$ (which is e_p^+) an arbitrarily assigned value[17] without changing the income statement and balance sheet in any essential way, it is only necessary to change the value of $R + R'$ provided that $MQ + M'Q'$ is set equal to $T(Q, Q')$ at the assigned values of Q and Q'. This step seems to be a reasonable one because it corresponds to the condition that average cost equals marginal cost at the long-run equilibrium position, and if the firms were free to choose the size of a factory this is the size they would prefer to choose. To increase e_a it is necessary to increase A and $J + J'$ by equal amounts and then to increase $R + R'$ as necessary to maintain $e_p + \bar{e}_p$ at the same value.

17   This is necessary to control the behavior of the market in case some firms have shortages as discussed in the section on the consumer market. Cf. *supra*, 95.

Most of the other entries on the income statement are fixed expenses which are easy to incorporate as indicated in the simple example given earlier. It seems satisfactory to use rather crude approximations for the working-capital requirements and for inventory costs.

Although it is usually desirable to specify the parameters in this fashion to be reasonably sure that the firms are viable, it is also desirable to introduce factors which will make equilibrium hard to achieve. Otherwise the simulation will not be a dynamic experience. This is the general role of the discrete elements in the model. Probably the most important of these discrete choices is the number of factories. A rather obvious way to make equilibrium hard to achieve is to set the "equilibrium" value of $Q + Q'$ equal to either 1/2, 3/2 or 5/2 the "optimal" capacity of one factory.[18] Then events within the actual simulation will determine which firms emerge with factories.

The participants in the simulation are, of course, not in a position to make very close estimates of the parameters. It is of some interest to see how departures from optimal strategies affect the value of Y. If the demand equations are regarded as given, then Y is a function of P, P' and A. Denote the optimal values of these variables by P_0, P_0' and A_0 and the values of Y and its various partial derivatives evaluated at this point by Y, Y_p, Y_{pp}, etc. Then the important terms in the series expansion of Y about the optimal point are (since the first partials all vanish)

$$Y (P_0 + x, P_0' + y, A_0 + z) - Y = (x^2/2) Y_{pp} + (xy) Y_{pp'} + (y^2/2) Y_{p'p'}$$
$$+ (xz) Y_{pa} + (yz) Y_{p'a} + (z^2/2) Y_{aa}$$

This expression gives the profit forgone by non-optimal decisions. Its components, which give the profits forgone by the various combinations of non-optimal decisions, can be expressed in terms of R, R', A, M, M', N, N' and C where $N = M_Q$, $N' = M'_{Q'}$ and $C = M_{Q'} = M'_Q$. The derivation is somewhat tedious, but it is easy to show that

$$(x^2/2) Y_{pp} = (1/2) (x^2/P^2) [(e_p + 1)^2 R + \bar{e}_p^2 R' - e_p^2 Q^2 N -$$
$$2e_p \bar{e}_p Q Q' C - \bar{e}_p^2 Q'^2 N' - e_p^2 Q M - \bar{e}_p^2 Q' M']$$
$$(xy) Y_{pp'} = (xy/PP') [(e_p + 1) \bar{e}_p (R + R') - e_p \bar{e}_p (Q^2N + Q'^2N' + QM +$$
$$Q' M') - (e_p^2 + \bar{e}_p^2) Q Q'C]$$
$$(y^2/2) Y_{p'p'} = (1/2) (y^2/P'^2) [(e_p + 1)^2 R' + \bar{e}_p^2 R - e_p^2 Q'^2 N'$$
$$- 2 e_p \bar{e}_p Q Q' C - \bar{e}_p^2 Q^2 N - e_p^2 Q' M' - \bar{e}_p^2 Q M]$$
$$(xz) Y_{pa} = - (xz/PA) e_a [e_p Q^2 N + (e_p + \bar{e}_p) Q Q'C + \bar{e}_p Q'^2 N']$$
$$(yz) Y_{p'a} = - (yz/P' A) e_a [e_p Q'^2 N' + (e_p + \bar{e}_p) Q Q'C + \bar{e}_p Q^2 N]$$
$$(z^2/2) Y_{aa} = (1/2) (z^2/A^2) [(e_a - 1) A - e_a^2 (Q^2 N + 2 Q Q' C + Q'^2N')]$$

The most important fact which these formulas show is that profit is affected as the square of the relative error of a decision. Thus if prices are set five per cent too high (or too low) then the loss is one fourth as great as when the relative error is ten per cent. The inter-

18   By optimal capacity is meant that value at which average variable cost is least.

action terms PA and $P'A$ enter only when marginal costs are not constant. When marginal costs are constant, then a ten per cent error in price affects profit by one per cent of $(1/2)$ $(e_p{}^+ + 1)$ $(R + R')$ while a ten per cent error in advertising affects profits by one per cent of $(1/2)$ $(e_a - 1)$ A. Thus the cost of errors is directly proportional to revenue (as would be suspected) and slightly less than proportional to price elasticity. Profits are more sensitive to errors when marginal costs are increasing (N and N' greater than zero) and less sensitive when they are decreasing. The terms involving N, N' and C will generally be smaller than the terms involving R and R'.

To make the model very sensitive to the values of decisions, it is necessary to make R and R' relatively large. This is done, as we have seen, by making the elasticities large so that in a certain sense from the model builder's point of view the risk from poor decisions is proportional to the square of the elasticities (or the revenue).

3.   The Simulation from the Computer Viewpoint

THIS SECTION GIVES a rather detailed technical definition of INTOP from a computer-oriented point of view. The definition is largely computer independent.[19]

A management game consists of two parts. The first is a list of variables whose values describe the state of the entities (companies) in the simulation and a list of parameters which partially describe the environment in which the entities exist. The second part is the set of rules which together with the parameters govern changes in the state of the entities in the game.

Many of the state variables are quantities which appear in conventional accounting statements. Certain others are measures of such things as the current effect of all previous advertising expenditures. The parameters include such quantities as the costs of factories, price elasticities, tax rates and so on. The program parameters, the company state variables and the players' decisions are stored on a reel of tape or on a deck of punched cards. The precise definition of the rules governing changes in the state variables is embodied in the computer program. The main purpose of this section is to express these rules precisely and in a more illuminating form than the program itself.

The rules, as well as the state variables and the parameters, can be divided into categories which correspond to the conventional way of viewing the companies and the environment. At the lowest level within each category the rules may be divided into elementary components we shall call tasks. Some of these tasks are performed for each company in the Home Office; others are performed for each area within each company. Within an area the tasks may be performed for each product or even for each model of each product.

---

[19] The fact that the most recent version of the program was written in FORTRAN II for the IBM 7090 inevitably influences the description.

The sequential nature of a computer program requires the tasks to be performed in a sequence which is in part arbitrary. To call attention to the *necessary* sequence we include arrow diagrams of the type used in critical-path scheduling. This is intended to illustrate the basic logic of the program and to ease the work of anyone who might wish to modify the program.

In the assignment of tasks to categories it is necessary to make certain arbitrary allocations. This is particularly true in activities which involve both a functional category and accounting. The reader will find it useful to consult the arrow diagrams where most of these interactions are indicated. Various parenthetic remarks will also be used to tie the different categories together.

Most of the tasks specify transformations of the state variables in individual areas within companies. Certain events in the simulation make it necessary to cross area boundaries within a company or to cross company boundaries. One way to implement tasks of this type is to collect in a table the relevant data from each participant in the action, to perform calculations on this data recording the results in another table and, finally, to return the results to the participants in the action. This mode of operation is indicated when computer memory is limited. It is not necessary when the complete list of variables and parameters can be stored in the computer memory at one time.

The overall plan of the FORTRAN program is as follows:
1. *a.* Read and check Master Control Card.[20]
   b. Read and check history or create history as indicated by control card. This step is omitted if consecutive runs are made.
2. *a.* Copy decisions on scratch tape. This step is necessary since different decision cards have different formats.
   b. Enter and check firm decisions.
3. Process Wonder Cards, a device used to change parameters and state variables in the run.[20]
4. Initialize appropriate accounts.
5. Process transactions involving Home Office.
6. Process transactions involving areas.
7. Perform all other tasks.
8. Write edited company reports.
9. Write edited history and unedited history for next period (if requested), then return to 1.

Before giving the detailed statement of tasks, it is useful to view the overall plan. The functional categories are:
1. Marketing
2. Manufacturing
3. Finance
4. Research and Development, Licensing and Market Research
5. Accounting

20   Cf. *infra*, Chapter 5.

Within the *marketing* section the inter-company sales decisions are used to calculate new values of the seller's state variables (sales revenue, cost of goods sold, shipping expense, Accounts Receivable, etc.) Next, intra-company sales are handled in a similar fashion, with the exception that sales in excess of inventory are not executed. The effective values of price and advertising are calculated, and these values together with the product grades, the economic indices and the marketing effectiveness factor are combined to yield each firm's orders for both products. Then a table of shortages is created by subtracting orders from the remaining inventory. Redistribution of shortages takes place, and then the final consumer sales are calculated and removed from inventory. Next, sales revenue, cost of goods sold, commercial and administrative expense and inventory expense are calculated. Finally, manufactured and purchased goods are placed in inventory (according to the priority rules which enforce the two-grade maximum), and the value of inventory and Accounts Payable are calculated.

Within *manufacturing* one builds and pays for plants, incurs certain fixed costs, calculates depreciation, produces goods of various types and grades, calculates the cost of these goods and makes the goods (and their costs) available to the marketing section.

In the *finance* section of the program, the area tasks and the home office tasks are listed separately. In the area list, the initial task is the first flow of funds. Then the cash transfers between the areas and the Home Office are made and any associated capital transfer taxes paid. Next investing or borrowing is done, followed by the second flow of funds. Then supplier credit is handled. Finally the calculations are made arising in income tax, the borrowing limit and the tax loss carry forward. In the Home Office, the special transactions (bank loans and inter-company loans) are processed first. Then dividends, investment and stock market confidence[21] are handled.

The *new product* and *market research* tasks begin by processing the special transaction (licensing) cards. This information is used to update the state variables in the individual companies. Then the market research expense is calculated. Next the research and development expenditure is made, and the new effective value of research expenditure and the probability of getting a patent are calculated. Then a pseudo-random number (between 0 and 1) is obtained and a patent for the next grade is granted if the computed probability exceeds this number. Finally the market research statistics are gathered, and the individual company reports are written.

The *accounting* tasks are those associated with the creation of the income statement and balance sheet. They include the calculation of current assets, current liabilities, total assets, total liabilities and simi-

[21] Cf. *supra,* 107, for a description of this concept.

lar items on the income statement. There are several interactions with non-accounting tasks. These are stated explicitly later.

One of the key aspects of any simulation model is the order in which the elementary transformations or tasks must be performed. In the INTOP model it is crucial to know that manufactured goods are placed in inventory after all sales have been executed because this reveals that goods manufactured in one period cannot be sold until the next period. Similarly it is fundamental that in the operating areas any necessary supplier credit is drawn upon after all other transactions which involve the cash account have been made. On the other hand in the Home Office, income taxes are paid from cash (rather than being charged to Accounts Payable) after supplier credit is calculated so that negative cash balances are possible. This is an unlikely occurrence, however, since supplier credit is invoked if necessary to make the cash balance before income taxes greater than some reasonable threshold.

There are a great many necessary orderings of this kind. The computer program enforces all of them, and the lists of tasks which appear in Figs. 21, 23, 25, 27 and 29 at the end of this chapter give one ordering system which is feasible. These lists do not give a complete picture, however, because they indicate a possible order but not a necessary one. Further they do not give the small number of precedence relations between tasks in the different functional areas which must be observed.

In the past few years the concept of "arrow diagrams" has arisen in other contexts in which it is convenient to depict graphically the order relations which *must* be observed in executing a sequence of jobs. These diagrams are often used in describing complicated engineering projects. The essential feature is that many of the very large collection of tasks are independent, but certain tasks must be completed before others can be started. The arrow diagram is a way of presenting this information in an easily understood form.

To show the conventions adopted in the diagrams given here, consider the problem a man encounters in getting dressed. The set of tasks to be performed will be denoted by a numbered list of articles of clothing ordered in such a manner that it is possible to put on the clothes in the given sequence. The list is:

1. Shorts
2. Undershirt
3. Left Sock
4. Right Sock
5. Shirt
6. Trousers
7. Left Shoe
8. Right Shoe
9. Tie
10. Coat

The diagram labeled "Dressing Tasks" in Fig. 20 depicts the necessary sequence. This figure is intended to convey the following information:

1. Any of the Tasks 1, 2, 3 or 4 may be done first.
2. Task 2 must precede Task 5.
3. Tasks 1 and 5 must precede Task 6.
4. Task 5 must precede Task 9 but Task 1 need not.
5. Tasks 3 and 6 must precede Task 7 but Task 4 need not.
6. Tasks 4 and 6 must precede Task 8 but Task 3 need not.
7. Task 9 must precede Task 10.

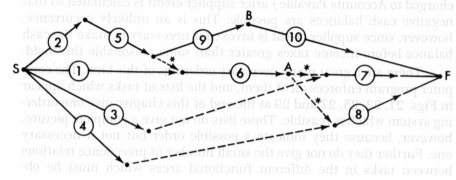

FIG. 20   *Dressing Tasks*

8. Another dashed line would appear from point A to point B if it is necessary to put on the trousers before the coat.

Figure 20 exhibits all of the features needed to construct arrow diagrams of the various sets of tasks in the simulation. These features are as follows:

1. Each solid line represents a task whose number is in a circle.
2. Each dashed line marked with an asterisk represents an artificial task which is needed to describe the necessary sequential relationships.
3. The unmarked dashed lines are merely a convenience which allows the diagram to be constructed using only straight lines.
4. The heavy black dots represent the completion of tasks. They are called "nodes." All tasks leading into a node (indicated by the arrows which point to nodes) must be completed before any tasks leading away from a node (again indicated by the arrows) can be executed.
5. The entire job begins at the start node labeled "S."
6. The entire job is completed when all tasks pointing toward the final node labeled "F" have been completed.

The diagrams for the tasks in the functional areas in the simulation are presented in Figs. 22, 24, 26, 28 and 30 at the end of this chapter. The circled numbers identify the tasks listed by functional area. The area tasks are shown separately; as the diagrams indicate, the sets of tasks are remarkably independent. The interactions are denoted by rectangles which contain the numbers of the tasks from another set that must be completed before tasks emanating from the node can be done. Thus on the diagram depicting the marketing tasks, Fig. 22, it is necessary to have calculated the cost of manufacturing goods before placing these goods into inventory. The diagram which exhibits the research and licensing tasks, Fig. 28, shows that the product grade to be manufactured is determined before the licensing of new grades is carried out.

One might expect accounting tasks to be more pervasive and indeed they are. The interplay is greatest between accounting and finance, since a number of accounting tasks must be completed before the financial tasks can be done and conversely. For example, supplier credit must be determined in the financial section before gross income can be determined in the accounting section, and gross income and taxes must be determined in the accounting section before taxes can be paid in the financial section. Further, taxes must be paid before current liabilities can be determined in the areas.

These diagrams do not show the sequence in which the tasks are performed for the different companies. The organizing scheme is very straightforward. A manageable group of tasks (as limited by computer memory) is selected and then all relevant tasks in the group are executed for each area within the first company, each area within the second company, and so on. Those tasks which must be performed for each product are executed first for product X and then for product Y. Within products, those tasks which must be executed for each plant are carried out in sequential order. Within plants (or products) the tasks are executed first for the standard model and then for the deluxe model.

The task lists which follow are divided into functional areas with only a modest number of tasks falling into the accounting category. Actually the program "discipline" is derived from the basic accounting philosophy. A majority of the state variables can be regarded as asset type or liability (equity) type accounts. The exceptions are such variables as factory age, price, etc. The following rule was adopted: No asset and liability accounts will be changed except by one of the four basic ways which accounting transactions may change accounts. This circumscribed the way in which tasks could be stated. It did make the description and construction of the program much easier. The lists of tasks which follow parallel the actual program very closely. The accounts (state variables) are changed, where possible, by one of four subroutines whose arguments are the names of the variables. The dollar amount involved in the transaction is always placed in the standard location Amount.

To make it possible to conform to this accounting discipline during the calculation of the balance sheet and income statement it was necessary to create special assets and liabilities called "balance accounts." In the process of calculating total operating expense, the discipline requires that this (asset) account be debited and some account be credited by an amount equal to the advertising expenditure. The (asset) account which it would be natural to credit would be advertising expense. But then we would lose the record (which we wish to print later) of the value of advertising expense. To get around this difficulty, an artificial "liability balance" account was set up. In this transaction this balance account is credited. Then as part of the initialization procedure of the next period, Task A2 debits this account and credits advertising expense by an amount equal to the advertising expenditure. This check was particularly useful in debugging the program. It is actually vacuous in the current program (except in consecutive runs) because the values of the variables in this category are not saved to be reintroduced in the next period.

Programming and debugging elaborate simulations on computers requires painstaking work. There are many "answers" to quests for efficient ways to proceed. Certain of these answers take the form of special programming systems such as Dynamo, Simscript, General Purpose Systems Simulator, etc. While these systems are very important, the conventions outlined in this chapter, together with the general principle that the program should be constructed in small modules, permitted a standard algebraic language to be a very practical tool.

FIG. 21   *Marketing Tasks** *

S 1] *Average Inventory Cost*

If Inventory Units > 0, Average Inventory Cost = Inventory Value/Inventory Units. If Inventory Units ≤ 0, Average Inventory Cost = Maximum Manufacturing Unit Cost.

S 2] *Industrial Sales for the Seller*

A) Set Amount = Average Inventory Cost × industrial sales decision

| Debit | Cost of Goods Sold |
| Credit | Value of Inventory |

B) Set Amount = Shipping Cost × industrial sales decision

| Debit | Shipping Expense |
| Credit | Cash |

C) Set Amount = Price × industrial sales decision

| Debit | A/R 2 |
| Credit | Industrial Sales Revenue |

* In all of the lists which follow, the capitalized words denote parameters and state variables, the noncapitalized ones, decisions.

FIG. 21   *Marketing Tasks* (Continued)

D) Set Amount = industrial sales decision
      Debit   Industrial Sales Units
              Credit   Inventory Units
      If Inventory Units < 0, do (E), (F) and (G)

E) Set Amount = − Sales Expediting Cost × Inventory Units
      Debit   Sales Expediting Expense
              Credit   Cash

F) Set Amount = − Average Inventory Cost × Inventory Units
      Debit   Inventory Value
              Credit   Cash

G) Inventory Units = 0

H) For later use, write transaction type, purchasing company, area, sales decision × price, product and grade

I) Write edited record

S 3] *Intra-company Sales for the Seller*
      This is the same as Task S 2 except that first the sales decision is replaced by min (decision, Inventory Units) and all references to Industrial are replaced by Intra-company. S 2 (E), (F) and (G) are not required.

S 4] *Advertising*
      Set Amount = advertising expenditure decision
      Debit   Advertising Expense
              Credit   Cash
      Calculate Effective Advertising

S 5] *Price*
      Set Price of Consumer Sales = decision
      Calculate Effective Price

S 6] *Consumer Orders and Redistribution*
      Here f is the approximation to the natural logarithm function described earlier in this chapter.

A) Calculate f(orders), a function of Effective Price, etc.

B) Calculate f(shortage) = f(Inventory   Units) − f(orders)
      If Price = 0, use 0 rather than Inventory Units
      If Inventory Units = 0, set Price = 0

c) Calculate z, the redistribution variable

FIG. 21 *Marketing Tasks* (Continued)

S 7] *Consumer Sales*

A) Set Amount = min (Inventory Units, redistributed
　　　　orders)
　　Debit　　　　　Consumer Sales Units
　　　　Credit　　　Inventory Units

B) If Inventory Units < 1, Set Amount = Inventory
　　Units
　　Debit　　　　　Consumer Sales Units
　　　　Credit　　　Inventory Units

c) Set Amount = Price × Consumer Sales Units
　　Debit　　　　　A/R 2
　　　　Credit　　　Consumer Sales Revenue

D) Set Amount = Average Inventory Cost × Consum-
　　　　er Sales Units
　　Debit　　　　　Cost of Goods Sold
　　　　Credit　　　Inventory Value

S 8] *Inventory Cost*

Set Amount = inventory holding cost (from formula)
Debit　　　　　　Inventory Expense
　　　　Credit　　Cash

S 9] *Commercial and Administrative Cost*

Set Amount = commercial and administrative cost
　　　　(from formula)
Debit　　　　　　Commercial and Administrative Ex-
　　　　pense
　　Credit　　　Cash

S 10] *Sales Offices*

Number of Sales Offices = min [max (Number of Sales
Offices + decision, 0), 9]

S 11] *Industrial Sales for the Purchaser*

A) Set Amount = Price × sales decision
　　Debit　　　　　Inventory Value
　　　　Credit　　　A/P 2

B) Set Amount = sales decision
　　Debit　　　　　Inventory Units
　　　　Credit　　　Industrial Purchases Units

c) Set Amount = Price × sales decision
　　Debit　　　　　Industrial Purchases Cost
　　　　Credit　　　Liability Balance

S 12] *Intra-company Sales for the Purchaser*

This is the same as S 11 except that all references to
Industrial are replaced by Intra-company.

FIG. 21   *Marketing Tasks* (Continued)

S 13] *Manufactured Goods to Inventory*
    A) Add Units Produced to Inventory Units
    B) Set Amount = Manufacturing Cost
        Debit   Inventory Value
           Credit   Liability Balance

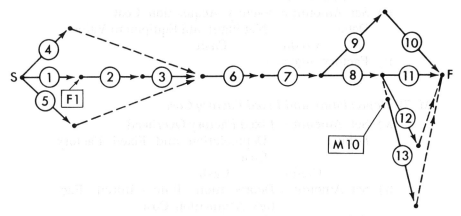

FIG. 22   *Marketing Tasks*

FIG. 23   *Manufacturing Tasks*

M 1] *Factory Construction Limit*
    A) Number of Factories Constructed This Period =
        min (decision, Number of Allowable Factories)
    B) Number of Allowable Factories = Number of
        Allowable Factories – Number of Factories
        Constructed this Period

M 2] *Methods Improvement*
    Set Amount = methods expense decision
    Debit   Methods Improvement Expense
        Credit   Cash

M 3] *Effective Methods Improvement*
    Calculate Effective Methods Improvement

M 4] *Production Grade*
    Grade of Units Produced = min (decision, Maximum
    Producible Grade)

M 5] *Factory Aging*
    If Factory Age > 0, add one to Factory Age

FIG. 23   *Manufacturing Tasks* (Continued)

M 6] *Factory Construction*

If Factory Age = 0 and if Number of Factories Constructed This Period > 0

A) Subtract one from Number of Factories Constructed This Period

B) Initial Factory Acquisition Cost = Factory Acquisition Cost

C) Set Amount = Factory Acquisition Cost
Debit   Net Plant and Equipment Value
        Credit   Cash

D) Factory Age = 1

M 7] *Depreciation and Fixed Factory Cost*

A) Set Amount = Fixed Factory Overhead
Debit   Depreciation and Fixed Factory
                     Cost
        Credit   Cash
B) Set Amount = Depreciation   Rate × Initial   Fac-
                  tory Acquisition Cost
Debit   Depreciation and Fixed Factory
                     Cost
        Credit   Net Plant and Equipment
                         Value

M 8] *Production Adjustment 1*

A) Units Produced in Previous Period = Units Produced

B) Units Produced = decision

M 9] *Production Adjustment 2*

A) Combine standard and deluxe Units Produced if
their grades are the same.

B) Scale total factory production to Maximum Factory Capacity

C) If Factory Age ≦ Construction Time, Set Units
Produced = 0

M 10] *Manufacturing Cost*

Set Amount = variable manufacturing cost (from
                   formula)
Debit   Manufacturing Cost
        Credit   A/P 2

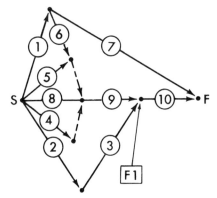

FIG. 24 *Manufacturing Tasks*

FIG. 25 *Financial Tasks*

Area Tasks

F 1] *First Flow of Funds*

A) Set Amount = A/R 1
   Debit   Cash
          Credit   A/R 1
B) Set Amount = A/R 2
   Debit   A/R 1
          Credit   A/R 2
c) Set Amount = A/P 1
   Debit   A/P 1
          Credit   Cash
D) Set Amount = A/P 2
   Debit   A/P 2
          Credit   A/P 1

F 2] *Cash Transfer*

Set Amount = cash transfer decision
Debit   Area Cash
       Credit   Home Office Control
Debit   Subsidiary Control
       Credit   Home Cash

F 3] *Capital Transfer Tax*

A) Set Amount = Home Rate × max (0, cash trans-
                fer decision)
   Debit   Home Capital Transfer Tax
          Credit   Home Cash
B) Set Amount = Area Rate × max (0, − cash trans-
                fer decision)
   Debit   Area Capital Transfer Tax
          Credit   Area Cash

FIG. 25 *Financial Tasks* (Continued)

F 4] *Previous Short Term Investment and Borrowing*

    A) Set Amount = Securities
      Debit   Cash
           Credit   Securities

    B) Set Amount = Bank Loan
      Debit   Bank Loan
           Credit   Cash

F 5] *Saving/Borrowing*

    A) Set Amount = max (0, − borrow/invest decision)
      Debit   Securities
           Credit   Cash

    B) Set Amount = max [0, min (borrow/invest deci-
                    sion, Borrowing Limit)]
      Debit   Cash
           Credit   Bank Loan

F 6] *Interest Income and Expense*

    A) Set Amount = Rate × Securities
      Debit   Cash
           Credit   Interest Income

    B) Set Amount = Rate × Bank Loan
      Debit   Interest Expense
           Credit   Cash

F 7] *Second Flow of Funds*

    A) Set Amount = $\alpha_1 \times A/R$ 2
      Debit A/R 1
           Credit A/R 2

    B) Set Amount = $\alpha_2 \times A/R$ 1
      Debit   Cash
           Credit A/R 1

    C) Set Amount = $\alpha_3 \times A/P$ 2
      Debit A/P 2
           Credit A/P 1

    D) Set Amount = $\alpha_4 \times A/P$ 1
      Debit A/P 1
           Credit   Cash

F 8] *Old Supplier Credit*

    Set Amount = Supplier Credit
    Debit   Supplier Credit
           Credit   Cash

F 9] *New Supplier Credit*

    Set Amount = max (− Cash, 0)
    Debit   Cash
           Credit   Supplier Credit

FIG. 25 *Financial Tasks* (Continued)

If Supplier Credit $\leqq$ Switch-over, Amount = First Rate $\times$ Supplier Credit
If Supplier Credit > Switch-over, Amount = Second Rate $\times$ Supplier Credit
Debit   Interest Expense
        Credit   Supplier Credit

F 10] *Income Tax*

Set Amount = Income Tax Rate $\times$ max (0, taxable earnings)
Debit   Income Tax
        Credit   A/P 1
(Taxable earnings are calculated in Task A9.)

F 11] *Borrowing Limit*

Borrowing Limit = Borrowing Ratio $\times$ max (0, Current Assets − Current Liabilities)

F 12] *Tax Loss Carry Forward*

Tax Loss Carry Forward = Write-off Fraction $\times$ min (0, Gross Earnings); (The result is zero or negative.)

Home Office

F 13] *Bank Loans*

A) Set Amount = loan decision
    Debit   Cash
            Credit   Loans Payable
B) Set Amount = interest decision
    Debit   Total Interest
            Credit   Cash

F 14] *Inter-company Loans Made by "Company From" (Cf. Decision Form 3)*

A) Set Amount = loan decision
    Debit   Investment Inter-company
            Credit   Cash
B) Set Amount = interest decision
    Debit   Cash
            Credit   Interest Income

F 15] *Inter-company Loans Received by "Company To"*

A) Set Amount = loan decision
    Debit   Cash
            Credit   Loans Payable
B) Set Amount = interest decision
    Debit   Interest Expense
            Credit   Cash

FIG. 25 *Financial Tasks* (Continued)

F 16] *Dividends*

Set Amount = dividend decision
Debit   Dividends Paid
         Credit   Cash

F 17] *Cumulative Dividends*

Add Dividends Paid to Cumulative Dividends.
(This is for historical purposes only.)

F 18] *Previous Investment*

Set Amount = Securities
Debit   Cash
         Credit   Securities

F 19] *Current Investment*

Set Amount = investment decision
Debit   Securities
         Credit   Cash

F 20] *Interest Income*

Set Amount = Interest Rate × Securities
Debit   Cash
         Credit   Interest Income

F 21] *Effective Dividends*

Calculate Effective Dividends

F 22] *Stock Market Confidence*

Set Amount = stock market confidence
Debit   Cash
         Credit   Paid-in-Capital

F 23] *Old Supplier Credit*

Set Amount = Supplier Credit + Minimum Balance
Debit   Supplier Credit
         Credit   Cash

F 24] *New Supplier Credit*

A) Set Amount = Minimum Balance + max (0, −
             Cash)
   Debit   Cash
         Credit   Supplier Credit

B) If Supplier Credit ≦ Switch-over, Amount = First
   Rate × Supplier Credit.
   If Supplier Credit > Switch-over, Amount = Second Rate × Supplier Credit.
   Debit   Interest Expense
         Credit   Supplier Credit

FIG. 25   *Financial Tasks* (Continued)

F 25] *Income Tax*
Set Amount = Income Tax Rate × max (0, taxable
            earnings)
Debit   Income Tax
    Credit   Cash
(Taxable earnings are calculated in Task A22.)

F 26] *Tax Loss Carry Forward*
Tax Loss Carry Forward = Write-off Fraction × min
(0, Gross Earnings); (The result is zero or negative.)

F 27] *Effective Earnings*
Calculate Effective Consolidated Earnings

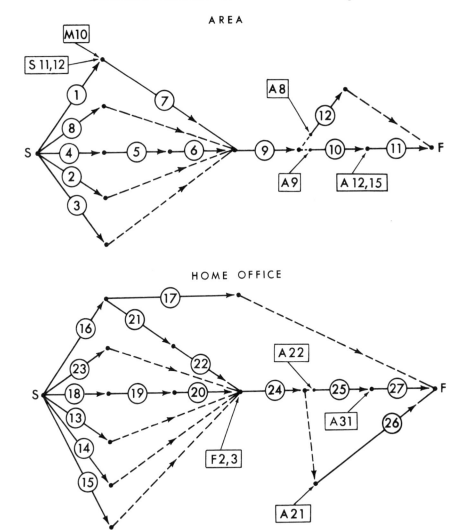

FIG. 26   *Financial Tasks*

FIG. 27   *New Product and Market Research Tasks*

R 1] *Licensing*

The required quantities are obtained from the special decision cards (Form 3). First the validity of the over-all transaction is checked for company numbers, product, and grade.

For Licensor:

A) Set grade licensed = min (decision, Maximum Producible Grade)

B) Set Amount = license payment

   Debit   Cash

        Credit   Licensing Income

For Licensee:

C) If grade licensed is greater than Maximum Producible Grade, set Probability of Receiving Patent = 0.

   Set Maximum Producible Grade = max (grade licensed, Maximum Producible Grade)

D) Set Amount = license payment

   Debit   Licensing Expense

        Credit   Cash

R 2] *Market Research Expense*

Set Amount = Basic Market Research Expenditure Decision (i.e., "Special consulting services" on Home Office decision form) plus sum of costs for specific items

Debit   Market Research Expense

      Credit   Cash

R 3] *Product Research*

Set Amount = research expenditure decision

Debit   Research Expense

      Credit   Cash

R 4] *Effective Research Expense and Probability of Receiving Patent*

Calculate Effective Research and Research Probability

R 5] *Patents*

If Probability of Receiving Patent is greater than Random Number, set Probability = 0 and Maximum Producible Grade = min (4, Maximum Producible Grade + 1)

R 6] *Market Research Statistics*

Calculate numerical values of Market Research Items

FIG. 27   *New Product and Market Research Tasks*
(Continued)

R 7] *Market Research Reports*
Write requested Market Research Items

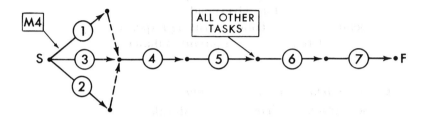

FIG. 28   *New Product and Market Research Tasks*

FIG. 29 *Accounting Tasks*

A 1] *Initialize Appropriate Liability Accounts*
In turn set Amount = State Variable bearing the label
"(L)" (see Appendix I)
Debit   State Variable
    Credit   Asset Balance

A 2] *Initialize Appropriate Asset Accounts*
In turn set Amount = State Variable bearing the label
"(A)"
Debit   Liability Balance
    Credit   State Variable

Area Tasks

A 3] *Gross Margin*
A) Set Amount = Sales Revenue
    Debit   Asset Balance
        Credit   Gross Margin
B) Set Amount = Cost of Goods
    Debit   Gross Margin
        Credit   Liability Balance

A 4] *Total Gross Margin*
Set Amount = Gross Margin
Debit   Asset Balance
    Credit   Total Gross Margin

FIG. 29   *Accounting Tasks* (Continued)

A 5] *Total Operating Expense*

Set Amount = C & A Expense + Advertising Expense
             + Shipping Expense + Inventory Ex-
             pense + Expediting Expense + Methods
             Expense + Depreciation and Fixed Fac-
             tory Overhead
Debit   Total Operating Expense
      Credit   Liability Balance

A 6] *Net Earnings From Operations*

Set Amount = Total Gross Margin
Debit   Asset Balance
      Credit   Net Operating Earnings
Set Amount = Total Operating Expense
Debit   Net Operating Earnings
      Credit   Liability Balance

A 7] *Total Net Operating Earnings*

Set Amount = Net Operating Earnings
Debit   Asset Balance
      Credit   Total Net Operating Earnings

A 8] *Gross Earnings*

Set Amount = Total Net Operating Earnings + In-
              terest Income
Debit   Asset Balance
      Credit   Gross Earnings

A 9] *Taxable Earnings*

Taxable earnings = Gross Earnings + Tax Loss Carry
                   Forward

A 10] *Net Earnings*

A) Set Amount = Gross Earnings
    Debit   Asset Balance
          Credit   Net Earnings
B) Set Amount = Income Tax + Capital Transfer Tax
    Debit   Net Earnings
          Credit   Liability Balance

FIG. 29   *Accounting Tasks* (Continued)

A 11] *Total Inventory Value*

Set Amount = Inventory Value
Debit   Total Inventory Value
        Credit   Liability Balance

A 12] *Total Current Assets*

Set Amount = Cash + Securities + A/R 1 + A/R 2 +
            Total Inventory Value
Debit   Total Current Assets
        Credit   Liability Balance

A 13] *Total Net Plant and Equipment*

Set Amount = Net Plant and Equipment
Debit   Total Net Plant and Equipment
        Credit   Liability Balance

A 14] *Total Assets*

Set Amount = Total Current Assets + Total Net Plant
            and Equipment
Debit   Total Assets
        Credit   Liability Balance

A 15] *Total Current Liability*

Set Amount = A/P 1 + A/P 2 + Supplier Credit +
            Bank Loans
Debit   Asset Balance
        Credit   Total Current Liability

A 16] *Retained Earnings*

Set Amount = Net Earnings
Debit   Asset Balance
        Credit   Retained Earnings

A 17] *Total Equity*

Set Amount = Retained Earnings + Home Office Con-
            trol
Debit   Asset Balance
        Credit   Total Equity

FIG. 29 *Accounting Tasks* (Continued)

A 18] *Total Liability and Equity*

Set Amount = Total Current Liability + Total Equity
Debit   Asset Balance
      Credit   Total Liability and Equity

Home Tasks

A 19] *Total Non-operating Income*

Set Amount = Interest on Intercompany Loans + Licensing Income + Interest on Securities
Debit   Asset Balance
      Credit   Total Non-operating Income

A 20] *Total Non-operating Expense*

Set Amount = Licensing Expense + Research Expense + Interest Expense + Market Research Expense
Debit   Total Non-operating Expense
      Credit   Liability Balance

A 21] *Gross Earnings*

A) Set Amount = Total Non-operating Income
Debit   Asset Balance
      Credit   Gross Earnings
B) Set Amount = Total Non-operating Expense
Debit   Gross Earnings
      Credit   Liability Balance

A 22] *Taxable Earnings*

Set taxable earnings = max (0, Gross Earnings + Tax Loss Carry Forward)

A 23] *Net Earnings*

A) Set Amount = Gross Earnings
Debit   Asset Balance
      Credit   Net Earnings
B) Set Amount = Income Tax + Capital Transfer Tax
Debit   Net Earnings
      Credit   Liability Balance

FIG. 29   *Accounting Tasks* (Continued)

A 24] *Addition to Retained Earnings*

    A) Set Amount = Net Earnings

      Debit   Asset Balance

          Credit   Addition to Retained Earnings

    B) Set Amount = Dividends Paid

      Debit   Addition to Retained Earnings

          Credit   Liability Balance

A 25] *Total Current Assets*

    Set Amount = Cash + Securities

    Debit   Total Current Assets

        Credit   Liability Balance

A 26] *Total Assets*

    Set Amount = Total Current Assets + Inter-company
                Investment + Subsidiary Control

    Debit   Total Assets

        Credit   Liability Balance

A 27] *Total Liabilities*

    Set Amount = Supplier Credit + Loans Payable

    Debit   Asset Balance

        Credit   Total Liabilities

A 28] *Retained Earnings*

    Set Amount = Addition to Retained Earnings

    Debit   Asset Balance

        Credit   Retained Earnings

A 29] *Total Equity*

    Set Amount = Common Stock + Paid-In-Capital + Re-
                tained Earnings

    Debit   Asset Balance

        Credit   Total Equity

A 30] *Total Liability and Equity*

    Set Amount = Total Liabilities + Total Equity

    Debit   Asset Balance

        Credit   Total Liability and Equity

A 31] *Consolidated Income Statement and Balance Sheet Quantities*

This task is done in the obvious manner, i.e., largely by totaling horizontally Area and Home Office accounts towards the consolidated columns on the right end of these output sheets.

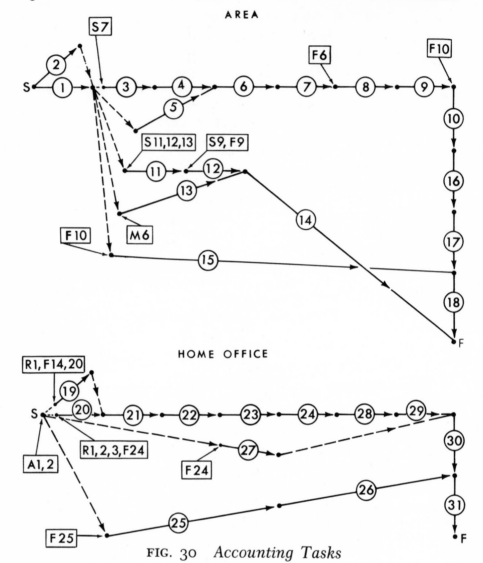

FIG. 30   *Accounting Tasks*

Chapter **4**

Game Administration

Introduction

THE EFFECTIVENESS of management simulations – like that
of any other educational technique – depends in large part on the skill
and imagination with which they are used. For all games a certain administrative effort is required merely to keep the play going. To maximize the learning potential of a game, the input of administrative
know-how and insight into educational processes needed is substantially greater than for routine play. The good game administrator must
have some of the qualities of an entrepreneur; in many respects he
may well be likened to the producer of a play.

Considering the vital role of competent and creative administration it is particularly unfortunate that the subject of game management has been given such scant attention. The discussion of the general problems involved has been fairly esoteric and unwilling to come
to grips with issues of practical detail which may spell the difference
between failure and success in game use. It is still true that for a majority of simulations only a set of player's instructions are generally
available. Indeed, we have failed to uncover a single administrative
manual going beyond cryptic technical pointers on how to make the
model involved function in actual play. This state of affairs was more
understandable in the frontier stage, when the problems of current
administration were frequently submerged among the greater issues
of game design and development. When the initial excitement of obtaining a working game model had died down, it seems that many a
designer lacked the patience for the follow-up work needed to make
use of his creation by others as easy and fruitful as possible. At a time
when it was important to gain acceptance for gaming per se there may

also have been a tendency on the part of proponents to minimize the administrative effort involved. As a result every new user had to start with two empty hands in the area of game administration, a time-consuming, costly and frequently frustrating experience.

The minimal administrative effort required — as well as the marginal yield in student learning experience of increased input of such effort — varies considerably from one simulation to the next. Significantly, the minimal effort required bears little relationship to whether the game is simple or complex, manual or computerized. It has more to do with the distribution of the onus of all computations and operations involved in the model between players and administrative staff (and, of course, the computer in machine games). It is also highly dependent on the quality of the model design itself. There are several determinants of the desirability of additional effort. *Ceteris paribus,* it seems to be true that (*a*) the more complex the model the greater the yield in terms of educational experience from such efforts, (*b*) the greater the degree of integration between the game and other elements of an educational program (or course), the greater the need for such efforts, and (*c*) the greater the number and extent of qualitative factors the administrator wishes to introduce in the course of the simulation the greater the additional effort.

An example of the fact that even simple manually operated games may involve considerable administrative effort merely to keep the play going is provided by the well-known Andlinger Game.[1] This game demands virtually continuous attention to administrative detail by the director during decision-making sessions as well as for perhaps a quarter of an hour between each decision period. In addition, the chief administrator must have an umpiring assistant for each of the participating teams. Experience indicates that even an administrator well-versed in this particular game needs at least half a day to indoctrinate fully the umpiring assistants.

The present chapter goes considerably further than earlier published writings in the discussion of game administration. The presentation gains concreteness by focusing on the management of INTOP. Nevertheless, the *types* of problems encountered in INTOP administration recur in a great many other games. Hence, the chapter should be of use to many administrators with no special interest in the Chicago simulation, to game designers and, not least, to the authors of the sorely needed administrative manuals about other simulations. To avoid reader tedium we shall not stop to emphasize broader applications at

---

[1] G. R. Andlinger, "Business Games — Play One," 36 *Harvard Business Review* (Mar.–Apr. 1958), 115–25. A marketing-oriented game, the original Andlinger design had the rather crucial limitation that price was not a variable as mentioned earlier, *supra,* 2, note 4. Several improved versions are known. Hans B. Thorelli has incorporated price as a variable. A mimeographed description of this version is available on request.

every point where this might be legitimate; the reader is also likely to be his own best guide in this regard.

The chapter attempts to pioneer in another important respect in trying to demonstrate how a game of INTOP's complexity and flexibility may be moulded into an integral part of a broader educational program. On this point there has been much discussion but little evidence in the past. Our exposition is based on experience in business policy and organization courses at Chicago and Stanford University as well as marketing management courses at Chicago. However, several of the observations made in that context should be applicable also in many other situations of intermittent play, in non-academic as well as academic environments.[2]

A principle in the selection of materials for the chapter has been to strike a balance between general observations and INTOP implications. For this reason, a number of detailed administrative routines pertaining to the simulation have been placed in the Appendix. Due reference to the exact location of this material will be given whenever appropriate.

Like all other chapters in the book, this one is written in such a manner that it can be read separately without undue loss of context. A prospective administrator of INTOP who is contented with a fully standardized run need not read the chapters following this one, provided that he has an effective computer liaison man who will read at least selected parts of Chapter 5 and related parts of the Appendix. If the administrator wants to introduce major change in the initial program or in the course of the game he should at least read the sections of Chapter 5 indicating how this may be done; virtually no knowledge of computers is required.

We are aware that the chapter is of awesome length. This should not discourage a potential administrator of INTOP or other sophisticated simulations, however. In large part the chapter has been written for reference use, rather than as a step-by-step guide. *The day-to-day problems of administration are actually handled within the confines of Section 2 of the chapter.* It must also be remembered that game administration is always a matter of teamwork and delegation. Depending on his own temperament and local resources available, each administrator will develop his own scheme of division of labor. It is hoped that his thinking in this regard will be stimulated by the prototype "job instructions" in Appendix V.

---

2 Like so many simpler games, INTOP has proved to perform satisfactorily in continuous play, although such play does not afford the opportunity to get the most out of the experience.

For an account of a 10-week executive development program in international business operations at International Minerals and Chemical Corporation using INTOP as a nuclear element see Hans B. Thorelli, "Simulate to Stimulate in International Marketing," in *Proceedings* of the American Marketing Association, December 1963.

1.   Preparatory Considerations

A. *Purpose*

The single most crucial task facing the game administrator is to determine as specifically as possible the purpose of running the simulation. In the early years of gaming an ill-defined purpose may have mattered little in view of the sheer novelty and general excitement of participation and a widespread feeling that the experience of playing any management game was somehow vaguely beneficial. With the development of games for a broad range of specialized as well as general uses, with the fad quality worn off, and with the increasing sophistication as to what may be accomplished by various types of simulations under different conditions of play, there is no longer any excuse for not thinking through the problem of objectives. This is all the more urgent as educators more generally flock to the notion that a balanced educational program requires an integrated mix of simultaneously used techniques (lectures, games, etc.).

Many of the basic considerations in deciding whether and for what purpose to employ management games were discussed in Chapter 1. The observation should be added here that once an educator has adopted gaming the uses to which he wants to put it usually tend to broaden. From this point of view there is much to be gained by choosing from the outset a general, flexible, modular-type simulation capable of diversified application. However, the selection of such a game in no way obviates the need for determining the specific purpose of running it in a given case. Of course, the determination of the role of gaming in an educational program and of the type and quality of game which may be used must often be made with an eye on resources at hand. These may place a limit on the range of discretion. On the other hand, the proven workability of play-by-mail of even such complex games as INTOP has eliminated what was formerly a powerful resource constraint, that is, the local availability of computer equipment of the type and capabilities required by a given machine-run game under consideration.

B. *Resources*

When the purpose of employing a given simulation in the particular educational context at hand has been established, the administrator will usually find it relatively easy to make necessary decisions with regard to the many sequel problems arising in game management. It is precisely to facilitate further this task that the present chapter was written. The specific resource requirements in running the game will be a prime concern.

To concretize the discussion we assume that the administrator wants to run INTOP as a part of a 10- or 12-week marketing management course in a school of business, making maximum use of the game as a self-teaching device and to illustrate general problems and principles discussed in lectures and course readings. Under such conditions it has been found at Chicago that the maximal personnel needs, in addition to the administrator, are as follows: computer liaison man, trade journal "editor," computer operator, key-punch girl, secretary and mimeographing clerk. Assuming only one set of decisions a week, no person involved need ever devote more than five hours a week to his function in game administration; most assistants will be used much less (the key-punch girl, for instance, only an hour or so). Thanks to the existence of the Wonder Card monitoring program in the INTOP model[3] even an administrator entirely unfamiliar with computers may serve as his own liaison man, given a willingness to increase his own input of time by a minimum of two or three hours a week.[4] There is certainly no inherent necessity to publish a trade journal in the course of the game, in which case there is need for neither editor nor regular mimeographing services. Much of the effect of a trade journal or industry association may be obtained simply by announcing environmental developments orally to the teams or by writing notes on the blackboard.[5] The key-punching and secretarial services may easily be combined and assigned to a single typist, who will still spend less than third time on INTOP matters. Hence the minimal personnel requirements are fairly modest, involving the part-time services of an administrator, a computer operator (whose services may be needed less than one hour a week) and a secretary. Even under such conditions INTOP will provide as rewarding an experience as any other game with which we are familiar. As suggested in the introduction to this chapter, many simple manual games require more personnel than complex computerized ones.

It was stated that the administrator need not be familiar with computers. Nor need the educator in charge of the program or course in which the game is played be the administrator, although this may usually be the case.[6] Further, while it is generally *desirable* that the administrator have personally participated in a run of the game before

3   Cf. *infra*, 219ff.

4   This would be the typical time needed to check team decision forms for clerical errors, proofread and sort key-punched cards and communicate with the computer operator. Beyond this minimum the additional time needed for computer liaison is directly proportional to the number and magnitude of environmental events necessitating change in the model structure of the numerical values of parameters which the administrator wants to introduce in the course of the game. While diligent use is made at Chicago of INTOP's great flexibility in this regard (giving rise to the notion of computer liaison as a special function and job assign-

ment), it should be remembered that *no* such changes are needed for the functioning of the basic model.

5   At Chicago the weekly *Gazette* will often run up to four or, occasionally, five pages. Cf. sample reprint in Appendix VI. Eliminating redundancy the core of the information in one issue could well be communicated orally in less than fifteen minutes.

6   At Chicago we have run the game in parallel with several classes, in which case only one of the instructors was responsible for current administration. Decisions on the introduction of environmental changes and other policy matters were handled jointly.

staging it himself, this is no requirement *sine qua non.*

Equipment and supplies also present resource requirements. Most manual games require the use of desk calculators — at least for continuous play — although occasionally it is possible to do without any specialized equipment.[7] Most computerized games in the past have been oriented toward a given brand of machine — occasionally even to a single model of a computer. This limitation is now gradually being overcome as more programs are being written in FORTRAN and other standard-type programming languages. Mail and telephone play has also removed the former cumbersome requirement that play take place in the physical proximity of a computer of the requisite type. The standard INTOP program is written in the FORTRAN computer language. Past runs of this program have made use of IBM 7090 machines in Europe and the United States. In principle any computer which will take FORTRAN programs and is equipped with large-scale memory should be able to accommodate the simulation. The program also exists in a version dovetailed to Remington Rand Univac computers. Due to the "bilingual" character of the program we have avoided tying the main discussion to any specific computer. Certain appendices are FORTRAN-oriented. Mimeographed instructions are available on technical details differing in the Univac version.

The INTOP program tape for either type of machine and certain mimeographed accessory materials may be obtained from the Graduate School of Business, The University of Chicago, Chicago 37, Illinois.

Player's manuals, decision forms and output sheets (the latter are furnished automatically in computerized games) are the only indispensable supplies in most games.[8] Frequently it is practical to furnish each team with a folder for additional forms, carbon paper, graph paper, etc.[9]

As regards space requirements, many administrators feel that "the best arrangement is to have each team in a separate office or room."[10] This may well be true of the vast majority of games which permit use of only three or four teams. Our own experience indicates that the banquet-type noise level in a room which permits seating of four or more teams at separate tables effectively prevents undue interference. To have all the teams in one room also facilitates administration by simplifying the handling of general announcements. In INTOP

---

[7] So, for instance, in the Andlinger game, cf. *supra* 2, note 4.

[8] Ample experience indicates that there is no need to provide teams with desk calculators, slide rules or other mechanical aids in intermittent play. While this may be desirable in some instances of continuous play it is also the case that in many continuous-play sessions teams do not have time to make complex enough computations to permit really effective use of such equipment. For a somewhat contrary opinion, cf. Joel M. Kibbee, Clifford J. Craft and Burt Nanus, *Management Games — A New Technique for Executive Development* (1961, hereafter cited as Kibbee-Craft-Nanus), 65f.

[9] Teams usually like to keep a copy of past decisions, hence the need for carbon paper. For suitable team folders in INTOP runs, see sample Secretary instruction in Appendix V.

[10] Kibbee-Craft-Nanus, 63.

more specifically it is also highly desirable in that it facilitates inter-company negotiations and transactions. Finally, a common room makes it superfluous to have any special briefing and review area, which otherwise is a necessity.

We have discussed personnel, time, equipment and space re-source requirements. It would be desirable also to give a cost estimate. A meaningful estimate is difficult to supply, however, without knowl-edge of the circumstances in a given case. Determinants include: type of game to be used, whether play is to be continuous or intermittent, what facilities are available locally, the rate structure employed by the computer center which may be used, etc. Out-of-pocket costs for sup-plies and personal assistance to the administrator in a simple manual game in continuous play for a day may be as low as fifty dollars. A complete run of 10–15 decision periods of intermittent play of a com-plex computerized game in some cases may incur costs of a thousand dollars or more. Most games – whether manual or computerized – fall somewhere in between. Frequently, as is our experience from the Chi-cago, Stanford and Stockholm Universities, it is possible to obtain computer time free of charge for educational purposes. Total out-of-pocket cost in a complete INTOP Standard run under such circum-stances may be limited to perhaps two hundred dollars for supplies and a student assistant for computer liaison work and trade journal editing. Due to the capacity of this simulation to accommodate a large number of participants, it is possible to run it in parallel for several classes (in one or several educational institutions), thereby lowering the cost considerably for each class.

c. *Team Number, Size and Structure. Mergers, Subsidiaries, Joint Ventures*

General observations on the number of teams in various types of games were made in Chapter 1.[11] The maximal number of teams in INTOP Standard is 25. In past runs, however, 15 has been the typical number. We have quite successfully experimented with as few as six and as many as 18 teams. Initial (basic) market potential and cross-elasticities are automatically adjusted according to the number of companies (including any monitor company) participating from the beginning of a run. If new companies are added in the process of a run (which may be done simply by filling out decision forms with the new company number, and providing the companies with whatever initial resources are deemed suitable) the basic market potential is automatically adjusted accordingly.[12] However, both radio and cleaner

11   Cf. *supra*, 19f.

12   Note for Univac users only: Stand-ard Univac tapes exist for 8, 12 and 15 companies, with corresponding dimen-sions of market potentials and cross-elasticities. In Univac runs it is not practicable to add to the number of companies in the course of the simula-tion. Instead, the administrator should use a tape which includes from the out-set the number of "spare" companies he may need later.

elasticities for the industry and each company remain the same, unless the administrator decides to adjust them by Wonder Cards.[13]

We believe that in order to achieve a desirable degree of competitive interaction between the companies in a run with a smaller number of teams than five, certain additional changes are desirable. One obvious boost to competition is to provide each company with greater initial resources. Customarily, starting capital is ten million dollars. With only four teams in the game this might well be increased to, say, 15 million dollars. Or the administrator may run a monitoring company representing Japanese competition. Either or both of these measures are likely to be sufficient to produce lively interaction. A more drastic means of forcing competition among few teams, of course, is to make structural changes in the model constraining the arena of team activity. For example, either one of the two product markets may be dropped, or a geographical area may be eliminated.

The number of participants within INTOP teams in the past has varied between one and seven.[14] There is no reason why the game should not provide a rewarding experience for teams with more than seven students, although internal organization and communications problems are likely to grow rapidly in larger groups, perhaps at the expense of learning from the subject matter and economic interrelationships in the game as such. Standard runs at Chicago have had 5–7 members per team, which seems to provide an excellent challenge in learning from the game itself as well as in problems of organization and decision-making in executive teams. Unless the object is to teach – or even to drill – a specific analytical technique, it is not advisable to have less than three participants in a company team, as this deprives students of the group decision-making experience, and the task of making effective decisions becomes quite onerous.

The composition of each team should be considered in advance. The Executive Program at Chicago is attended by men with a wide variety of backgrounds in the functional areas of management. The men are ordinarily distributed over the teams in such a manner that each major management function is represented on each team. If teams are allowed to organize as they see fit, this sets up a tendency toward functional organization (rather than organization by product

13   In the absence of adjustment an (inadvertent) effect of adding new companies is that inter-company cross elasticities will become less prominent. This is not apt to cause any problem as long as the number of companies added is small in relation to the number of original participants.

Subtraction of companies in the course of a run is not apt to cause any problem as long as *pro forma* output is permitted to remain, and the number of companies deleted is small in relation to the number of original partici-

pants. For the procedure involved, cf. *infra*, 217.

14   Research carried out in collaboration with Professors Norman M. Bradburn and Jack Sawyer at the University of Chicago on 3-, 5- and 7-member teams showed that larger teams more often than not were more successful than smaller ones on a broad range of performance criteria. Generally there was a strong indication that the INTOP model is complex enough to make real division of labor meaningful within the teams.

or area), with each "expert" in charge of his customary area of interest. As a prime benefit of games is to help participants "see the other fellow's point of view" in real life, however, the administrator may wish to specify that no one is to be given an assignment corresponding to his area of professional specialization. In this way, too, teams are encouraged to take a more open-minded view of organization problems.

In a reasonably extended run — stretching over twelve or more decision periods — we have generally obliged the teams to rotate management in the middle of the game, at the same time giving them the option of reconsidering their organization structure. This has doubtless enhanced that part of the simulation experience relating to decision-making processes, although rotation may entail a slight sacrifice in training in the subject-matter areas of management represented in the game.[15]

The administrator may wish to go further in the direction of organizational flexibility by introducing discretionary or compulsory exchange of executives between teams. Discretionary exchange actually represents a step toward simulating the executive job market. The problem of incentives may not be insuperable. While INTOP teams cannot offer fancy salaries or generous expense accounts, an executive might well be interested in moving from a junior position in one team to one providing greater authority in another, or from a low-morale team to one with a more congenial atmosphere.[16] The risk that such arrangements may interfere with the sensibilities of some persons must be observed.[17] The fact that a pirated executive may hurt his former "employer" competitively is only realistic.

Mobility both among executives and in the industry may also be promoted by changing the number of companies during the simulation through mergers and/or by permitting teams of disgruntled managers to form new companies.[18]

15 A more far-reaching idea is that of switching the entire teams at mid-game, Company 1 taking over Company 2, Company 2 taking over Company 3 and so on. Such an experiment might be especially worthwhile when the simulation is run primarily to emphasize training in "situation management."

16 The status aspect of compensation may, however, be simulated if so desired. Teams are then obliged to pay executive salaries each quarter, which simply are deducted in the "consulting services" box on the Home Office Decision Card. It may be wise to oblige the companies to pay their presidents at least $20,000 per period, and their lowest-paid executives at least, say, $2,000 per period, but otherwise leave the compensation structure to company discretion.

17 This problem is also encountered if the administrator allows the class to divide into teams based on the mutual personal preferences of participants, although this method is frequently practiced (sometimes by default).

A practical observation: given the chance, game participants will often select partners on the basis of the law of least resistance. In executive training programs it is not unusual to see real-life members of a given firm, or given management function, or type of business flocking together. This is not conducive to maximal benefit from gaming or other forms of organized exchange of experience.

For a further discussion of organization simulation by gaming, see Appendix VII.

18 On mergers as a possibility, see INTOP Memo 5, reproduced in Appendix VI.

The capacity of the International Operations Simulation of accommodating large numbers of companies opens some very exciting and unusual possibilities in that it permits the establishment of corporate *subsidiaries* and *joint ventures* of the original company teams. Among the preparatory considerations of the administrator should be whether he wants to prevail on this feature, which is clearly an optional "extra."

Subsidiaries and joint ventures with a corporate framework separate from the parent companies (hence separate company numbers and computer outputs) might serve many of the purposes which are generally associated with such organizations. Their existence is ordinarily based on diminishing returns or, conversely, economies of scale phenomena or on the desire to share risks. In INTOP the establishment of a subsidiary R & D operation (in addition to that at the regular Home Office) may well make sense for a company wishing to specialize in that function, as may indeed a duplicate marketing organization for a sales-oriented concern. This is no more remarkable than the fact that it pays General Electric to market GE and Hotpoint appliances separately. The administrator may also wish to add economies of scale beyond the standard INTOP framework to make subsidiaries or joint ventures attractive. Most conveniently this may be done by manipulating the marketing effectiveness factor (see Section 4E of this chapter), as this discriminates at the company level. It is also possible to introduce economies of scale in manufacturing (e.g., by reducing fixed factory overhead) if the new company is in effect building plants 4, 5 and 6 for a given product in a given area (assuming that the parent concern already possesses the maximal three permissible on any given set of outputs). The latter type of common economies must, however, be re-implemented each quarter by Wonder Cards.

As long as the number of subsidiaries and/or joint ventures is not large relative to the number of *teams* the administrator will not encounter any major side-effects as regards market potential and elasticities in the model (cf. the discussion in the first paragraph of this subsection). If the number of such organizations may fairly be expected to be large, the administrator may wish to incorporate some of these "extra" companies from the outset, while any extraordinary additions are made in the course of the run. This will help to maintain a balanced set of market dimensions. Should the market potential still seem to be too large it may easily be adjusted by Wonder Card.

The administrator may decide to place an upper limit on the number of subsidiaries and/or joint ventures to be permitted. He may then introduce a hefty corporate registration fee or simply auction off the corporate shells. Different registration fees may also be charged depending on the use to be made of a new venture (R & D, marketing, production, operations only in one area, etc.).

Again, it should be emphasized that mergers, subsidiaries and joint ventures are in the nature of possible but certainly not necessary side benefits of the versatile INTOP model. The first time the adminis-trator stages the simulation, and indeed in all runs of less than 8–10 periods, he may well wish to exclude such variations on the basic company structure.

D. *Equal Start or Handicap Play? Predetermined or Discretionary Objectives?*

In most game runs teams start out from a basis of equality in terms of both size and mix of resources. INTOP runs in the past have invariably been based on the assumption that each company has just been organized and has succeeded in mobilizing the ten million dollars in starting capital. There is, however, no obvious reason why other alternatives should not be considered. Indeed, the vexing problems of evaluating management performance, in real life as well as in gaming, might be better highlighted if the teams were started out with different resource allocations. The simplest way of trying out this idea would be merely to ask the teams of one course to take over where the teams of a prior run had left off.

Two somewhat more sophisticated ways of proceeding suggest themselves in INTOP, both based on the extraordinary variety of entre-preneurial opportunity in that simulation. One is to commit the start-ing capital (identical for all companies) of the teams in advance in a systematically differentiated pattern. This might be varied according to general riskiness (high in Brazil, low in the U.S.), degree of liquidity (high for a wholesaler with small inventories, low for a world-wide manufacturer of vacuum cleaners), extent of diversification, etc. In this case participants might be allowed to join whatever team they would prefer; it may be hypothesized that risk-minded persons would be attracted to high-risk situations and vice versa.[19]

The other method is essentially to leave the initial resource allo-cation indeterminate. After teams have been selected in any manner deemed suitable by the administrator, they are invited to submit a

19   Other patterns of initial resource allocation are suggested by Paul S. Greenlaw, Lowell W. Herron and Rich-ard H. Rawdon, *Business Simulation* (1962, hereafter cited as Greenlaw-Herron-Rawdon), 189: "In a total en-terprise type of game, the extent to which the industry already possesses considerably more capacity than mar-ket demand can utilize will tend to emphasize the competitiveness of the marketing decisions to be made and will likewise play down the importance of any expansion planning. If the sit-uation is structured further in this di-rection, it is possible to begin play in the midst of a depression with a history of net losses for all companies over a period of time preceding the start of the actual play, and perhaps heavy inven-tory accumulation. In contrast, em-phasis might be desired on the evalua-tion of proposed investment alterna-tives dealing with capital equipment additions and a high degree of market expansion."

stock-sale prospectus setting forth their objectives, plans, capabilities, needs of capital, etc. On the basis of the quality of the argumentation in the prospectus, the administrator (or such outside expertise as he may call in for the purpose) then decides what amounts investors might reasonably be expected to place at the disposal of each team. This procedure does have at least two minor drawbacks, however. It injects a strong personal element (the judgment of the administrator or board of experts) at a crucial stage of the simulation, and it also requires ample advance study of game documentation by participants, who are presumably eager to engage in actual play with minimum delay.

2.   Administering a Standard Run of INTOP

A. *Orienting Participants*

To get off to a flying start in a new position an executive must assimilate in a brief period a vast amount of information about the company he is joining, about the industry in which it is active, the products it makes and so on. This immersion in "the rules of the game" is equally desirable for prospective participants in management games. Indeed, as in INTOP where several years of real-life operation are compressed into a dozen decision-making sessions, rapid and thorough orientation is a prerequisite to effective participation.

In accordance with the psychology of learning as well as practical experience this introductory process usually may be shortened most effectively by diversified use of learning media. Whenever possible the *Player's Manual* should be distributed well in advance to the participants for individual reading. In a transatlantic mail run of INTOP it was demonstrated that highly motivated individuals can proceed directly from such study to play of a quality well above the average of other participants in the same run who had the additional benefit of both an oral presentation and more rapid feedback of game data. Generally speaking, however, it is highly desirable to supplement individual study with an oral presentation allowing ample opportunity for questions from the floor. If there is no time for study of the game documentation before the presentation, experience indicates that participants have to place greater reliance on "learning by doing" during the first decision periods of the simulation than is otherwise necessary. To derive maximum benefits from participation the elementary rules of the game should, however, be digested as fast as possible. In this respect management games are no different from baseball or bridge. In cases where participants are relatively unprepared the administrator (or his assistants) should be ready to devote more effort to preventing trivial but fateful mistakes from creeping into team records during the first few decision periods.[20]

There is no "one best way" of making the oral presentation. Until he finds his own style the administrator may wish to stick fairly closely to the outline and materials of Chapter 2. He may also point out that to a certain extent life itself is indeed but a "game." The Dill-Hilton-Reitman study of young career executives makes it fairly clear that the more successful men are those who consciously and continuously re-examine their own relations *to* as well as *in* a decision-making system (such as a company team in INTOP), and also examine the interaction of that particular system with its external task environment.[21] This leads naturally to a restatement of the fact that while INTOP is indeed presenting teams with types of problems, considerations and general interrelationships characteristic of real-life business there has been no intention to reproduce in the game with any degree of faithfulness any given industry or market. The point is rather for participants to learn from experience and analysis in the simulation, to take the features of their operating environment in the game as "given" and then proceed to do their best with it. This is indeed not too different from what goes on in reality. A further problem.that needs discussion before play begins is that of performance criteria and evaluation.[22] A full presentation of the simulation with time for questions may take as much as an hour and a half. However, a workable briefing may be performed in half that time under favorable circumstances.

B. *Organization and Objectives of Teams*

Considerations relating to team size and number and the assignment of participants to particular teams have already been discussed.[23] Unless team members know each other quite well in advance it is advisable that the first item on their agenda be the discussion and

---

20   One way of "cutting corners" at the beginning of the run is to assign the task of recording team decisions to preselected individuals, thereby saving other participants the trouble of learning the technicalities of handling decision forms. However, as process and content are interrelated in decision-making this will tend to reduce the learning experience of the other participants to some extent. It may also mitigate against certain types of team organization which the group might have found preferable on more functional grounds. Finally, such a procedure *may* infringe on the benefits of participation accruing to the "record-keeper."

In highly simplified games it is sometimes possible to let the teams "learn by doing" by letting them play four or five periods "without obligation," and then start over again with the "real" run. This is usually too costly and time-consuming a process in complex games. Often, too, there would be no corresponding opportunity in real life as an executive takes over a new job. Occasionally it may be worthwhile to give the teams in complex simulations an opportunity to "warm up" by making a set of decisions adding a period to an old run.

21   William R. Dill, Thomas L. Hilton and Walter R. Reitman, *The New Managers. Patterns of Behavior and Development* (1962).

22   Cf. *supra*, 31, and *infra*, 195ff.

23   Cf. *supra*, 19f.

definition of objectives. This will give the members time to get acquainted with each other, a generally desirable prelude to formal organization of the group.

How much time the teams should be allowed for such initial activities as defining objectives and organizing depends entirely upon the purpose for which the game is being run. In part, but only in part, an overly brief allocation of time for these purposes at the beginning of the simulation may be compensated for by the teams' devoting attention to these problems on a more informal basis as the game goes along.

Even where INTOP is used for continuous play in a one- or two-day session it would rarely be advisable to provide for less than one hour for definition of objectives, organization and the formation of at least an embryo of a long-range plan. If the simulation is to be part of an integrated university course or a training program, where such matters as goal formation, organization and long-range planning are themselves the objects of lectures or discussions at a principal level, teams may need double this time, in addition to time used in preparation for and follow-up of the meeting.

The minimal accomplishment in the area of objectives would seem to be for the team to set down in written form a definition of its business in terms of such dimensions as what product and geographical markets it will pertain to, what functions it will perform in various areas, what clientele it will aim at (in terms of family consumers or distributors, the demand for standard or deluxe products, etc.) and a gross estimate of where the team plans to be at a given future date in terms of assets, sales, etc.

To increase the degree of rationality in the selection of initial stances the administrator may encourage a voluntary exchange of data on company intentions at this formative stage.[24] A certain degree of specialization is forced on the teams by the fact that starting capital is limited. If time is provided even at this early stage for at least informal negotiation between various teams for standing supplier arrangements, inter-company loans, etc., the degree of specialization will usually be considerably greater than otherwise.[25] It is also prudent to provide each team with a sample copy of all types of standing agree-

---

24 This may be done most conveniently by means of the blackboard, where companies so inclined may register their intentions under such headings as: will focus on product X (Y), on Area 1 (2, 3), will go global, will look for suppliers (buyers, licenses, licensees, funds, borrowers). As in reality, it cannot be expected that all companies will want to reveal their plans.

25 No company may want to restrict its role to that of a pure distributor (although the combination manufacturer in one area, distributor in an-

other is quite common). If the administrator wants to encourage such a stance, this may be done most easily by his offering to auction off a pool of products to would-be distributors in quarter 3. He may represent a British, Scandinavian or Japanese supplier. In this manner the initial disadvantage of a non-producing company of a one-quarter shipping lag may be overcome. After quarter 3, distributors may obtain their goods from the regular companies in the game.

ments,[26] as this helps to visualize the details of long-term arrangements with other groups. Companies may be further assisted in the selection of suitable stances if they are reminded of INTOP Memo 2 on Common Economies.[27]

After determining its objectives each company team should give some thought to internal organization and division of labor. Here again, the amount of time and energy invested must depend on the purpose for which the game is run. It would seem desirable that the administrator at least point out such major alternatives as organization primarily by area, by function and by product, as illustrated on the outside back cover of the *Player's Manual*. The special significance of the president in an INTOP company should also be emphasized: he is alone responsible for the delivery of decision forms on time, and his signature is required on all inter-company transactions.[28]

As to make the teams grapple with the problems of organization has in itself been a purpose in past runs no standard organizational scheme has been developed. This has been done, however, for the Carnegie game where a standard organization is more natural since program routines focusing on particular management positions have been developed and the range of alternate objectives facing the teams is narrower. Clearly, the details of organization will also depend on the number of team members.[29] In order to stimulate the maintenance of effective division of labor (as opposed to committee management of each and every problem in the game) teams should supplement their organization plan with a set of job descriptions. Again, if time does not permit this, the administrator may provide the teams with standardized job descriptions suitable to a variety of different organization structures.

The administrator who plans to provide for rotation of team managements at some stage of the game should consider whether he wants

26 Standard agreements of this kind are reproduced in Appendix IV. The administrator may also elect to stimulate specialization in R & D by giving the teams samples of a research specialization agreement, also reproduced in Appendix IV.

27 Reproduced in Appendix VI and on the inside back cover of the *Player's Manual*.

28 Of course, this does not mean that he has to make all decisions (or fill out decision forms) or personally negotiate all transactions. However, to enable the administrator (as well as other outsiders) to remain beyond any internal conflict emerging in a team it is normally imperative that one of its members be formally responsible for external relations. Where a main purpose of the game is organization simulation the administrator may wish to relax this emphasis on the formal leadership position of the president.

It is recognized that a strong president may wish to change the team objectives as previously arrived at, and may successfully impose his will on the team. All that the rules require is that any change in objectives in the course of the game be delivered to the administrator to assist him in his evaluation of performance.

29 To illustrate, a team with seven members might well consider making R & D and licensing the only concern of one of its executives, even if the company is also engaged in worldwide manufacturing and marketing operations. A smaller team similarly engaged could not afford to make R & D and licensing a separate assignment.

to divulge this intention in advance. To do so may induce dysfunctional behavior in some instances, while in others it may stimulate a healthy amount of intra-team competition, with the various executives vying for the more powerful or interesting positions in the group after reorganization.

c. *Telescoping Initial Decision Periods*

In standard runs of INTOP it is advisable to telescope the decisions of the first three quarters (Q1-3)[30] into one decision-making session. Once a team has chosen its objectives, making the first three sets of decisions becomes a fairly routine matter, and involves little extra strain beyond filling out three sets of forms rather than the single set which they will normally fill out.[31] The number of periods to be telescoped is suggested by the length of the plant construction period. Telescoping more than three quarters is not recommended, as teams both want and need to have a clear view of their production cost picture before making major pricing decisions.

During the first few sessions many groups will not yet have developed efficient decision-making machinery. To instill the requisite degree of discipline to produce decisions on time the administrator may split up the telescoped session into three segments requiring one set of decisions to be submitted at the end of each time segment.

Early decision-making efforts will be facilitated if the administrator draws the attention to INTOP Memo 1 on the front inside cover of the *Player's Manual*.

It is important that the administrator facilitate a realistic exchange of information among the teams during the initial sessions. For this purpose companies should be encouraged (although not forced) to make public announcements concerning their plans, either orally or in a "Press Release and Advertisements" section on the blackboard. Immediately after Q1 decisions have been delivered, the administrator should announce all plant construction initiated by company, product and area. This is only realistic, and provides an opportunity for the teams to go into "underdeveloped" areas at an early stage of the simulation.

To prevent what may perhaps be regarded as excusable mistakes in decision-making during the first session the administrator may wish to remind the teams of the following elements of the standard rules:

The Brazilian securities deposit requirement for plant construction (applies for every plant under construction or on stream in each of the first three quarters).

Chase-A-Martini Bank requires a minimum balance of $50,000 in home office cash account at the end of each quarter.

---

30   In the following, the notation "Q" followed by a number will frequently be used to denote a given quarter.

31   If the teams start with a predetermined resource allocation enabling them to market goods in the first quarter of operations, telescoping should be avoided at the beginning of the simulation.

A team should provide enough area cash in Q3 to cover fixed cost of production as well as that part of variable manufacturing cost which is payable immediately. (The percentage in Accounts Payable depends upon the area.)

Generally speaking, experience indicates the wisdom of supplying ample cash for area and home office operations in the beginning quarters – only what is clearly excess cash should be placed in home office securities.

The choice of marketing channel (or mix of the three available channels: agents, captive sales organization, using other team as distributor) is predicated mostly on minimizing cost (in the short run)[32] as there is no inherent difference in sales promotion ability between various channels.

Teams probably wish to subscribe to the *Gazette* in Q3.

Chase will not negotiate any bank loans until Q5, when the result of initial marketing operations are in.

The administrator concerned with minimizing the dysfunctional (in terms of team reaction often dismal) consequences of clerical mistakes in filling in forms or cards (the terms are used interchangeably) may wish to add some of the following reminders:

Teams should look upon the forms as the crucial link in a man-machine system of a general variety which will become increasingly common in the computer era. Hence, to write correct instructions is indeed a managerial challenge. Instructions must be legible – at the risk of the teams. (Stress that the readers will be key-punch operators not familiar with the game.)

Instructions must be unequivocal – at the risk of the teams. (There will be *no* "doctoring" of decisions.)

Teams should always hand in *originals* of all decision forms, as digits are easily misplaced on copies. (Such dislocations will confuse the key-puncher, but hardly the teams themselves.)

Teams should be careful not to hand in duplicate sets of any decision forms inadvertently. This point is especially relevant to inter-company transactions as all forms submitted will be processed.

Teams making no decisions in Q2 in an area where they initiated plant construction or other operations in Q1 should be careful to fill in *Company No.* and *Period No.* for the area on the Operations Card. (If these data are left out all prior decisions will be repeated automatically.)

The repeat convention of the computer applies to the Operations and Home Office cards only. All inter-company transactions have to be renewed quarter by quarter if they are to be repeated.

Hence, quarterly transactions under *any* standing contract require a new Inter-Company and Special Transactions Card *each* quarter during the validity of the contract.

Almost without exception, the computer reads "zero" in empty spaces on decision forms [33] – hence a one-digit number should be placed in the

---

[32] In the long run, such questions as the degree of permanence and expected volume of company engagement in a given area, the risks inherent in tying up with another company over extended periods of time and many other broader questions presumably enter the picture.

[33] An empty price box is taken to mean "hold any available goods in inventory this quarter" (as the result otherwise would be an outright give-away). In sign boxes an empty space is also read as 0, which here *always* has an operational meaning, such as "add."

far right-hand space of a box, a two-digit number in the two right-hand spaces, etc. This also applies to Marketing Research items.

Teams should not forget, or misinterpret, the sign boxes, which should be used always (and only) when there is a number to be written in the accompanying box for financial transactions or regional sales offices.

Boxes on the decision forms can *only* take digits and, occasionally, a minus sign. They can *never* take a letter or any other symbol (such as X_0, which some teams are tempted to put in the grade box on area cards). Indeed, if a letter does get key-punched this will likely result in costly computer stoppage.[34]

Subscription to the *Gazette* is Marketing Research Item 1. This digit should be written in space 38 (*nothing* to be written in spaces 34-36) on the Home Office Decision Card.

This may well seem like a formidable list of reminders. However, most of the points are fairly self-evident in the context in which participants encounter them. Indeed, as they are all included in the *Player's Manual* the administrator should exercise some discretion in repeating the information. If he is overly solicitous he will soon find participants turning to him as a "walking encyclopedia" rather than bothering to consult the manual. This may be acceptable in a continuous run for top executives, but certainly not in intermittent play in a class of mature students. A workable compromise is frequently simply to put some of the more vital points on the blackboard.

It may finally be noted that the R & D programs of some companies may result in a product improvement in Q1 or Q2 which they will not be able to utilize in Q3. A simple but adequate solution is to grant National Science Foundation Awards of $50,000 or so to teams which develop improvements in the first two quarters.[35]

D. *A Standard Decision Session*

1] LENGTH OF SESSION

If circumstances permit it may occasionally be wise to allow teams certain flexibility with regard to time during the first decision-making sessions. As observed by C. Northcote Parkinson, however, work tends to expand to fill whatever time allotted to it, and this "law" seems particularly applicable in management games. For this reason, it is highly desirable to impose fairly strict discipline with regard to timing as soon as feasible. In this way it is generally also possible to stimulate

[34] For this reason, Computer Liaison will check that no letters or symbols other than minus occur on the form; cf. Computer Liaison instruction in Appendix V.

[35] Alternatively, companies conducting R & D programs may be encouraged to make their Q3 production decisions on the *assumption* that they will develop X_1 and/or Y_1 in Q1 or Q2.

Should they fail to do so, the computer will simply provide for X_0 or Y_0 production instead. Indeed, the companies may, if they so wish, indicate both X_0 (Y_0) standard and X_1 (Y_1) deluxe production. Should X_1 (Y_1) not materialize in Q1 or Q2 the computer will simply add the standard and deluxe decisions, making only X_0 (Y_0) up to maximal capacity of each plant.

more effective team organization and data processing. If there is no reasonable constraint on time committee management of even the most trivial matters is likely to result.[36]

There are simple but highly effective means of enforcing time limits. A mild form of penalty is simply to impose a fine of, say, fifty thousand dollars in lieu of profit opportunities missed by a slow-moving executive group.[37] A more severe, and yet perhaps more realistic, punishment is to refuse to accept late decision forms. This in effect means that the decisions made last quarter in area and home office operations are allowed to stand. They will, in fact, be repeated automatically by the computer.[38]

Assuming intermittent play, a standard decision-making session in INTOP should never be shorter than half an hour.[39] One hour would be more typical. Especially in the early sessions teams can effectively use up to an hour and a half. Background experience of participants, the amount of time they can devote to preparatory work between sessions and the detailed purposes of running the simulation will suggest optimal time in a given run. Ancillary assignments, such as making decisions for several quarters in one session, study of consolidated outputs of competing firms[40] or the drafting of plans and organization charts (if made in class), will naturally require extra time. To maintain mental discipline it may be helpful to set aside a given part of the session for such activities.

2] COUNSELING TEAMS

A number of administrator activities represent counseling in various forms. These activities are of considerable significance in influencing the yield participants will obtain from the simulation. Whenever possible the administrator should take pains to examine computer outputs before each session as part of a continuing evaluation. Some of his notes may be communicated with the teams as the game goes along rather than at the end of the run. The effect on performance and morale is almost always salutary, even where the comments imply criticism. This effect may be further enhanced by occasional public praise or "needling" of individual companies.

In any run of a complex simulation there will inevitably be some complaints. The standard version of INTOP has proven "bug-free" in

---

[36] Dysfunctional behavior will also result if the sessions are too brief; cf. *supra,* 21f.

[37] This may simply be taken out of home office cash and retained earnings by means of Wonder Card 4A.

[38] The only exception to automatic repetition is inter-company transactions. This presents no problem if the non-dilatory team has handed in these forms. If not, the administrator may either accept late delivery of these particular forms or arbitrate the damage suits which are likely to be filed in the following quarter.

[39] Some of the special considerations in continuous play were discussed in Chapter 1.

[40] Cf. *infra,* 162, 178f.

many runs. Occasionally, however, some peculiar combination of play may produce unreasonable results, as it is practically impossible to foresee every conceivable constellation of several hundred variables. Furthermore, experimentally-minded administrators sometimes may make changes in game parameters a bit too radical. Some complaints may originate in the nonchalant way a team has filled out its forms, or an error by the key-punch operator or computer liaison man.[41] At times the administrator may find that he himself is the cause; he may, for instance, not have communicated properly the impact of a given environmental change which he has introduced. In the interest of equity and morale complaints should be handled judiciously.

Ordinarily, the administrator will find that he is able to make a decision on a complaint on the spot. Where this is not possible, it is advisable to have the team state the complaint in writing, specifying not only what they think is wrong but also what they think should have been correct procedure. Preferably, reference should be made to relevant parts of the *Player's Manual* (not infrequently, renewed consultation of the manual will take the wind out of an erstwhile complaint).[42] In more complex cases, it is generally helpful to the administrator, and a useful exercise for the team, for the plaintiff to prepare cash-flow statements for the operations (area, home office or entire company) and periods involved.

Time and computer expense generally make it impractical to rerun an entire set of decisions to correct an individual complaint. In practice, most corrections are made ex post facto. This being the case, the preferable form of correction is an addition to or deduction from cash (representing damages, lost profit opportunity, etc.). Such cash corrections are extremely simple to make in the areas as well as in the Home Office.[43] While *any* position on the balance sheet, income statement or ancillary data sheet is easy to change, it must be remembered that more complex adjustments – such as adding goods to inventory – generally tend to affect a whole series of accounts. It may simply not be worthwhile to trace through the consequences of such an adjustment, as in most cases a reasonable estimate of its monetary implications may be made.

Ordinarily, there will be no conflicts *between* teams giving rise to complaints as long as the rules governing inter-company transactions are followed. Teams should be reminded about the fact that the administrator will assist in the enforcement of standing contracts only if they have been properly registered. There may occasionally be legitimate cause for disagreement among the parties, however, such as with regard to the impact of a strike on a supplier contract, import prohibi-

[41] In not a single instance has the computer been to blame in the past.
[42] It would be perfectly legitimate for the administrator to impose a fine on complaints negligently conceived, although the modest number of complaints in the past has not justified such action.
[43] Wonder Cards 4B and 4A, respectively, are used.

tion or similar environmental event. Depending on the purpose for which the simulation is being run the administrator may make a snap decision or prefer to conduct a moot court session with the parties (or have a third party from among or outside the circle of participants in the game do so). In any case, it should be pointed out before the administrator takes any action that the tendency in modern business is for the parties to iron out among themselves disagreements over contract interpretation.

The administrator may engage most actively in team counseling by adopting the role of consultant.[44] As in real life, calling in an outside consultant occasionally seems to be the only means of resurrecting an ailing company in INTOP, whatever the reasons for its incapacity to act intelligently or aggressively may have been. To maximize the learning experience of participants the consultation should take the form of prodding questions rather than outright guidance.[45]

3] STANDARD ADMINISTRATIVE ROUTINES: CHASE-A-MARTINI BANK

Companies may secure outside financing principally by borrowing from each other or from Chase-A-Martini, the leading Liechtenstein bank. The Bank is ordinarily represented by the administrator.[46] In standard runs of INTOP the Bank will not grant any loans until Q5, when it has an opportunity to examine the initial sales records of its clients. To simplify credit management the administrator may decide to introduce standard credit lines. The limit may be defined, e.g., as a given percentage either of total equity in the Home Office or of paid-in-capital whichever is greatest.[47] Larger loans may be granted after special negotiation with the Bank to companies which submit well-documented plans for the use of funds. A standard bank loan contract is reproduced in the Appendix.[48]

4] INTER-COMPANY TRANSACTIONS

To stimulate long-term planning and functional specialization teams are encouraged to enter standing contracts. Standard forms are provided for inter-company loans, supplier, licensing and R & D speciali-

---

44 The Marketing Research section of the *Player's Manual* suggests in this capacity he adopt the nom-de-guerre of Arthur DeBig. To maintain equity among competing teams a hefty fee should be charged under the heading "special consulting services" on the Home Office Decision Card.

45 Cf. *infra*, 174.

46 Cf. however, *infra*, 194.

47 In quarters 5–7 a workable limit is 15 per cent of total equity in the Home Office or ten times paid-in-capital. To keep credit expansion within bounds the limit may later be reduced.

48 Cf. Appendix IV. The borrowing company is responsible for quarterly follow-up on the contract; see *Player's Manual*, 29.

zation arrangements.[49] All the administrator (or his assistant) needs to do when two teams have entered a long-range agreement is to check that a standing contract form has been properly filled out and signed, and that an inter-company transactions form (Decision Card No. 3) has been made out to effectuate the part of the total contract scheduled to be executed during the current quarter. The file of standing contracts serves a dual purpose. It enables the administrator to keep tabs on contract performance and to assist in the enforcement of contracts when a party defaults for no good reason. It also provides a set of useful records for the review and evaluation of the entire run and of individual company participation therein.

5] MARKETING RESEARCH AND CONSULTING SERVICES

Most marketing research is handled by the computer, acting on the instructions of the teams. However, the two standard items relating to test marketing and variable production cost are non-programmed, and a form listing the information must be distributed to teams ordering it.[50] The administrator should make a policy decision as to whether teams should be able to obtain this information immediately when ordered or whether it is to be given to them with a lag of one quarter. (In the standard listing all other items have such a lag.) Retaining the lag places a premium on long-range planning, but it is also likely to lead to costly mistakes on the part of teams which start to produce "dud" grades of their products while waiting for the information. To encourage teams which do show the foresight and initiative of ordering these items, the information has generally been made available immediately in recent runs at Chicago.[51] If this is the decision of the administrator it should be publicly announced to all teams.

As suggested in the Marketing Research section of the *Player's Manual*, the administrator may from time to time be approached by teams interested in obtaining data not included in the standard listing of items. Whether and on what conditions the data will be supplied is his own decision.

6] PLANT DISPOSAL AND RENEWAL, MERGERS

Among the "fringe benefits" of INTOP are the possibility of plant dis-

---

[49] Reproduced in Appendix IV. In the interest of realism the minimal permissible contract period for patent licenses is two quarters.

[50] Items 17 and 18 in the Marketing Research "catalog of services," cf. *supra*, 79. The cost of these items is charged automatically. The form is reproduced in the Computer Liaison instruction in Appendix V. That instruction also gives directions for filling out the form.

[51] The underlying notion is then that the consulting firm by fortunate coincidence (or perhaps by virtue of earlier commission from the World Federation of Appliance Manufacturers) has already executed the requisite studies when the data are ordered. Alternatively, the teams may be charged an extra fee for immediate delivery (presumably to defray the extra cost of accelerated research by the consultants). This extra fee may be deducted in the consulting services box on the Home Office Card.

posal and renewal and mergers. Clearly, a rewarding and viable simulation may be run without these features. If the administrator does not wish to permit plant disposal (and renewal), teams should be notified accordingly, as the *Player's Manual* suggests that this feature is ordinarily available. If plant disposal is to be permitted, INTOP Memo 4 should be distributed to the teams.[52] No such notice is necessary with regard to mergers, which are not mentioned in the manual. If and when mergers are to be permitted (in past runs usually not before Q7), teams should be notified of the opportunity.[53]

E. *Administrative Aide-mémoire*

1] LOGISTICS

The following items should be available at each decision-making session:

Company folders
Computer output for last quarter
Decision forms submitted last quarter
Standing contract file and extra forms
Extra decision forms
Dictionary of parameters and state variables (Appendix I of this volume)
(Gazettes)

In intermittent play it is often practical to have teams deposit their folders with the administrator between sessions.[54] If a team member is entrusted with the folder there is always the risk that he will be unable to attend the following session. As each team member will ordinarily have his own copy of computer outputs the inaccessibility of the company folder does not prevent participants from doing preparatory homework between sessions.

Whenever possible, team copies of computer output should be distributed in advance of decision-making sessions to encourage preparatory work.[55] In addition, the administrator will find it desirable to have his own output available for team counseling activity. In a standard run, the administrator's own output in each period consists of the following items:

Complete set of individual company outputs[56]

52 Reproduced in Appendix VI. For administrative instructions for handling plant disposal see Computer Liaison instruction.

53 Cf. *infra*, 192. INTOP Memo 5 (reproduced in Appendix VI) should be self-explanatory.

54 For contents of a company folder, see *supra*, 144.

55 Directions for assembling team outputs are included in the instruc-

tions for the administrator's secretary; cf. Appendix V.

56 These consist of balance sheet, income statement and the ancillary data and Marketing Research 1 sheets. In addition, each company ordering any of items 2–16 in the Marketing Research catalog of services receives the data ordered on a separate Marketing Research Sheet 2. For sample company output, see Appendix II.

Complete output of marketing research data

Cross-company consolidated balance sheet and consolidated income statement[57]

Record of inter-company transactions and Wonder Card changes

Current values of program parameters and company state variables (history)

Complete output for all individual companies and the consolidated financial statements are clearly indispensable for an understanding and evaluation of current events in the game at either a general or a particular company level. The standard set of company outputs includes a sheet of marketing research information giving complete price information as well as data on product qualities being manufactured by each company. The administrator's copy of the second sheet of marketing research output includes all data relating to items 2–16 in the Marketing Research catalog of services.[58] The inter-company transactions record yields a complete file of all bank loans, inter-company loans, interest and principal payments, licenses, royalty payments, shipments of goods and payments thereof during the quarter as actually recorded by the computer.[59]

Immediately preceding the inter-company transactions record the computer will print out a complete register of any and all so-called Wonder Cards fed into the machine before it began processing the decision sheets of each company for the period. Hence the administrator has a record of whether changes introduced by him in model parameters as well as any adjustments he may have made in the accounts of individual companies were accurately received by the computer. The latter information is especially handy in adjudicating complaints.[60] For such purposes it is also valuable to have on hand the decision forms submitted by the teams in the past period.[61] Any discrepancies between the forms as submitted and the data actually fed into the computer – due to intervening human factors – will be revealed by a comparison of the forms submitted and the decision seg-

---

57   On command the computer will include a copy of these industry-wide data with each individual company output. Cf. *infra*, 212 and 215. For sample consolidated output see Appendix III-A.

58   Cf. *supra*, 78f. It is to be remembered that in standard runs each team may order a maximum of three of these items in any one decision period. The administrator's computer output will also contain a record of the items ordered by each company.

59   This listing is more convenient for survey purposes than the stack of original inter-company transactions decision cards and has the additional advantage of resolving any doubt as to what data was actually fed into the

machine concerning these transactions (editing and key-punch mistakes may have intervened).

60   Companies sometimes are unable (or possibly unwilling) to establish that a given adjustment has actually been effectuated. The printout of Wonder Cards shows beyond doubt whether this was the case. For details of the Wonder Card routine, see Chapter 5, Section 2.

61   Despite admonitions to the contrary, teams occasionally will forget to take copies of their decision forms. To minimize the possibility of repetition, teams should also be made aware of simple clerical mistakes they may have made in filling out the forms; cf. Computer Liaison instruction.

ment of the history. If the administrator is uncertain as to the exact location on the history output of a given decision, all he has to do is to consult the "Dictionary."[62]

A more detailed discussion of computer outputs follows in Chapter 5.[63]

The file of standing contracts entered into in past quarters is useful in adjudicating rarely occurring inter-company disputes. Extra forms should be available for contracts which may be entered into during the current session. An extra supply of the three quarterly decision forms is also necessary, as some teams will run short regardless of how many forms were originally supplied in their company folder.

Current Gazettes (if a trade association journal is a feature of the run) need not be brought to the session if — as typically is the case — the teams received their copies with outputs distributed in advance. On the other hand, the administrator may occasionally have a need to consult a file of back issues.

2] POINTERS FOR PARTICIPANTS

Some administrative and technical features of the game which it may be desirable to bring to the attention of the companies were mentioned in the discussion of the initial decision session in the earlier part of this chapter. A few of those points may warrant occasional repetition. The following additional pointers may prove useful:

Directions as to how to read team outputs may be found in Chapter IV of the *Player's Manual*.[64]

Teams may reconsider objectives and long-range plans at any time, but should file a record of changes made with the administrator.

If there appears to be a tendency toward committee management of even trivial questions teams should be reminded of the importance to both learning and performance of effective organization.

A summary of automatic routines in the model as contrasted to volitional action on the part of participating teams is covered in the next subsection. (While the *Player's Manual* makes this distinction wherever necessary in describing the various functional parts of the model, it does not discuss the subject separately.)

Re-emphasize that as long as a company has only one model of a product in a given area inventory it is a *standard* model, regardless of what the grade (X_3, Y_4, etc.) it may be.

Review the conditions under which two grades may be merged into the lower of the two to maintain the maximum-two-grades-per-area-in-any-given-quarter limitation, and also the various way in which this calamity may be avoided.[65]

62   The dictionary is reprinted as Appendix I. The details of the dictionary are discussed in Chapter 5, Section 2.

63   Cf. *infra*, 211ff.

64   The administrator may, however, add that minus signs often occur at the extreme left end of the space reserved for any given account on the output. Hence, if a negative number has only one or two digits, the minus sign may be more than an inch to the left.

65   The subject is amply covered in the *Player's Manual*, 10.

Teams may be reminded of the fact that to take a license may be a means of accelerating one's own R & D program, as a subsequent improvement will be of the next *higher* grade than that for which the license was taken (if obtained during the period of validity of the license).

In quarters 3, 7, 11, etc., teams should be reminded that it is *Gazette* subscription time (if the journal is used in the run).

If no trade journal is being published, the administrator should list any environmental changes contemplated in the next quarter (or quarters) on the blackboard.

A section of the blackboard should always be reserved for advertising and other public announcements teams may wish to make.

F. *Programmed Routines vs. Deliberate Decisions*

One of the superior features of INTOP is that the administrator can completely disengage himself from the processing of the myriad of data involved in even a single play of the game. Virtually *all* manipulation of data — with the exception of such information about environmental change as the administrator may himself want to introduce — is handled by the man-machine system represented by the teams and the computer. This is indeed in sharp contrast to most manual games where voluminous calculations must be made by the administrator and/or a staff of assistants to process the data generated even in quite simple models. Indeed, substantial administrator engagement in fairly routine processing of data is required even in a number of computerized games.

While there is no inherent reason why the administrator of a standard INTOP run should be familiar with the intricacies of processing, his ability to counsel the teams may be somewhat contingent on an understanding of different types of interaction between the teams and the computer as well as the areas of the game system in which the computer works fairly independently of the team.[66] A basis for such understanding is provided by examining various aspects of the system in the light of the continuum from data processing according to pre-programmed routines to processing pursuant to deliberate decisions or volitional actions on the part of the teams.

Some routines are virtually automated. This is the case with the repeat convention with regard to area operations and home office affairs when a team fails to hand in forms signalling changed desires as regards these activities. Note that the repeat convention applies indiscriminately to all prior decisions on these cards. After much experimentation with various compromises none of which seemed very satisfactory, it was decided to adopt this universal repeat rule as the most easily understood and remembered in case of non-submittal of

[66] The teams may also more or less deliberately process data independently of the computer, as when they prepare cash-flow estimates, sales forecasts, etc. Cf. *infra*, 173, 180, 199f. It is to be noted that virtually no routine processing is *required* of the teams to make the system function.

Operations and Home Office Decision Cards. Admittedly, the convention in rare instances may lead to such extreme consequences as the building of a new plant in Q_t merely because a plant was built in Q_{t-1}, and the team failed to hand in an Operations Card for Q_t. However, there is a limit to the madness in that the computer will restrict the number of plants of any one product to three in any one area. Also, the team may dispose of the plant at a reasonable discount if the repeat action was involuntary. In addition, two standard and continuous routines are largely beyond the purview of current decision-making by the teams, i.e., those pertaining to depreciation and fixed production cost.

At the opposite end of the spectrum are inter-company transactions. From the viewpoint of the computer program such transactions are completely dependent on volitional action on the part of the teams. Virtually nothing is repeated without such action – not even quarterly transactions under standing contracts.[67]

Ordinarily, the problem of automatic vs. volitional repetition of decisions is of little practical significance. Teams generally are eager to exercise autonomous control over all issues before them, even if reconsideration results in simple repetition of many decisions.[68] The teams make decisions, and the computer will execute their instructions. It will then establish the consequences of team action as well as interaction in the marketplace and feed back the results. Before executing instructions, the machine will usually check that the teams stayed within permissible bounds. If a decision goes beyond these bounds the computer will often reduce it to the maximal limit currently in force.[69] This occurs, for example, if a team attempts to produce a greater output than maximal plant capacity or to produce in a plant not yet "on stream," if the grade indicated for production is higher than the maximal grade of product improvement possessed by the team, and if the amount a team would want to borrow in an area exceeds that to which it is entitled. The computer will also enforce the limitation of maximum two grades per product per area in ending inventory in any given quarter where a team would otherwise have more than two grades. In a few instances instructions will be executed only after calling into play emergency programs designed to discourage companies from overextending themselves. Principal illustrations are the

67   If the administrator finds the last mentioned feature unsatisfactory, he may, of course, have all inter-company transactions checked *before* computer processing, with a view towards administrative enforcement of all standing contracts. In standard INTOP runs the administration has participated in enforcement only upon legitimate ex post facto complaints of non-fulfillment by one of the parties. This has been felt to be the most realistic approach.

68   This does not preclude long-range planning, cf. *infra*, 176f.

69   Illustrative exceptions: if a price of more than $99 is indicated, only the last two digits will be taken into account, and what a company will write into the grade manufactured column on an Operations Card will show up on the Market Research 1 sheet regardless of whether the company was actually able to produce the grade in question.

supplier credit and sales expediting programs. These programs have the additional merit of preventing the possibility of negative cash or of a buyer in inter-company sales not obtaining the goods contracted for – eventualities regarded as dysfunctional by the designers of the simulation.

G. *Changing Game Parameters. Role of Monitor Company*

The basic tape needed to stage the INTOP simulation contains all data needed for a successful run in accordance with the *Player's Manual.* It is virtually true that not a single parameter requires change either before or during the game. However, the administrator is free to change any or all of the 450 program parameters at any time with generous latitudes of discretion. A great number of changes which he may wish to consider both before[70] and in the course of the run[71] are discussed elsewhere. So is the simple Wonder Card routine of effecting change in the model.[72]

Even in a highly routinized run of the simulation most administrators will wish to introduce business cycle fluctuations and long-term change in market potential. By means of the economic index parameters this is easily accomplished for both products and areas.[73] A table indicating the specific index numbers used in several past runs of the simulation is supplied with the standard program tape.

A monitor company managed by a member of the administration is an effective and versatile instrument for many purposes in game management. Such a company may be used any time when the number of participating companies is 24 or less. To maximize its usefulness, monitor should be given certain unique resources from the outset, and a few elementary decisions should be registered on regular decision forms in the first quarter.[74] Neither the administrator nor the teams need be concerned about its existence unless and until circumstances suggest use of this "big stick."

A typical use of monitor is the licensing of product improvements as a management consulting service.[75] More importantly, monitor may serve as a regulator of market potential. If an area is saddled with too much inventory the administrator may have monitor engage in government purchasing or represent importers in Britain or some other area outside the regular game structure.[76] Conversely, if an area re-

[70] Cf. Chapter 5, Section 3.

[71] Cf. *infra*, 192f.

[72] Cf. Chapter 5, Section 2.

[73] Cf. Computer Liaison instruction, Wonder Card section.

[74] For specific instructions see Computer Liaison instruction.

[75] This may be done simply by a reg- ular inter-company transaction card. If there is no monitor, Wonder Cards have to be used both for the license transfer and to reduce the licensee's home office cash and retained earnings accounts by the amount of the license fee.

[76] Here again Wonder Cards might be used, although this procedure would be more cumbersome.

mains underdeveloped, monitor may represent Japanese competition, either selling directly or, preferably, through companies willing to act as distributors in the area. Similarly, if collusion develops among companies in an area the mere threat of Japanese competition as represented by monitor would ordinarily suffice to break up the cartel. Incidentally, collusion has been a surprisingly rare occurrence in past runs – in spite of all teams usually meeting in the same room.

H. *Processing Cycle and Administrative Routines*

When the teams deliver their decision forms at the end of a session the processing cycle begins. The steps involved in INTOP Standard are set forth in the table in Fig. 31.

FIG. 31 *The INTOP Processing Cycle*
(FORTRAN PROGRAM ON IBM 7090 COMPUTER*)

Steps	Description	Approximate Time Required in Minutes			
		CL	Sec.	Ed.	KP Comp.
1	Editor prepares environmental changes and team contributions for *Gazette*....			60	
2	Audit of decision cards..............	20			
3	Preparation of Wonder Cards..........	20			
4	Sorting cards for key-punching.........	10			
5	Key-punching				50
6	Proofreading cards, re-punch mistakes (if any)	20	20		5
7	Sorting punched cards for computer run (not necessary but desirable)........	10			
8	Computer run				5
9	Fast-speed printing				20
10	Assembling outputs by company........		10		
11	Editor reviews outputs, writes company news and gossip....................			60	
12	Typing *Gazette* masters, mimeographing and collating		150		
13	Distribution of outputs and *Gazette* to teams		(30)		
14	Updating game historical statistics......		30		

Legend: CL = Computer Liaison; Sec. = Secretary; Ed. = Editor; KP = Key-punching; Comp. = Computer and ancillary machine operation.

* On smaller FORTRAN-compatible computers Step 8 would take more time. The Univac program requires an additional step, i.e., the production of a decision tape, which adds approximately 15 minutes each period. Also, computer running time (Step 8) would be 15–25 minutes in that program, actual time depending on the number of companies.

It is assumed that 8–12 companies are participating. A number of steps would require longer time if the number of teams is markedly greater (notably output printing). The time gains resulting from fewer companies would be minor.[77] Detailed explanations of all steps in the cycle are given in the standard Computer Liaison, Editor and Secretary instructions in Appendix V; a few general comments follow.

The table assumes that a trade journal is in fact being used. If not, there is no need for an editor, and aggregate secretarial time may be cut in half. Before the editor can prepare a write-up of environmental changes the administrator must have made up his mind as to what changes to introduce in various decision periods, and in what periods the teams should be warned (if at all) about the changes. Clearly, the time needed for Step 1 is largely dependent on the number and complexity of such changes, and the extent to which teams hand in contributions to the *Gazette*.

The audit of decision cards is crucial. Twenty minutes is standard time. As some environmental changes – such as strikes and import prohibitions – are most conveniently enforced by checking that no decision cards contain conflicting data, Step 2 will take longer time when such changes are introduced. If there are no environmental events of the type that require change in model parameters and no adjustments to be made of individual company outputs, Step 3 is eliminated; twenty minutes represents average time in a typical University of Chicago run with a fair amount of parameter change each quarter.

In performing Step 11 the editor is likely to find several hot items for the *Gazette* in even a cursory review of this aggregate output. The thirty minute time allocation for Step 13 is stated in parentheses. It applies only to distribution by mail. If the outputs will be given out directly to team members this operation clearly takes no time of any consequence. Even when mail distribution is contemplated the time required will vary considerably, depending on the system used and the number of copies involved. If only one copy per team is distributed, or if all of the several copies intended for a team are sent to one address (that of the president, for example), data transmission by mail may require only ten or fifteen minutes of secretarial work.

In most runs of INTOP Standard in the past each participant has received a complete set of his company's output sheets as well as a copy of the *Gazette* (if his company was a subscriber) each decision period. Mail distribution has been used in several runs where classes met only once a week. In a few instances this meant mail distribution to 70 participants – still requiring only about an hour per week.

Finally, the secretary will ordinarily make certain statistical compilations for game historical purposes, as indicated in the next subsection (and in the prototype Secretary instruction in the Appendix).

Applying a "critical path" view of the several parallel and sequential steps involved, we find that total processing time for a decision

[77] For a more detailed discussion of computer and printing time see Chapter 5, Section 1.

period cannot conveniently be cut below two and one-half hours in a standard run. If the game is to be played continuously, and in other cases where it is desirable to hold processing time to a minimum, several time-saving measures may be considered. Elimination of the *Gazette*, leap-frogging between decision periods, making decisions for several quarters each session and simplification of the game model itself are all fairly drastic means. However, even when all these means are resorted to simultaneously, participation in the exercise may still be a worthwhile experience to judge by testimony from U.S. Steel executives playing the game under such conditions. Appreciable time-savings may be obtained by less far-reaching arrangements. Wonder Cards incorporating all environmental changes contemplated in the course of the exercise may be made out and key-punched in advance. As many steps as possible should be carried out in parallel. Aggregate processing time may be reduced further by increasing personnel resources. Such time-consuming steps as 1, 5, 6, 11 and 12 all stand to benefit from an increase in resource input.[78]

Eliminating the *Gazette*, and cutting other administrative corners, INTOP Standard may be fully processed in 75–90 minutes, even with as many as 15–20 companies participating. Such a schedule does assume that the key personnel involved have had some prior experience of running the simulation.[79]

An administrative policy question of some significance to processing time but also with broader implications is how many copies of computer output should be printed.[80] A good rule of thumb is to print as many copies of the regular company financial and market research outputs as there are members per team (at least as long as this number is no greater than five) plus two or three copies for the administration.[81] For emergency purposes it is, however, clear that one can make do with one copy for the teams and one for the administration. There is no appreciable gain in such conservation where three-part or four-part output paper is available. If at all possible, such paper should definitely be used. It is advisable that the administrator and his computer liaison man each are given a copy of the program parameter and state variables (history) output from each quarter.[82]

The discussion in this section has focused on functions to be per-

78   Step 14 – updating game statistics – may be done during decision sessions in continuous play, hence outside the regular processing cycle.

79   It is not necessary to eliminate the *Gazette* even where time is of the essence. The journal may, of course, be produced while teams are in decision sessions. The lag in certain information thus introduced need not necessarily detract from realism.

80   The Step 9 printing-time estimate was based on one round of printing only.

81   The administrator needs one or two (a continuous strip is a minimum; an additional set assembled by company is preferable), and the work of Computer Liaison and/or the editor may often be speeded if a third administrative copy is available.

82   Company financial output constitutes the main part of what from a computer point of view is labeled PART 1 of the output, while history constitutes PART 2. Cf. the technical discussion of outputs in Chapter 5, Section 1.

formed during the processing cycle rather than *by whom* they should be performed. Clearly, the latter question has to be answered largely in terms of the resources locally available. A thoroughly tested arrangement with regard to all aspects of routine administration in runs of INTOP Standard is indicated by the conglomerate of model instructions for Computer Liaison, Editor and Secretary reproduced in Appendix V. What the administrator himself will do in large measure depends on the purpose for which the simulation is being staged and on what part of the total game management burden he wants to take on personally. For this reason no attempt was made to write any model instruction for the administrator. Rather, this chapter provides the necessary background needed to enable each administrator to write the type of instruction which seems most proper to his own needs.

I. *Short Runs — Some Observations*

In many executive development programs in industry it will not be possible to run the International Operations Simulation for more than perhaps six to eight decision periods. To maximize the learning experience as well as the involvement of participants the administrator of such a short run might well consider some modifications of INTOP Standard procedures.

The administrator may, for instance, consider giving all teams X_1 and Y_1 product improvements from the outset. Or he may have Arthur DeBig offer these patents for sale or license even in the first quarter. In this way teams will get a feel for the problems and opportunities involved in the management of both standard and deluxe models at an early stage. Alternatively — or in addition — he may decide to raise the rate of probability increase for any given amount of R & D or set a relatively low threshold for obtaining patents.[83]

In choosing environmental events to be introduced in the course of the run the administrator should also keep in mind that in an INTOP Standard run many companies will usually be operating at a cumulative loss as late as the sixth quarter, as it takes time to recuperate heavy initial expenses. In a short run he may therefore wish to avoid cost-increasing labor settlements and other events which markedly decrease the munificence of the operating environment.

To increase the number of profit-making opportunities at the beginning of the simulation the administrator may use the monitor company as a Japanese supplier from whom the teams may buy until they get their own productive capacity (in which case the outside supplier may no longer be willing to cooperate with them).

The simulation will get off to a really fast start if the companies are provided with plants as well as inventory from the beginning.[84] If

---

[83] Cf. the discussion of the R & D function in Chapter 3, *supra*.

[84] A somewhat similar effect may be achieved by setting plant construction time to 0 or to one period.

this seems desirable, the administrator should consider whether to make the initial pattern of resource allocation identical for all teams, or whether he prefers to start simply by letting them take over where the teams in a previous run left off.

These are merely a few illustrations of the many things which may be done to accelerate events in short runs. While quite effective most of the measures suggested involve very little effort on the part of the administrator.

J. *Accumulating Game History for Control and Evaluation*

In most game runs – and especially those which constitute a part of a broader educational program – the administrator will want to be able to follow developments in detail. This certainly is necessary if he wishes to influence the course of events by injecting suitable environmental developments, by counseling the teams, etc. Historical data are also needed in any intelligent attempt at evaluating team performance.[85]

A wealth of data for such purposes are generated continuously in INTOP. All the administrator needs to do is to keep track of the flow of information, develop a file system and, if necessary, reorganize the materials for his own control and review purposes. The most important records in the simulation are those describing the interaction within the man-machine system. The administrator should keep a copy of the continuous strip of all output produced each quarter. If possible, he should have a second copy of company financial output disassembled and the several output sheets reassembled by company. It is quite helpful to have a game history organized both chronologically and by company. The company-oriented history may also be used for distribution to the auditing companies in the cross-company management audit described in the last section of this chapter.

A set of all copies of the *Gazette* should be retained. If no journal is used in the simulation, a record should be made of all environmental changes introduced, the quarter in which the teams were prewarned of each change (if at all) and the quarter in which the change took effect. Such a record is indispensable to any evaluation of team response to environmental stimuli. The file of standing agreements in inter-company transactions should also be preserved.

The statements of company objectives, plans and organization (if any) furnish a basis for evaluation.

In runs of INTOP Standard at Chicago we have found some minor special compilations of data useful. A record of company orders of Market Research 2 Items 17 and 18 is helpful as indicative of planning

---

[85] For a detailed discussion of performance evaluation, cf. Section 5 of this chapter.

and foresight among the teams.[86] Every administrator will develop his own preferences as to special compilations of data. A recurring assignment of the administrator's secretary in past runs has been to prepare and update the following tables:[87]

Retained earnings and paid-in-capital

Total assets

Plant construction, disposal and replacement by company, product, area and quarter

Industry inventory in units, by product and area

If so desired these and scores of other data may be compiled each quarter from the history part of the output.

The administrator may wish to present some of the statistical series in chart form to the class during the run or at the review session. If the number of companies exceeds four or five it is not advisable to break the data down on a company basis, as the charts will soon be too cluttered for comfort. In runs of INTOP Standard charts when used have been confined to industry totals.

3.   Regulating the Flow of Decision-making Data

A.   *Information Systems and Their Manipulation* [88]

A sophisticated management game is an excellent means of demonstrating that the essence of decision-making is the procurement, processing and evaluation of data. Similarly, such an exercise can effectively demonstrate such vital dimensions of decision-making data as relevance, timeliness, accuracy, reliability and cost. With the IN-TOP simulation it is possible to go one step further and emphasize the interdependence of information flows and the internal organization patterns of corporations. This is facilitated by the deliberate structuring of input and output forms with a view towards organization simulation.[89]

INTOP possesses another important feature of realism in the very wealth of information generated in the course of the simulation. The torrential flow of data has two important effects. It teaches participants that selectivity is of the essence. Too many teachers as well as students of management are influenced by the gospel that mere maximization of data accumulated is beneficial in decision-making. Even when a team has decided what data are most relevant to its activities it will find that systematic organizing and processing of these raw data

---

86   To keep such a record is a function of Computer Liaison in the model instruction.

87   Cf. prototype instruction for Secre-

tary.

88   Cf. Kibbee-Craft-Nanus, 106–10.

89   Cf. Appendix VII.

is a powerful area of payoff in "professional" management.[90] Incidentally, the fact that systematic handling of data pays off is a powerful stimulus to long-range planning.

The administrator of INTOP is in the position of varying the flow of data along each one of its major dimensions. Just how he decides to regulate it in a given case should reasonably depend on the purpose of the run and the circumstances under which it takes place, notably with regard to time available for decision-making and between game sessions.

B. *Varying the Rate and Types of Information*

In a sense, the prospective participant in a sophisticated management game is like an executive about to take a job with another company. There is a bewildering amount of structural information to be mastered about the new situation before either individual can effectively participate in the processing of operating data and decision-making. How should the newcomer be introduced to the "facts of life"? According to one view "Complexity should be introduced gradually to avoid overwhelming the student at the beginning of the game. This corresponds to the way an executive learns his own job."[91] There is no doubt a grain of truth in this. But it is also true that the facts of the situation are there from the outset in all their complexity. We lean towards the view that to learn to be selective is important to any decision-maker. Thus, we introduce most of the complexity in the basic structure of the simulation from the beginning. Without this information it would also make less sense for the teams to engage in serious long-range planning from the outset.

Participants generally derive basic structural information about the simulation from the *Player's Manual* and accessory documents.[92]

---

90 This does not mean that there is not room for intuitive management in INTOP. There certainly is. But it does mean that among companies which really try to go in for a professional approach there is a clear-cut correlation between quality and quantity of analytical work on the one hand and successful performance on the other. For less positive experience in the early UCLA games (corroborated in runs of these games at Chicago), cf. James R. Jackson, "Business Gaming in Management Science Education," in Proceedings of the Sixth International Meeting of the Institute of Management Sciences, *Management Sciences — Models and Techniques*, Vol. 1 (1960), 250–62, 254.

91 Professor Albert N. Schrieber as quoted in *Proceedings of the Conference on Business Games as Teaching Devices Sponsored by the Ford Foundation and the School of Business Admin-* *istration, Tulane University* (1961), 133.

92 Teams often find INTOP Memos 1 and 2 helpful at the organizing session. These memos are reprinted on the inside covers of the *Player's Manual*. At this time it is also advisable to distribute one or two samples of all standing contract forms used in the game to each team. If plant disposal will be a feature of the run it may be appropriate to give out Memo 4 at that time also.

In Q4 Memo 3 may be distributed as well as a suggested Worksheet for Demand Studies (cf. Appendix VI) to stimulate analytical work and data processing.

If mergers will be a feature of the game Memo 5 must be handed out. In standard runs in the past this has not been done until Q7 or Q8, although teams have been told from the outset that mergers would be allowed in the latter part of the game.

This information is sufficient for effective participation. Some administrators may wish to enrich it even further before the beginning of the run. While this has not been done in standard runs it is easily accomplished by giving out histories of past runs to the teams.[93] Accuracy and reliability of this information will depend on whether and to what extent the administrator resets the model parameters in the new run. If he wishes to, he may make the information available only at substantial cost.

Participants will inevitably vary in their willingness and ability to assimilate the structural information. Not infrequently they will request information from the administrator which they could themselves obtain by further study of the manual or output data. The nature of the clientele and the purpose of the run should determine the readiness with which the administrator responds to their questions. Sometimes a useful rule of thumb is to answer only questions pertaining to the formal routines of filling in forms while discouraging other inquiries.[94] After a few sessions the administrator may charge a consulting fee for each question answered.

Even in standard runs most administrators will wish to introduce at least a minimum of environmental change (strikes, changes in inter-area transfer costs, etc.).[95] While the model poses few constraints as to the number and extent of such structural changes there are indeed limits to the capacity of teams to adjust. An important question in considering any given change is whether — and how far in advance — teams should be warned. Another is the degree of accuracy and reliability of warnings. At least in the U.S. and the EEC open conflict in the labor market is fairly rare except in times of breakdown in bargaining for contract renewal. Expiration dates for collective bargaining contracts are known well in advance. Management also has some advance inkling of the possibility of a strike, although full certainty is never at hand until the strike is actually declared or a new contract signed. On the other hand, governments rarely if ever give advance notice of pending devaluation or revaluation of currencies. Such moves often follow protracted periods of speculation and rumor — although it is equally true that many rumors in this area turn out to be without foundation.

An outstanding weakness in business today is the poor state of competitive intelligence. In most firms a wealth of data concerning competition is in the hands of employees. Unfortunately, however, each employee has only one or a few pieces of the total puzzle in his hand, and no concerted effort at systematic assembly and analysis is ever made. Yet competitive developments are as crucial to business success as changes in consumer likes and dislikes or business cycle fluctuations. INTOP offers a splendid opportunity to highlight the sig-

---

93 Clearly, outputs from past runs may also serve as an excellent base for case discussion of a more conventional character, quite apart from gaming.

94 Cf. *supra*, 156.

95 Cf. Section 4C of this chapter.

nificance of competitive data — both about the industry as a whole and about individual rivaling companies. The two market research sheets in the regular output were designed with this point in mind. The special routine for producing consolidated financial statements about competing companies has a similar purpose. Indeed, companies may well be encouraged to exchange operating data on a recurring basis. This is a likely avenue of further management progress in the real world.[96]

In the area of competitive intelligence trade association journals generally provide an effective contrast to systematic exchange of data. Thus, the information about individual companies supplied in the INTOP *Gazette* in standard runs of the simulation has been fairly much of a random character, and many of the data and rumors published have actually been of questionable reliability. As frequently is the case in real life, industry-level information on the other hand has tended to be both more systematic (e.g., industry forecasts, aggregate inventory data, etc.) and reliable, if often far from accurate.

An important means of varying the rate and types of information fed into the game system at the individual company level is consultation by the administrator or other outside experts. Occasionally a team may also find it possible to engage in consulting as a sideline activity, notably in cases where the main business of the teams is that of financing or R & D. Sometimes two or more teams will share marketing research data and expenses.

The important variables of timeliness and cost may be regulated in different ways.[97] The price tags for marketing research items and the *Gazette* may easily be changed by means of Wonder Cards. As suggested by the Marketing Research section of the *Player's Manual*, dated information may be sold at reduced rates[98] and the cost of special consultation services may be freely negotiated. The timeliness of data may be affected by the introduction of lags in the distribution of data (e.g., Marketing Research 1), by leap-frogging, by making test marketing

---

96 Cf., e.g., the "exchange of experience" arrangements stimulated in much of European industry under the auspices of the former Organization for European Economic Cooperation a decade ago — arrangements which continue to flourish in a number of countries. Such exchange of data between U.S. firms would have to be established in such a way that it would not conflict with the antitrust laws. In point of actuality, these laws permit a much more penetrating exchange of data than the average legal counsel is aware.

Exchange of information may be encouraged as well as directed by arranging "conventions" of the World

Federation of Appliance Manufacturers, of the Brazilian Manufacturers Association, etc.

97 For a simulation emphasizing the cost of research and information, see F. E. Balderston, "Communication Networks in Intermediate Markets," 4 *Management Science* (Jan. 1958), 154–71.

98 If a monitor company is being used, the sale of obsolete data is facilitated by having that company order Item 2 of Market Research 2 in one or two sets each quarter; Item 2 is the only information which takes appreciable time to reproduce. This is suggested in the Computer Liaison instruction.

reports and production cost estimates available immediately or with a lag[99] and so on.

c. *Extending the Time Span of Plans and Decisions*

The basic significance of time and timing in all decision-making may be emphasized by stimulating or requiring long-range planning by the teams. The introduction of leap-frogging[100] and/or data processing forms to facilitate sales forecasting and cash-flow projections will stimulate many teams to do an aggressive planning job. This may also be generated by requiring the submission of formal plans for one to three years of operation.

Planning and policy-making may also be forced on the companies by extending the time span of decisions. The pressure on participants may be varied from relatively low (alternative 1) to relatively high (alternative 3) as follows:

(1) By requiring teams when making their decisions for Q_t also to hand in *preliminary* decisions for Q_{t+1}. They will be asked to submit final decisions for Q_{t+1} only after receiving their regular output from Q_t. To make this a worthwhile exercise the administrator should emphasize that part of the evaluation of team performance will be directed toward the deviations between the sets of preliminary and final decisions. As all good plans should have some flexibility, it should be emphasized that deviations will not be penalized per se. However, one may be justly critical of deviations based on bad planning. To escape such criticism it is desirable that companies hand in a set of assumptions about the outcome of Q_t and about conditions in Q_{t+1} when they deliver their preliminary Q_{t+1} decisions. They may also be given the opportunity to submit ex-post rationalizations of their deviations, although these should reasonably be examined rather critically.

(2) By requiring the teams to submit *final* decisions for Q_t and Q_{t+1} in one session, with no intervening feedback. Most exacting for the teams, perhaps is to be allowed *no* latitude as to the Q_{t+1} decisions. It may still be more rewarding to them if they are permitted to attach certain decision rules to their Q_{t+1} decisions, these rules to serve as instructions to the administrator or his assistant before Q_{t+1} is processed. An example of such a decision rule: "If ending inventory of X_2 in the U.S. is more than 25,000 units in Q_t, lower the price we have given for Q_{t+1} by five dollars." To avoid becoming overburdened by such instructions the administrator may limit their number or type.

(3) By requiring teams to submit *one* set of decisions which will be processed two to four times, i.e., decisions which will be valid for one half to one year. Feedback will be deferred until all quarters have been processed.[101] In making use of this alternative it should be remembered that certain dysfunctional consequences may arise from

99   Cf. *supra*, 73; *infra*, 337f.
100   Cf. *supra*, 23.
101   Sequential processing of several

quarters is quite simple, and actually results in a saving of computer time; cf. *infra*, 216.

indiscriminate repeating of decisions. This is apt to be really trouble-some only in the case of new plant construction. To avoid undesirable repetition of such decisions the administrator may prohibit new plant construction during the part of the simulation when decisions are auto-matically re-implemented. This will not cause any appreciable prob-lems if companies have been given advance notice, enabling them to add new plants in Q_{t-1}.[102]

There is, of course, a possibility that companies engaged in R & D will develop a product improvement in Q_t. This need cause no concern. Companies expecting an improvement may simply make decisions for Q_{t+1} on the assumption that the patent is obtained in Q_t. Should it fail to materialize, the computer will automatically arrange for production of the highest possible grade possessed by the company in Q_t.[103]

Some restraint in the introduction of environmental changes in the exercise may be desirable when companies are asked to make de-cisions for two or more quarters. Indeed, when teams have no oppor-tunity to prescribe changes in decisions from one quarter to the next it would seem appropriate that the environment be held constant — perhaps with the exception of minor business cycle fluctuations. When participants do have the opportunity to differentiate the decisions by quarter they should still be given reasonable extra time for the con-sideration of the impact of environmental changes beyond the current quarter of their operations.

---

102 The rationale may simply be a strike in the building trades in Q_t, or that no construction permits are issued by the authorities in that quarter.

If he prefers, the administrator may permit plant construction in Q_t, avoid-ing repetition in Q_{t+1} by duplicating the Operations Cards with the excep-tion of the plant construction column. However, this introduces an extra proc-essing operation.

103 Only one minor dysfunctional consequence may occur. Suppose the company has X_2 in Q_{t-1}. It expects to get X_3 in Q_t, and wishes to devote half its productive capacity in Q_{t+1} to mak-ing X_2 as standard and half of it to making X_3 as deluxe. The company fails to get X_3. In this instance all pro-duction will be of grade X_2, and the company will only get a standard model produced. The presumed ad-vantage of carrying a standard inven-tory of this grade (as compared to lower ones) must be weighed against the advantage of carrying both stand-ard and deluxe. If the company wants to make sure it has both models it should make at least a minimal amount of X_0 (or X_1), as standard and indicate X_3 as deluxe. (Again, X_2 will be produced if X_3 does not show up.) Of course, it may prefer to buy some X_0 (X_1) from the outside. Not even this case is quite problem-free, however. Suppose the company actually does get X_3 in Q_t and produces it in Q_{t+1}. Any X_2 products remaining unsold at the end of Q_{t+1} will then be merged with the X_0 (or X_1). This, in turn, may be avoided by setting a price for X_2 in Q_{t+1} calculated to clean out inventory. The subtleties of the situation place a premium on planning and risk calcu-lation skills.

If the administrator so prefers, he may reduce the element of uncertainty by instructing the computer either to give patents to all companies which have achieved a given probability or to suppress any product improvements in Q_t. This may be done simply by setting the parameter PR05 Threshold Proba-bility at a given low percentage or close to 1. Cf. *supra,* 170; *infra,* 241.

D. *Media of Regulation*

There is ordinarily little need to vary the standard quarterly output sheets distributed to each team. To emphasize the value of data on competitive offerings the administrator may occasionally withhold distribution of the Market Research 1 sheet (or hand it out with a lag). He may increase the flow of the semi-standardized marketing research data on the Market Research 2 sheet by simply requiring that the companies order certain items (or by setting their cost at zero).[104] He may also prevail on the opportunity which the computer program provides to double the number of Market Research 2 items available to individual firms each quarter from three to six.[105] Financial statements and ancillary data output by and large cannot be changed with regard to their general format in the present model without reprogramming.[106] However, the data may be easily disassembled by product and/or area by simply cutting output sheets apart, if it is felt desirable to restrict team members individually to data pertaining to their own position in the organization.[107] While it is technically simple to provide a program for such disassembled output no such routine has been written, as the regular output has been found appropriate to both standard and a variety of special-purpose runs. A special program does, however, permit the printing of the consolidated columns of the balance sheet and income statement of each company with appropriate headings on a single output sheet. In this way financial data of the type customarily found in annual reports may be cross-circulated among participating

---

104   In the past it has often been felt worthwhile for the administrator to *oblige* the companies to procure Marketing Research Item 2 (sales broken down by company, product, model and area) as a complement to the consolidate balance sheet and income statement for all companies which the teams were given in Q4, Q8, Q12 etc.

105   This is done most easily by mimeographing a Home Office Decision Card with three additional double boxes, marked with columns 43-44, 45-46 and 47-48, respectively. In standard runs only three items are used in order to impress upon participants that it is desirable to plan their marketing research, as this is not an activity which can simply be turned on and off like a faucet.

106   Only exception: administrators not enamored with direct costing may switch to absorption costing, cf. *infra*, 258, 281.

107   This will create problems of internal communication which are further enhanced if the number of messages between members are restricted by cutting decision time or by placing them in different rooms; cf. Appendix VII.

The latest version of the Carnegie Tech game offers students some opportunity of programming their own output formats. This flexibility is gained at the expense of a fair amount of time spent on this ancillary activity. Such an arrangement would be less feasible in INTOP where extraordinary flexibility in entrepreneurial objectives and organization patterns is a prime feature. Cf. Kalman Cohen and Merton H. Miller, "Management Games, Information Processing and Control," Behavioral Theory of the Firm Working Paper No. 33 (mimeographed, June-Aug. 1961), Graduate School of Industrial Administration, Carnegie Institute of Technology.

INTOP accounting formats may be rearranged by means of "plugboards" hooked up to the output printer, although this takes some doing. Also, whatever rearrangements an administrator may wish to undertake must apply uniformly to *all* teams.

companies at appropriate intervals.[108]

The *Gazette* of the World Federation of Appliance Manufacturers has been the principal medium of supplying data concerning environmental changes, Wall Street-type gossip and information volunteered by individual companies (advertisements, press releases, complaints, etc.) in runs of INTOP Standard at Chicago. A copy of the *Gazette* as well as a prototype instruction for the editor are reproduced in Appendix VI and V, respectively. These documents should give an adequate view of the types of information typically appearing in the journal, which has generally been published each quarter beginning with Q4.[109] The *Gazette* offers ample opportunity for systematic manipulation of availability, timeliness, reliability and accuracy of data of interest to the teams – from economic forecasts to intelligence about the operations of individual companies. While we have not yet employed it as such it is also clear that one might experiment with the journal as a trade association disciplinary device. This could be done in a relatively subtle manner, e.g., in the form of a fictional interview with the Secretary of the Federation concerning price-cutting or the troublesome inventory situation in the industry. It might also be done in a more brazen fashion, suggesting that prices in the industry are about to be raised a given percentage, or that a leading member of the industry plans to lower its price a given number of dollars. It must be kept in mind, however, that such activities soon would be in contravention of U.S. antitrust laws – and, indeed, of the new EEC provisions concerning restrictive business practices as well.

Ordinarily, subscription to the *Gazette* has been a voluntary matter. At times, however, it has been made obligatory merely to simplify administration. There is, of course, nothing to prevent the administrator from distributing it gratis to the teams, although this skirts the notion that valuable information tends to be costly. If subscription is voluntary, the administrator faces the problem of what environmental information he should reasonably give non-subscribers. Clearly, for example, the entire industry should be made aware well in advance when collective bargaining contracts expire. On the other hand, there seems to be no good reason why the economic forecasts should be made available to non-subscribers. This type of question can best be answered on a case-by-case and common-sense basis.

Experience indicates that some companies need outside stimulation in order to develop effective data processing routines and make use of reasonably sophisticated analytical techniques. This stimulus may be provided in the form of a checklist of items worth considering (including, e.g., sales forecasting, cash-flow projections, demand analysis, cost analyses of manufacturing and distribution). As a further assist, the administrator may provide one or two sample forms. A

---

[108] Consolidated financial statements are reproduced in Appendix III.
[109] When decisions are to be made for several quarters in one session, a corresponding number of issues have been consolidated into one.

prototype form for convenient tabulation of raw data for demand studies generally given the teams in past INTOP runs is reproduced in Appendix VI. As always, the purpose of running the simulation in each case should determine to what extent the work of the teams should be facilitated. The preparation of worksheets may in itself be a useful exercise for the teams, given enough time. Also, the administrator must decide to what extent any prefabricated worksheets should be suggestive of a given type of analysis. The demand-studies form supplied at Chicago is deliberately fairly unstructured, thus lending itself to a variety of sales forecasting, demand-schedule analysis and marketing research purposes. The form is also not in any way suggestive of a given type of company organization or set of objectives, as we have thus far been anxious to leave these matters to the discretion of the teams.

E. *Evaluating Comprehension and Processing of Data. Feedback from One Student Cohort to the Next*

To derive maximum benefit from a management game it is imperative that participants assimilate the rules and structural information as rapidly and as thoroughly as possible. This information will not of itself be of any value to the students in their business careers, yet familiarity with the nature of the simulation is a prerequisite to learning anything from it of such value. If a group of top executives are playing the game the instructor can hardly afford to subject their knowledge of the exercise to a formal test. In a college class such a test may have a healthy needling influence, however. To be of greatest benefit it should come at a fairly early stage. A test with half a dozen true-false statements (varied from one student cohort to the next) has been used at Chicago.[110]

In order to stimulate effective data processing and analysis and to evaluate team effort in this area, the administrator may request copies of any worksheets and other analytical tools which the companies may have developed. Clearly, participants should be advised of such an intent well in advance.

Continuous evaluation of comprehension and data processing is facilitated if the administrator takes note of the types of questions participants will ask him in the course of the run. A wealth of material for evaluation may also be gathered by simply observing individual teams in decision sessions. After the first few sessions team discussions are not appreciably affected by the presence of the administrator.

A question bound to arise in any institution making use of the same game several times is that of feedback from one student cohort to the next. In the case of INTOP this is not a serious problem. By simply changing a few elasticities and the "pay-off" rate of R & D (pre-

---

[110]   A sample test may be obtained from Thorelli. Typical statement: "The fixed costs of production per unit of output are higher in Brazil than anywhere else, but the variable manufacturing costs are lower." (False.)

serving the *relationships* between the parameters indicated by the *Player's Manual*) the character of the simulation is changed sufficiently to make viable strategies quite different from one run to another, even though not a letter or number be changed in the documentation. If the administrator is willing to have a mimeographed set of amendments to the *Player's Manual,* there is, of course, no limit to the amount of change he may introduce. Our experience suggests that even when *no* change is made the value of feedback from one run to another may be limited simply because the nature of competition and company strategies will vary widely in a game of INTOP's complexity.

While for some purposes it might be useful to inform participants of certain parameter numbers and features of the model not revealed in the *Player's Manual,* prudence would seem to indicate caution in this regard if the simulation will be used with any regularity at a given institution. We do not believe that this book's being publicly available should present any major problem. True, a keen reader would doubtless gain some differential advantage. It may be asked whether this is not as it should be, considering the extra effort required. The book has been written deliberately in such a manner as to avoid giving a participant reader an *undue* advantage.[111] This is also the reason why certain documentation is available only to game administrators.[112]

4. Enriching the INTOP Experience

A. *Integration of the Simulation in a Broader Educational Context*

All too often management games are staged in splendid isolation — entirely disassociated from any real discussion of underlying theory or principles. This has been quite a common phenomenon, e.g., when the large computer manufacturing firms have demonstrated their games. Failure to achieve more than spurious contact with basic issues in such a context is understandable, as the time factor generally required runs of a continuous nature. We believe that continous play is of lasting value only when the simulation involves drill-type exercise in the application of a single analytical technique or managerial device, such as a formula for economic order quantity. But game-play has often been entirely disassociated from what students encountered in lectures, reading and writing assignments, etc., even in executive development programs and in university courses where the necessary time for achieving a desirable degree of closure between the various means of instruction was available. This is not surprising: games rep-

---

111   Any administrator who feels that we have been unsuccessful in this regard may take some comfort in the fact that the substantial price of this volume is apt to discourage most students from buying it. He may also make sure that local library copies are not made available to participants.

112   This documentation includes such items as suggested economic index numbers and the data needed to fill requisitions for Marketing Research Items 17 and 18.

resent an entirely new technique of instruction with which educators have had to familiarize themselves over a period of years. Moreover, the effective integration of a new simulation with other educational tools is likely to take about as much time as the development of the simulation model itself.

At the present time enough experience does exist about the Carnegie and Chicago games, however, for any educator to make effective use of these exercises in a well-integrated fashion. In this section we will show how INTOP has been made an integral part of academic courses at Chicago.[113] *Many of the ideas advanced may be equally well applied when the simulation is staged in other contexts, such as executive development programs.* As minimal limits for the effective use of INTOP in combination with other educational tools (lectures, readings, role-playing, written assignments dealing with underlying principles or practice, etc.), we would suggest a three-day seminar or mail-play over an extended period of time with occasional get-togethers for discussion of the basic issues of management illustrated by the simulation. An additional reason for an account of our experience is that many of the ideas we have tried out could be applied directly, or in some modified form, in the use of other simulations of at least moderate complexity and flexibility.

B. *Means of Integration*

The two main applications of INTOP at the Graduate School of Business at Chicago thus far has been in courses on advanced marketing management and business policy and organization.[114] The following discussion of these courses is solely for purposes of illustration,[115] included in the hope that it will serve as a starting-point for other educators. In the advanced marketing management course classes meet three hours each week for eleven weeks; in the business policy and organization course they meet six hours a week for ten weeks. Both types of classes meet twice a week. Both courses make use of lecture-discussions, readings and written assignments related to the subject matter of these lectures and readings as well as to INTOP. In the "double-header" policy and organization course students are also expected to write a term paper.

The advanced marketing management course is a voluntary

[113] Whether a game is run as a separate course, as at Carnegie, or as an integral element of a course is dependent both on taste and the more detailed purposes of using the simulation. Generally speaking, greater effort is required to achieve closure with other means of instruction if it is run separately.

Since the fall of 1962 the International Operations Simulation has been used as an integral part of the organization and policy course at the new International Center for the Advancement of Management Education (ICAME) in the Graduate School of Business at Stanford University.

[114] A special version of the game described in the last section of Chapter 6 below has also been used in a course in industrial marketing management.

[115] It should be noted, e.g., that at Chicago different teachers approach these courses differently, whether or not they are making use of INTOP.

offering to regular MBA students. Prerequisites are two economics courses or a marketing and an economics course and at least one course in accounting. The number of registrants generally varies between 15 and 40.[116] The business policy and organization course is obligatory, constituting the capstone course of the Executive Program of the School. Most participants are middle management executives between 30 and 45 years of age. Each cohort comprises 70–75 students.

In both courses we have had one INTOP decision-making session per week of 1–1½ hours duration.[117] Students receive outputs and the *Gazette* later in the same week, either at the second class meeting or by mail (or from the student mail file in the office of the Dean of Students). Whether or not it is practicable for the teams to meet out of class, students are thus assured of the opportunity to spend their weekend in preparation for the next decision session.

I] THE ADVANCED MARKETING MANAGEMENT COURSE

This course aims at relating marketing to the overall entrepreneurial mission of the firm and to the other major functional areas of management (finance, production, etc.). Another major aim of the course is the integration of the subfunctions of marketing (product planning, sales, marketing communications and research, etc.) into an overall marketing management perspective. In general, organizational, behavioral and institutional factors in marketing and entrepreneurial decision-making move to the forefront in this course.[118] Students are informed in advance that "one half of the course grade will depend on qualitative performance in INTOP and related assignments to you and to your team." In gross terms, one half of class time is devoted to lecture-discussions, the other half to the playing of INTOP. A typical schedule of lectures, decision sessions and weekly assignments is shown in Fig. 32.

As the outline suggests, lecture-discussions, game and weekly assignments are closely interwoven in this course. Indeed, readings

[116] Occasionally when sections of this course are given in parallel at the Midway campus and at the downtown Chicago campus of the School the game has been run to comprise teams from both classes.
[117] In some of these sessions several sets of quarterly decisions have been made for reasons indicated earlier.
[118] A Winter 1962 reading list included the following obligatory (plus a good number of optional) items:
Texts:
Kelley, Eugene J., and Lazer, William, *Managerial Marketing: Perspectives and Viewpoints* (Richard D. Irwin, 1958).
Still, Richard R., and Cundiff, Edward W., *Sales Management* (Prentice-Hall, 1957 or later edition).

Required readings:
Clewett, Richard M., *Marketing Channels for Manufactured Products* (Irwin, 1954), Parts I (pp. 5–79) and III (pp. 365–504).
Fayerweather, John, *Management of International Operations* (McGraw-Hill, 1960), pp. 1–12, 56–79, 207–21, 356–87, 435–64.
Smith, R. A., "The Incredible Electrical Conspiracy" (*Fortune*, May 1961).
Thorelli, Hans B., "How Marketing Managers Can Adjust to Fluctuations in Business Conditions" (Am. Mktg. Assn. Conference *Proceedings*, Los Angeles, 1961).
Thorelli, Hans B., et al., *International Operations Simulation (INTOP) Player's Manual* and other related materials as assigned.

FIG. 32   *Advanced Marketing Management — Sample Course Schedule*

Session	Class Schedule	Assignments by Week
1	L: Marketing in the economy and as a business function. Business objectives and the marketing management concept.	Study INTOP rules.
2	L: INTOP presentation. Teams organize.	
3	Q1-3: Decisions.	Business and marketing objectives. Agenda for Q4.
4	L: Overall planning in business. Marketing plans. The marketing mix and subfunctional plans.	
5	Q4: Decisions.	2-year business and marketing plans.
6	L: Organization of the marketing function at the company level. Measuring marketing performance.	
7	Q5: Decisions. INTOP rules test.	Organization plan and job descriptions.
8	L: Marketing channels and systems.	
9	Q6-7: Decisions.	Review of Q6-7, preview of Q8. Memos on marketing in INTOP firms.
10	L: Use of marketing research and competitive intelligence in business.	
11	Q8: Decisions.	
12	Mid-term examination on readings and lectures.	
13	Q9: Decisions. Class discussion: Ethics in marketing.	Annual report. Rotate management in teams.
14	L: Sales forecasting and demand analysis.	

FIG. 32   *Advanced Marketing Management—Sample Course Schedule* (Continued)

Session	Class Schedule	Assignments by Week
15	Q10: Decisions.	Revised business and marketing plans. Worksheets and analytical tools used in data processing and decision-making.
16	L: International business: criteria for selecting local *modus operandi*.	
17	Q11: Decisions. Class discussion: Elements of a marketing management audit.	
18	L: Interdependence of market structure and marketing strategy.	
19	Final examination on readings and lectures.	Preparation for marketing management audit.
20	Q12: Decisions. Class discussion: Structure and strategy in INTOP markets.	
21	Cross-company marketing management audits.	
22	Review and evaluation of the simulation and the course as a whole	

Legend: L = lecture-discussion; Q = quarter in INTOP simulation.

have also been selected with a view to feeding into this integrated pattern. A prerequisite to achieving the desirable closure is the maintenance of a proper temporal sequence between the lectures introducing or analyzing given areas of subject matter and the related weekly assignments. The lecture titles would appear to be self-explanatory.

All except the first and last of the assignments are written. They are typically two or three pages long, although company business plans and annual reports (comprising contributions by all team members) may run into a dozen pages or more.[119] Company presidents are formally responsible for the drafting of company objectives and organization plans, as well as the occasional quarterly reviews and previews of operations, although their documentation is based on discussion within their executive teams.[120] The presidents also organize the business planning and management audit efforts of their teams. However, each team member submits the more detailed plan for his own area of decision-making. The presentation of the management audit is an oral affair conducted in class.[121] In weeks when the company presidents have exclusive assignments other team members are given different tasks, i.e., writing an agenda for their own activities in Q4, writing their own job descriptions in Q5 and preparing memoranda on problems of marketing management in their firms in Q8. Some typical topics of such reports: the interaction between marketing and finance (or production), what our company expects of its channels of distribution, the role of inter-company transactions in our operations, our program for marketing research and its use in decision-making.

2] THE BUSINESS POLICY AND ORGANIZATION COURSE

The purpose, subject matter, means of instruction and requirements of this course are set forth broadly in an official announcement, a sample of which is reproduced below.

PURPOSE. The broad purpose of this course is to synthesize and integrate all work in the Executive Program in a top management perspective.

SUBJECT AREAS. The major subject areas are, first, general organization theory, philosophy and practice and, second, the application of such general management thought in conjunction with previously acquired functional knowledge to overall business objectives and strategy in specific situations.

---

[119] One of the elements of the annual report should be the preparation of a truly *annual* income statement (by consolidation of the four last quarterly income statements obtained from the computer). Indeed, if the administrator does not wish to assign the teams the task of preparing a full annual report he may well confine himself to commissioning them to prepare annual income statements at suitable intervals. This procedure was first adopted by Professor John E. Jeuck at Chicago, to whom we are grateful for the suggestion.

[120] In the downtown evening operation of the Graduate School of Business at Chicago, it is not always practical for the teams to meet out of class for such discussions. When this is the case part of the decision-making class sessions are set aside for this purpose.

[121] Cf. *infra*, 202ff.

MEANS OF INSTRUCTION. From the viewpoint of instruction the course consists of three parts:

1. Lectures and group discussions on organization theory, philosophy and practice.
2. Readings in the same area.
3. An International Operations Simulation (INTOP).

No assignments of reading for particular evenings will be made – each student is responsible for scheduling his study in time for the final exam.

Of total time in class, lecture-discussions will probably take about 55 per cent, INTOP and related activities about 45 per cent.

REQUIREMENTS AND EVALUATION. You are required to write a *term paper*, which is due two weeks before the termination of the course.

Part of the grade in the course will depend on your participation in INTOP and related assignments. The criteria relate to such factors as purposiveness, goal achievement, ability to plan and apply analytical techniques, understanding of the rules and interrelationships in the simulation model, the quality of your written assignments pertaining to the game and the rating you receive by your team colleagues. Evaluation of your INTOP performance is NOT related to "winning" the game.

You may be given minor personal assignments from time to time in class discussion groups, etc.

In principle, the final exam is addressed to the entire course, but it will be focused largely on organization theory, philosophy and practice. The final takes place one week before the completion of the program.

Readings and term papers in the course are primarily addressed to organization theory and business philosophy and ethics.[122] With the

122 A 1961 reading list includes the following items:

Required Texts:
Drucker, P. F., *The Practice of Management* (Harper, 1954), 3–254, 341–92.
Pfiffner, J. M., and Sherwood, F. P., *Administrative Organization* (Prentice-Hall, 1960).
Woodward, Joan, *Management and Technology* (London: Department of Scientific and Industrial Research, 1958).
Game and case materials as assigned.

Additional Required Readings:
Bush, Vannevar, "Of What Use Is a Board of Directors" (mimeographed; supplied).
Dale, E., *The Great Organizers* (McGraw-Hill, 1960), 1–216, 261–72.
Mason, Edward S., "The Apologetics of 'Managerialism'" (reprint supplied courtesy of the *Journal of Business*).
Smith, R. A., "The Incredible Electrical Conspiracy," *Fortune*, May 1961.
Thorelli, H. B., "The Tantalizing Concept of Productivity," 4 *Am. Behavioral Scientist* (Nov. 1960), 6–11.

Recommended Readings:
The New European Market – A Guide for American Businessmen (Courtesy Chase Manhattan Bank).
Anshen, M., and Bach, G. L., *Management and Corporations, 1985* (McGraw-Hill, 1960).
Dale, E., *Planning and Developing the Company Organization Structure* (American Management Association, 1952).
Dean, J., *Managerial Economics* (Prentice-Hall, 1951 and later eds.).
Haire, M., ed., *Modern Organization Theory* (Wiley, 1959).
March, J. G., and Simon, H. A., *Organizations* (Wiley, 1958).
Simon, H. A., *Administrative Behavior* (Macmillan, 1957).

FIG. 33 *Business Policy and Organization – Sample Course Schedule*

Session		Class Schedule	Related Assignments
1	L:	Concept of the modern corporation. Business philosophy and objectives.	Study INTOP rules (distributed a week in advance of the course).
	L:	Presentation of INTOP. Assignment to teams.	
2	L:	Structuring approaches in organization (purpose or product, function, geographical area, etc.). Job descriptions – their contents, uses and limitations. INTOP teams discuss their philosophy and organization preliminarily. Then organize.	Presidents: business philosophy and goals, organization chart; all team members: personal job descriptions.
3	Q1-3:	Teams settle on philosophy and first year objectives. Decisions.	
4	L:	Long-range planning. INTOP staff work and inter-company negotiations (60 minutes). Small-group discussion: The special problems of family firms.	Two-year business plan.
5	Q4:	Decisions.	
	L:	Data processing systems for decision-making.	
6		INTOP rules test (15 minutes). Staff work and design of data processing systems (60 minutes).	Worksheets and analytical tools used in data processing and decision-making.
	L:	Intra-corporate economics and transfer problems.	
	Q5:	Decisions.	
7	L:	Organization – the concept reconsidered (crucial characteristics such as division of labor and coordination, biological analogies, etc.).	

FIG. 33   *Business Policy and Organization – Sample Course Schedule* (Continued)

Session	Class Schedule	Related Assignments
8	L: Centralization and decentralization – what are the determinants? INTOP staff work (30 minutes). L: International business operations. Private enterprise and overseas economic development.	
9	Q6-7: Decisions. L: The Scientific Management School I.	
10	Small-group discussion: Determinants of "span of control." INTOP staff work (30 minutes). L: The Scientific Management School II.	
11	Q8: Decisions. L: The Human Relations School.	
12	INTOP staff work, including review of consolidated data of competing companies. Prepare for annual report (60 minutes). L: Contemporary organization theory I. Small-group discussion: Can experience gained in one organization be transferred to another?	
13	Rotate management in INTOP companies. Reorganize if desired. Reconsider objectives (30 minutes). Q9: Decisions. L: Contemporary organization theory II.	Annual report.

FIG. 33   *Business Policy and Organization — Sample Course Schedule* (Continued)

Session		Class Schedule	Related Assignments
14	L:	Soviet and American management. INTOP staff work (30 minutes). Presentation of best annual reports.	
15	Q10:	Decisions.	Revised business objectives, organization plan and job descriptions (where applicable).
	L:	The concept of productivity. Small-group discussion: Business ethics.	
16	L:	Authority, responsibility, accountability. The paraphernalia of organization planning. INTOP staff work (30 minutes). Small-group discussion: Organization and decision-making in 1980.	Revised two-year plan.
17	Q11:	Decisions and preliminary Q12 decisions.	Term papers due.
	L:	Administering change.	
18	L:	Purpose and process of a management audit. INTOP staff work, including review of consolidated data of competing companies. Prepare for management audit (60 minutes). Presentation of most interesting term papers.	
19	Q12:	Final examination on lectures, discussions and readings. Decisions.	Prepare for management audit.
20		Mutual evaluation by the executives in each team (20 minutes). Management audit of INTOP companies.	

Legend: L = lecture-discussion; Q = quarter in INTOP simulation.

readings furnishing the background for lectures and small-group discussions, and INTOP with related weekly assignments, the course constitutes a well-integrated whole despite the rather amorphous nature of its subject matter. A typical schedule of class work and weekly assignments based on twenty three-hour sessions in ten weeks is shown in Fig. 33. The INTOP simulation is directly illustrative of at least two-thirds of the total number of lectures in this course. Comments regarding the length and nature of the related assignments in the marketing management course are again applicable.

It may be noted that both course outlines are based on an initial resource allocation to the INTOP teams of ten million dollars, with full freedom for the companies to choose their own objectives and organization. The administrator may wish to leave the game even more unstructured by forcing the companies to negotiate for their initial funds on the basis of their objectives and plans.[123] He may, conversely, impose a tighter structure on the game by prescribing similar or different objectives and modes of operation for the companies. If companies are to retain discretion with regard to objectives, organization and job descriptions he may well stimulate their thinking by handing out sample documentation in these areas.[124]

Outlines corresponding to those just presented applying the simulation to finance, production, accounting and international operations courses will be developed as soon as time and opportunity permit. In the meanwhile the concrete illustrations given here of two highly viable courses express a basic philosophy that a balanced portfolio of educational tools applied in an integrated fashion is worth striving for. It seems clear that sophisticated simulations will play a major role in the implementation of such a philosophy in management education in years to come.

c. *Introducing Qualitative Factors*

We have pointed out that there are no other limits to the introduction of qualitative change in the world of INTOPIA than the imagination of the administrator and the ability of participants to react. Ordinarily the administrator will have no difficulty in finding a suitable rationale for the changes introduced. Fig. 34 illustrates qualitative factors confronting the teams in a typical run at Chicago.

If the administrator wants to make temporary changes in the market potential of an area or product he may use a monitor company representing for instance a governmental buying unit or a Japanese competitor. Countries in balance-of-payment difficulties may introduce import quotas or temporary import prohibitions. Seasonal variations may be superimposed on the general economic fluctuations simply by

123 Cf. *supra*, 149f.

124 Sample statements of business philosophy and goals and position descriptions are reproduced in Appendix VI.

FIG. 34   *Environmental Developments in a*
Typical INTOP Run

Environmental Development	Quarter of Gazette Notice	Quarter of Occurrence
Brazil prohibits capital export Q4-5*	4, 5	4, 5
Brazil subsidizes the construction of new plants with $100,000 per plant, Q4-5	4, 5	4, 5
Arthur DeBig offers to develop patents X_3 and Y_3 by Q7†	4	7
Strike warning in U.S. radio manufacturing industry‡	5, 6-7	8
No building permits in Q6-7§	4, 5, 6-7	6-7
Rumor EEC currency revaluation	6-7	
Brazil permits capital export, but introduces 5 per cent capital transfer tax||	6-7	6
New radio stations open in Brazil#	8	8
EEC currency revaluation**	8	8
Brazilian government securities written down by 20 per cent††	9	8
Slowdown warning in EEC cleaner industry‡‡	8, 9, 10	10
Rumor Atlantic Economic Community to be established	8, 9	
Mergers conditionally permitted§§	8	9
Atlantic Economic Community established||||		10

*The capital export prohibition is likely to be an especially severe constraint in standard runs, in which companies are obliged to place considerable funds in Brazilian government securities as a condition for plant construction in Q1-3.

†Sample *Gazette* notice: *"Caveat Emptor.* Arthur DeBig, the internationally infamous consulting firm, makes the following offer: an R & D contract to develop X_3 by Q7 for $600,000 (with a refund of $200,000 should they fail to do so). For a meager $800,000 they will sign a contract to develop Y_3 by Q7 with the added assurance of a $250,000 rebate if they prove unsuccessful. The offer is available in Q4 and for one company only for each product." The administrator may also decide to make the contract available to several companies, presumably at a lower rate. Any improvement he actually wishes to "develop" is simply fed in on the customer company's ancillary data sheet in Q7 by Wonder Card.

‡The administrator may decide a strike will take place, in which case companies are simply told not to produce X in the U.S. during Q8 and any additional quarters he may wish to keep the industry in a state of frenzy. He may decide against a strike at the last minute, concluding a new labor agreement resulting in higher variable X manufacturing costs in the U.S. He may also have the conflict settled by simulated bargaining sessions, in which he (or some team not active in the X manufacturing industry in the U.S.) represents the union negotiating with a committee representing the American X manufacturing companies. Note that while individual firms may be singled out for strikes, a change in variable manufacturing cost will always affect all companies making a given product in a given area (unless the administration is willing to write special Wonder Cards for each affected company every quarter).

§In several runs of INTOP Standard Q6 decisions have been rerun in identical form as Q7, cf. *supra,* 176f. This can be done most reasonably by eliminating plant construction during these two quarters.

changing the economic index.[125] Structural change in demand — again calling only for a single Wonder Card[126] — may be rationalized in such terms as the development of electro-static vacuum-cleaning devices of a built-in type outside the Y industry (or, conversely, by announcing that one of the higher Y grades represents such a cleaner, or that a higher X grade licks the problem of making a reliable FM portable radio). By making the market potential larger than in the standard version of the game, the administrator may focus the attention of the teams primarily on the broader environment; by making it smaller he leads them to concentrating on battling competition.

As a possible stimulus to other game administrators (and designers) we submit a few additional illustrations of qualitative developments which may be easily implemented in INTOP:

Random plants destroyed by acts of God.

Regional sales manager hired away from a team (implemented by reducing the number of regional sales offices of the team in an area).

Internal Revenue refuses to accept intra-company sales from the U.S. to another area at below cost.

The United States prohibits imports of goods priced lower here than in the country of origin.

Brazilian election uncertainties with parties having radically different views on the desirability of foreign private investment in the country.

Dissension within the EEC, resulting in higher intra-area shipping costs, higher variable manufacturing costs, etc.

Payments to government officials in certain areas for public relations, protection or expediting purposes.

---

[125]   Q4, 8, 12, etc., may be Christmas quarter, Q5, 9, 13, etc. tax-collecting period in U.S., Q6, 10, 14, etc., tax-collecting period (with depressed sales) in the EEC, and so on.

[126]   This will regulate basic market potential (Dictionary symbol PS01) for any product in any area.

||Simply introduced by Wonder Card, the effect of the tax will appear on a standard line of the income statement.

#Effect: a jump in demand for radios and an increase in advertising elasticities in Brazil (as the advertising dollar will go further with greater radio coverage).

**Several effects may be imagined, e.g., lower variable manufacturing costs (as overseas raw materials decrease in price), lower costs of transfers to the EEC (or higher from the EEC), changed valuation of assets, new local interest rates, etc.

††Presumably a drastic anti-inflationary move, effectuated by writing down by 20 per cent any local securities investments on the Brazil part of the Operations Decision Card and subtracting by Wonder Card 4B a corresponding amount from area cash and retained earnings of the companies concerned.

‡‡Should the administrator decide a slowdown is in order he need only inform teams of the new maximal Y plant capacity limits in the EEC. Cf. note ‡ above.

§§In past standard runs mergers have only been allowed a) at a late stage of the game and b) between a chronically unprofitable and a profitable company. Cf. INTOP Memo 5, Mergers (reproduced in Appendix VI), which should also be distributed to the teams when mergers become permissible.

|| ||Obvious effect: drastic lowering of the transfer costs between U.S. and the EEC (preferably to the intra-area transfer cost level).

Wave of hijacking in the U.S., resulting in the disappearance of a certain per cent of inventory.

Government price control in Brazil.[127]

Behind-the-scenes intervention by U.S. Government in labor disputes in order to reach a "voluntary" settlement of a non-inflationary nature involving both wages and prices.

Perhaps after this discussion it should be re-emphasized that a perfectly viable run of INTOP may be undertaken without *any* environmental change. Indeed, as often as not the problem is to make administrators exercise reasonable self-restraint in the introduction of disrupting influences in the simulation!

D. *Making Use of Outside Experts, Role-playing, In-baskets, etc.*

In past runs of INTOP Standard, faculty members at Chicago have added new qualitative dimensions to the simulation by roleplaying as board chairmen, Liechtenstein bankers, labor negotiators and management consultants. At Carnegie, groups of faculty members have served as boards of directors goading the student teams. At that school, too, accounting students have also been assigned to undertake full-scale and continuous management audits of participating teams. The latter experiments, spearheaded by Neil C. Churchill, Merton H. Miller and Robert M. Trueblood, have apparently provided both the auditors and the audited with a rewarding educational experience.[128]

Participation in a complex game actually involves a continuous role-playing exercise in a managerial position. This experience may be enriched further by special assignments. A team may be asked to stage an executive committee meeting before the class concerning the pros and cons of going into Brazil, of building a new plant, of the R & D and licensing program of the company and so on. In such a situation each student plays his customary role in the team. Participants may be given special role-playing assignments as union leaders, bankers, consultants, etc. They may also act out moot court sessions in case of contract violation in inter-company transactions.

The sense of realism and the educational experience of participants may be enriched further by calling on outside expertise to perform certain functions in the game. A representative of an advertising agency may evaluate advertising campaign plans in a marketing management course, a banker may be invited to pass on proposed financing arrangements of teams in a finance course and so on.[129]

Game administrators who want to emphasize qualitative aspects

[127] This might be introduced at a fairly late stage in the game, and perhaps in the form of a simple ceiling price. This would presumably have interesting consequences with regard to the product grades and advertising policies of companies active in the area.

[128] Mimeographed accounts of these experiments may be obtained from Carnegie. Formal publication is forthcoming.

[129] Cf. *supra*, 25, 149f.

of management still further may make use of the in-basket technique. In this manner teams may be asked to pass on discipline problems in their plants, ethical issues in government-business, manufacturer-distributor or plant-community relations and so on. Performance in such exercises may be incorporated as one of the criteria of the instructor's evaluation of the teams. Alternately, the effect of decisions in these areas may be taken into account by adjusting quantitative performance indicators of individual teams in the simulation as indicated below.

E.   *Adjusting Quantitative Performance of Individual Companies to the Quality of Their Decisions*

The INTOP model offers at least three principally different ways of adjusting the quantitative performance of individual teams to the quality of their decisions. First, the administrator may manipulate a team's "effectiveness index," thereby directly affecting the marketing performance of the company.[130] Secondly, he may regulate paid-in-capital. While the standard purpose of this function is to reflect stock market confidence in the company, the administrator may make it serve the dual mission of reflecting general goodwill among the public. If he chooses to make this use of the function the teams should be advised accordingly. Thirdly, he may mete out damages (in connection with contract violation) or fines (for antitrust violations, etc.) simply by changing the cash (and retained earnings) account in the Home Office or the area involved.[131]

In past standard runs of the game we have not had reason to regulate the marketing effectiveness factor. As such action does place individual teams on a different competitive basis, it would seem imperative that they be informed in advance of the criteria to be applied in any use of the index. Perhaps each team should even be informed of the exact numerical change in their effectiveness rating when such changes are made.

5.   Performance Evaluation

A.   *Performance Criteria*

The problems of performance measurement have been treated very lightly in the literature on management games. We perceive at least three reasons for this. First, surprisingly little is known about the evaluation of intellectual and creative effort in general and

130 For the simple mechanics involved, see Computer Liaison instruction.

131 Wonder Cards 4A and 4B make this a trivial operation. Awards – e.g., the $10,000 prize of the Public Relations Society of America for the best annual report—may be given in the same manner.

of managerial activity in particular.[132] Secondly, such an insightful observer as Dean Dill — having in mind especially the evaluation of game performance as a determinant of grades in academic course-work — and others with him have appeared to question the very notion of performance ratings.[133] A third reason for an otherwise astonishing lack of discussion of this subject derives from the fact that in *some* games performance appraisal *is* indeed quite simple. We are thinking of games involving drill in the use of a single analytical device, such as an economic order quantity or inventory control formula, and some exercises involving quite simple models. Broadly speaking, the more complex the simulation the more intricate the problems of evaluation. This rule, of course, applies to real-life situations as well: the job of the production manager is harder to evaluate than that of the piece-rate worker on the assembly line. In truly complex games — such as the Chicago simulation — there is indeed no practicable way of finding out what "optimal" play would be in any given situation. It might even be argued that one of the important things participants may learn from such a game is the fallacy of the Scientific Management School (and, unfortunately, of some latter-day Operations Research rene-gades) that there is always "the One Best Way" in problem-solving. The game administrator may simplify the task of evaluation somewhat by imposing identical objectives on all teams. Although this might be a reasonable procedure in certain stripped-down as well as laboratory-type runs it does introduce an undesirable element of artificiality.[134]

The discussion in this section is based on the assumption that performance appraisal is either desirable or a practical necessity (as it may be in some academic contexts).[135] It is certainly of a highly preliminary nature. We are experimenting with different approaches and a variety of criteria, and feel that it would be presumptuous to deal with any one of them in detail. Also, what standards of appraisal to use as well as their relative ranking is ultimately a question of judg-ment and values.[136] It is also a question related to the purpose of run-ning the game and the use to be made of the ratings. If a simulation

[132] Cf., e.g., Hans B. Thorelli, "The Tantalizing Concept of Productivity," *American Behavioral Scientist* (Nov. 1960), 6–11.

[133] "(I)t is not clear that we should try to grade at all. Since games tend to stimulate high levels of interest and involvement, grades may not be neces-sary to induce students to work hard. Our insistence on grades and on vari-ous kinds of grading standards is not alway supported by some important theories (e.g., B. F. Skinner's) of the effects of reward and punishment. It is not even always consistent with what we teach under the heading of 'moti-vation' in our courses in human rela-tions and management." Tulane Uni-versity Conference *Proceedings, op. cit.,* 34.

[134] It should be remembered, how-ever, that (too) many game models do set up quite rigid constraints on the selection of objectives.

[135] It should also not be forgotten that most human beings seem to have a dualistic outlook towards measure-ment of our own performance: we fre-quently tend to resent it while at the same time we have an irresistible crav-ing for being evaluated.

[136] Of course, those being evaluated have a legitimate claim to being in-formed in advance what the evaluator's standards are.

is used as a means of testing risk-willingness among decision-makers the criteria of evaluation must reasonably be somewhat different from what they would be if the same simulation is used in a college course in business organization and policy. There are a number of practical issues connected with evaluation such as when, by whom, and by what means or on what evidence it should be undertaken. In complex simulations – as in real life organizations – there is also the frequently awkward problem of appraising individual vs. group performance. These matters will be touched on wherever this seems natural in the main discussion of criteria.

B. *Objectives and Degree of Goal Achievement*

In highly simplified games the objective of each team may be both unambiguous and identical with that of every other team, making evaluation a reasonably easy task. A complex general management simulation such as INTOP is at the opposite end of the pole. To clarify one's thinking there is reason to distinguish two types of overall performance criteria, one general, the other specific.[137] The general criteria are substantially identical with those which the stock market, financial analysts or prudent investors would apply, such as profitability or growth in assets or sales, growth potential, market share and so on. As everyone knows there is no universal agreement on what the relative significance of these general performance yardsticks should be.[138] For this reason, and because such an exercise can be quite instructive in itself, it may often be desirable to have a class discussion of these general criteria of business performance where the time is available. Our experience indicates that this is not *necessary*, however, as participants almost invariably will carry on such a discussion spontaneously in the course of the simulation, and indeed make their own informal appraisal of the teams in terms of such criteria.

The generally accepted standards provide a necessary, but not a sufficient, basis for performance appraisal. In any industry or trade each firm has its own explicit or implicit objectives. In INTOP, too, it is perfectly feasible for one company to conceive of itself as a corner appliance store in Rio while another aspires to be Global Electric. A family of specific performance criteria may be derived from the goals each firm has set for itself. Note that achievement of objectives need not in itself constitute superior performance. If objectives are defined with sufficient modesty and vagueness their attainment may be a trivial feat. At Chicago teams have been informed that the nature of

137 The discussion in this subsection is condensed in the *Player's Manual*, 2.
138 If he so wishes, the administrator may naturally decide that a given mix of suitable criteria is to govern evaluation in the simulation. For instance, absolute or relative achievement in terms of profitability and market share may be weighted with certain coefficients and combined in an overall yardstick.
  Given a clear definition of criteria and relative weights it would indeed be a fairly simple matter to build an "evaluation subroutine" into the INTOP FORTRAN program.

their objectives as well as their degree of goal attainment will be taken into account in evaluation.[139] Their statement of objectives are examined with the following considerations in mind:

level of ambition, absolutely and as related to resources at hand
internal consistency
specificity and "actionability"
imagination
strength of supporting arguments

In considering performance in terms of both general criteria and the self-determined objectives of the companies *action potential for the future at the end of the simulation* should be particularly emphasized. This will underscore the point that we are dealing only with a fairly brief period of the life of modern, "perpetuate" corporations. Unrealistic cutbacks on levels of inventory maintained, R & D, advertising, etc. in the last quarter of play are completely avoided in this way.[140] In addition, class discussion of suitable indicators of strong and weak action potentials may be quite rewarding.[141]

c. *Quality of Plans and Play*

A prime criterion for the appraisal of a plan is whether, and to what extent, it is conducive to the attainment of the objectives of the organization. A budget indicating the proposed procurement and use of resources should probably be an integrated part of any business plan. Assumptions and forecasts should be explicitly stated;[142] their reasonableness may be judged in the light of the company position and the availability of environmental data at the time the plan was made. The projects and measures contemplated in the plan should be scheduled in a logical sequence allowing reasonable time for the achievement of subgoals. The plan should capitalize on, and in execution re-enforce, any differential advantage enjoyed by the company in relation to its competitors.

These are some guideposts for the evaluation of the quality of a planning job whether in real life or in a sophisticated simulation. It should be noted that "realism" need not necessarily be aimed at in planning by game teams, however. It does not seem reasonable to penalize a team outlining a scheme for systematic experimentation in order to gain a better understanding of the game structure merely because in real life the company would not have an analogous oppor-

---

[139] Cf. *supra*, 187.

[140] In the last quarter it may also be advisable to check on "paper profits" which may be made in INTOP as in real life by means of intra-company transfers at more than cost.

[141] Indicators include credit worthiness, inventory position, productive capacity, age of plants, variable manufacturing costs, patents, standing con-

tracts with other companies, captive sales organization in place where justified by sales volume and a great number of conventional analyst's ratios.

[142] Unless assumptions and forecasts are made explicit it is not possible either to use the plan as a tool of performance measurement or to know when it should be revised in view of changing circumstances.

tunity.[143] Like business objectives, plans may also be examined from the viewpoint of internal consistency, specificity and workability and the strength of any supporting argumentation.

A certain amount of flexibility is characteristic of any viable organization. As pointed out in the *Player's Manual,* companies must be given an opportunity to revise their objectives and/or plans from time to time.[144] Whenever such a change is undertaken it should, however, be documented, and the reasons for the change spelled out.

The problems of evaluating actual vs. planned performance of an INTOP team are quite analogous to those encountered in real life when plans are made yardsticks of managerial evaluation. Degree of deviation between plan and execution is clearly relevant. Frequently the more interesting question is whether the deviation is simply due to poor performance (if actual falls short of planned) or to environmental developments which reasonably could not be foreseen at the time of planning or easily coped with when they occurred.[145] Ability to recognize and respond to environmental change — whether generated by the competitive interplay itself or by external stimuli introduced by the administrator — is clearly an important qualitative aspect of performance.

What additional dimensions of the quality of play should be taken into account is partly a matter of taste, partly dependent on the nature of any assignments related to the game. The next two subsections deal with evaluation of related assignments and some specific indications of quality of play in INTOP.

D. *Quality of Related Assignments*

As previously suggested, integrated use of a simulation tends to be reflected in a variety of ancillary assignments to participants.[146] To a considerable extent, the standards to be used in appraising such work are identical to those educators apply in grading term papers or theses generally. There is no reason to discuss such criteria here. It may also be pointed out that participants often develop worksheets, analytical techniques, internal reporting systems, etc., even though such activities have not been explicitly assigned to them. The instructor may well wish to take such evidence into account in any formal

143 An administrator who feels differently should make it clear in advance that only plans which could hope to meet the acid test of reality are acceptable.

144 Cf. *Player's Manual,* 2, note 2.

145 Conversely, if actual performance exceeds planned performance this may be due to excellence in management, to poor planning, to favorable environmental circumstances or any combination of these factors.

Our observations concerning flexibility and the desirability of viewing deviations from intended courses of action in relation to assumptions made at the time intentions were announced and to subsequent environmental change are also applicable if the administrator wishes to make an evaluation of tentative vs. definite decisions in multi-quarter play; cf. *supra,* 176f.

146 Illustrations from university courses are given in Section 4B of this chapter.

evaluation of team performance.

Of the specific assignments given Chicago teams only the annual report is in need of further comment. Students are asked to view the preparation of these reports not as an exercise in public relations but as an opportunity to conduct an internal management audit. It is emphasized that this implies a self-evaluation explicitly relating company performance during the period reviewed to business philosophy, objectives and plans as previously submitted to the administrator.

Both in academic courses and in executive development programs it is frequently desirable to extend performance appraisal beyond the teams to individual participants. (Clearly, team performance will generally also be one of the criteria used in appraising individual participants.) Several of the written assignments in the Chicago courses are eminently suitable for individual contribution. Even though this is explained to the students, teams will occasionally hand in a business plan or an annual report as a collective product without any identification of individual contributions. In such cases we have assigned an equal grade on the assignment to all members of the team, based on the assumption that they all did in fact contribute. At the same time it has been pointed out to participants that where a team (or real-life company) has achieved an efficient internal division of labor — presumably based on a clear concept of overall objectives and plans — each executive is enabled to render an independent contribution. Hence individual contributions, whenever they are in fact possible, are examined with somewhat greater favor than collective reports. Other opportunities for individual evaluation are provided by rules tests,[147] mutual evaluation by team members,[148] and by questions and comments on the part of participants regarding the rules and models used in the simulation and their relation to underlying theoretical and practical issues. If this is not regarded as sufficient the instructor may contemplate giving an examination at the end of the simulation, possibly in the form of a case based on the operations of some imaginary firm.[149]

E. *Indications Inherent in the INTOP Model*

The INTOP model itself by setting up a system of constraints and opportunities requires responses which may furnish indications

[147] Cf. *supra,* 180.

[148] Cf. Section 5F below.

[149] Cf. Professor Paul S. Greenlaw accounting for his "Experience with Gaming in a Senior Undergraduate Course" in the Tulane University Conference *Proceedings, op. cit.,* 87: "In the examination, each student was given a game operating statement, and asked to: 1) analyze the current position of the firm; 2) indicate his decisions for the forthcoming period; and 3) show what analytical facts he employed in developing 1) and 2) above, and why they were of value to him. Although I am not sure how valid a measurement of gaming performance this examination provided, it did seem to replicate quite closely the kind of situation with which the players had been confronted throughout the play." Perhaps two operating statements would give a better result than one, as they provide the students with a dynamic view of the firm's operations.

of the quality of participation of individual companies. As long as companies are given freedom to choose different objectives and modes of operation, however, a majority of these benchmarks will be of value only in appraising a limited number of teams. Still, a few of the indicators are more broadly applicable in performance evaluation and may warrant restatement here:

1. Ability to schedule the flow of funds in such a manner that the company has neither an excess of cash nor has to resort to excessive supplier credit. Note that supplier credit may occasionally be warranted, notably if the return on the funds thus obtained is greater than the interest. However, the simultaneous occurrence of supplier credit and investments in government securities is almost invariably evidence of bad planning. Similarly, it is poor planning not to prevail on any available opportunities for area or home office bank loans in quarters when supplier credit is incurred.

2. Ability to adjust price-quantity relationships in a sensible way avoiding both stock-outs and excessive inventory charges.

3. Ability to avoid excessive suboptimization in company operations.

4. Ability to make effective use of common economies and unique advantages through inter-company transactions. For example, if a company's R & D program is yielding product improvements which the firm cannot itself effectively utilize due to limitations of capacity, it would be logical to license the patents to others.

5. Ability to live up to inter-company agreements.

6. Ability to avoid clearly unbalanced spending in some areas of the business, such as R & D or methods improvement.

7. Ability to make a reasonable marketing channel decision and minimize C & A expense in relation to stability and volume of sales in various areas.

8. Ability to avoid production and/or marketing of "dud" grades of either product. This requires the foresight to order test marketing and/or consultant's estimates of production costs[150] before any decisions to produce or purchase these grades.

9. Ability to make effective use of marketing research and consultative services in general.

10. Ability to avoid sales expediting. To prevail on this function is generally, although not invariably, an indication of negligence.

Occasionally a team's performance may be severely affected by error or negligence in filling out decision forms. The administrator may have adjusted the records of the company during the simulation to compensate for dysfunctional consequences of such behavior. If not, he may wish to take this into account in evaluation. In either case, it should be remembered that ability to live with the computer — including the formulation of correct instructions of the simple kind used in INTOP — is rapidly becoming a performance criterion in many executive positions in real life.

[150] Items 17 and 18 in the catalog of Marketing Research Services, respectively.

F. *Mutual Evaluation of Executives Within Teams*

Mutual evaluation of executives within teams may be of some assistance in cases where a rating of the performance of individual members of groups participating in a simulation is desired. If students are made aware at the beginning of the simulation that such sociometric scoring will be employed at the end, experience suggests that this may have a positive motivational effect even in runs where no formal grades or ratings are to be established by the instructor.[151]

A form used experimentally with some success at Chicago is reproduced in Fig. 35. Twenty minutes seems to be sufficient time for participants to complete the form. For evaluation purposes only Items 1–3, 7 and 9 have been used. It may well be that the remaining "noise" items can be eliminated. (They were originally inserted for a secondary purpose.) While no direct attempt has been made as yet to validate this instrument, we may state that there has been a substantial degree of correlation among the mutual appraisals of the members within most teams. The item concerning knowledge of game rules (Item 1) has also shown rather high correlation with results on the INTOP rules test given each participant individually at a fairly early stage of the game.

G. *Management Audit and Review of the Simulation*

Dissatisfaction with game critique sessions of the conventional type,[152] and the notion that systematic evaluation of team performance would itself constitute a worthwhile student experience, has prompted us to make the management audit of a competitive company the last major assignment in runs of INTOP Standard at Chicago.[153] Each team is told that for purposes of this assignment they represent a management consulting firm called in to make a thorough evaluation of the company assigned to them.[154] While auditing in a more narrow technical sense is not neglected, the emphasis of the exercise is on the evaluation of overall management performance. It is pointed out that the company to be audited must be appraised as much in terms of its own specific objectives and plans as in such categories as profitability, growth and other general criteria.

Typically, each pair of auditing and audited companies are given ten minutes of class time (to be shared equally) for criticism and comments. In addition, a few minutes should be open for questions and comments from the floor and by the instructor (if he wishes to engage

---

151 We are not aware of any research indicating whether advance awareness of future rating by colleagues may also have dysfunctional consequences, such as subduing certain forms of creativity.

152 Cf. *supra*, 23f.

153 To what extent these audits should in turn influence the instructor's evaluation would seem to be a matter of discretion.

154 To avoid the possibility that the exercise develop into a tug-of-war, care is taken that no company be audited by the team which in turn was audited by it.

FIG. 35 *INTOP Group Analysis**

Your Name_____   Company #_____

You are assured that all data on this sheet will be held in *strict confidence.*

Kindly list each member of your firm in alphabetical order, *including yourself.* For each of the characteristics listed, rate each member on a scale from 0 (lowest) to 100 (highest), where the number indicates your estimate of the proportion of the members of the entire class who fall below the rated individual on the given characteristic. A rating of 50 is to be regarded as average for all class members; over the entire class, *but not necessarily within any given teams,* half the members should receive lower than 50 and half higher than 50. *No two persons may receive the same rating* on the same characteristic; i.e., no number may appear more than once on a given line.

Please note that if this form is not filled in in accordance with instructions it will be disregarded.

	Name								
1	Knowledge of INTOP Rules								
2	Use of Analytic Techniques								
3	Influence on Company Decisions								
4	Willingness to Take Risks								
5	Originality of Ideas								
6	Contribution to Group Morale								
7	Ability to Plan Ahead								
8	Ability to See Points of View Other than Own								
9	Overall Value to Company								

*Several suggestions by Professor Franklin B. Evans at Chicago are gratefully acknowledged.

in the discussion). In a run with fourteen or fifteen companies there may not be 2½–3 hours of class time available for a management audit; our experience indicates that in such a case it is more instructive to have a few full-blown audits than to cut down the time available for each audit.[155] The division of tasks in the preparation of the audit may be left to the teams themselves. The distribution of roles in the public discussion may be established in a similar manner. To stimulate the thinking of the teams, the instructor may suggest various ways to

[155] All companies may, of course, be asked to *prepare* audits. The instructor may prefer not to divulge in advance what companies will be called upon to perform in the public discussion.

organize the audit. One member of the auditing team may focus on objectives, another on plans, a third on data-processing, or the audit may be structured around functional or geographical areas or by product and so on.

To make the audit a worthwhile effort the auditing team should have access to as complete a set of records as possible concerning the company to be examined. The latter company should also be obliged to answer questions arising in the course of preparations. The auditing team should be given a set of all computer outputs concerning the company,[156] and should also have access to worksheets and records used by it. The administrator should provide copies of statements of business objectives, two-year plans, organization charts, position descriptions and annual reports.

The auditing team will have considerable general background information about the industry in its own files. In runs of INTOP Standard these materials have included the *Gazette* and consolidated outputs for each company for Q4, Q8 and Q12. The auditing company's own output history should also be included as a source of valuable comparative data. In addition, all companies have been required to order the complete breakdown of industry sales by company, area and products in the quarter prior to the audit (Item 2 in the catalog of Marketing Research Services).[157] At Chicago we have also distributed mimeographed copies of industry statistics compiled in the course of the game.[158] The instructor may further draw the attention of the teams to some of the indications of performance quality inherent in the INTOP model.[159]

Whenever circumstances permit the integration of the simulation in a broader educational framework and also the use of a thorough management audit there is relatively little need for additional review. The instructor may wish to discuss briefly his own evaluation of the particular run of the game just concluded and invite participants to evaluate the course and submit their ideas for its further enrichment. For the latter purpose it may be preferable to use a questionnaire anonymously completed.

When pressures of time and circumstance are such as to prompt using the simulation as a self-contained educational instrument the game review as classically conceived will naturally assume a more strategic role.[160] We would still re-emphasize, however, that it refutes the purpose of a dynamic exercise to attach as much weight to the

---

[156] We have generally required the audited company to give one of its sets to the auditors. Alternatively, the administrator may simply retain a set of all company outputs from all periods to be distributed to the appropriate teams at management audit time.

[157] If the administrator so wishes, he may set the cost of these data in the last quarter at zero by a Wonder Card.

[158] Cf. instruction for Secretary, Appendix V.

[159] Cf. Chapter 4, Section 5E. See also Kibbee-Craft-Nanus, 219ff. One approach to the management audit which some students may find helpful is that of W. P. Leonard, *The Management Audit* (1962).

[160] For a good restatement, see Kibbee-Craft-Nanus, 87ff.

critique session as many administrators have in the past. The learning by doing, the *continuous* review by the teams themselves, enriched by critical observations by the administrator in the course of the game, more than anything else will determine the quality of the experience gained by participants.

Chapter **5**

Computer Operations and Wonder Cards. Parameter Choice and Change

Introduction

THIS CHAPTER ATTEMPTS to fill two distinct but related purposes. The first of these objectives is to provide an overall view of computer operations and of the simple but exceedingly versatile mechanics of effectuating change in general program parameters as well as in specific data on individual team outputs. Computer operations are surveyed in the first section of the chapter, emphasizing the differential information flows through the system focused on the administrator and the participating teams, respectively. The second section is devoted to the instruments of change — that is, the "Dictionary" listing of all parameters and current company accounts or "state variables" and the companion "Wonder Card" which the administrator may use to cause change in any parameter or state variable.

The second objective of the chapter is to demonstrate an approach to parameter choice and change. Such a way of reasoning is needed by any administrator who wishes to make full use of the unusual versatility of the INTOP model — whether his concern is to create variations on the standard theme represented by the *Player's Manual* or to re-arrange the 450 parameters and build a basically different simulation. For convenience, the discussion uses INTOP Standard for purposes of illustration. This procedure also permits us to indicate ranges of values for individual parameters; the administrator using the standard model may find it advisable to stay within these ranges. It is hoped that the man who wishes to design a basically different simulation will still find the suggested way of reasoning of considerable help as a point of departure. Chapter 6 illustrates how a great variety of such simulations may be structured around the INTOP model. However, the approach to parameter choice and sizing presented in this chapter may be useful to designers of management simulations based on entirely different models as well. Parameter choice and change is discussed in the third and largest section of the chapter.

The reading of this chapter and, indeed, the administration of the International Operations Simulation requires no familiarity with computers. Nor does the processing of INTOP data require any familiarity with the simulation on the part of the computer operator who simply follows a routine procedure indicated on a control card and delivers the output statements as they emerge from his printing equipment.

Most INTOP administrators will probably find it wise to read the first two sections of this chapter. If he contemplates *no* change of basic program parameters — or solely marginal ones, such as manipulation of the economic indices in the various geographical areas — the administrator may well disregard the entire section on parameter choice and change. Some administrators may find that section useful essentially for reference purposes in instances when a specific change is contemplated in the course of a run. Game designers and general readers may wish to familiarize themselves with the first two sections, but restrict their attention in the last one to the approach taken, leaving aside the detailed illustrations.

Sections 1 and 2 of this chapter are oriented towards the FORTRAN version of the INTOP program. Corresponding information for the Univac program — which differs in a number of details — is available in mimeographed form from the Graduate School of Business at the University of Chicago.

1. General Overview of Computer Operations

A. *The Flow of Information*

Conceptually the computer operation is a recursive input-output process, as suggested by Fig. 36. Inputs are provided each period *t* by the *decision cards* pertaining to that period, by the so-called *history* produced as part of the output in the preceding period *t* − 1 and by the computer *program* which embodies the basic simulation model. The histories produced in successive periods provide the only continuous record of events during a run of the simulation. The history consists of three parts. One segment contains the numerical parameter values currently used in processing the program. Another contains the latest values of the "state variables," i.e., the variables which record the different characteristics of each company for each period of a given run of the simulation. The third part is a register of decisions made by participating company teams during the period.

Computer processing is governed by the program, which remains unchanged throughout the course of a run. Each period the program

FIG. 36 *Overall View of INTOP FORTRAN Operations*

Point of Time Period *t*

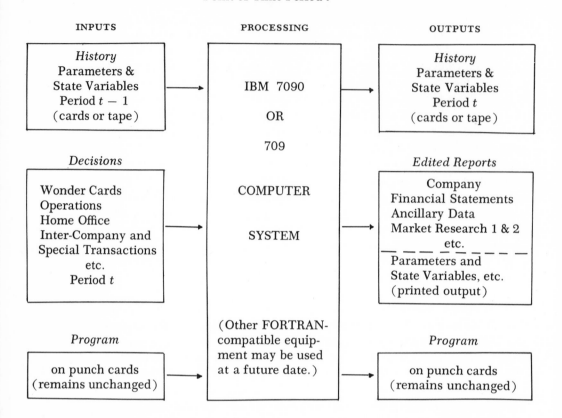

takes the new decision cards and the parameters into the model for processing, and then calculates a new set of state variables for each company expressing the transformation which has taken place from the state variables of the preceding period.

The players and the administrator may use four different types of decision forms to stimulate changes in the simulation. Of these, the Operations, Home Office and Inter-Company and Special Transactions forms (Forms 1-3) will be used by the company teams. They will also be used by the administrator, if he chooses to operate a monitor company. Samples of these forms are reproduced in the *Player's Manual* and Appendix IV.

The fourth type of decision form, the so-called Wonder Card, may be used by the administrator only, in order to effectuate change in program parameter values or in individual company records. The nature and uses of Wonder Cards are discussed in the second section of this chapter.

Conceptually, as Fig. 36 indicates, the output for each period is also tripartite, each part corresponding to a certain part of the input. The program emerges unchanged. The new history will be needed as the point of departure for the processing cycle of the subsequent period. The third part of the output, i.e., the edited and printed reports, is of greatest interest to participants and administrator alike. Its crucial ingredients are the financial statements, ancillary report and marketing research data of each and all companies (arranged by company) and the administrator's special printout of current parameter values and state variables (arranged by variables rather than companies). Sample company-oriented output in the FORTRAN program is reproduced in the Appendix.[1] So are the Dictionary *headings* of parameters and state variables.[2] Sample state variables output from an actual run of the simulation will be obtained when the test run included on the master program tape delivered from the Graduate School of Business at the University of Chicago is processed on local computer installations.[3]

The remainder of this section is devoted to a somewhat more detailed discussion of inputs and outputs, equipment requirements and certain operating problems of more general interest. The more detailed matters of routine are dealt with in the Computer Liaison instruction reproduced in Appendix V.

B. *Inputs*

The most vital part of the INTOP simulation is the program tape. It embodies the master program governing computer operations. It also embodies *a special program to create the initial history of any INTOP Standard run.* Such a history, properly dimensioned in relation to the number of companies which are to participate in a given run, is automatically created at the command of the administrator in the first period of the run. This means (1) that there will be a set of outputs for each company, (2) that the companies will all be given $10,000,000 as starting capital[4] and (3) that numerical parameter values are dimensioned in accordance with all background data in the *Player's Manual* and consistent (as regards aggregate market potential and several other characteristics) with the number of companies participating. As the program tape itself contains the history input for the first period of a run there is no need to deliver a separate history to users.

Technically speaking, certain built-in processing routines may differ from one computer installation to another. In addition, it would frequently be a nuisance to use a tape program in the regular routine of a run, as this would tend to disrupt the continuity of computer proc-

---

1 Appendix II. Sample Univac output for company teams is reproduced in the *Player's Manual.*

2 Appendix I.

3 Similarly, output of current parameter values – which should clearly be kept out of sight – will be printed out automatically for the benefit of the administrator in each period of a given run (including the test run referred to in the text).

4 If the administrator wishes to change this or other parameter values indicated in the *Player's Manual* he may do this simply by Wonder Cards, as indicated in Section 2 of this chapter.

essing of other material than the simulation itself. Continuous feed requires a *card* program. For these reasons *the program should be compiled on (binary) cards* before the actual INTOP run is begun. This deck of program cards is then used in identical form as one of the basic inputs each period.[5]

In the very first decision period, then, basic inputs are only the program cards and decision cards. Part of the output of period 1 is the history for the period. That history (and its successors) will constitute the third vital ingredient of input in period 2 (and all successive periods). While the computer will produce history output in either card or tape form at the administrator's command, cards are generally preferable for reasons similar to those applicable to the program itself.

Assuming that all materials exist in punch-card form, the inputs are loaded into the card-to-tape converting equipment in the order indicated by Fig. 37. All data will be fed onto a single tape for processing purposes. Processing itself is a strictly routine operation which need not be discussed here.[6] A note may, however, be added concerning the Master Control Card which is a cardinal means of communication between the administrator on the one hand and the operator-computer system on the other.

The Master Control Card is reproduced in Fig. 38. The comments on the lower part of the card would seem largely self-explanatory. The administrator may choose any suitable identification of the run; it will appear on his own output only. *Some* identification is necessary, although it need not take up all columns allowed. Change in number of companies in the course of a run is discussed later in this section.[7] In standard runs of the simulation only the first, third and fourth history options will be used. The fourth option is *only* used in the first period of an INTOP Standard run. Alternatively, it is of course also possible to use a history from a prior run (e.g., make the last period of a prior run represent the first period of a new one) or any history especially designed by the administrator. In these cases the first option should be used.[8] After the first period the first option is standard in most runs. However, if several decision periods are to be processed consecutively in one computer operation, the third option should be used for the *second* and all following periods.

The last four items on the Master Control Card are discussed under computer outputs below.

[5] There are approximately 1,100 binary cards in the program. The simple directions for compiling the program may be found in the Computer Liaison instruction in Appendix V.

[6] Some observations in processing are made in the Computer Liaison instruction at points where doubt might conceivably arise in the operator's mind. Basically, the processing of INTOP is a self-contained, automatic process.

[7] Cf. *infra,* 216f.

[8] Note that if the administrator has in mind only minor deviations from INTOP Standard – e.g., changing the amount of starting capital – it is usually most practical simply to effectuate them in the form of amendments to the standard initial history. This is done by means of Wonder Cards as part of the decision-card input in the first period. In such a case the fourth option is again used for that period.

FIG. 37   *Computer Input Specifications*

In a run of INTOP Standard using punch cards for all data (as envisaged in the text) the computer input in any one period must be ordered in the following manner:

1. Identification Card (of the type used in the local computer installation).

2. Execute Card.

3. Binary *Program* Cards (approx. 1100 – identical in each period)
   First Card: ★ CHAIN (1, 2)
   Last Card: ★ DATA

4. Master Control Card.

5. *History* (90–100 basic cards, plus 60–70 cards per participating company – automatically produced each period).
   First *and* last cards of history are identical; in addition to some of the data from the Master Control Card they carry a pattern of key-punches in the form of three big V's for easy identification.
   Note. In the first period of an INTOP Standard run history is *created* by the program – no separate history input.

6. Current *Decision* Cards (number of cards depends on number of companies, inter-company transactions and Wonder Card changes).
   Decision Cards may be entered in *any* internal order.

7. Blank Card. (Signal to computer that current period data are now fed in, and to proceed to data for next period(s) if several periods are run consecutively.)

When several periods are to be processed *consecutively* on the machine the following steps are added for *each* period.

8. Master Control Card, with new period number (and appropriate input and output options indicated).

9. New Decision Cards.

10. Blank Card.

Notes. 1. It is crucial that the internal order of program and history cards not be disturbed.
2. The Identification and monitor cards (identical in all periods of a run) are discussed in the Computer Liaison instruction.

c. *Outputs*

The basic computer output consists of a single tape.[9] This tape carries all information for participating teams (PART 1) and the history produced during the period (PART 2). After the printing of the requisite number of copies of both parts of this tape has been concluded,

[9] The punch-card program remains unchanged for use in subsequent periods.

FIG. 38 *Master Control Card*

Item		Decision	Card Column
a.	Identification of Run	☐☐☐☐☐☐	1- 6
b.	Period No.	☐☐☐	7- 9
c.	Number of Companies This Period	☐☐	10-11

d.	History Input Option
	    1 = From Cards
	    2 = From Tape Unit 9 (A5)
	    3 = Already in (consecutive run)
	    4 = Create History (Period 1 only)
		☐	12

e.	History Output Option
	    1 = Punch Cards
	    2 = On Tape Unit 10 (B5)
	    3 = Leave it in (consecutive run)
		☐	13

f.	No. of Copies of First Set of Reports (PART 1)	☐☐	14-15
g.	No. of Copies of Second Set of Reports (PARTS 1 and 2)	☐☐	16-17
h.	Consolidated Output With All Company Reports 0 = No; 1 = Yes	☐	18

COMMENTS

a. Identification in letters and/or numbers only. Must be same each period of a run. Mu~~
   never be left blank.
b. First period may be given any number. From then on periods *must* be numbered i~~
   numerical sequence. (Period No. now *must* be one unit greater than last time.)
c. Number of companies must never be less than 2.
d. Computer will hang up (*a*) if there is *no* number in the box, (*b*) if any other num~~
   ber than 1-4 is used, (*c*) if the wrong option is used.
e. Analogous with *d.*
f-g. Computer Operator's instructions *not* automatically implemented. Check that Operat~~
   is aware of meaning of these signals (cf. Computer Liaison instruction).
f. First set of reports is largely intended for the *company teams.*
g. Second set of reports is intended for *administrators only.* Also includes first set.
h. Mark with a one (1) only when you want all *company teams* to get consolidated ba~~
   ance sheets and income statements. *One* set of these reports for administrative use ~~
   always included in each copy of the first set of reports.

the tape is used for the production of the history to be used as input
the next period. As indicated on the Master Control Card (Fig. 38) the
history should be left in the computer in all (but the last) periods in
case of multi-period processing. In the last period of consecutive processing the administrator will presumably wish to get a history output
which will serve as input next period. The standard history output op-

tion is the first one, i.e., punch cards.[10] When punch-card history has been made and company and administrator outputs have been printed in the requisite number of copies the output tape is no longer needed.

Only three additional items remain on the Master Control Card. They may be commented on most appropriately against the background of Fig. 39, which gives the detailed specification of the edited and printed output. The first of the remaining items on the Master Control Card is a signal to the computer operator to print the requisite number of copies of the first set of reports (PART 1 on Fig. 39).[11] If the number of members on the company teams is no more than half a dozen and multi-part paper is available, the number of copies requested of the first set of reports may well be made equal to the number of members on a team. If saving on printing time and/or cost is of the essence, an advisable minimum is two copies per team.[12]

The next item on the Master Control Card is a signal to the operator to print the requisite number of copies of the second set of reports, which includes both PART 1 and PART 2.[13] Ordinarily two copies of the second set of reports are sufficient for the needs of the administrator, Computer Liaison and *Gazette* editor (if there is such a member of the administrative team). The state variables output of the history part is especially valuable, in that it permits cross-company comparison on any one of the several hundred accounts appearing on the financial statements and ancillary data sheets. With the Market Research 1 and 2 and cross-company consolidated balance sheets and consolidated income statement which always are included in the administrator's output, his record of developments during the period cover virtually the entire range of the simulation. The history output is also of great help if the administrator wishes to supply the teams with additional statistics (via the *Gazette*, in consulting or otherwise). For example, the history output gives complete inventory statistics by company, area, product and model, and it also reports the current number of sales offices by company and area. By simply totaling the respective columns on the history, one may obtain the industry-wide data.

For the record, the history finally also yields a complete register of company decisions during the period on the Operations and Home

---

10   The standard program will produce decimal punch cards, usable at all 7090 and 709 installations. In some installations (such as the University of Chicago) it is possible to use binary punch cards for history. The advantage of the latter is that only a few hundred cards will be required, while decimal card history with a fair number of companies participating generally takes well over a thousand cards.

11   If multi-part paper is being used, the sample computer operator guide included in the Computer Liaison instruction directs the operator to divide the number indicated on the Master Control Card by the number of copies obtainable in each printing on the multi-part paper.

12   As indicated on Fig. 39, PART 1 also contains a few sheets of information intended for the administrator only. Surplus copies of these may simply be discarded.

13   Hence the administrator gets full company output with each copy of the second set of reports. This is convenient, as it enables him to store a record of *all* output of the decision period on a single continuous strip.

FIG. 39   *Computer Output Specifications*

PART 1.

Program Loading Map (may be discarded) ⎫
Identification page
Rejected decision forms of types 1 and 2 (Operations and Home Office), if any
Register of Wonder Card changes
Register of Inter-company and Special Transactions
Company 0   Market Research 1
Company 0   Market Research 2 (*all* computerized items)
Consolidated Balance Sheet for all companies, one copy
Consolidated Income Statement for all companies, one copy ⎭

For administrator only

Company 1   Balance Sheet ⎫
Income Statement
Ancillary Data
Consolidated Balance Sheet (optional)
Consolidated Income Statement (optional)
Market Research 1
Market Research 2 (if ordered by the company) ⎭

For company teams (and administrator)

Company 2   Balance Sheet
Etc. (same for all companies)

PART 2.   (HISTORY)

Parameter names and current values of each parameter in the model (always 2 sheets) ⎫
State variables by name and current value for each company participating (60–120 sheets, depending on number of companies)
Register of company decisions in the current period (6–14 sheets) ⎭

For administrator only

Notes: 1.   "First set of reports" on the Master Control Card refers to PART 1 above. It is intended mainly for the teams. "Second set of reports" on the Master Control Card includes both PART 1 and PART 2. It is intended for the administrator *only*.

2.   A sample of most of PART 1 output is reproduced in Appendices II and III. The "Dictionary" of parameter and state variable names (although not values, for discretionary reasons) constitutes Appendix I.

3.   The register of company decisions reproduces the decisions as recorded by the computer. This will reveal any mistakes in key-punching from the decision forms. The register makes it superfluous to save the punched decision cards themselves for game history purposes. The punched decision cards should, however, be saved until *all periods* in a run have been processed, in case there would ever be a need to rerun one or more periods.

Office Cards.[14] Decisions made in inter-company and special transactions appear on a special register in the administrator's segment of PART 1 of the printed output (see Fig. 39).

The last item on the Master Control Card gives the administrator an option to provide *each* company with cross-company consolidated financial statements of operations during the period indicated on the Control Card. This is often done every fourth period (i.e., "annually"). The implementation of this command is automatic, i.e., independent of the computer operator.

D. *Equipment Requirements, Processing Time*

The INTOP FORTRAN program is written in the FORTRAN II, Version 2, language as adapted to IBM 7090 and 709 computers. The Univac program may be employed with Remington Rand Univac I-III computers.[15] Univac operations are discussed in mimeographed materials obtainable from the Graduate School of Business at Chicago. The first two sections of this chapter are confined to the FORTRAN version. It is likely that the FORTRAN program may be run on a number of smaller IBM computers (such as the 7070 and 7074) as well as on several types of equipment made by other computer manufacturers. Oftentimes this will require special adjustments in the program due to differences in processing routines, memory capacity and so on. Occasionally little change may be required, but the maximal number of companies participating in the run may have to be reduced markedly. (It may be noted that most complex management games permit no more than 4–6 teams in the first place.) The experience of others with equipment other than the 7090, 7094 or 709 will be recorded for the benefit of potential users.

Most 7090 and 709 installations are equipped with an IBM Tape 1401 auxiliary computer. The existence of a 1401 computer is assumed in this chapter. Where such equipment is not at hand operations may require more time and/or modifications in the basic INTOP program. We have learned from personal experience that the much-touted versatility of so-called universal computer languages should not be blindly accepted as a given.

The 1401 is used for card-to-tape converting (and vice versa) as well as for output printing. Input cards are converted to tape for the run on the 7090. All inputs go on a single tape. Ordinarily, all output information is also recorded on a single tape. The 1401 will first print

14 Should any key-punching mistake have been made this will be revealed by comparing this part of the history printout with the original decision forms.

15 The Univac program is written for Univac I, and in a language unique to that computer. According to the Remington Rand Univac Division of Sperry Rand Corporation, the program may be run on Univac II by throwing a switch on that computer which in effect transforms it into a Univac I, and on the Univac III by means of a Univac I simulator. At the time of writing the designers of INTOP have not had personal experience with Univac II and III.

output and then automatically switch to producing punch-card history for use next period.[16] In some installations the history part of the output will be produced on a separate tape, which in turn is mounted on the 1401 for the conversion to punch-card history.[17]

Processing time may be viewed as composed of one basic segment independent of the number of participating teams and another element roughly proportional to the number of companies. The loading of input constitutes the first segment. Approximate time for loading is 2½–3 minutes. Computation operations on the 7090 require less than a minute. The recording of data on the output tape takes approximately 3 minutes for 15–18 teams and perhaps 4 minutes for 25 companies, 2 minutes for 10 and a minute and a half for half a dozen companies or less. Typical total processing time is 5–6½ minutes per decision period. In consecutive processing of several periods loading occurs only once.

Output *printing* time is dependent largely on the number of companies participating. One full set of outputs (PART 1 and PART 2) will require approximately 1¼ minutes of printing time per company.[18] PART 1 alone will ordinarily take about two-thirds as much time to print as PART 1 and PART 2. The fact that printing time is fairly long indicates the importance of using multi-part output paper. Tape-to-card conversion of history also varies somewhat proportionately with number of companies. Experience indicates that some 4 minutes are required to produce punch-card history for 15–18 companies.

E. *Changing Number of Companies. Consecutive Processing of Several Periods. Changing Period Numbers and Identification*

The INTOP program in its FORTRAN version permits the administrator to add new companies at any time during a given run of the simulation, as long as the total number of company teams does not exceed 25.[19] New outputs will be provided simply by increasing the number inserted in the box marked "Number of Companies This Period" on the Master Control Card. It should be observed, however, that no assumption as to the initial characteristics of later-added companies is built into the model. If the administrator wants a new company to have the same initial characteristics as did the others at the beginning of the simulation these characteristics may be given the company by Wonder Cards.[20] The same procedure may be used to give

16 History output option number 1 is used in these cases.

17 History output option number 1 is still used. The use of option number 2 is discussed in the Computer Liaison instruction.

18 This time may be 1½ minutes in periods when cross-company consolidated reports are included with each company output.

19 In special versions of the simulation the number of companies may be a great deal larger; cf. Chapter 6.

20 This is detailed in the Computer Liaison instruction.

the company any other characteristics compatible with the model. In some respects, e.g., as regards plant age, it is even possible (if desired) to give the newcomer characteristics similar to those it would have had had it participated from the beginning of the simulation. Aggregate market potential is automatically and proportionately increased.[21]

Occasionally an administrator may wish to decrease the number of companies participating. This is a simple matter if it is the company (or companies) with the highest number(s) which is to be eliminated. In such a case, the box marked "Number of Companies This Period" on the Master Control Card is simply filled in with the new, lower number. This "wipes out" the companies affected completely, and total market potential is readjusted downwards automatically.[22] Often enough a drop-out company is not the one with the highest number. In these instances it would clearly be inappropriate to use the Master Control Card procedure of restricting the number of companies, as this would eliminate all the teams with higher numbers than the drop-out company as well as that company. As a defunct company will not influence the performance or behavior of the remaining teams in any appreciable manner (assuming eight or more companies) there is actually little *functional* need to eliminate it.[23]

The number of participating company teams is an important dimension of any game simulation. As we have seen, it is in effect a variable subject to the administrator's discretion in INTOP. Time is another important dimension which is a variable in the Chicago simulation. It is possible to vary the impact of the time factor on business decisions by distributing the effect of such decisions as well as of environmental events with time lags varying all the way from zero to half a dozen periods.[24] More relevant in the present context is the fact that it is also possible to "telescope" time by having the teams make decisions for two or more periods in a single decision-making session

---

[21] Should the administrator not wish this increase in total markets to take place he may readjust all or any of the basic sales quantity parameters (PS01) by means of a single Wonder Card. See also *supra*, 92 and 145.

[22] If this is undesirable, the basic sales quantity parameters (PS01) may be adjusted by Wonder Card.

[23] If the administrator wishes to reduce the total market potential he may, of course, do so by Wonder Card.

Note that in the *first* period after a company has dropped out *pro forma* Operations and Home Office Cards indicating Company No. and Period No. only should be included among the inputs to prevent re-implementation of the last set of decisions made by the company.

The Computer Liaison instruction contains suggestions for "cleaning up" the printed outputs of a defunct company. Again, there is little *functional* need for such a cleanup, as long as it has been made clear to participants that the defunct company may simply be disregarded.

[24] Examples of parameters which may be varied to reflect the influence of time: plant construction period, business cycles, effects of advertising, methods improvement, R & D, stock market confidence, the distribution in time of accounts payable and receivable. Cf. section on Time and Change in Chapter 3.

and then process these decisions sequentially in a single computer operation.

Two cases of such "consecutive processing" may be distinguished. The decisions may differ from one period to the next. Going back to Fig. 37, we find how the computer input is arranged in this case. For each new period after the first (which is arranged as usual) Steps 8–10 are to be followed. In discussing history input and output options on the Master Control Card, we indicated that history must be left in the computer in all but the last of the consecutive periods.[25] Occasionally it may be desired that decisions for a given period be re-implemented in *identical* form for one or more additional consecutive periods. Steps 8 and 10 on Fig. 37 must again be followed. If there are no Inter-Company and Special Transactions Cards among the decision inputs in the first of the periods to be processed consecutively, Step 9 may be skipped over as Operations and Home Office Decision Cards are always automatically re-implemented in the absence of new directions. Any Inter-Company and Special Transactions Cards which are to be re-implemented must, however, be duplicated for each period and inserted at Step 9.[26] Complete output for all periods may be printed out after any multi-period processing operation.

Occasionally it is desirable to *change period numbers* in the simulation. This is usually the case, for instance, when the outputs of the last period of a prior run are to serve as the starting-point of a new run. All that should be done to achieve such a change is to take out the first and the last cards of the history (these cards are identical, and are punched with three big V's for easy identification) and substitute in their place cards which are identical in all respects, except that they should carry one less than the number of the first period of the new run instead of the number of the last period of the prior run.[27] If the identification of the new run differs from the old one it should be changed in the same manner.[28] Should the number of companies participating in the new run be different from the prior run this should be taken into account *only* by indicating the new number on the Master Control Card in the first period of the new run. If the number of companies in the new run is to be greater than in the prior one the administrator must decide what the initial characteristics of the additional companies should be. Such characteristics may then be given these companies by Wonder Cards in the first period of the new run.[29]

---

[25] Cf. *supra*, 211f.

[26] For additional observations on telescoped decisions see *supra*, 176f.

[27] Hence if the intended period number is 1 this should be marked on the Master Control Card, while the cards referred to in the text should carry a zero (0).

[28] Period number and/or identification may be changed in the course of a given run in the same fashion.

[29] If no such characteristics are given these companies, their state variables will all be zero.

2. Dictionary and Wonder Cards: Instruments of Change

FLEXIBILITY IS AN outstanding characteristic of the International Operations Simulation. On the basis of the computerized model an administrator may design any number of different simulations to suit his particular purposes. A number of examples of this versatility of the program are illustrated in Chapter 6. Equally important is the fact that at any given time during a given run of INTOP Standard (or of any variation of the model) he is able to change any or every one of the 450 parameters in the program as well as almost every one of the 500-odd state variables expressing the current condition of any given participating company.

This adaptability of the model would be of little practical significance in the absence of machinery to routinize change. The system designed for this purpose permits any person — even one without *any* acquaintance with computers — to carry out whatever changes in program parameters or company accounts deemed desirable.

A. *Dictionary*

To undertake a desired change the administrator needs to know exactly what program parameter(s) or state variable(s) needs adjustment to implement his will. The INTOP Dictionary is designed to supply this information. A copy of the Dictionary with explanatory comments is reproduced as Appendix I. It is essentially a listing of all parameters in the program and all state variables on company financial statements and ancillary data sheets.[30] The layout of the Dictionary is summarized in Fig. 40. The engineering of change will often also require knowledge of the current *values* of program parameters and/or state variables. These values are reported each period on the history output, which is arranged sequentially in the same order as the Dictionary. The same Wonder Card form may be used to change either program parameters or state variables.

B. *Wonder Cards*

The standard Administrator's Wonder Card is reproduced in Fig. 41. This card will change any program parameter or individual company state variable at the beginning of any period. Indeed, as will be seen later a single Wonder Card may often be used to change several parameter or state variable items at once.

It is useful to distinguish six different applications of this versatile tool:

First, to implement major restructuring of the simulation or ex-

---

30 The Dictionary also lists all state variables which cannot be observed by company teams, such as "effective advertising" (VS11).

FIG. 40 *Outline of the INTOP Dictionary*

1. *Program Parameters*

a. Manufacturing Parameters

b. Financial Parameters – Areas

c. Financial Parameters – Home Office

d. Marketing Parameters

e. Marketing Research Cost Parameters

f. Research and Development Parameters

2. *Company State Variables*

a. Marketing State Variables

b. Manufacturing State Variables

c. Research and Development State Variables

d. Financial State Variables – Areas

e. Financial State Variables –Home Office

f. Accounting State Variables

(Indicate subtotals and totals on area income statements and balance sheets and home office income statements and balance sheets, respectively. The Dictionary also lists the accounting state variables constituting the consolidated income statements and balance sheet. These consolidated state variables are not reprinted separately in the history output as their values are indicated on the master cross-company balance sheet and income statement which represent part of the administrator's special output each period.)

3. *Company Decision Variables*

a. Manufacturing Decision Variables

b. Marketing Decision Variables

c. Financial Decision Variables

d. Research and Development and Marketing Research Decision Variables

(This part of the Dictionary is of little interest from the viewpoint of administering change, as changes which the administrator wishes to make in original company decisions may most readily be made directly on the decision forms. Decision variables cannot be changed by Wonder Cards.)

tensive modifications of parameter and/or state variable values before the processing of first period decisions of a given run begins.[31]

Second, to implement parameter changes reflecting environmental developments in the course of a given run.

Third, to introduce probabilistic processes in other than the R & D

---

31 Some of the simulations illustrated in Chapter 6 call for such major changes.

function[32] or, conversely, to make the R & D function deterministic.

Fourth, to make adjustments in individual state variables of one or more companies in the course of a given run.[33]

Fifth, to implement major structural change of individual companies in the course of a run.[34]

Sixth, to implement inter-company transactions. While Wonder Cards may be employed for this purpose, the use of a monitor company in combination with the standard Decision Form 3 for inter-company and special transactions is generally the natural and efficacious way of effectuating inter-company transactions.[35]

The administrator should keep in mind that most changes of the last three types involve adjustments of income statements and balance sheets, in which case a *dual* change is necessary to balance accounts. For instance, an addition to cash may be balanced by an addition to retained earnings.[36]

As suggested by Fig. 41, a Wonder Card may be used for a single change of a single parameter or state variable, multiplying, adding to, subtracting from or replacing the item to be transformed. This is perhaps the most frequent application of these cards. A typical example of such a change involving a program parameter occurs if the administrator wishes to increase the advertising elasticity for product X in Area 3 (but *not* in any other area, nor for product Y).[37] An example of a single change involving a state variable is that of changing the marketing effectiveness index for Company 5 for their sales of Y in Area 2

---

[32] The administrator may, for example, decide that in each period there should be a 5 per cent probability that the manager of any sales office is hired away by competition, retires or dies. By simply multiplying the number of sales offices of a company by 5 and consulting a table of random numbers in the ordinary fashion (checking the last two digits in the number examined) one may determine in an equitable manner what offices and companies, if any, will be affected in any given period. Alternatively one may say that in each period there is a $.95^n$ probability of all sales office managers retaining their jobs, where n stands for the number of sales offices. Thus, no office would be eliminated if $.95^n$ is larger than a uniformly distributed random number between 0 and 1. (Even simpler than using a Wonder Card to implement the result in this particular case is to indicate the closing of the appropriate number of sales offices on the Operations Decision Forms of the companies affected.) An intriguing possibility is that of selecting economic index numbers (af-

fecting all companies equally) or marketing effectiveness factors (affecting individual companies differently) by a similar process.

The R & D function may be made deterministic simply by bringing the parameter PR05 Threshold Probability into play. (E.g., giving PR05 the value of 0.25 means that any company achieving an R & D effectiveness of 25 per cent or more will automatically get a patent.)

[33] Chapter 4 abounds in illustrations of environmental and company behavior which may call for changes of the second and fourth types.

[34] Plant disposal and the cleaning-out of the records of defunct companies illustrate this type of change, cf. Computer Liaison instruction.

[35] Re monitor company, see *supra*, 166.

[36] A great advantage in using Decision Form 3 for the fifth type of change is that the computer will automatically handle the balancing of accounts.

[37] The Dictionary symbol is PS20.

FIG. 4I   *Administrator's Wonder Card*

INTOP DECISION CARD NO. 4

Heading Code: (6 for Parameters; 7 for State Variables)   ☐ 1

Time Period Number   ☐☐ 2 3

Dictionary Symbol (note: applies to all items changed)   ☐☐☐☐ 4 5 6 7

Type of Item Changed   *Initial Item (or single item)*

Grade Index: (0, 1, 2, 3, or 4, use for PM16 & PS06 only)   ☐ 8

Model: (1 is standard; 2 is deluxe)   ☐ 9

Factory: (1, 2 or 3)   ☐ 10

Product: (1 is X; 2 is Y)   ☐ 11

Area: (1 is U.S.; 2 is EEC; 3 is Brazil)   ☐ 12

Company: (1, 2, . . . , 25) *State Variables Only*   ☐☐ 13 14

Multiple for Old Item: (If replacement or addition/subtraction is intended, write 0 for replace and 1 for addition/subtraction in col. 26)

Final Item, If Consecutive Changes

Grade: ☐ 15

Model: ☐ 16

Factory: ☐ 17

Product: ☐ 18

Area: ☐ 19

Company: ☐☐ 20 21   ☐☐ 22   ☐☐ 24   ☐ 26

FIG. 41 *Administrator's Wonder Card* (Continued)

New Items: (In sign box 0 if addition; − if subtraction)

First Item Number   0| [ ] 27   [ ][ ][ ] 29 31 33 35

Second Item Number   0| [ ] 36   [ ][ ][ ] 38 40 42 44

Third Item Number   0| [ ] 45   [ ][ ][ ] 47 49 51 53

Fourth Item Number   0| [ ] 54   [ ][ ][ ] 56 58 60 62

Fifth Item Number   0| [ ] 63   [ ][ ][ ] 65 67 69 71

Sixth Item Number   0| [ ] 72   [ ][ ][ ] 74 76 78 80

Any column left blank will be interpreted as zero. All numbers are integers unless a decimal point is indicated.

Notes: (1) Under *Multiple for Old Item* all items designated in cols. 8-21 are multiplied by the same constant value. (2) Under *New Items,* if only the *first item number* is filled in, the changes will be interpreted as *replacing, adding or subtracting* this single constant value to all items included between the type designations in cols. 8-21. (3) Also under *New Items,* replacement or addition/subtraction of *different* numbers may be performed on a maximum of *six consecutive items* having a common dictionary symbol. Specify the items in cols. 8-21.

This two-page display of the standard Wonder Card is not ideal for reproduction. Sample mimeographed and/or printed Wonder Card forms are included in the INTOP Users Package delivered with the program tape.

(but *not* for any other company, nor in any other area, nor for Company 5 sales of product X).[38]

The Wonder Card also permits several types of *multiple* changes. This is of special importance to save time and effort when the purpose is to restructure the entire simulation or to undertake identical changes in the records of many companies. The principal constraint on multiple change effectuated by a single card is that *the several changes involved must relate only to a single Dictionary symbol* (such as PS15, VA12). A great number of these symbols are common denominators for several parameter or state variable items; the heading "basic sales quantity" in the Dictionary (symbol: PS01), for instance, is common to six parameters determining the market potential per company for each of the two products in each of the three geographical areas. Similarly, the heading "income tax" (symbol: VF15) is common (for any given company) to three income tax accounts, one for each geographical area.

Another limitation on the use of single Wonder Cards to cause multiple change is that while a given card may be used for either multiplication or replacement or addition and subtraction it is not possible to apply either two or all three of these principal modes of change simultaneously on any given card.[39]

A third important constraint on multiple change by a single card relates to *the extent of variation permitted among the contemplated changes*. If multiplication is involved each item (parameter or state variable) to be changed may be changed only by a common multiple, i.e., the relative change in each item will be identical. As indicated by Fig. 41, the multiplier may have up to five digits, i.e., the range of the multiplier is .0001 to 99999.[40]

Replacement and addition (subtraction) are generally used much more frequently than multiplication to institute change. For this reason two optional procedures of making such changes are provided, pertaining to *identical* change of a number of items and to *differential* change of up to six items, respectively. Identical change by replacement or addition (subtraction) is quite analogous to the only type of change possible with multiplication. As in the case of multiplication the aggregate number of identical changes achievable with a single Wonder

[38] The Dictionary symbol is VS13.

[39] Addition and subtraction may be used concomitantly.

[40] The decimal point, when used, requires one column. By repeated multiplication on more than one Wonder Card, the items affected may be multiplied by even smaller or greater numbers, until the maximal number of digits printed on the output sheets or permitted in various parts of the program itself becomes the ultimate constraint. For instance, program parameters may not exceed 9,999,999.

Card may be quite considerable; they could be many hundred when state variables are involved.[41]

Differential change by replacement or addition (subtraction) may be undertaken on a maximum of *six consecutive items* embraced by a common Dictionary symbol (whether parameter or state variable items). The fact that up to six items may be changed when the Dictionary symbol involves program parameters in effect means that no more than one card is ever needed to change *all* parameters with a common symbol by replacement or addition (subtraction).[42] When more than three companies participate in a run of the simulation no game-wide adjustment of a state variable involving more than one account for each company is possible by a single card.[43] However, at every turn the administrator may use several cards; any differential change which can be made on one card can also be implemented by filling in several cards, each making only a single change of a single parameter or state variable item. Replacement and addition (subtraction) may involve up to eight-digit integral numbers (99,999,999) and up to seven-digit decimal numbers (.0000001).[44] This range includes virtually all numbers which may be changed most sensibly by replacement or addition (subtraction).[45]

Differential change involves *consecutive* items. The definition of "consecutive" in any given situation is specified by the order of processing of Wonder Card items in the computer program. In a nutshell, processing is determined by the following sequence (abbreviations as used in the Dictionary):

Company	(C)
Area	(A)
Product	(P)
Factory	(F)
Model	(M)

---

41   To take an admittedly extreme example: assuming that the administrator wished to readjust (or replace) the state variable "previous production amount" (symbol: VM07) with an identical amount for all of 25 companies in all 3 areas, and for all 3 factories for each of the 2 products and the 2 models of each of these products, the total of these 900 changes could be implemented by a single Wonder Card.

42   The maximum variation embraced by any parameter symbol is ordinarily defined by the six product-area combinations; see, e.g., PM01, PS01. Sole exception: grade differentials for manufacturing and marketing (PM16, PS06), which represent 10 items each and hence require two cards.

43   If a state variable involves only one account, such as "common stock" (VF25) a differential game-wide change may be made by a single card if the number of companies does not exceed six. If the number of teams is greater, additional cards must be used.

44   Note again that the decimal point involves the use of one column. No program parameter may exceed 9,999,999.

45   The only numbers beyond this range in the entire INTOP Standard framework are certain coefficients in the manufacturing cost function (PM04, PM06 and PM08) and the "inventory square term" (PS32). If the administrator wishes to change these parameters multiplication should be used; cf. Computer Liaison instruction.

We may observe that this sequence is identical with that obtained by reading from the bottom towards the top of the items listed on the Wonder Card under the heading "Type of Item Changed."[46] When more than a single change of a single type is to be made, then, the order of processing means that the computer will always search in this particular sequence for the first sign of variation appearing on the Wonder Card (between the "Initial Item" and the "Final Item" designations) and give first priority to the changes indicated by that variation. Assume, for example, that the administrator wishes to change the number of regional sales offices (VS14) of Companies 7, 8 and 9 in Areas 1 and 2. The logic of processing follows:[47]

Co. 7   Area 1
Co. 8   Area 1
Co. 9   Area 1
Co. 7   Area 2
Co. 8   Area 2
Co. 9   Area 2

Taking a similar example relating to parameter change, let us assume that the administrator wishes to change by different amounts the economic index (PS24) for all product markets in all areas. Using the same logic, the processing order is clear:[48]

Area 1   Product X
Area 2   Product X
Area 3   Product X
Area 1   Product Y
Area 2   Product Y
Area 3   Product Y

The master processing logic is indicated by Fig. 42, which indicates the full sequence of an imaginary set of changes running the gamut of the Wonder Card program.[49] It should be observed that whenever the Dictionary indicates that a program or state variable symbol does not include all of the subscripts Company, Area, Product, Factory and Model the logic simply excludes the items concerned, but otherwise remains the same. Thus, for example, "maximum producible grade" (VR01) varies only by company and product, and a Wonder Card involving VR01 is processed in that order.

46   The item "Grade Index" is a characteristic of only two program parameters (PM16 and PS06) and of no state variables. For this reason it is disregarded in the text.

47   These consecutive changes would be specified as follows on the card: a "1" in col. 12, a "7" in col. 14, a "2" in col. 19 and a "9" in col. 21.

Note that if the same changes are to be made in Areas 1 and 3 (but not Area 2) two cards must be used, as Area 2 precedes Area 3 in consecutive processing.

48   These consecutive changes would be specified as follows on the card: a "1" in col. 11, a "1" in col. 12, a "2" in col. 18 and a "3" in col. 19.

49   Thus several hundred changes would be involved, whereas in reality the limit is *six consecutive changes* anywhere within the scheme when *differential* change is involved.

FIG. 42 *Wonder Card Processing Logic*

| Co. | 1 | Area 1 | Product 1 | Factory 1 | Model 1 |
| Co. | 2 | Area 1 | Product 1 | Factory 1 | Model 1 |

.
.

| Co. 25 | Area 1 | Product 1 | Factory 1 | Model 1 |
| Co. 1 | Area 2 | Product 1 | Factory 1 | Model 1 |

.
.

| Co. 25 | Area 2 | Product 1 | Factory 1 | Model 1 |
| Co. 1 | Area 3 | Product 1 | Factory 1 | Model 1 |

.
.

| Co. 25 | Area 3 | Product 1 | Factory 1 | Model 1 |
| Co. 1 | Area 1 | Product 2 | Factory 1 | Model 1 |

.
.

| Co. 25 | Area 1 | Product 2 | Factory 1 | Model 1 |
| Co. 1 | Area 2 | Product 2 | Factory 1 | Model 1 |

.
.

| Co. 25 | Area 2 | Product 2 | Factory 1 | Model 1 |
| Co. 1 | Area 3 | Product 2 | Factory 1 | Model 1 |

.
.

| Co. 25 | Area 3 | Product 2 | Factory 1 | Model 1 |
| Co. 1 | Area 1 | Product 1 | Factory 2 | Model 1 |

.
.

| Co. 25 | Area 1 | Product 1 | Factory 2 | Model 1 |
| Co. 1 | Area 2 | Product 1 | Factory 2 | Model 1 |

.
.

| Co. 25 | Area 2 | Product 1 | Factory 2 | Model 1 |
| Co. 1 | Area 3 | Product 1 | Factory 2 | Model 1 |

.
.

| Co. 25 | Area 3 | Product 1 | Factory 2 | Model 1 |
| Co. 1 | Area 1 | Product 2 | Factory 2 | Model 1 |

.
.

| Co. 25 | Area 1 | Product 2 | Factory 2 | Model 1 |
| Co. 1 | Area 2 | Product 2 | Factory 2 | Model 1 |

.
.

| Co. 25 | Area 2 | Product 2 | Factory 2 | Model 1 |
| Co. 1 | Area 3 | Product 2 | Factory 2 | Model 1 |

.
.

| Co. 25 | Area 3 | Product 2 | Factory 2 | Model 1 |

FIG. 42 *Wonder Card Processing Logic* (Continued)

Co. 1	Area 1	Product 1	Factory 3	Model 1

⋮

Co. 25	Area 1	Product 1	Factory 3	Model 1
Co. 1	Area 2	Product 1	Factory 3	Model 1

⋮

Co. 25	Area 2	Product 1	Factory 3	Model 1
Co. 1	Area 3	Product 1	Factory 3	Model 1

⋮

Co. 25	Area 3	Product 1	Factory 3	Model 1
Co. 1	Area 1	Product 2	Factory 3	Model 1

⋮

Co. 25	Area 1	Product 2	Factory 3	Model 1
Co. 1	Area 2	Product 2	Factory 3	Model 1

⋮

Co. 25	Area 2	Product 2	Factory 3	Model 1
Co. 1	Area 3	Product 2	Factory 3	Model 1

⋮

Co. 25	Area 3	Product 2	Factory 3	Model 1
Co. 1	Area 1	Product 1	Factory 1	Model 2

etc., etc.

Note that while program parameters *never* vary by company, state variables *always* do.

While "Grade Index" appears as a type of item on the Wonder Card it is not included in Fig. 42, as this item is related only to two parameters, i.e., PM16 and PS06. The processing logic applies in these cases as well, with grade number the last item in the processing sequence.

A capsule summary of our discussion of the uses of Wonder Cards may be written in algebraic form. Any change in a Dictionary symbol (program parameter or state variable) involves an evaluation of this basic formula:

$$N_t = C_1 \ (N_{t-1}) + C_2$$

Here N_t is the new number and N_{t-1} is the original number. C_1 and C_2 are numbers provided by the administrator to institute the transformation of N_{t-1} to N_t. Of these, C_1 is involved in *all* changes: it is the multiplier when changing by multiplication; it is set to one (1) in addition (subtraction); and it is set to zero (0) when N_t is to be created by the replacement of N_{t-1} by another number (i.e., by C_2).[50] When C_2 is 0 or a constant number other than 0 *identical* changes may be made to any number of consecutive items having a common Dictionary symbol by multiplication, replacement or addition (subtraction).[51] A set of items having a common Dictionary symbol may be changed by adding and subtracting to them or replacing them with different C_2 values.[52] The items in the set must be consecutive and must not exceed six in number.

Past experience indicates that a few Dictionary symbols are changed quite often, while the great majority are manipulated only occasionally. The most commonly changed program parameters in INTOP Standard runs are the economic indices registering business cycle developments; the most frequently changed state variables generally are the area cash (and, for balance, retained earnings) accounts of individual companies. For the convenience of administrators who make frequent use of the simulation, special variants of the Wonder Cards have been designed which drastically simplify the making of the latter two types of changes. The special cards are described in the Computer Liaison instruction. Economic indices may be varied quite simply by using the regular card.[53] The description of the standard Wonder Card given in this section has been quite elaborate in the interest of INTOP administrators and the designers of other simulations alike. The Computer Liaison instruction also contains some further observations and illustrations.

As indicated in Fig. 39[54] the administrator will receive in each period of a run a complete register of any Wonder Card changes of program parameters or state variables which he may have instituted during the period. This register is valuable both for purposes of verification[55] and for the historical record of the run of the simulation in which the changes were made.

---

[50] As indicated by Fig. 41, C_1 is represented by columns 22-26 in multiplication, and by column 26 in addition (subtraction) or replacement.

[51] When C_2 is a constant number other than 0 columns 27-35 on the Card are used. C_2 is 0 only in multiplication.

[52] When more than one C_2 value is involved, these values are written in the spaces labeled "Second Item Number" (cols. 36-44), "Third Item Number" (cols. 45-53), etc.

[53] Cf. *supra*, 226 and Computer Liaison instruction.

[54] Cf. *supra*, 214.

[55] Occasionally a mistake may be made in filling out a particular Wonder Card or in the transfer of the data thereon to a corresponding punch card. Whenever such a mistake makes the card non-acceptable the administrator will be duly informed by a "Reject" sign on the output, and the computer will also type out a copy of the rejected card to facilitate correction in the subsequent period. It is a good idea always to check the Wonder Card register, as mistakes may be made which are not objectionable to the program. Hence they will be implemented and may remain undetected in the absence of such examination of the output. Should the administrator (or his assistant) fail to observe a mistake, participating teams are usually quick to draw it to his attention.

3. Parameter Choice and Change

A. *Introduction*

An outstanding characteristic of the International Operations Simulation is its flexibility. Literally hundreds of different games may be structured around the basic model. Even if the administrator does not wish to stray beyond the *Player's Manual* (with or without a mimeographed sheet of amendments) a broad range of alternate values for most parameters in the model may be adopted. If he is interested in a basically different type of simulation than that described in the *Player's Manual* (and Chapter 2 above) — such as many of the simulations outlined in Chapter 6 — it may be appropriate to assign to many parameters entirely different sets of values than customarily used and, indeed, to eliminate some parameters entirely. Whatever his intentions, the administrator is *obliged* to abide only by a limited number of constraints imposed by the basic model itself, such as the maximum number of areas, products and factors (cf. Subsection B below). The remaining 450 parameters are at the command of the administrator.

The purpose in this section is to indicate how this model may be manipulated, to outline a process of selecting and changing parameters to create a viable competitive environment for any purpose the administrator may have in mind. At the same time it is hoped that the discussion will serve as a stimulus to the designers of other models, both in their own model-building and in their possible effort to explain to others whatever opportunities for variation their models may possess. We are presenting a way of reasoning and some guideposts useful to anyone wishing to gain mastery of a maze of possible parameter values and relationships. Once the reader has a basic notion of the simulation he would like to develop, this guide will allow him to cut his own path. The administrator who is interested only in making adjustments in isolated parameters in a run of INTOP Standard should also find this guide useful. He must constantly keep in mind, however, that the elements of the model are all interdependent. Hence, extreme change of an isolated parameter even if within the range suggested as permissible may have undesirable side-effects unless the various interrelationships of that parameter with other parts of the model have been duly considered.

The fundamental problem facing the model-builder is to transform all qualitative statements into precise logical and quantitative values. All description and instruction must eventually become mathematical. Thus, a qualitative statement like "product X sales should be relatively sensitive to price" must be transformed into the numerical values of price elasticities and cross-elasticities. Other statements, of course, like the depreciation rate are already in numerical form.

Our procedure rests on two basic assumptions: first, that a principal objective of the average company participating in the simulation is to conduct a viable and organically growing operation while making a reasonable return on investment; and secondly, that the administrator wishes to provide an operating environment in which it is indeed possible for the typical participating company to achieve such an objective. These assumptions allow us to use the relationships among parameters and state variables which are presented in the first part of Chapter 3.

An analogy may be helpful in understanding the overall process. Certain assumptions (viability of the average firm) and logical identities (income statement and balance sheet equalities) impose given relations among the state variables. Other considerations (certainly personal taste) fix the values of many. The task is to choose the remaining variables so that all relationships are satisfied. Problems will arise if there are too many or too few variables and parameters which have been given fixed values. The problem is analogous to that of a mathematical construct: a solution to a system of two linear equations in five variables requires that three variables be chosen. In general, if more than three variables are chosen there is no solution; if fewer than three variables are fixed there is no unique solution.

This section presents a way of reasoning about parameter selection which can be used by the non-mathematically oriented administrator, as well as by those who are adept in equation manipulation. A few terms frequently used may need a word of explanation. For want of a better phrase the expression *decision rule* (abbreviated DR) is used to denote opportunities for reconsideration of parameter values in the computer program. The forty decision rules will be arranged sequentially somewhat in order of relative importance as conceived by the model designers. Others may find that for their purposes the relative significance of various elements is quite different. While this might change the order in which some parts of the presentation might be read most suitably, the basic approach should remain the same. It is especially important that the interdependence of key parameters in various parts of the simulation be observed. The discussion of decision rules, added to the treatment in Chapter 3, serves to point up such linkages. In addition, each decision rule indicates either a *range* of permissible parameter values or, if that range is extremely broad, the range of values believed most applicable when variations on INTOP Standard compatible with the *Player's Manual* (rather than far-reaching redesign) are contemplated.[56] For convenience the Dictionary location of the parameter affected is restated wherever applicable, although this information may also be derived by going directly to the INTOP Dictionary in Appendix I.

The presentation of this general approach to parameter choice and change will take the reader through eight major steps: (1) to isolate the parameters having the greatest influence on the economy and

56 Maximal limits of discretion are indicated simply by the word "Range" in front of the numbers specifying the limits. Where the variation possible is of very broad scope, the phrase "Standard Range" is used in front of numbers indicating suitable limits within the framework of the *Player's Manual*.

the firm and to determine the area and product variations between them (pp. 232-39); (2) to consider the constraints inherent in the model (pp. 240-43); (3) to quantify such basic sizing parameters as price, quantity, revenue, initial capital and plant costs (pp. 243-53); (4) to determine the cost and profit margins for the firm by means of income statement summary accounts (pp. 253-54); (5) to quantify the specific operating expenses (pp. 254-55); (6) to derive experimentally or from the INTOP equations in Chapter 3 the remaining parameters which have not already been determined by decision rules (pp. 256-59); (7) to consider a hypothetical balance sheet in order to quantify plant, Accounts Receivable, Accounts Payable and working capital requirements (pp. 259-66); and (8) to set the values of various safety valves which will keep the model from "blowing up" or behave dysfunctionally (pp. 266-69).

Concrete illustration is highly desirable in the exposition of such an approach. As much redesign of the simulation will start out from the INTOP Standard version — that is, the parameter values in the program as delivered — we shall use it for purposes of illustration. In doing so we can be quite specific for seven out of the eight steps in the process, without furnishing participants in standard runs of the simulation undue guidance. Discretionary considerations prompt more sketchy illustration in the discussion of the sixth step in Subsection C. The chapter concludes with a brief discussion of some of the more drastic shortcuts which simplify features and eliminate parameters (as contemplated in some of the simulations outlined in Chapter 6) and of the control parameters or safety valves which prevent the model from deviating from a realistic course when extreme decisions occur. This section should be of particular interest to administrators interested in designing simulations different in kind rather than degree from that described in the *Player's Manual* but still based on the INTOP model. The question of safety valves is also (or at least should be) of concern to every game designer.

B. *The Framework of Parameter Selection*

1] AREA AND PRODUCT VARIATIONS

The parameters in the model are too numerous to be dealt with simultaneously. We must pick the most important ones first and subsequently expand our analysis to include the other parameters. In compiling the list of crucial parameters, a major aim should presumably be to obtain a balanced representation from the functional areas, marketing, production and finance, and to include all features to be emphasized in the simulation.

Our choice for INTOP Standard is the list of thirty parameters (numbered V1, V2, . . . , V30 for this discussion) in the tables in Figs. 43 and 44. An administrator may increase or decrease this list according to his own taste. The approach pursued here remains the same regardless of the number of parameters singled out for special attention.

Each of the crucial parameters has six *dimensions*, one each for the three operating areas and the two products. The administrator's task is to estimate the variations among the dimensions as he considers each crucial parameter independently. But it is easier, as a prelude to deriving the actual numbers, to assign relative weights among the dimensions. This is the purpose of the tables in Figs. 43 and 44. As a practical device a hypothetical scale from one to nine is used to give some quantification to the technique. In this system the range 1 to 3 indicates low values for parameters concerned; 4 to 6 moderate values; and 7 to 9 high values. A zero (0) means that the variable is not used. A dash (−) means that only area variations are possible and, hence, that X and Y products have identical parameters. Whenever the same relative value is used across all columns (e.g., V22), actual parameter numbers in each dimension are equal.

Given the scale, it was a fairly simple matter to fill in the tables for our example in tune with the background information given in the *Player's Manual* (and in Chapter 2 above, pp. 62ff) and an overall commitment to assign certain consistent characteristics to the areas and the products. An important consideration, of course, was to inject considerable international and product differentiation while still maintaining a consistent and believable representation of these dimensions.

The method of determining the relative values of the crucial parameters consists of the following steps:

(1) The crucial parameters are grouped by their approximate functional areas as shown in Fig. 43. The marketing parameters are V1-V11, the manufacturing parameters V12-V22, and the financial parameters V23-V30.

(2) The scale devised for the purpose was then used to order the values within the six dimensions.

(3) Figure 44 was constructed from Fig. 43 by regrouping the crucial parameters according to their relative values. Hence the organization of the table is governed by the aforementioned scale of low, moderate and high values. This allows us to compare what parameters we have emphasized and de-emphasized in any of the six dimensions. A profile of each dimension emerges, a set of characteristics which will define each competitive environment. In Fig. 44 we have given only one example (product Y in the U.S.) of the six profiles that may be made. The others may be constructed in the same straightforward manner, but different parameters, of course, will fall into the low, moderate and high range.

(4) Figure 43 of inter-dimensional variation and Fig. 44 of intra-dimensional variation represent two points of view in approaching the problem of sizing parameters. In the process of arriving at a final set of values, the administrator will wish to balance and compromise his conceptions of area and product variation with his conceptions of a

FIG. 43 *Sample Worksheet for Area and Product Variations, by Function*

(USING INTOP STANDARD FOR PURPOSE OF ILLUSTRATION)

Parameters	U.S. X	EEC X	Brazil X	U.S. Y	EEC Y	Brazil Y	Dictionary Symbol
Marketing Parameters							
(V1) Base Quantity in Consumer Sales Function	6	4	2	9	7	3	PS01
(V2) Base Price in Consumer Sales Function	1	2	3	6	7	8	PS02
(V3) Base Advertising Amount in Consumer Sales Function	4	3	2	8	6	4	PS03
(V4) Price Elasticity – Industry, Both Models	3	5	7	2	3	5	PS07
(V5) Grade Elasticity – Industry, Both Models	3	5	7	2	3	5	PS11
(V6) Redistribution Elasticity – Industry, Both Models	3	5	7	2	3	5	PS15
(V7) Advertising Elasticity – Industry, Both Models	4	6	3	6	2	4	PS19
(V8) Other Product Price Elasticity – Firm, Both Models (Y affects X)	6	4	1	–	–	–	PS21
Other Product Price Elasticity – (X affects Y)	–	–	–	4	3	2	PS21
(V9) Commercial & Administrative Captive Cost/Unit	3	5	5	6	6	8	PS25
C & A: Agency, Cost/Unit Combined	3	4	4	4	5	7	PS26
C & A: Agency, Cost/Unit Isolated	3	5	6	7	7	9	PS27
(V10) Inventory: Cost Per Unit	1	2	3	4	5	6	PS31
(V11) Shipping: From Area 1	1	3	4	2	6	9	PS33
Shipping: From Area 2	3	1	4	6	2	9	PS34
Shipping: From Area 3	4	4	1	9	9	2	PS35
Manufacturing Parameters							
(V12) Minimum Cost Per Unit	1	2	3	7	6	8	PM03
(V13) Optimum Production Level – One Model	5	3	1	8	6	2	PM05
(V14) Optimum Production Level – Both Models	5	3	1	8	6	2	PM07
(V15) Area Effect for Grade Cost Differentials*	0	0	0	0	0	0	PM11

FIG. 43 *Sample Worksheet for Area and Product Variations, by Function* (Continued)

(USING INTOP STANDARD FOR PURPOSE OF ILLUSTRATION)

Parameters	U.S. X	EEC X	Brazil X	U.S. Y	EEC Y	Brazil Y	Dictionary Symbol
(V16) Obsolescence Cost Rate	4	4	4	2	2	2	PM12
(V17) Factory Construction Time	2	2	2	2	2	2	PM13
(V18) Methods Improvement:							
Max. Cost Reduction Limit	7	6	4	5	6	3	PM14
Optimal Methods Expense	4	2	1	6	5	3	
(V19) Factory Acquisition Cost	5	4	2	8	7	2	PM17
(V20) Maximal Factory Capacity	5	4	2	9	7	2	PM18
(V21) Fixed Cost for Factories	6	4	2	8	6	2	PM19
Fixed Cost Per Factory (If Inventoried)	0	0	0	0	0	0	PM01
(V22) Depreciation Rate	6	6	6	6	6	6	PM20
Financial Parameters†							
(V23) Capital Transfer Tax — Area To Home	0	0	0	—	—	—	PF01
Capital Transfer Tax — Home To Area	0	0	0	—	—	—	PF14
(V24) Fraction of A/R 2 Added to A/R 1	0	7	6	—	—	—	PF02
Fraction of A/R 1 Added to Cash	4	5	3	—	—	—	PF03
(V25) Fraction of A/P 2 Added to A/P 1	0	7	6	—	—	—	PF04
Fraction of A/P 1 Subtracted From Cash	4	5	3	—	—	—	PF05
(V26) Savings Interest Rate	3	3	5	—	—	—	PF06
(V27) Borrowing Interest Rate	3	4	5	—	—	—	PF07
(V28) Supplier Credit Interest Rate Below Switch-over Amount	6	6	6	—	—	—	PF08
Supplier Credit Switch-over Amount	7	7	4	—	—	—	PF09
Supplier Credit Interest Rate Above Switch-over Amount	9	9	9	—	—	—	PF10
(V29) Income Tax Rate	8	7	4	—	—	—	PF11
(V30) Fraction of Losses Available As Tax Credits	5	3	0	—	—	—	PF12

*A zero means that a parameter is not used in INTOP Standard.
†Area financial parameters apply irrespective of products (only area variations are possible).

FIG. 44 *Worksheet for Area and Product Profiles,*
Illustration: Product Y in Area 1 (The United States)

	Y in U.S.	Dictionary Symbol
I. *Major Variables in the High Range (7–9)*		
V 1) Base Quantity in Consumer Sales Function	9	PS01
V11) Shipping: From Area 3	9	PS35
V20) Maximal Factory Capacity	9	PM18
V28) Supplier Credit Interest Rate Above Switch-over Amount	9	PF10
V 3) Base Advertising Amount in Consumer Sales	8	PS03
V13) Optimum Production Level – One Model	8	PM05
V14) Optimum Production Level – Both Models	8	PM07
V19) Factory Acquisition Cost	8	PM17
V21) Fixed Cost for Factories	8	PM19
V29) Income Tax Rate	8	PF11
V 9) Commercial & Administrative: Agency, Cost/Unit Isolated	7	PS27
V12) Minimum Cost Per Unit	7	PM03
V28) Supplier Credit Switch-over Amount	7	PF09
II. *Major Variables in the Moderate Range (4–6)*		
V 2) Base Price in Consumer Sales Function	6	PS02
V 7) Advertising Elasticity – Industry, Both Models	6	PS19
V 9) Commercial & Administrative: Captive, Cost/Unit	6	PS25
V11) Shipping: From Area 2	6	PS34
V18) Optimal Methods Expense	6	
V22) Depreciation Rate	6	PM20
V28) Supplier Credit Interest Rate Below Switch-over	6	PF08
V18) Methods Improvement: Maximum Cost Reduction	5	PM14
V30) Fraction of Losses Available As Tax Credits	5	PF12

FIG. 44 *Worksheet for Area and Product Profiles,*
Illustration: Product Y in Area 1 (The United States)
(*Continued*)

	Y in U.S.	Dictionary Symbol
V 8) Other Product Price Elasticity — Firm, Both Models (X affects Y)	4	PS21
V 9) C & A: Agency, Cost/Unit Combined	4	PS26
V10) Inventory: Cost Per Unit	4	PS31
V24) Fraction of A/R 1 Added To Cash	4	PF03
V25) Fraction of A/P 1 Subtracted From Cash	4	PF05
III. *Major Variables in the Low Range (1–3)*		
V26) Savings Interest Rate	3	PF06
V27) Borrowing Interest Rate	3	PF07
V 4) Price Elasticity — Industry, Both Models	2	PS07
V 5) Grade Elasticity — Industry, Both Models	2	PS11
V 6) Redistribution Elasticity — Industry, Both Models	2	PS15
V11) Shipping: From Area 1 (i.e., intra-area)	2	PS33
V16) Obsolescence Cost Rate	2	PM12
V17) Factory Construction Time	2	PM13
IV. *Major Variables Not Used in INTOP Standard**		
V15) Area Effect for Grade Cost Differentials	0	PM11
V21) Fixed Cost Per Factory (If Inventoried)	0	PM01
V23) Capital Transfer Tax — Area To Home	0	PF01
V23) Capital Transfer Tax — Home To Area	0	PF14
V24) Fraction of A/R 2 Added to A/R 1	0	PF02
V25) Fraction of A/P 2 Added to A/P 1	0	PF04

*Reasons for the inclusion of these variables among those considered crucial are set forth in the text on p. 239.

dimension's consistency. Worksheets of the type illustrated by the tables in Figs. 43 and 44 at once point up the great number of relationships possible between crucial parameters and assist the administrator in organizing them.

When we consider the inter-dimension variation in INTOP Standard as represented by Fig. 43, two types of relations are predominant. On one hand there are some parameters which emphasize international variation – as contrasted to product differentiation – such as the Base Sales Quantity (V1), the Price, Grade and Redistribution Elasticities (V4, V5 and V6), the Factory Acquisition Costs (V19) and the Fixed Factory Costs (V21). On the other hand some parameters stress product differentiation more than international variation: the Base Price (V2), the Base Advertising Expense (V3), the Commercial and Administrative Costs (V9) and the Minimum Production Costs (V12). Some parameters like Inventory Costs (V10) and Shipping Costs (V11) are hybrids which stress both these relationships. A few, like the Depreciation Rate (V22) have no variation at all. Again, it should be emphasized that these relationships are subject to the discretion of the administrator.

In a similar way we can look at the direction of flow from high to low (or vice versa) between the six dimensions. On most parameters the U.S., EEC, and Brazil are ranked in this order. Generally Y products have greater value than X products in the same area. These two relations form a general pattern underlying the selection of the relative values in Fig. 43.

A different picture is presented by Fig. 44. When prepared for each dimension such profiles will assist materially in determining what each competitive environment should look like. Taking our example of Y in the U.S., we can describe the profile which results from the high, moderate and low groupings of the crucial parameters as well as some pertinent eliminations from the list.

(I) The product rates high in consumer demand (V1) and requires large expense on advertising if that is to be effective (V3). While its price is fairly moderate (V2), it is costly to produce (V12) and distribute (V9). Although plant costs (V19) are the highest in the INTOP world, capacity limitations (V20) and optimal production levels (V13, V14) are also the most liberal. Fixed costs (V21) are emphasized relative to the variable cost element. The costs of emergency supplier credit (V28) are rather steep (although not nearly as steep as in Brazil), and as one would expect, so is the tax rate (V29).

(II) A more moderate effect is present for the variables of advertising elasticity (V7) and inter-product price elasticity (V8). In manufacturing, both the gain from methods improvement expense (V18) and the depreciation rate on plants (V22) have a significant influence. In line with one's expectation the costs for captive and combined distribution (V9) are lower than unit agency costs. A generous tax loss provision (V30) eases the effect of the burdensome tax rate. Finally, unit inventory costs (V10) are also in the moderate category.

(III) Relative to other products and areas in the INTOP simulation, the elasticities of price (V4), grades (V5) and redistribution (V6) are low. Further, in such a developed economy factory construction time (V17) is short − in spite of high capacity ratings − while the plant obsolescence rate for Y (V16) is relatively low. Interest rates (V26 and V27) tend to be lower in this advanced economy than elsewhere. All intra-area shipping costs (V11) are small in comparison to global shipping rates.

(IV) A few parameters, while potentially significant, are eliminated from consideration here. Since the option for direct cost accounting was chosen, the fixed cost parameter (V21) in the manufacturing function is set to zero. The manufacturing grade cost differential (V15) generally is not used in INTOP Standard, although it could be an important feature in other simulations. Because the United States is a highly developed financial area, only a one-quarter credit lag is available on accounts receivable and payable. The A/R 2 and the A/P 2 steppages (V24, V25) are therefore bypassed. The capital transfer tax (V23) is usually introduced during the simulation and, thus, has not been given a value.

In principle, the inter-dimensional discussion thus accounted for may be extended to a comparison between Liechtenstein (Home Office) on one hand and the operating areas on the other, insofar as parameters are common. In INTOP Standard this relationship is governed by the notion that overall financial management is generally a centralized corporate function in diversified and otherwise decentralized concerns. Operating functions in Liechtenstein are mainly restricted to finance and research and development. The latter function as well as certain parts of financial management (e.g., dividend policy) are uniquely the prerogative of the Home Office. As regards those aspects of financial management which are common both to the Home Office and the operating areas, the Home Office generally enjoys certain advantages due to scale and specialization. Thus we find that the Liechtenstein savings interest rate (V26) is higher than in the areas, as is the supplier credit switch-over amount (V28). The Liechtenstein corporate tax (V29) is low, and carry-over provisions (V30) are extremely liberal (100 per cent) to encourage companies specializing in financial and/or R & D operations and generally to stimulate patent license arrangements and the transfer to the Home Office of surplus funds from the areas.[57] Supplier credit rates are also lower than elsewhere.

[57] Typically, most companies will usually run a deficit at the Home Office, which is essentially a corporate overhead organization for companies also engaged in area operations.

2]   CONSTRAINTS IMPOSED BY THE MODEL AND THE
     DECISION FORMS

Certain constraints relevant to parameter selection are inherent in the design of the INTOP model and the structure of the decision forms commonly (although not necessarily) used. These constraints set upper limits on some parameters and consequently define a range of administrator discretion. They are vital determinants for the ultimate quantification of parameters, because they constitute the frame of reference within which specific parameter choices will be made. In other simulations there will be other such overall constraints — usually of a more confining nature than here. Clearly, these broad limiting factors are a joint concern of administrators and designers of games.

The discussion will make use of the concepts of *decision rule* and *range* as defined earlier.[58]

DR 1:   *Choose the number of companies participating in the simulation (including a monitoring company, if desired).*

Range: 2–25 (for Univac operation 2–15)
                        The administrator signifies on the Master Control Card[59] the number of companies participating in a given period of a given run.

In educational play, the desirable number of members on each company team should determine the number of participating companies rather than vice versa.[60] The unusually great number of companies permitted by the INTOP model allows full application of this rule.

DR 2:   *Choose the combination of area and product dimensions desired.*

Standard Range: 1, 2 or 3 areas; 1 or 2 products·
                        No specific parameter controls this decision rule, although the range does restate an overall constraint. If the administrator wants to restrict any dimension(s) it is sufficient to ignore the area(s) or product(s) on the decision forms. (Alternatively, new decision forms blocking out an area or product may easily be prepared.) Chapter 6 illustrates how the number of products may be increased beyond the usual two.

While our example has presumed a full complement of three areas and two products, the administrator can vary conditions of their

58   Cf. *supra*, 231.
59   Cf. *supra*, 212.
60   Cf. *supra*, 19f, 146.

use. Given that parameters exist for all dimensions, it is easy to begin the simulation with only two areas and one product and then sometime during play expand to three areas and two products. In past runs at Chicago we have sometimes begun with two products in the U.S. and the EEC and opened up Brazil to vacuum cleaners and transistor radios only in the fourth quarter. Another intriguing possibility is to eliminate an area or product during play, perhaps as the result of nationalization in one of the areas.

DR 3:   *Choose the maximum number of product improvements (grades) that each product may attain.*

Range: 0–4 for either X or Y.
                      No specific parameter controls this decision rule, although the range does restate an overall constraint. The effect of each grade on sales (PS06) and manufacturing cost (PM16) is subject to administrative control.

Since product improvements are only attainable through research and development in the Home Office, the elimination of this feature means that the grades will always be zero.[61] If it is desired to limit the maximum number of grades of either product to less than four, the most efficient method is simply to inform participants of the highest grade contemplated. If desired, it is also an easy matter to set the probability of attaining an improvement (VR04) to zero after a company has reached the limit.[62] Again, the option is available to hold off introducing one or several of the higher grades until late in the play. If the administrator wishes to eliminate product improvements entirely he may simply set Research Probability (PR02) at zero or miminal R & D expenditure (PR03) at a high value.

DR 4:   *Choose the maximum number of factories which could be constructed per product and area by each company.*

Range: 0–3 factories

Dictionary Location: VM01

A typical example of variation with this decision rule is to allow initially a two-factory maximum for radios (product X) and a three-factory maximum for cleaners (product Y) in order to differentiate more sharply the production potential between the two products. At a latter stage the third factory for radios might be introduced to reflect

61 Cf. *infra*, 284.
62 If the company persists in spending money on R & D after reaching the contemplated maximum number of product improvements, it may be necessary to reset its VR04 at zero every three periods or so.

the greater growth rate in the radio market. The interesting feature of this parameter is that it permits *variation between individual companies* on a crucial variable. This is one of the opportunities in the simulation (initial capital, VF16 and VF25, and the marketing effectiveness index, VS13, are others) enabling one to distribute differential competitive advantages between the companies and study on a systematic basis the performance differences which result during play. Since INTOP Standard treats all companies equally, however, this inviting opportunity has not been used much yet.

DR 5:   *Choose the maximum number of regional sales offices in each area.*

Range: 0–9
                   No specific parameter, but the range indicates an overall constraint.

The administrator can restrict the number of sales offices by controlling the state variable VS14 for all or individual companies during the simulation or by modifying the Operations Decision Card and/or the *Player's Manual.*

DR 6:   *Choose the number of items of marketing research information that a team may buy in one period.*

Range: 0–6 items of two digits each
                   No specific parameter; but the range indicates an overall constraint.

The administrator implements his choice by changing the Home Office Decision Card, if necessary. A place is provided in the program for six items of two digits each in columns 37–48. Since INTOP Standard uses only three items, one must make the appropriate adjustment in the number of decision boxes for a different choice on this decision rule. Clearly not only the number of items available, but also the cost of each item (PR12 to PR29) will determine how much the companies are inclined to request marketing research information.

DR 7:   *Set the time period number for the beginning of the simulation.*

Range: 00–99 or two digits
                   The Master Control Card is used for indication of time period number.

The value of the time period has no effect on the simulation other than to act as a counter. If the administrator were to begin the simulation after the companies had developed past histories, he might set this parameter ahead to perhaps 20, indicating five years of past industry expansion.

DR 8:   *The decision form places a limit on price for standard or deluxe grades of two digits.*

Ranges: From 00¢–99¢ to $0000–$9900

DR 9:   *The decision form places a limit on the number of items to be manufactured per factory for either standard or deluxe grades of two digits.*

Ranges: From 00–99 to 0,000,000–9,900,000 units

Most administrators will probably accept the values of DR 8 and DR 9 as given in INTOP Standard (i.e., the price range as $00–$99, and the production range as 00,000–99,000 units). However, with a slight program modification it is possible to move the decimal point to the right or left to accommodate different ranges of these decision rules. Thus, it is feasible with the INTOP model to simulate a low priced, high volume product like commercial laundry soaps or a high priced, low volume product like freezers instead of the radios and cleaners that are the basic products in INTOP Standard. Even with considerable juggling of price and production parameters there is little risk in FORTRAN operations that the administrator will encounter the ultimate constraint, i.e., that on total revenue.

DR 10:   *The computer equipment places a limit on total revenue (or the maximum price times the maximum sales quantity) in any given decision period of $9,999,999,999. (In Univac operations $9,999,999.)*

In INTOP Standard no company has ever reached close even to the indicated ceiling for Univac operations; this might happen if starting capital were markedly increased.

It may finally be observed that there are two other overall constraints, as indicated by the Operations Decision Card, i.e., the two-digit limit on methods improvement ($99,000 maximum) and the three-digit limit on advertising expense ($999,000 maximum). Neither one of the two is likely to restrict the selection of parameters in practice. As both of these constraints apply to each area and product separately the *overall* ceiling is actually six times these figures.

3] FINANCIAL STATEMENTS AND RELATED PARAMETERS

With knowledge of the basic constraints and the key area and product variations (V1-V30), we can turn our attention to the next four steps in quantifying the crucial parameters. We shall discuss in sequence in this section the parameters associated with sizing characteristics of the model, the summary income statement accounts, the specific operating expenses and the balance sheet accounts. The task is to create a conception of a particular company and its competitive behavior at a time when it has fully developed its potential in the market place. In particular, we construct the hypothetical balance sheet and income statement for this company. In so doing we shall commit ourselves to values of the crucial parameters and supply the necessary information to complete the choice of parameters for the INTOP equations.

It should be quite clear that in creating an ideal company image in order to pick parameters we are not trying to predict or determine individual company behavior in practice. Some companies will do much worse and some much better under actual competitive play. The value of the financial statement construction is that it approximates a middle-ground of company performance and thus provides a rationale for parameter selection in terms of a proper balance between the strategic variables in the model.

The technique that we shall use here will be a slight variation upon the analysis set forth in Chapter 3. In that chapter the elements of the model were divided into fixed and variable components, permitting the direct application of marginal reasoning. The parameters in the C & A and the manufacturing costs equations easily lend themselves to this division. Other asset variables such as R & D, advertising and methods-improvement expenses must be approximated by using their effective values obtained from the time-lag parameters. A residual element of subjectivity is inescàpable due to the discontinuities (notably as regards products, areas and factories) deliberately incorporated into the model. The principal advantage of this straightforward mathematical approach is that it allows specific parameter values to be calculated in one step and from one system of simultaneous equations derived from the logic inherent in financial statement relationships.

The approach adopted here is based on a few initial discretionary parameter choices and period 12 financial statements of an hypothetical, average-performing company. The discussion of the financial statements and the parameter values chosen to accord with them follows a process of orderly reasoning. We use the equations in Chapter 3 only to calculate the elasticities of the consumer market function and the cost-curve coefficients of the manufacturing function (in the next subsection). The advantage of the approach pursued here is that it enables the non-mathematically oriented administrator to make just as successful parameter choices and changes as those which may be made with greater mathematical sophistication. Either method will lead to acceptable results because the INTOP model is viable within a wide range of parameter values.

Our starting point is the selection of two crucial balance sheet constituents, i.e., total assets and total revenue (DR10), a choice presumably based on a preconceived view of the type of industry and company one wishes to simulate. The balance sheet is broken down further by allocating total assets to fixed assets and current assets and by allocating total liability and equity to common stock, long-term debt and current liabilities. The first choice for the income statement is a "reasonable" rate of return which is reflected in new income. This quantity and the tax rate together with the revenue dictate the total cost. The division of total cost into variable cost and fixed cost is discretionary, but it will determine the price elasticity as noted in Chapter 3. Finally, the detailed cost elements as presented on the income statement must be selected.

An illustration of this technique is contained in the tables in Figs. 45, 46 and 47, representing financial statements of a "middling" company in a standard run. Certain simplifying assumptions have been made consistent with the area and product variations previously derived. We assume that the company has allocated its initial capital and subsequent profits by period 12 to develop a capacity to operate fully in all six dimensions. In every dimension it has two producing plants and sells its products entirely in the consumer market. The company develops all dimensions equally, so that no differential advantage accrues to it by specializing in a few dimensions.

Many features are ignored to strip the model down to its essentials. The company engages only marginally in inter-company transactions and not at all in the financial functions of borrowing or investing money. Further, it is assumed that research and development has yielded no improvements in the past, so that all products made and sold still have a zero grade. The company is operating in a steady state as if it had made the same decisions for the last three periods. Therefore, various time lags have stabilized and the flow of cash in Accounts Receivable and Accounts Payable has become constant. A result of these assumptions is that we have considerably understated the profit potential of this company's operations.

Similarly, we have assumed that within its limitations this company has attained an efficient allocation of its resources. It operates with low production costs at an economical plant capacity utilization in each dimension. It maintains the economy-model prices prevailing at the beginning of the simulation. It controls its operating expenses and cash flow efficiently, avoiding the costly mistakes that plague less astute management. On the other hand, it must be emphasized that the company's resources are thinly distributed, making it sensitive to competitive inroads in any one of its markets.

With both profits and costs understated in relation to anticipated extremes of behavior, we hoped to create a wide variety of conditions for which the simulation would be viable. In addition, by choosing a reasonable profit criterion around 10 per cent of total sales after taxes for the medium-performing company, one could expect that most companies, even those under fairly poor management, would be able to survive. In actual experience, we have encountered companies with anything from $4,000,000 to over $30,000,000 in total assets after 12–15 periods of play. (These figures should be seen against the initial resource allocation of $10,000,000 to each company in INTOP Standard.)

FIG. 45   *Hypothetical Company Forecasted Income Statement for Period 12 in Thousands of Dollars*

	U.S. X	EEC X	Brazil X	All X	U.S. Y	EEC Y	Brazil Y	All Y	Total X+Y
Total Units Sold	30,000	18,000	13,000	61,000	50,000	36,000	16,000	102,000	163,000
Total Sales	720	504	416	1,640	2,250	1,800	880	4,930	6,570
Cost of Goods Sold	180	126	117	423	820	486	376	1,682	2,105
Gross Margin	540	378	299	1,217	1,430	1,314	504	3,248	4,465
C & A Expense	99	72	52	223	200	162	88	450	673
Shipping Expense	10	10	5	25	28	28	14	70	95
Advertising Expense	50	40	33	123	120	90	50	260	383
Methods Expense	20	15	8	43	72	50	16	138	181
Inventory Expense	7	7	6	20	36	29	12	77	97
Depreciation Expense	120	100	70	290	180	150	70	400	690
Fixed Expense	95	65	55	215	150	100	50	300	515
Net Operating Expense	401	309	229	939	786	609	300	1,695	2,634
Total Net Earnings	139	69	70	278	644	705	204	1,553	1,831
Marketing Research	–	–	–	5	–	–	–	5	10
R & D	–	–	–	25	–	–	–	50	75
Gross Earnings	139	69	70	248	644	705	204	1,498	1,746
Taxes	72	31	21	124	335	317	61	713	837
Net Earnings	67	38	49	124	309	388	143	785	909
Dividends	–	–	–	–	–	–	–	–	150
Total Retained Earnings	67	38	49	124	309	388	143	785	759

Note. While illustrative these data are fictitious. Total Units Sold is based on the assumption that the company has two plants in all dimensions by period 12. The numbers deliberately deviate from optimal plant operation (in order not to divulge this information to participants), although Cost of Goods Sold is based on optimal capacity utilization. The administrator may find currently used optimal capacity numbers in PM05 and PM07, and currently used optimal cost in PM03.

FIG. 46   *Hypothetical Company Forecasted Income Statement for Period 12 in Per Cent of Price and in Dollars Per Unit Sold*

	U.S. X		EEC X		Brazil X		All X		U.S. Y		EEC Y		Brazil Y		All Y		Total X+Y	
	%	$	%	$	%	$	%	$	%	$	%	$	%	$	%	$	%	$
Sales Price	100	24.0	100	28.0	100	32.0	100	26.9	100	45.0	100	50.0	100	55.0	100	48.3	100	40.3
Cost of Goods Sold	25	6.0	25	7.0	28	9.0	26	6.9	36	16.4	27	13.5	42	23.5	34	16.5	32	13.0
Gross Margin	75	18.0	75	21.0	72	23.0	74	20.0	64	28.6	73	36.5	58	31.5	66	31.8	68	27.3
C & A Expense	14	3.3	14	4.0	12	4.0	14	3.7	9	4.0	9	4.5	10	5.5	9	4.4	10	4.1
Shipping Expense	1	.3	2	.6	1	.4	1	.4	1	.6	2	.8	2	.9	1	.7	1	.6
Advertising Expense	7	1.7	8	2.2	8	2.5	7	2.0	5	2.4	5	2.5	6	3.1	5	2.5	6	2.3
Methods Expense	3	.7	4	.8	2	.6	3	.7	3	1.4	3	1.4	2	1.0	3	1.4	3	1.1
Inventory Expense	1	.2	1	.4	1	.4	1	.3	2	.7	2	.8	1	.7	2	.7	2	.6
Depreciation Expense	17	4.0	20	5.6	18	5.4	18	4.7	8	3.6	8	4.2	8	4.4	8	3.9	10	4.2
Fixed Expense	13	3.2	13	3.6	13	4.2	13	3.5	7	3.0	6	2.8	6	3.1	6	2.9	8	3.1
Net Operating Expense	56	13.4	62	17.2	55	17.5	57	15.3	35	15.7	35	17.0	35	18.7	34	16.5	40	16.0
Total Net Earnings	19	4.6	13	3.8	17	5.5	17	4.7	29	12.9	38	19.5	23	12.8	32	15.3	28	11.3
Marketing Research							1	.1							1	.1	1	.1
R & D							2	.4							1	.5	1	.5
Gross Earnings	19	4.6	13	3.8	17	5.5	14	4.2	29	12.9	38	19.5	23	12.8	30	14.7	26	10.7
Taxes	10	2.4	6	1.7	5	1.6	7	2.0	15	6.7	17	8.8	7	3.8	14	7.0	13	5.1
Net Earnings	9	2.2	7	2.1	12	3.9	7	2.2	14	6.2	21	10.7	16	9.0	16	7.7	13	5.6
Dividends																	2	.9
Total Retained Earnings	9	2.2	7	2.1	12	3.9	7	2.2	14	6.2	21	10.7	16	9.0	16	7.7	11	4.7

Note. While illustrative, these data are fictitious.

FIG. 47   *Hypothetical Company Forecasted Balance Sheet for Period 12, Items in Per Cent of Assets and in Thousands of Dollars*

	U.S.		EEC		Brazil		Home Office		Consolidated	
	%	$	%	$	%	$	%	$	%	$
Cash	4	266	2	121	6	239	1	100	5	726
A/R First Quarter	25	1,782	12	658	18	648			19	3,088
A/R Second Quarter		–	13	691	14	518			7	1,209
Inventory, X	3	204	3	168	3	126			3	498
Inventory, Y	13	951	10	567	9	329			11	1,547
Total Current Assets	45	3,203	40	2,205	50	1,860	1	100	45	7,368
Net Plant and Equip., X	22	1,560	24	1,300	25	910			23	3,770
Net Plant and Equip., Y	33	2,340	36	1,950	25	910			32	5,200
Subsidiary Control							99	10,000		
Total Assets	100	7,103	100	5,455	100	3,680	100	10,100	100	16,338
A/P First Quarter	10	693	4	210	6	228			7	1,131
A/P Second Quarter		–	4	220	5	182			2	402
Total Current Liability	10	693	8	430	11	410			9	1,533
Common Stock	27	1,910	37	2,025			99	10,000	61	10,000
Retained Earnings	63	4,500	55	3,000	21	770	1	100	30	4,805
Home Office Control					68	2,500				
Total Liability and Equity	100	7,103	100	5,455	100	3,680	100	10,100	100	16,338

Note. While illustrative, these data are fictitious.

There is no reason why other administrators must agree with our assumptions in making use of the technique just presented. The intent has been merely to illustrate a general approach to the problem of parameter selection, an approach which would appear at once reasonable in theory and workable in practice. We could just as well have assumed that the company produced and marketed products of grade two at correspondingly higher costs, that it made more use of the financial functions, that it was active only in one product or in two areas, or that it had a profit criterion of 15 per cent. No attention has been given to the possibility of additions to working capital through long-term bank loans or new issues of stock sanctioned by the administrator in the initial periods. For any reasonably consistent set of assumptions the financial statements will give a gross approximation to the competitive environments in the six area and product dimensions, and the parameters which reflect these statements will give the administrator a simulation with the characteristics that he has ascribed to it.

To arrive at specific values for the data in the prototype financial statements, within the constraints imposed by the model, by the decision forms and by the purpose and preferences of the administrator himself, we know of no better way of proceeding than by trial and error. If the administrator wants to create a simulation going beyond the framework given by the *Player's Manual*, adjustments in the format of the tables in Figs. 45–47 may be necessary. We have found it helpful to look at these model statements in two ways. One is to consider the absolute dollar values of each variable; the other is to consider the balance sheet variables as a percentage of total assets and the income statement variables as either a percentage of total sales or in terms of cost per unit sold. Although the administrator may prefer one representation to the other, it may be useful to construct and compare both of them. The actual numbers are not representative of INTOP Standard, but of a past version of the simulation. Participants in the game will not obtain a competitive advantage from studying them.

The sequence followed in spelling out the detailed implications of the preceding discussion is not crucial. It does, however, seem natural to begin with starting capital.

DR 11:	*Choose the initial amount of capital in the Home Office with which each company will begin the simulation. This amount of cash is equal to the common stock of the corporation.*
Standard Range:[63]	$5,000,000 to $15,000,000
Dictionary:	VF16 which equals VF25

---

63 For an explanation of the Standard Range concept, see *supra*, 231, note 56.

The initial amount of capital influences the rate of expansion for the individual companies and, hence, is not an arbitrary choice. At the beginning of the simulation a company must have the capital to build plants (or buy inventory) and the working capital for production (and/or holding inventory) until revenues are collected. The acquisition costs for plants, therefore, must be chosen with this capital constraint in mind. In INTOP Standard a company should theoretically be able to build initially at least one plant in each of the six dimensions, but have insufficient funds to build two. As profits accrue a company should be able to expand to two plants in each dimension as assumed in Figs. 45–47. In line with this assumption about the company growth rate, it is possible to express the total acquisition costs for plant construction as a per cent of the invested capital.

DR 12: *The total cost for constructing one plant in each of the six dimensions should be 50–75 per cent of the initial capital.*

This suggested range for plant costs is based on the notion that a reasonable approximation of the ratio of plant cost to working capital is 2:1. That is, for every two dollars originally invested in plant and equipment, one dollar is needed to make and market the product. It is possible, then, with this capital constraint to begin activity in each area and product dimension but impossible to develop them all immediately. The specific plant costs in each dimension are chosen according to the relative weighting ascribed to area variation V19 in the table in Fig. 43 as well as the overall constraint of long-term indebtedness permitted by the administrator.

DR 13: *Choose the plant costs for each dimension subject to DR 12 and the area variation V19 in Fig. 43 (5, 4, 2, 8, 7, 2).*

Standard Range: From $500,000 to $2,500,000 per plant. (Actual INTOP Standard numbers range from $700,000 for X and Y plants in Brazil to $1,800,000 for Y plants in the U.S.)

Dictionary: PM17

Particularly important for beginning the income statement construction are the variables of base sales quantity (PS01), base price (PS02) and total revenue (R), since all expenses and the projected profits are based on these values. Also, because $R = (PS01) (PS02)$, once any two of these values are selected, the third is determined.

The choice of the initial base price for product grade zero involves a consideration of the base prices for the four higher grades. The model uses two parameters to identify the base prices. The first parameter is the actual base price (PS02) of the product grade zero; the second is the price index (PS06) which measures the relative price differentials between the five grades. If we call the values of the price index P_0, P_1, P_2, P_3 and P_4, and set P_0 equal to one, we can express the base prices of the higher grades P_1, P_2, P_3 and P_4 as multiples of the initial base price P_0. Further, the base price of a grade equals (PS02) times its price index value. Since P_0 is set to one, for convenience, P_0 equals (PS02). The model operates so that the base price has this meaning in the consumer sales function: when any of the five grades are marketed, the basic price for any grade, P_0, P_1, P_2, P_3 or P_4, *ceteris paribus*, will sell the same quantity (PS01). The value of the higher grades, therefore, is that the same sales quantity will bring in a higher total revenue.

The choice of PS02 and PS06 will depend upon the limits of DR 8 (price range) and the area variation V2 (base price). When we consider the values of the price index, we must remember that there are only one hundred price increments available ($0–$99 in INTOP Standard), and that the price index is the same for all dimensions. Also, since we desire product X to have greater appeal to buccaneering companies than product Y, the span of the price index will be greater for X than for Y. An easy way to set the price index is to compare the economy-grade price P_0 and the maximum product improvement price P_4.

DR 14:	*Set the price index values P_0, P_1, P_2, P_3 and P_4 for product X and product Y in terms of the price span between P_0 and P_4.*
Standard Range:	P_4 is 2 to 3 times P_0 for X; P_4 is 1.3 to 1.8 times P_0 for Y.
Dictionary:	PS06

The values of P_1, P_2 and P_3 are successively higher within the range of DR 14, *except* for the grade(s) of X and of Y which are selected to represent marketing "duds." We set the index value of these "duds" close to P_0.[64] Since the costs of all grades continue to rise (cf. DR 20), it is uneconomical to produce these two grades — a fact that the companies will discover in an efficient way if they invest in marketing research, and in an expensive way if they go ahead and produce and/or market these grades without such research.

We now choose a base price (PS02) which will quantify the values of the price index in DR 14. The area variation V2 gives us the additional information. The base prices for all five grades should generally fall well within the limits of DR 8.

---

[64] The administrator may readily derive what the "duds" are in INTOP Standard as delivered by examining the confidential data on Marketing Research Items 17 and 18, which are a part of the INTOP User's Package.

DR 15:   *Select the prices of the lowest grade P_0, according to the variation V2 (1, 2, 3, 6, 7, 8).*

Standard Range: \$20–\$35 for X; \$45–\$60 for Y (i.e., the prices of Y are approximately two times the price of X in each area).

Dictionary: PS02

In a similar manner we consider the values of the base sales quantities (PS01). They depend upon the limit DR 9 which allows for one hundred production increments in each plant (0–99,000 units in INTOP Standard),[65] the area variation V1 and an estimate of the total industry sales potential for both products. Since we have a relatively free choice for the values of total sales potential, we can introduce sales figures which grossly approximate actual conditions for the transistor radio and vacuum cleaner markets. Because the United States sales figures were more readily available, we used them for this estimation of the sales parameters.

DR 16:   *Determine the total industry sales potential per period for transistor radios (X) and vacuum cleaners (Y) in the United States.*

Standard Range: 350,000 to 1,000,000 units for X; 650,000 to 1,300,000 units for Y.

Dictionary: No parameter — basic sales quantity is set on a company basis (see below).

In practice, total industry sales potential becomes a derivative of the base sales quantity set on a company basis (although the administrator may wish to select the latter after considering the former, and the number of companies participating). Sales quantities in the other areas are related to those of the United States by variation V1. In FORTRAN operations industry sales potential is *automatically* adjusted in direct proportion to the number of participating companies, and is the sum of company base sales quantity times the number of companies. This automaticity prevails whether the administrator wishes his creation to remain within the confines of the *Player's Manual* or go beyond it.[66] Should he prefer industry market potential to grow slower or faster than the number of companies he may regulate it most conveniently by means of the economic index (PS24).[67]

---

[65] Clearly, there should be a reasonable relationship between sales potential and plant capacity, see *infra*, 260. Cf. Schedule of Costs, etc. in Chapter 2 and the *Player's Manual* and footnote to Fig. 45 above.

[66] Cf. *supra*, 92, 145.

[67] In Univac operations this is not automatic. However, INTOP Standard Univac tapes are available dimensioned for 8, 12 and 15 companies, respectively.

DR 17:   *Select the base sales quantities per company and period according to the variation V1 (6, 4, 2, 9, 7, 3).*

Standard Range: 10,000 to 35,000 units per quarter for X; 15,000 to 55,000 units per quarter for Y.

Dictionary: PS01. (The base quantities apply to both standard and deluxe grades sold. Since PS01 is the parameter for the standard grade only, PS01 is exactly one-half the base quantities calculated in this decision rule.)

From the sales quantities (PS01) and the prices (PS02) of product grade zero, we have calculated the total revenues for the income statement in Fig. 45. To provide some check upon the feasibility of these numbers, we compare the total revenue in all dimensions to the amount of initial invested capital and find that the decision rule provides a satisfactory criterion.

DR 18:   *The total revenue by period 12 should be between 40 and 80 per cent of initial invested capital.*

A glance at Figs. 45 and 47 indicates that total revenue is about 65 per cent of invested capital in our hypothetical company. For another check one might wish to calculate the sales to asset ratio, which turns out to be about 1.6:1. Such checks are needed to ascertain that initial capital (DR 11) will be adequate for the volume of sales we have chosen. Clearly, if the revenue to capital ratio were as low as 10 per cent or as high as 150 per cent, the companies would starve in competition or feast together on profits in an unchallenging world.

The total revenue for each dimension now becomes a standard of comparison for deriving the other income statement variables. In Fig. 46 percentages and cost per unit analysis are used to relate all variables to revenue or price. In this way the allocation of costs in the six dimensions is facilitated. We begin with the variable cost in the manufacturing function and proceed to consider all the other income statement variables.

DR 19:   *Choose the minimum variable manufacturing cost as a per cent of price, considering variation V12 (1, 2, 3, 7, 6, 8).*

Standard Range: 25–30 per cent for X; 25–45 per cent for Y

Dictionary: PM03

From the minimum manufacturing cost (PM03) for grade zero we can determine the minimum costs for the four higher grades by considering the parameter for the cost index (PM16). The values of the cost index C_0, C_1, C_2, C_3 and C_4 are analogous to the price index values P_0, P_1, P_2, P_3 and P_4 in DR 14 and, just as DR 15 defined P_0, so DR 19 defines C_0. In selecting the cost index, we are in effect deciding upon the gross margin for each of the product grades.[68] Because product X has a higher growth rate than product Y, we have elected to make the relative gross margin for product X in INTOP Standard much greater than that of product Y. From DR 14 we have adequate information for this decision rule:

DR 20:	*Set the cost index values C_0, C_1, C_2, C_3 and C_4 for product X and product Y in terms of the cost increase between C_0 and C_4.*
Standard Range:	C_4 is 2.5 to 4.5 times C_0 for X; C_4 is 1.5 to 2.5 times C_0 for Y.
Dictionary:	PM16

The values of C_1, C_2 and C_3 represent progressively higher costs within the range of DR 20. If it is desired to vary the cost index by area as well as by product, parameter (PM11) — i.e., variation V15 in Fig. 43 — is brought into play. A look at the manufacturing cost equation in Chapter 3 should be sufficient to indicate how this parameter might be chosen.

Having established the revenue and variable manufacturing cost figures, we can estimate the value of total net operating expenses. In general, in INTOP Standard manufacturing costs will tend to balance the net operating expenses. That is, as product X has low variable manufacturing costs, it will have a high value for net operating expenses (and vice versa for product Y), as indicated by Fig. 46.

DR 21:	*Choose the percentages of total net operating expenses relative to price in all dimensions.*
Standard Range:	50–70 per cent for X; 30–50 per cent for Y

Before proceeding to discuss the individual operating expenses we may complete the general character of the income statement with respect to taxes and profits. Ignoring the Home Office for the time being, a simple calculation from DR 19 and DR 21 gives us the gross earnings.

DR 22:	*Calculate gross earnings in each dimension as a per cent of price.*
Standard Range:	5–25 per cent for X; 20–40 per cent for Y

[68] Naturally, the gross margin for the "dud" grades will be much narrower than for the other grades.

While it would be interesting to discuss product and area variations for total net operating expenses as well as gross earnings in some
detail, discretionary considerations vis-à-vis participants in the simulation prompt us to desist. The administrator interested in these variations as they appear in INTOP Standard as delivered is invited to check
major operating expense parameters on the history printout for quarter
1 on the test run.[69] Should the administrator wish to change these
parameters DR22 is a reminder to him to select new values which still
permit a viable operation in all dimensions. (Should he desire to make
operations in some dimension *not* viable, the simple calculation of
gross earnings again provides a helpful check.)

DR 23:	*Select the tax rates for each operating area somewhat in line with the actual rates prevailing in the simulated countries (or regions).*
Standard Range:	30–52 per cent among the three operating areas
Dictionary:	PF11

At the time of writing the real-life corporate tax rate in the
United States is being reconsidered. INTOP Standard tapes will carry
the rate at the time of delivery. If this rate deviates from that stated in
the *Player's Manual* the administrator will be reminded to inform
participants about the change. At any time, of course, the administrator may himself change these rates by Wonder Card.

DR 24:	*Calculate the profit margins in each dimension so that the total average profit on both products after taxes is about 10 per cent.*
Standard Range:	5–25 per cent

Clearly DR 19 through DR 24 must be considered together in the
determination of suitable profit margins in the various dimensions.
These rules form an interdependent framework which will vary as the
administrator adjusts any one of the five major variables on the income
statement (revenues, manufacturing costs, net operating expenses,
taxes and profits) to conform with his ideas of a dimension's characteristics.

We retrace our steps to consider the percentage estimates of the
seven individual expenses that make up total net operating expenses,
keeping in mind the constraint imposed by DR 21.

The commercial and administrative expenses (C & A) in Figs. 45
and 46 are calculated according to the "combined" agency rates
(PS26) which apply when a company markets both products. The

69   He may also write to the Graduate
School of Business at the University of
Chicago.

"isolated" rates (PS27) which prevail when only one product is marketed will be slightly higher. Whether the "captive" rates (PS25) which apply when a company has its own sales organization are more or less economical than agency depends on the stability and volume of sales as well as the number of sales offices in the areas.[70]

DR 25:	*Choose the "combined" C & A expense for each product dimension as a per cent of the selling price, according to the variation V9 (3, 4, 4, 4, 5, 7).*
Standard Range:	12–14 per cent for X; 8–10 per cent for Y (Fig. 46)
Dictionary:	PS26

Shipping expenses between the producing areas are significant primarily when Brazil is involved. Intra-area shipping expenses are fairly negligible. In INTOP Standard we assume – at least at the beginning of the simulation – that transfer costs to and from a given area are equal. The total shipping expenses in Fig. 45 are estimated rather arbitrarily by assuming an average cost of $5.00 for transistors and $14.00 for cleaners, with a volume of 2,000 units shipped to the U.S. and the EEC and 1,000 units shipped to Brazil during the period.[71] (Actually, the extent of shipping activity is very hard to predict.)

DR 26:	*Choose the costs to prevail at the beginning of the game for area shipments from the United States in line with V11 (1, 3, 4, 2, 6, 9). Costs from the other areas should be chosen in analogous fashion.*
Standard Range:	1–5 per cent of selling price of economy models (Fig. 46)
Dictionary:	PS33, PS34 and PS35

In the course of the simulation these transfer costs may be varied on a unilateral or multilateral basis to simulate tariff restrictions or a reciprocal trade policy. Similarly, the opportunity to differentiate the rates in both directions between two areas may be used to set up a strong economic incentive for new overseas plants, movements of capital, etc. The manipulation of the transfer rates gives the administrator a powerful tool for introducing some of the unpredictable elements of international competition and trade policy.

When the base values of advertising expenses (PS03) for the con-

[70] Cf. Chapter 3, 98f.
[71] In point of fact transfer cost is charged against the area *from* which goods are shipped in the INTOP model. This is largely an accounting convention, however, as in the general case the seller must be expected to get his costs covered.

sumer sales function are determined it should be borne in mind that advertising applies equally to both standard and deluxe products marketed.

DR 27:   *Choose the advertising expenses as a per cent of total revenue in each dimension according to V3 (4, 3, 2, 8, 6, 4).*

Standard Range: 6–9 per cent for X; 4–7 per cent for Y

Dictionary: PS03

The cost of manufacturing either product in a plant can be reduced (or plant obsolescence retarded) by spending money on methods improvement. The maximal cost reduction attainable may be varied by product and area (PM14), as indicated by the discussion of the methods improvement function in Chapter 3.[72]

DR 28:   *Select the optimum methods expense as a per cent of total revenue considering V18 (4, 2, 1, 6, 5, 3).*

Standard Range: 2–6 per cent for X; 2–4 per cent for Y

Dictionary: No specific parameter, but PM14 and this decision rule determines PM15, i.e., the methods improvement expense which will yield half of the maximal cost reduction, as indicated in Chapter 3.

Prediction as to the amount spent for inventory expenses can be only approximate, lacking more precise knowledge of actual market interaction in a "typical" run of the simulation. We estimate the number of units left in inventory at the end of the period liberally at around one quarter of the total sales. The cost per unit of holding this inventory is the parameter value we must select.

DR 29:   *Choose the cost for storing unsold inventory as a per cent of price, consistent with variation V10 (1, 2, 3, 4, 5, 6).*

Standard Range: ½–2 per cent for both X and Y

Dictionary: PS31

The depreciation (non-cash) expense for each plant in a period is a linear function of the plant acquisition costs (cf. DR 13). For INTOP Standard the depreciation rate is set at the same value for all dimensions (V22).[73] Nevertheless, even with identical linear rates, the

[72] Cf. *supra,* 104.
[73] Cf. *infra,* 277.

total depreciation expenses must be a reasonable per cent of total revenues. Assuming that a company has two producing plants in each dimension, we can calculate the depreciation expenses and the depreciation rates by this decision rule.

DR 30:   *Select the depreciation expense based on two producing plants in each dimension as a per cent of total revenue and the depreciation rate as a per cent of plant costs according to the variation V22 (6, 6, 6, 6, 6, 6).*

Standard Range: 10–20 per cent of total revenue for X depreciation expenses; 5–10 per cent of total revenue for Y. Actual depreciation rates for both X and Y are in the 3–8 per cent range.

Dictionary: PM20

The last item of the operating expenses is the fixed cost per plant for which two options are available. The first is the direct costing method discussed below; the second is the traditional method of including fixed costs (PM01) as part of the inventoried value of the products produced.[74] Our choice is to use the direct costing method, which conveniently provides for some economies of scale if more than one plant is built. Each of the possible three plants for a product has a separate fixed cost associated with it. We first estimate the fixed cost for having two producing plants, since this was the assumption made in constructing the income statement. One may then readily proceed to select the fixed costs for one and three producing plants.

DR 31:   *Choose the value for the fixed costs for two producing plants in each dimension according to the variation V21 (6, 4, 2, 8, 6, 2), still assuming reasonable capacity utilization.*

Standard Range: 10–15 per cent of total revenue for X; 5–10 per cent of total revenue for Y

Dictionary: PM19

DR 32:   *Introduce economies of scale for one and three producing plants, given the value for two producing plants.*

Standard Range: For one plant: 10–30 per cent *less* than DR 31 for X, 15–50 per cent *less* than DR 31 for Y. For three plants: 8–15 per cent *more* than DR 31 for X, 10–20 per cent *more* than DR 31 for Y.

Dictionary: PM19

[74] Cf. the manufacturing equation, *supra,* 101f.

Up to this point the concern has been with the operating areas. To complete the income statements in Figs. 45 and 46, we must consider three variables uniquely relevant to home office activities: marketing research expense, research and development expense and dividend payments. We have few criteria to judge the magnitude of the home office variables since they are independent of the other features in the simulation. Significantly, the income statement provides the only logical link between these and other expenses.

Our preference is to make marketing research information available to participating companies cheaply. For this reason marketing research expense per quarter in INTOP Standard is modest. The Schedule of Costs[75] shows current values of the cost parameters (PR12–PR29) assigned to the marketing research items.

Research and development as well as dividend payments are significant expenses, being hypothetically scaled at between 2 and 6 per cent and dividends between 2 and 3 per cent of total revenue. From estimates of these expenses it is possible to select the parameters for R & D (PR01–PR04) and for dividends (PF22–PF26). The details of parameter selection in these areas should be fairly clear from the discussion of the equations for these two home office functions.[76]

The income statement completed, we may consider the variables on the balance sheet in Fig. 47. Four of these variables constitute elements of our framework for parameter selection, i.e., inventory, net plant and equipment, Accounts Receivable and Accounts Payable. The other items on the sheet are derivatives from previous decision rules or conventional accounting rules.

The value of common stock and initial capital are obtained from DR 11. Home office control and subsidiary control provide the accounting mechanism for allocating capital to the operating areas. Cash and retained earnings are residual accounts which have little significance in parameter selection. We have arbitrarily taken the retained earnings, as estimated from the income statements, to be the accumulation of profits for five periods. It is hardly possible to be accurate about retained earnings, as companies will lose money in the early stages of their development and regain it later when they engage in marketing.

The estimates of inventory values are based on optimal plant production which we must now consider. Most significant is the relation between the base sales quantity (PS01) and the plant capacity level (PM05). The choice available is reflected in the two positions: (1) sales and optimum production capacity (in our example for two plants in each division) could coincide and (2) sales and production could be out of tune in that sales could fall between optimum capacity levels for one, two or three plants. In the former case, companies would sell

[75] Cf. *Player's Manual*, 49ff, and Chapter 2.
[76] Cf. Chapter 3.

exactly what they produced, *ceteris paribus,* once they found the level of plant utilization yielding optimal production cost, and there would be no question of how many plants to build. In the latter case it would be difficult for companies to decide how many plants to build, and they would face the dilemma of accumulating inventory because they produced too much, or of losing sales to competitors because they produced too little. There are many ways in which companies may circumvent this dilemma, such as by inter-company sales or purchases, price adjustments or production at non-optimal capacity. Thus, the latter alternative has been chosen in INTOP Standard as the more challenging.

DR 33:   *Choose the optimum plant capacities in each dimension as a per cent of the base sales quantity (DR 17) according to the area variation V13 (5, 3, 1, 8, 6, 2).*

Standard Range: 40–80 per cent (for each of two plants)

Dictionary: PM05

The next step is to choose the values of the maximum plant capacity (PM18) based on DR 33 and the variation V20. For this decision the administrator enjoys considerable discretion, even if he has in mind staying within the bounds of the *Player's Manual.*[77]

The basic notion that our "representative firm" is in a steady state automatically yields data on number of units in inventory, which we now multiply with minimal production cost (on the brazen assumption that the goods were obtained at that figure — whether produced by the company or bought from the outside) to get the balance sheet value of inventory. Similarly, net plant and equipment comes from DR 13 and DR 30 on the simplified assumption that the two producing plants have been depreciating for seven periods. The only other major variable of concern on the asset side of the balance sheet is Accounts Receivable. It may be derived after considering all these variables as a per cent of total assets in Fig. 47.

Net plant and equipment have the greatest share of assets (50–60 per cent), if only because of our original emphasis on large plant acquisition costs (DR 13). Due to the fairly high obsolescence rate on factories (PM12) — chosen to stimulate companies to sell old plants and to buy new ones — we would expect our estimate of plant value (based on an average of seven periods) to be about as low as this figure would go. Inventory value appears as a mere 10–25 per cent of total assets (note direct costing effect). We may now estimate the value of assets in Accounts Receivable (25–35 per cent). From this figure we can choose the per cent steppage between *A/R* 2, *A/R* 1 and

[77] Cf. *Player's Manual,* 49. A mimeographed amendment distributed to participants is sufficient if the administrator wants other than the standard maximum plant capacity figures.

cash (PF02 and PF03), in keeping with the area variation V24. A similar calculation follows for Accounts Payable (V25), with a rate of steppage (PF04 and PF05) equal to that of Accounts Receivable in INTOP Standard.

It may be observed that we could have chosen the parameters for Accounts Receivable and Accounts Payable in a different way, as derivatives from the income statement instead of the balance sheet. In such a case one might formulate this decision rule:

DR 34:   *Choose the amount of steppage between A/R 2,*
                    A/R 1 and cash as a per cent of total revenue
                    according to V24, and the amount of steppage
                    between A/P 2, A/P 1 and cash as a per cent of
                    manufacturing cost according to V25.

Standard Range: 55–85 per cent in all areas

Dictionary: PF02, PF03, PF04 and PF05.

Both methods should be used to derive the values for these parameters. This is merely an illustration of the cardinal fact of life in parameter selection and scaling: the interdependence of parts in the entire model. No matter what the framework of analysis employed, the administrator will discover that he deals with a complicated puzzle of interrelated parts, and that fitting the pieces together involves trial and error plus a clear conception of the simulation's purpose.

We have developed a framework for parameter selection which begins with the isolation of crucial parameters and the definitions of area and product variations among them. Then, by considering the key constituents of the model, we were able to construct a financial statement for a hypothetical, not overly imaginatively run, company which in turn led to the quantification of many parameters. Ours is just one way of reasoning. We hope an administrator will be encouraged to adapt it to his own needs and to find out for himself how well the INTOP model can adapt to him.

c. *Additional Considerations in Parameter Selection*
1] ELASTICITIES AND REMAINING PARAMETERS IN THE
   FUNCTIONAL MANAGEMENT AREAS

The discussion in preceding subsections has allowed us to select many of the key parameters in the INTOP model. The selection process is one of trial and error, which may require continual adjustment if all parameters are to be compatible. To push the work further it is desirable, if not necessary, to consider the equilibrium analysis as well as some of the equations presented in Chapter 3.[78]

78 For the equilibrium analysis, see
supra, 112ff.

The formulas of Chapter 3 indicate that the decision rules we have chosen for price, quantity and advertising parameters determine price and advertising elasticities. But the administrator may have his own conception of what these elasticities should be in a particular dimension and what area and product variations (inter-dimensional differentiation) should exist between these elasticities. Accordingly, he may wish to adjust them. This may be done either experimentally by manipulation of the elasticity parameters or by changing determinants of elasticities. If the administrator changes elasticities by direct manipulation of the elasticity parameters he should be aware of the fact that even relatively small changes may have a fairly drastic effect on markets and company operating conditions.

To change the determinants of elasticity is often a fairly complex process. For instance, if a given price elasticity is regarded as too small in absolute value, one may change it while holding company income constant by raising both revenue and fixed costs by the same amount. Such a change will also tend to make decision-making in the particular operating environment affected more risky as pointed out in Chapter 3.

While the number of elasticities in the consumer sales function may seem imposing, they are all calculated from information already known, the variations of industry elasticities (V4 to V8) and the parameters PS01, PS02 and PS03. The redistribution and grade elasticities are set equal to the industry price elasticities in INTOP Standard, although one could also contemplate choosing them proportional to advertising elasticities or some other criterion. Individual firm elasticities are always greater than industry elasticities. These two types of elasticities move in parallel directions, at least in INTOP Standard. It is advisable to keep the price elasticities between product X and product Y (V8) relatively low (in the range from 0.01 to 0.1) since the effect of this variable will vary widely with the number of companies actually marketing products.[79] The elasticity of the economic index (PS23) need not be used (i.e., it may simply be set equal to one as in INTOP Standard),[80] since corresponding effects – if desired – can be built into the economic index values which the administrator

---

[79] If the X-Y cross elasticities are set higher than in the suggested range, they will tend to be over-dimensioned in relation to individual product price elasticities usually considered more important. This dysfunctional effect would increase with the number of companies actually operating in an area. Note that while cross-elasticities are automatically adjusted for number of participating companies at the beginning of a run, no such adjustment is made if new companies are added in the course of a run. This is not apt to create problems as long as the number of companies added is small in relation to the number of original participants.

[80] This parameter is useful chiefly when the administrator wishes to introduce time-parallel business cycle developments of different amplitude in the different areas.

supplies each period (PS24) to inject cyclical variations in local economies.[81]

The manufacturing equation is not complicated if we examine each part separately. It breaks down into a long-run cost curve, a short-run cost curve and simple multiplication terms for grade differences, obsolescence and methods improvement. A most important consideration is the variation in the cost curves when either a standard and/or a deluxe grade is produced. The administrator has the option to emphasize a single grade production or joint standard-and-deluxe production in one plant, to emphasize short-run costs at the expense of the long-run or to vary the shapes of the two cost curves at non-optimal levels of production. It may be logical to have steeply rising long-run cost curves accompany slowly rising short-run cost curves (and vice versa). Certainly, the steeper the cost curves, the closer maximal capacity should be to optimal capacity, at least in the INTOP world (due to constraints in the model, which seem reasonably realistic).

The rate of obsolescence (V16) is intimately related to the depreciation rate (V22). The greater the obsolescence rate (i.e., the rise of production costs with age), the greater the depreciation rate may well be, since plants which deteriorate rapidly should not have much asset value. Also, the maximum cost reduction from methods improvement should balance the contribution to increased costs from plant obsolescence in some reasonable fashion. There is a point (in INTOP Standard around period 12) where all methods improvement expense is typically needed not to reduce costs but to cancel out the factor of obsolescence.[82] Above this point plants become increasingly uneconomical to run and there will be growing reason for the administrator to introduce the option of plant elimination enabling companies to return to more agreeable production costs.[83]

Within the marketing functions it has proved both workable and fairly realistic in INTOP Standard to establish shipping costs in some reasonable relation to profit margins among the areas viewed per unit of each product. As regards commercial and administrative expenses the chief concern is the relationship between the agency rates and the captive sales force rates. In particular, one must decide the sales volume for which it is economical to change from agency marketing to a captive sales force and what number of sales offices should be most economical at different volumes in the various areas. The formula

---

[81] Suggested index data are included in the INTOP User's Package. They are based on the notion that business cycles tend to vary not only in amplitude but also as to timing between various geographical areas.

[82] What should be done to implement any specific change in depreciation-obsolescence relationships may be easily derived from the discussion of the manufacturing cost function; cf. *supra*, 104.

[83] Cf. INTOP Memo 4, reproduced in Appendix VI, and the guide to plant disposal by Wonder Cards in the Computer Liaison instruction in Appendix V. For *maximal* production economies companies would be well advised to consider plant renewal several periods earlier than period 12 in INTOP Standard.

given in Chapter 3 is a straightforward one.

Among the financial parameters we are especially concerned with the interest rate structure (V26, V27 and V28). There must be a range of rates between the parameters for bank borrowing and government securities investment making *inter-company* loan transactions reasonably attractive to both borrower and lender. INTOP Standard has four ranges of interest rates: the securities interest rates (1.0–1.7 per cent per period), the "gap" for inter-company negotiations (1.7–3.0 per cent), the borrowing rates (3.0–4.0 per cent) and the supplier credit rates (5 per cent or greater). With the gap between investment and borrowing parameters in the open market there is strong incentive to negotiate. If for some reason the administrator wishes to discourage inter-company loans he may, of course, close the gap.

The major issue in selecting parameter values for the research and development equation is the rate at which product improvements should occur (i.e., the time-lag parameters). A prime determinant is likely to be the number of periods the simulation is to be run. The numbers in INTOP Standard are based on a run of 12–15 periods, with on the average one product improvement every three to four periods for each company engaged in R & D on an optimal basis.[84] There are diminishing returns on investment in R & D after a certain expense (PR04), and it takes a minimum expense (PR03) to get any increase in research probability at all. The administrator has the choice of differentiating product X and product Y research on these variables as well as of controlling their rates.

The dividend equation emphasizes two kinds of relationship. First, the dividend time-lag parameter (PF22) determines how much the continuity of dividend expenses influences the amount of cash returned to the companies. The earnings time-lag parameter (PF23) performs a corresponding function with regard to earnings. Second, the minimal and maximal threshold ratios of dividend expense to effective earnings (PF24 and PF25) determine the effect of a company's dividend policy. Assuming continuously profitable operations, companies will do best by adopting a dividend policy directly proportional to last period's earnings. The stock market confidence ratio is determined by PF26. The administrator may wish to begin with a low pay-out ratio in the initial periods when companies are developing and increase it later when they have achieved some stability.[85] If, as in INTOP Standard, the maximum addition to cash is actually greater than dividends paid, the administrator may conversely wish to lower

---

84 Note the opportunity for cross-licensing. This creates an uncertainty factor in parameter selection, as the relative willingness of companies to engage in license transactions varies markedly from one run to another.
Cf. also the "Time and Change" and R & D discussion of Chapter 3.

85 He may correspondingly wish to set PF24 (and perhaps PF25) fairly low in the beginning of a run, increasing them to INTOP Standard (or even higher) values only toward the end of the run.

the pay-back ratio if companies were to begin using the dividend function for speculative purposes. However, this has rarely occurred thus far, and the pay-back ratio has been left constant throughout each run.

The last variables we shall comment upon are the time-lag parameters which influence price, advertising, methods improvement, R & D and stock market confidence.[86] All time lags have this property: the smaller the value of the time-lag parameter, the less the time lag imposed on the particular variable. Further, a quick rate of expansion implies a quick rate of decay. If a variable like methods-improvement expense has a small time lag, it will reach steady state more quickly and also dampen out more quickly when the methods expense is terminated. The converse is true also. If the administrator wants the effect of an expense to linger long after the expense is terminated, he must necessarily have the effect build up slowly and choose a high value (i.e., close to 1) for the time-lag parameter.

2] THE ELIMINATION OF PARAMETERS

The administrator may not wish to use all features of the model in his simulation. He has three methods of eliminating those features which he wishes to exclude: (1) to set corresponding parameter values to zero (and, occasionally, at some arbitrarily high figure) by Wonder Cards, (2) to prepare new decision forms on which the undesired features do not appear or (3) to instruct the participants to ignore particular features on the standard decision forms.

Of these methods only that involving elimination by parameter change needs illustration here. For example, if a monitoring company were to act as single buyer, substituting for the consumer market function (which may be the case, e.g., in a production-management simulation), the administrator need only set the base sales quantity (PS01) to a diminutive positive number.[87] Similarly, if he were to act as the sole supplier (e.g., in some marketing-management oriented simulations), he might eliminate the production function by setting factory capacity (PM18) equal to zero. The R & D feature is eliminated for all practical purposes if the minimum useful research expenditure (PR03) is set arbitrarily high (e.g., $1,000,000), as is the stock market confidence function if the pay-out ratio (PF26) is set at zero.

For illustrations of simulations involving varying degrees and types of change or simplification in the basic model the reader is referred to Chapter 6. We may only add here that an interesting possibility is the elimination of whole sets of parameters cutting across many aspects of the model. For instance, all time lags, most common economies and all inter-company transactions in the simulation could be eliminated while still retaining a perfectly workable model.

---

86 The Dictionary locations are PS04, PS05, PM10, PR01, PR02, PF22 and PF23. Cf. Chapter 3.

87 Setting PS01, PS02 or PS03 to zero might "blow up" the model.

3] SAFETY VALVES

Unlike most other management simulations taking the form of games, the INTOP model is equipped with adequate safety valves, i.e., mechanisms preventing obviously dysfunctional results. There are at least two good reasons for such safety valves in game models: many equations may lead to unacceptable (in the sense of blatantly unrealistic) results at their extreme values, and the financial statements may show negative entries where none would normally occur. This type of outcome we have guarded against by introducing special parameters in the program. These will be discussed below. First it should be added, however, that INTOP has what might be labeled *a universal safety valve* in the Wonder Card procedure, which permits ex post adjustment of *any* result considered undesirable. The use of Wonder Cards has already been discussed.[88] Let us merely note that the safety valve parameters differ from the Wonder Cards by being preventive rather than curative in character.

Three of the safety valve parameters apply to manufacturing: the maximum production costs; the penalty cost for a commitment to ship goods to another company when the inventory is insufficient to fill the order; and the special penalty cost for such inter-company shipments in cases where the seller has never had *any* production in the area from which his goods are shipped.[89] Three more are in the financial realm: forced loans from suppliers which require that Accounts Receivable be mortgaged in order that the company attain a liquid cash position; a minimum cash requirement in the Home Office imposed by the Bank to cover any tax liability a company may have in Liechtenstein; and a limit on area bank loans based on the amount of working capital in the operating areas. Each of these safety valves will be discussed in turn.

Since the manufacturing cost equation has the shape of a parabola, very low or very high rates of production might produce astronomical costs. To prevent such an unrealistic occurrence we introduce a parameter for the maximum cost per unit for any production (PM02). Referring to the manufacturing function,[90] we observe that the "actual" production cost is calculated in its entirety; then this cost is compared with the cost limit. If the "actual" cost is greater than this limit, the limit becomes the production cost. We will want to choose the maximum production cost so that a substantial penalty is incurred for extremely low or extremely high production levels. At such low levels it could be assumed that the goods were turned out by manual labor, or conversely by excessive overtime operation. As this parameter applies to all grades, the additional cost for the higher grades must also be included in choosing its value.

88 Cf. *supra*, 219ff.

89 The assumption in the last case is that the penalty costs were incurred by the company having had the goods made by inexperienced subcontractors outside the X and Y industries.

90 Cf. *supra*, 103.

DR 35:   *Choose the maximum cost per unit as a func-*
                       tion of the minimum cost per unit (DR 19).

Standard Range: 5–6 times the minimum cost for X; 2½–4 times
                       the minimum cost for Y

Dictionary: PM02

One of the INTOP features which simplifies administration is the rule that all shipping between companies must be carried out. Occasionally, however, a company will commit itself to shipments which it does not have in inventory. When this happens, it incurs a sales expediting expense on the income statement as an extra cost for readying the required products over and above their regular manufacturing cost. This penalty again is unrelated to the product grade involved.

DR 36:   *Set the sales expediting cost per unit as a per*
                       cent of the minimum production cost (DR 19).

Standard Range: 80–120 per cent for both X and Y

Dictionary: PS30

Another anomaly may occur under the shipping rule when goods are expedited from an area where the company has never produced any goods of the type involved. In this case, too, the production cost per unit must be known so that it can be added to the sales expediting cost. But with no previous manufacture, the production costs would come out as zero if no safety valve were provided. Hence, we substitute a penalty cost per unit to discourage this type of expediting. It is set equal to the maximum manufacturing cost (PM02) corresponding to the use of handicraft means of production. This is a safety valve built into the program.

Among the safety valve mechanisms in the financial function the most important is supplier credit. Its function is to insure that a company does not have negative cash balances on its financial statements, and to penalize companies engaging in poor financial planning. To prevent the occurrence of negative cash, suppliers will reluctantly extend credits, but only at premium interest charges. There are two interest rates for supplier credit which will operate depending upon the amount of the cash deficiency. We call the point where the higher interest rate goes into effect the switch-over amount. As other financial parameters this switch-over amount varies as between the areas and Liechtenstein, but not as between the products.

DR 37:   *Choose the switch-over amount for supplier cred-*
                       it as a per cent of Accounts Receivable in the
                       operating areas according to variation V28 (7,
                       7, 4). Set the switch-over amount in the Home
                       Office higher to reflect the presumed greater ac-
                       cessibility to funds of centralized financial man-
                       agement.

Standard Range: 10–50 per cent in the operating areas;
                       $1,000,000–$1,500,000 in the Home Office.

Dictionary: PF09, PF18

DR 38:   *Choose supplier credit interest rates high enough
                       to make the use of such credits generally, though
                       not unconditionally, unattractive, and in any
                       case higher than standard bank rates.*

Standard Range: In the operating areas: 5–7 per cent below, 7–
                       10 per cent above switch-over
                       In the Home Office: 4–6 per cent below, 6–9 per
                       cent above switch-over

Dictionary: PF08, PF10, PF17, PF19

If the administrator wishes to eliminate the second supplier credit rate, the switch-over amount may be raised to an arbitrarily high value (such as $9,000,000).

In the Home Office an additional problem sometimes arises from the interaction of supplier credit, taxes and the desire to keep the cash balance positive. Since the supplier credit expense, which appears under miscellaneous interest, is needed to calculate the tax expense on the income statement, we must know the supplier credit expense first. But we cannot know it, because the tax expense can contribute to supplier credit. We are forced into a dilemma, as we desire the tax expense to be taken out of cash. In the operating areas we solve this dilemma by putting the tax expense into Accounts Payable 1, but unfortunately the Home Office has no such account. Any tax liability must come out of cash, so that we must require a minimum cash balance in Liechtenstein large enough to cover any tax expense. Since it is unlikely that the gross earnings in the Home Office will exceed $500,000, we can derive this Decision Rule:

DR 39:   *Choose the minimum cash balance in the Home
                       Office based on the tax rate and an assumed
                       limit on gross earnings.*

Standard Range: Tax rate times $500,000, i.e., the requirement is
                       $50,000

Dictionary: PF20

Since the area bank loans are an automatic feature of INTOP, any amount of credit may be solicited on the Operations Decision Card. A prudent banker, however, would not grant just any loan request. We introduce in each area a parameter to limit the maximum amount of such loans to a certain per cent of working capital for each company in the area. In INTOP Standard this loan limit is the same for all operating areas in *percentage* terms, although the limit may be varied by area. As working capital tends to be grossly correlated with market potential of the areas the dollar limit will vary accordingly.

DR 40:	*Choose the parameter which limits the amount of area bank loans as a per cent of working capital (current assets minus current liabilities).*
Standard Range:	20–60 per cent of working capital
Dictionary:	PF13

The administrator will see that the safety valves serve a variety of purposes, all of which contribute to making a realistic simulation. But there is a further purpose: the safety valves at once reflect and enhance the flexibility of the INTOP model, underwriting its functioning even within wide ranges of parameter values. These safety valves give the administrator assurance that he can choose parameters to create a great many different viable simulations. The next and last chapter is included as a stimulation in this direction.

Chapter **6**

A Modular

Multi-Purpose Simulation

1. Modular in Design, Multiple by Purpose

THE INTERNATIONAL OPERATIONS SIMULATION is modular; modular in the basic sense that the overall model is composed of a series of distinct elementary segments which may be eliminated or recombined in different ways.[1] The major modular sections are represented by the products, geographical areas and business functions. These sections are in turn modularized in that they are comprised of building blocks many of which may be eliminated or drastically modified without rewriting the computer program (e,g., the accounts payable and receivable routines in the finance modules, the patent and standard-deluxe features of the product modules, tax carry-forward provisions in area modules). The degree of integration and interdependence among the modules may often be varied within quite broad limits (e.g., by regulating transfer costs between geographical areas). In addition, INTOP as a whole is an extraordinarily flexible instrument both in terms of the number and range of individual parameter changes possible and the ease with which such change may be made.[2] Modular design in general and flexibility in detail permit each administrator to write his own bill of particulars.

Whether the simulation should be changed and what types of

---

[1] It is not modular in the more narrow and technical sense of being a conglomerate of a few score *standard* computer subroutines. Also, the elimination of any given module in the model will not necessarily reduce machine processing time, as the computer ordinarily will have to go through the "dead" parts of the program on a routine basis. Computer output formats will remain basically the same regardless of what parts of the program are being used, unless editing routines are rewritten (or so-called "plugboards" are used to rearrange the formats).

[2] Cf. Chapter 5.

changes should be undertaken are questions to which there can be no general answer. In any given case the answer must depend primarily on the purpose for which the use of the exercise is being contemplated. Precisely because of the versatility of INTOP it is out of the question here to attempt to counsel the reader on all applications and the modifications in the game which they may require. Rather, we shall proceed by exemplification of simulations run for different purposes and some of the concomitant changes possible within the basic INTOP framework. Many — although not all — of these variations have in fact been tried out at Chicago. We predict, however, that others will soon carry this work further than we have been able to and that a major pool of applications experience will be built up. The following sections of the chapter will be devoted to general management simulations with a flavor different from that reflected in the standard *Player's Manual*, to production, marketing and other functional management simulations, to simplified games and, finally, to a brief discussion of INTOP-INDUSTRIAL, the most complex game-type simulation staged at Chicago thus far.

2. General Management INTOP Simulations

THE TYPE AND MIX of problems encountered at the general management level of two different firms are never identical — not even if the firms are of substantially the same size and active in the same industry. This does not in itself mean that there can be no general principles of management or that experience gained in one situation is worthless in every other. But it does mean that one general management simulation may differ widely from another, even though both may be equally "realistic." INTOP permits considerable change in emphasis within the overall framework of the game without losing its original character of a general management simulation.

A. *Emphasis on Organization*

INTOP was designed with organization simulation and research in mind. Its use for organization simulation and planning purposes in business is discussed in Appendix VII. In the present context our focus is on organization problems in educational programs. The reader interested in research in the organization theory area may wish to read both the appendix and the comments which follow.

A basic postulate is that organizational objectives, task environments and internal structure-behavior patterns are interdependent. A fourth major set of interacting variables is composed of the personal characteristics of the members of the organization. As the last-named variables may be manipulated by the game administrator (according to the educational or business backgrounds of participants, etc.) without changing any features of the simulation itself there is no need to discuss them here. Neither do we need to develop the fact that varying the size of teams is likely to produce interesting variations in organization structure and decision-making patterns.

Runs of INTOP Standard present teams with a variety of internal and product market environments. Companies are allowed to choose objectives freely, and a considerable differentiation in this regard is typical. It is not surprising – at least not to us – that internal organization and behavior patterns also vary greatly.[3] Assuming the validity of our basic postulate, more systematic observation of organization-environmental relationships would be possible by requiring teams to have identical objectives and initial resource commitments. By making the areas even more different than they are in INTOP Standard teams might be stimulated to emphasize area administration; by differentiating the products more product-oriented management might come to prevail; or by emphasizing the complexity of the management functions an even more pronounced trend toward functionalism as a prevailing structuring approach than at present might appear. Similar effects may well be obtained merely by de-emphasizing product differences (similar elasticities, growth patterns, etc.) and functional complexity in order to make the significance of area variations more clear-cut, or by de-emphasizing area variations (government-business relations, market size, etc.) and functional complexity in order to make product differences appear more pronounced. Clearly, a great range of combinations are possible. Generally speaking, it seems fair to assume that the greater the differences between the areas as well as between the products, and the greater the depth of the several management functions represented in the model, the greater the attention will viable teams pay to problems of organization, decision-making processes and internal communication. This is well in line with the contention in the introductory chapter that an emphasis on reasonably realistic organization problems requires complex simulation models.

The International Operations Simulation would seem especially well adapted to highlighting in education as well as in research two key areas of intra-organizational conflict and coordination, namely that of innovation management and that of the internal "scramble for resources." As regards the management of innovation it may be sufficient to refer to the *Player's Manual* in this context.[4] Internal conflict and coordination problems may be emphasized further than in INTOP Standard by setting up a more drastic tug-of-war between the "payoff" alternatives of various management functions, products and areas. For instance, marketing may be set against production by making the advantage of having both standard and deluxe models vital in the

---

[3] Other circumstances equal, there appears to be a certain trend from organization by function to organization by area in the course of a game in which teams are free to reorganize as they feel the need arise.

[4] *Player's Manual*, 7. Cf. *supra*, Chapter 2.

marketplace, while the concomitant production of standard and deluxe in a given factory is made drastically more expensive than single-model production, and finance may be set against both of the other functions by increasing inventory carrying charges while at the same time raising the rate of interest obtainable on government securities. The marketing-production cleavage may be further increased by making the grade differentials for patent improvements move in opposite directions as regards consumer attractiveness and manufacturing cost. X may be made even more of a growth product (with initial disappointments) and Y even more of a stable "necessity of life." Europe may be made even less risky, while Brazil is made even more so, etc.

It may also be noted that team choices of organization structure seem to be influenced by the way decision-making information is structured. For example, while the standard Operations Card 1 incorporates functional as well as product decisions for *all* areas, thus (hopefully) being nondirective, an earlier Area Operations form (reproduced in Fig. 48) by treating each area as a separate entity apparently suggested area-oriented organization to many teams. While it is necessary to stick to existing column numbers in indicating decisions made, an organization researcher may well contemplate the design of alternate formats of the decision cards to study the effect of format bias on organization structure and behavior. Where the research design requires a fairly rigid division of authority or compartmentalization among team members, the researcher may wish to block out certain areas of the standard forms according to a predetermined pattern before distributing them to the executives of each company.

B. *Emphasis on Diversification*

Geographical diversification may be encouraged by high fixed costs of production in combination with relatively low transfer charges and agency fees. Inelastic demand functions coupled with fairly steeply accelerating inventory charges tend to produce a similar effect. Product diversification is promoted by increasing the common economies available in the commercial and administrative (C & A) cost area and/or the cross-elasticity of demand for the two products. Functional diversification may be encouraged by lowering the rate at which expenses are incurred in any given function and/or by eliminating intercompany transactions. Another stimulus is to make captive sales organization more advantageous than alternate forms of distribution even at low rates of operation. Depending upon the area, product and functional makeup of the parties involved, diversification may also occur through mergers.

C. *Emphasis on Product Interdependence*

By changing the cross-elasticity of demand of X on Y (and/or vice versa) it is possible to vary the relationship between the two prod-

FIG. 48   *Experimental Area Operations Form*

(INTOP DECISION CARD NO. 1)

Item   *Decision*

USE PENCIL, NOT INK!   9 ▢
                                                                         1

Company No.   ▢▢
                                                                         2-3

Area No. (US is 1, EEC is 2, Brazil is 3)   ▢
                                                                         4

Period No.   ▢
                                                                         5

Cash From (0) or To (−) Home   0 ▢   (000's)   ▢▢▢▢
                                    6   7-10

No. New X Plants   ▢   No. New Y Plants   ▢
                                   11   12

Borrow (0) or Invest (−)   0 ▢   (000's)   ▢▢▢
                                   13   14-16

Methods Improvement   (000's)   X ▢▢   Methods Improvement Y   ▢▢
                                  17-18   19-20

Production

Grade X Std.   ▢   Grade X Del. ▢   Grade Y Std. ▢   Grade Y Del.
              21   22   23

Units (00's) of X   Std.   Del.   Std.   Del.   Std.   De
    Plant 1 ▢▢▢ ▢▢▢   Plant 2 ▢▢▢ ▢▢▢   Plant 3 ▢▢▢ ▢▢
                25-30   31-36   37-42

Units (00's) of Y   Std.   Del.   Std.   Del.   Std.   De
    Plant 1 ▢▢▢ ▢▢▢   Plant 2 ▢▢▢ ▢▢▢   Plant 3 ▢▢▢ ▢▢
                43-48   49-54   55-60

Marketing

Price X Std. ▢▢   X Del. ▢▢   Y Std. ▢▢   Y Del. ▢▢
        61-62   63-64   65-66   67-68

Advertising (000's)   X ▢▢▢   Advertising Y ▢▢▢
                         73-75   76-78

ucts over a broad range from strongly supplementary to strongly competitive. Indeed, their degree of interdependence may be made to vary by areas, reflecting the fact that while some products may be regarded as supplementary by Americans, lower-income Brazilians may look upon them as alternatives. Interdependence may also be varied by manipulating the common economies in distribution.

A different type of interaction results if one of the products is made a component of the other. This introduces several new dimensions in the simulation, such as inter-company and intra-company marketing of components, make-lease-buy decisions and some rather exacting scheduling problems. A special version of the Chicago simulation, INTOP-INDUSTRIAL, has been developed to incorporate these features. It is described in some detail in the last section of this chapter.

D. *Emphasis on Bargaining*

Bargaining may be emphasized by making inter-company transactions attractive,[5] by stimulating intra-company negotiations and by introducing role-playing in situations ancillary to the game. Role-playing in the form of participants simulating management and union representatives, management consultants, CHASE-A-MARTINI Bank, etc. has already been discussed.[6] The administrator may stimulate intra-company negotiations by placing a premium on autonomy within the teams. This may be accomplished by such means as introducing capital transfer taxes from all areas to home (and, possibly, in the reverse direction as well) in the third or fourth quarter of the game or by a rule that no goods may be transferred out of an area without the consent of local management.

The attractiveness of inter-company transactions may be enhanced by stimulating functional specialization among the companies and by the introduction of environmental changes demanding more than routine adjustment on the part of the teams. Greater functional specialization among the teams may be induced in several ways. For example, inter-company financing activity may be stimulated by stiffening the terms of area and home office bank loans. The scale economies of production may be made even more pronounced. C & A costs for agents and captive sales organization may be increased. The minimal amount necessary to obtain a modicum of probability increase each quarter in R & D may be raised. Teams specializing as distributors may initially be given access to a special pool of inventory supplied by a Japanese firm whose costs keep increasing as the quarters go by, thereby stimulating the distributors to find alternate sources of supply among the other teams.

If he so prefers, the administrator may simply *assign* specialized roles to all teams. In this manner he can save himself the trouble of re-dimensioning the parameters of the model. Specialization may be re-emphasized by eliminating intra-company transfer of goods.

Many environmental events stimulate inter-company transactions. For instance, strikes may induce imports, the lowering of transfer costs promotes international trade and capital export prohibition in Brazil tends to produce inter-company borrowing.

E. *Emphasis on Experimentation.* *Non-Interactive Settings*

The purpose of staging a management game need not be to subject participants to a "well-rounded" simulation of environmental

---

[5] It may be observed that we have often had 50–100 inter-company transactions per decision session even in runs of INTOP Standard at Chicago.

[6] Cf. *supra*, 25, 149f, 194.

differences such as that hopefully achieved in a model with three international regions and two different products. The purpose may rather be to stimulate systematic experimentation within a reasonably unified and controllable framework. This may be achieved by making all three areas in the game identical, for example, by resetting all parameter values in Areas 2 and 3 to conform to Area 1 parameters. Thus each company is offered the opportunity to experiment with three different sets of policies in three identical operating environments each decision period. The room for systematic experimentation may be doubled by also making all characteristics of the two products identical.

It is likely that runs of this type would tend to turn the attention of the teams away from some general organization and management problems. On the other hand, participants would be freer to concentrate on the subject matter of business economics per se.

Ordinarily, one would not wish to see a general management game non-interactive. Non-interactive simulations may be highly desirable in the case of self-contained mathematical models of business and in the case of games aiming at the exercise of a particular analytical tool, such as an inventory control formula. Generally, however, in game simulations of broader management activity it must be considered an important facet of realism that the model *is* interactive.

Nevertheless, it is clear that for research purposes it may be quite valuable to be able to keep a large segment of even a general management game under control by making the simulation non-interactive. In the case of INTOP this is perfectly feasible. Each team may be confronted with an identical market situation, as long as no more than six teams are involved, by making both products and all three areas identical. Identical competition may be pre-programmed in each market in several ways. The administrator may run an identical monitor company in each market or he may run up to 19 such companies, each with identical or different strategies. Competition may also be entirely eliminated simply by providing a given market potential in each area and inviting the teams to attempt to optimize their performance.

As each run in a non-interactive game can be completely standardized there is no limit to the number of observations a researcher may make by repeated runs.

If there are a maximum of six teams each operating in segmented markets independently of each other, the administrator has vastly increased opportunities at his disposal of permitting qualitative influences at the individual company level. He may now set manufacturing cost differentially for each company, if he so desires, in accordance with certain criteria of production management ability, such as the foresight displayed in production scheduling and forecasting, or performance in in-basket type problem-solving exercises pertaining to supervisory or grievance problems, quality control, collective bargaining, etc. He may regulate commercial and administrative costs individually according to corresponding criteria of marketing management proficiency (this in addition to the ever-present possibility of manipulating the marketing effectiveness factor). In finance, supplier credit rates may be similarly differentiated.

These examples are merely illustrative of a great many ways in which the simulation might be used in non-interactive settings.

3.   Functional Management INTOP Simulations

WHILE INTOP IS A general management game it is represented well enough in the areas of production, finance and marketing to permit direct use of the standard version of the simulation in educational programs emphasizing any one of these functions. A detailed example of such use in an advanced marketing management course was given in a previous chapter.[7] Use of the general model in a functional management game appears especially desirable when a purpose of the run is to demonstrate the interaction and interdependence of the function in question with other areas of management.

Where the purpose is to emphasize intra-functional problems and when the time available for decision-making is limited, it is often preferable to use a simulation focusing on the function to be examined. As we shall try to indicate, the basic INTOP model lends itself extremely well to such functional simulations. In each case, the modifications required are surprisingly modest, even though they may drastically change the nature of the game.[8] Generally, modification proceeds in two directions: to emphasize the function under study and to reduce the role of the other functions. As usual, our discussion is limited to exemplification of the opportunities available.

A. *Production*

Measures by which the production management aspects of the basic model may be enhanced without any amendment of the computer program include:

Differentiation of obsolescence and depreciation rates by *areas* as well as products.

Permitting accelerated amortization under certain circumstances. (This can only be done by industry-wide manipulation of depreciation rates, or by Wonder Cards each quarter at the individual company level.)[9]

---

7   Cf. *supra*, 183ff.

8   The minimal changes necessary in or amendments to the *Player's Manual* in functionally specialized games as a rule are also easily accomplished. Ordinarily, no change in decision or output forms is required; participants are instructed to disregard any parts of the forms not applicable in a given run.

9   If marketing takes place by the sale of output at a fixed price, or if selling is confined to Area 1, the administrator may introduce significant variations in the production management environment simply by labeling the "areas" differently, say "Alternative 1" (or 2, 3). Alternative 1 may not allow accelerated amortization, while this may be possible under Alternative 2, etc.

Making the plant investment decision more critical by informing the companies from the outset that due to increase in real estate values (and, in Brazil, runaway inflation) factory acquisition cost will increase each quarter by 3 per cent of original cost in the U.S., by 5 per cent in the EEC and by 10–12 per cent in Brazil.

Application of direct costing during the early quarters of a run and absorption costing during the latter quarters, thus highlighting problems of inventory evaluation.[10]

Making the plant disposal and renewal problems more interesting by differentiating disposal value by products, and by offering "second-generation" plants of quite different characteristics from those offered in the first round as regards acquisition cost and construction time.[11]

New plant technology may be introduced either by parameter change after a certain number of quarters or by having the "alternatives" mentioned in note 9 above represent different generations of plant technology and setting their parameters from the beginning.

Differentiation of construction time of plants for areas and products.

Introduction of additional scheduling problems by making X represent a component or a raw material of Y.[12]

Introduction of quality control problems.[13]

Making more information on production costs and their determinants available by consulting services.

A limit on flexibility is provided by the fact that general parameters as a rule may be changed at the individual company level only by Wonder Cards each quarter. The only exception is variable manufacturing cost, which may be changed artificially by manipulating the number indicating plant age. This may be done on a once-for-all basis for any given company, reflecting a special labor agreement or other differentiating circumstances.

To depress the significance of marketing in a production-oriented game the marketing management function may be eliminated entirely. This may be done most easily by a monitor company representing all customers, with monitor buying a certain quantity from each producer at a given price (which may vary with business fluctuations, industry supply, etc.). Less severe restrictions in the marketing area may be introduced by cutting out selected submodules, such as advertising, captive sales organizations and inter-company sales. Another variation is to permit selling only in *one* area, while production may be carried on under varied conditions in all three.[14]

[10] Cf. *infra*, 281.

[11] For standard rules of plant disposal, see INTOP Memo 4, Appendix VI.

[12] This idea is illustrated by INTOP-INDUSTRIAL in Section 6 of the chapter.

[13] The number of production line rejects may be varied by chance or (inversely) in relation to methods improvement expense. The elimination of rejects may be effectuated simply by treating it technically as an inter-company sale to the monitor company (any price paid being the salvage value of the rejects).

[14] Transfer cost may be set to zero. Note that the one-quarter lag in product transfer cannot be eliminated.

The role of the finance function may be diminished by eliminating area and home office bank loans, inter-company loans, the stock market confidence function and securities investments. The accounts payable and receivable routines should probably not be completely eliminated, but might be simplified to comprise only one quarter. Tax legislation is also of direct concern to production management, which speaks against oversimplification in this area. In some instances the requisite degree of simplification may be obtained by making the financial parameters identical in all three areas.

B. *Marketing*

There is a greater variety of marketing management problems in INTOP Standard than in many specialized marketing games. Nonetheless, it is possible to emphasize the marketing function even further. A principal means of doing this is to bring the marketing "effectiveness factor" into play. In this manner, variations in the quality of marketing strategies pursued may be translated into corresponding variations in sales.[15] The factor may be varied for each product in each area and for each individual company.

In INTOP Standard the consideration governing the choice of distribution channels is primarily that of cost, as there is no inherent difference in sales promotion ability of agents and captive sales organizations.[16] In a marketing management game the administrator may wish to endow a captive organization with greater sales promotion ability than agents (or vice versa).[17] This may be accomplished simply by varying the marketing effectiveness factor for companies establishing their own sales organization in a given area. Preferably, the factor should be varied somewhat in relation to the number of offices employed; the adjustment might even be in a negative direction if the company has only one or two regional offices. The captive sales force may also be a superior means of marketing communications. Hence, it may occasionally be enabled to feed back competitive intelligence, such as the sales volume of a given rival by area and product in the past quarter.

An alternate way of making the choice of distribution channels more critical, and also making specialization as a distributor company more interesting, is to permit only specialized distributors to have captive sales organization. This forces integrated suppliers to choose between selling via the computerized agents or through other companies acting as distributors.[18] A more modest step in the same direc-

---

15   For a simple example cf. *supra*, 195.

16   When another team is used as distributor there is also the problem of risk involved.

17   This may call for a readjustment of C & A cost parameters.

18   The administrator may wish to raise all agency fees in the *Player's Manual* by, say, 50 cents per unit for radios and $1.50 for cleaners. He may also drastically reduce the fixed cost and the opening and closing costs for sales offices, and perhaps attach an increase in the marketing effectiveness factor to captive sales organizations.

tion is to make the acquisition of a captive sales organization profitable only at very large turnover volume, perhaps attaching a 2–4 per cent sales advantage (via the marketing effectiveness factor) to each sales office in an area.

A monitor company is of particular value in a marketing game as a source of outside competition, governmental purchasing, new export markets and so on.

The complex coordination, bargaining and inventory management problems in manufacturer-dealer systems in marketing are the object of the Distribution Systems Simulation outlined in Section 5 below. The many differences which practitioners have long recognized as existing between industrial and consumer marketing are brought to the fore in INTOP-INDUSTRIAL, which has provided the backbone of an industrial marketing management course at Chicago.

The administrator of a marketing game may wish to de-emphasize other management functions. Constraints on the finance function have already been discussed.[19] If he so desires, the administrator may eliminate the production function entirely by simply making goods available at a fixed (or auctioned) price through a monitor company. At the opposite end of the continuum of change he may eliminate certain individual features such as the methods improvement function, the change costs due to variations in output, fixed plant expense and the possibility of plant disposal. Intermediary alternatives are also possible. Production functions may be simplified by being made identical (or merely differentiated by scale) in the three areas, or all production may be restricted to one area.[20]

c. *Finance and Accounting*

More than any other business function, financial and accounting management in combination are widely represented in the basic INTOP structure. Without any doubt the use of the simulation as a functional game in this area may be a rewarding one. The financial function may be further emphasized by making the quality of capital budgeting, cash-flow projections, internal control arrangements and other vital aspects of financial management determine the extent and terms of resource allocation, whether by stock capital or home office bank loans. The administrator may also make area bank and securities interest rates vary with business cycle fluctuations. Accounts receivable and payable flows may similarly be varied during the simulation. The imagination of participants may be challenged by asking them to specify likely consequences of inflation or currency devaluation in an area, given the fact that all INTOP accounting is executed in dollar terms.

[19] Cf. *supra*, 279.

[20] There is no imperative need to set inter-area transfer costs to zero, as all companies are affected in an identical manner. The one-quarter lag in shipments from one area to another cannot be eliminated.

Being somewhat in the nature of an artificial appendix, the computerized stock market confidence function in INTOP is not worth emphasizing in a financial game. There are, however, other ways in which stock market confidence (or lack thereof) may be reflected. Companies may be authorized to issue additional stock — presumably on the basis of a well-reasoned stock prospectus submitted to the Liechtenstein Securities Commission, as represented by the administrator. If the past performance of the company and its stock prospectus inspire confidence, this may be reflected in a premium paid for the shares. A simple example: a well-run company decides to issue new shares in the amount of $1,000,000 at par. The administrator, feeling that investors are willing to pay a 15 per cent premium, uses Wonder Cards to add $1,150,000 to home office cash, $1,000,000 to capital stock at par and $150,000 to paid-in-capital. The level of public confidence in a company may also be reflected by the terms on which the administrator is willing to grant home office bank loans.[21]

The prominent role of inter-company loans as a form of financing may be enhanced further by encouraging teams to experiment with various types of restrictive and "banker control" clauses, profit-sharing arrangements, etc., in addition to conventional loan conditions.

The intricate tax problems connected with intra-company shipments between subsidiaries in different jurisdictions may be demonstrated, as may some issues in holding company control and operation in the management of Liechtenstein home offices. Companies may be confronted with changes in corporate tax rates, carry-over provisions and accelerated and/or area- or product-differentiated depreciation schemes,[22] which may or may not influence their day-to-day decisions and investment behavior.

The differences between direct and absorption costing in the production area may be brought out.[23] While existing output formats cannot be changed with regard to contents they may be rearranged by means of so-called plugboards.[24]

The understanding of participants of the accounting structure of the model may be put to the supreme test by embezzlement carried out

21   The authors are indebted to Drs. Leonard Marks, Jr., and Maneck Wadia of the International Center for the Advancement of Management Education at Stanford University for the suggestions in this paragraph.

22   Cf. *supra*, 277.

23   Cf. *supra*, 277f. Direct costing, sometimes more properly called *variable costing*, is the inventory costing method which applies only variable production costs to product; under this method fixed factory overhead is not assigned to product. Direct costing differs from absorption costing, sometimes called *conventional costing*, be-

cause fixed factory overhead is charged against sales immediately instead of being assigned to the inventory cost of units produced. Cf. *supra*, 101f.

Also, marketing cost analysis is often facilitated by a delineation between fixed and variable costs. Unfortunately, the program does not permit the isolation of the fixed cost element in maintaining a captive sales organization in a direct manner. However, companies may themselves maintain such a record.

24   In this manner, too, it is possible to eliminate entirely accounts not at all used in a given run of the game.

by the administrator through the (inappropriate) use of Wonder Cards.[25]

More than other major functions (personnel perhaps excluded) finance and accounting are inextricably intertwined with all other aspects of management. For this reason it would seem inadvisable to reduce in any drastic way the non-financial aspects of INTOP when the simulation is used as an educational device in financial or accounting management. This statement applies especially to decision areas involving capital investment or fixed expenses. On the other hand, one might well wish to eliminate such secondary current expense functions as methods improvement and advertising.

4. Simplification

FOR MANY GOOD REASONS an administrator may wish to make use of a simpler simulation exercise than that represented by INTOP Standard. By simplification the time needed for each decision-making session may easily be reduced to half an hour.[26] If the total number of participants in a run is small, allowing for only one or two persons per company, there is also reason to consider simplification. Somewhat paradoxically, simplification is also the solution to the very large numbers problem; in the last part of the section we present an INTOP game for up to 72 teams of 1–4 persons each, playing in half-hour sessions. Even in cases where time and number of participants do not impose any unusual constraints, simplification may sometimes be worth considering. By eliminating certain parts of the model those aspects which the administrator wishes to emphasize may be highlighted. By reducing the number of interacting variables simplification has the additional merit of making cause-effect relationships more clear cut to participants.

Simplification of the various functional modules was amply discussed in the preceding section. In the present section we shall carry the discussion further by illustrating four additional major avenues of simplification, in each case leading to a useful and viable simulation of a distinct character.

A. *A Domestic Regional Management Simulation*

A prime purpose of the basic INTOP model is to illustrate the problems of divisionalized and diversified concerns. We believe that

---

25 Most elementarily, the administrator may simply siphon off funds from cash and retained earnings in an area until "caught."

26 It could be reduced even further. If this is done most of the unique features of the simulation — inter-company transactions, the entrepreneurial emphasis, international operations — would have to be eliminated, however.

Processing time on the computer will not be appreciably reduced by simplification, as the machine will still have to go through all basic routines, and as the output formats to be printed will remain the same even though not all accounts may be used.

the problems confronting such companies in international operations in some respects are more severe than anywhere else; in fact this was an important consideration in the design of the game. Clearly, however, these international aspects introduce elements of complexity which it may often be desirable to avoid. The simulation may indeed be simplified appreciably if limited to some major features of diversified domestic concerns divisionalized on a regional and/or product basis.

It is not difficult to specify how INTOP may be "domesticated." Such international features as varying corporate tax rates, carry-over provisions, and capital transfer taxes should clearly be eliminated. In addition, inter-area disparities in interest rates, economic indices, supplier credit regulations, accounts payable and receivable routines and inventory charges should be either eliminated or reduced to proportions actually existing within a single commercial jurisdiction, such as the United States. Inter-area transfer charges — no longer comprising tariffs and other international handling charges in addition to freight and insurance — should be reduced to levels reasonably close to intra-area shipping rates. The administrator may also wish to consider reducing some of the more drastic differences between the areas as regards production and marketing functions. Technology, labor and materials costs, consumer styles of life, selling costs, etc., would generally vary less between regions within one country than internationally. On the other hand, a few of these sharp differences may be retained in order to highlight the effect of divergence in the variables concerned. Participants should be made aware of any such special emphasis in the simulation.

Moving the Home Office back to the United States (or any other area) from Liechtenstein offers no great problem. Tax rates have to be equalized. All companies will also have to accept separate accounting for home office operations, even though they may not always themselves make such a clear distinction in their own organization plans and internal bookkeeping. From a legal and taxation viewpoint it is convenient to look upon the Home Office as a holding company.

For a domestic game a special player's manual should be prepared. This will not be difficult. Using the standard manual as a basis, the administrator will find that some parts may simply be eliminated. As the subject matter in all essential parts will be retained, modification rather than outright rewriting is called for. In fact, many pages, such as some of those relating to inter-company transactions and the directions for filling out decision forms, may be used without any change.

B. *A Single-Product Simulation*

It may be desirable to retain the international aspects and all essential features of the basic model and yet conduct major surgery on it. This might be the case, for instance, if the number of participants is relatively small, but an emphasis on international competition makes it useful to have a fairly large number of companies. It may then be helpful simply to cut the standard model in half by confining the exercise to one of the products.

The only major loss suffered by such an arrangement is that it eliminates one of the major dimensions in organization structuring. However, the basic choice between area and functional organization remains, as do the problems of data processing and delegation. If the administrator feels that this accent on organization is insufficient, the alternative is to use the standard version of the game, increasing the number of members per team and correspondingly limiting the number of companies.

There is no need to prepare any special documentation in a one-product simulation. Participants should merely be instructed to disregard the parts of the *Player's Manual* and of the decision and ouput forms pertaining to the product eliminated.

c. *A Multi-Product Simulation*

As we have seen, the number of products may be curtailed without a single change in either the basic program or player documentation. It is also possible to design a game with six different products, although this operation is not quite as painless. Such a simulation might be preferable if the purpose is to demonstrate widely differing types of products in terms of the associated market structures or production functions within the confines of one geographical area.[27] The principle involved is to treat the X and the Y industries in each so-called area as a separate entity. Thus X in "Area 1" may be electric mixers, while in "Area 2" it is Swiss cheese, and in "Area 3" it is dress shirts; Y may be differentiated in an analogous manner. Clearly, no inter-area transactions can be permitted, and R & D would have to be restricted (if used at all) to one of the X and one of the Y products.[28]

Production and marketing data for each of the six products would be separately reported on the income statement and ancillary data sheets. However, financial management would be commingled by "area" for each "pair" of X and Y products, and, of course, ferreting out separate data on the balance sheet would be quite difficult. It is for this reason that such a game should be considered only where the prime purpose is the demonstration of varying production and/or marketing conditions for different products. While it should not be necessary to change input and output formats, one would presumably

[27] While retaining international differences between the three areas would be perfectly feasible it would not seem to make much sense in the circumstances.

[28] If the administrator and the players are willing to maintain separate patent records for each product, patent improvements may be extended to all products by the administrator selling licenses.

have to rewrite the *Player's Manual* rather extensively.

D. *A Single-Area Simulation*

The simplest viable game based on the INTOP model is confined to one product in a single area. In addition, certain features of the functional modules may be eliminated, such as the choice of channels and the possibility of multiple plants or bank loans. Automatically, intra-company transactions are also eliminated in such a game. The Home Office may either carry on a holding operation of the type indicated in Subsection A above, or it may be entirely eliminated in the manner indicated in Subsection E below.

If the international aspects of the standard simulation are of little concern, if product diversification is of greater interest than regional operations and if the number of participants is limited, a single-area, two-product approach would seem most preferable. It is also perfectly feasible to strike an intermediary compromise, such as a two-area game with one or two products.

As long as two areas are involved there is no need to prepare a special player's manual; participants should be told to disregard the third area (and the second product, if it is to be eliminated). If the game is confined to one area, a new manual should be prepared. The comments in the last paragraph of Subsection A above are applicable.

E. *A Game for 72 Teams*

Each area module in INTOP Standard comprises all the perquisites of a full-blown general management game with one or two products. Prevailing on this feature, the simulation may be run with up to 72 teams simultaneously. The possibility of employing such a large number of teams represents an important advantage in at least four types of situations:

(*a*) if the number of participants is very large, i.e., anywhere between 100 and 200 persons;
(*b*) if the simulation is to be run in parallel in several classes or at several different institutions;
(*c*) if the simulation is used for research calling for a great number of observations at the team level; and
(*d*) if it is desired to spread the cost of staging the simulation as widely as possible.

We believe that there is great merit in cooperative runs between different institutions to share costs. The Chicago game affords ample opportunity for such arrangements while still retaining its character of a sophisticated and challenging simulation.

By allocating the teams by area there is ample room for 24–72 different companies. Depending on the circumstances, the simulation may comprise only one game, or two[29] or three parallel games. Area characteristics may be made identical, or they may be different as preferred (e.g., the U.S.-EEC-Brazil configuration of the standard version may be retained). The areas may be isolated from each other; this may be most reasonable where different sets of teams are located in different cities. However, it is perfectly feasible to retain all international features, including sales transactions between teams in different games, if so desired. In all cases, inter-company sales between teams in the same area can be carried on as usual.[30]

Computer outputs are produced in the same manner as usual. Consequently, three teams are accounted for on each set of outputs. If in some case this would be held objectionable, output forms may simply be cut in three parts.[31] While theoretically up to 75 teams could be used, it is advisable to reserve the last set of outputs for monitoring purposes.

The 72-team game calls for one major simplification: the elimination of a separate Home Office and the functions performed by it in INTOP Standard. While, if it is so desired, home office operations may be retained by up to 24 companies, it would clearly be anomalous to retain a common superstructure for up to three entirely separate and distinct companies. Ordinarily, too, this simplification is to be welcomed in runs of the magnitude discussed here.

Viable marketing research and R & D functions may be retained even though separate home offices are eliminated. Marketing Research 1 sheets will be produced as usual (unless deliberately suppressed). A standard set of up to six Marketing Research 2 items may be provided each company every quarter gratuitously or for a fee. Alternatively, each team represented on a set of output sheets may order up to six items every third quarter. Payment may be made simply by transferring cash from the team's area to its non-existent Home Office!

Several arrangements to handle R & D may be imagined. The most reasonable, and at the same time most practical, is for the administrator to license the teams patents of various grades according to a predetermined schedule (or on the basis of competitive bidding).[32] There is no room in this exercise for the stock market confidence function.

As each "area" column on the output sheets represents a self-sufficient operation the game is set up with an allocation of starting

---

[29] A dual game may consist of one two-area and one single-area or of two single-area runs. In a two-area run the limit will be either 24 or 48 companies depending on whether or not each team is confined to one area from an accounting viewpoint.

[30] Loans and patent licenses on an inter-company basis are not feasible.

[31] This might be desirable where parameters for each area have been made identical.

[32] Note that teams having been licensed only for lower grades than those granted other companies appearing on the same ancillary data sheet should be instructed not to make use of grades higher than those they have in fact been licensed for.

capital to each of the 72 companies.[33] Should it be desirable, the administrator may later change the resource allocation at any time by making use of the capital transfer boxes on the Operations Decision Card. Teams are instructed not to use these boxes except for payment for market research and consulting services.[34] As long as the inter-area differences of INTOP Standard are retained there is no need to rewrite the *Player's Manual*. If all areas are made identical the manual may, of course, be correspondingly simplified.

5.   A Distribution Systems Simulation

THE BEHAVIOR OF MARKETING and physical distribution systems composed of such interacting elements as manufacturers, wholesalers, retailers and consumers is receiving increasing attention both from students such as Alderson, Balderston, Forrester and Ridgway[35] and practitioners. The designers of one elementary distribution systems game say about their creation that it

enables the participant to view each segment of a distribution channel as a contributing part of an integrated system. It enables him to examine the time-sequence patterns of such a system, which involves the physical production and distribution of goods. It reveals the effects of various order and inventory policies. It provides a tool for experimentation in the operation and control of the factors affecting a distribution system. It may be used as either a decision or a non-decision simulation (with fixed decision rules). As a teaching device it is highly flexible.[36]

The INTOP Distribution Systems Simulation outlined below will perform all of these functions. It will also do what for purposes of realism in such systems simulation is much more important, that is, providing each participating component in any one manufacturer-dealer system with viable alternatives for survival. Manufacturers have

33 The funds are directed to the cash and home office control accounts on the balance sheet. This may be accomplished most simply by indicating a transfer of funds from the fictional Home Office on the Operations Decision Card in the first quarter of the game. It can, of course, also be done by Wonder Cards.

34 On the balance sheet such transfers affect the home office control account. It should be pointed out to participants that this is a technical deficiency from an accounting viewpoint. Alternatively, the administrator may make retroactive corrections by Wonder Card, making the deduction appear in retained earnings and restoring the home office control account.

35 Wroe Alderson, *Marketing Behav-*

ior and Executive Action (1957), especially Chapters III and V; F. E. Balderston, "Communication Networks in Intermediate Markets," 4 *Management Science* (Jan. 1958), 154–71; Jay W. Forrester, *Industrial Dynamics* (1961); Valentine F. Ridgway, "Administration of Manufacturer-Dealer Systems," 1 *Administrative Science Quarterly* (Mar. 1957), 464–83.

36   Paul S. Greenlaw, Lowell W. Herron and Richard H. Rawdon, *Business Simulation* (1962), 175. (Parentheses added.) A major weakness in the simulation designed by these authors is that while it may be made to provide for competition between tripartite manufacturer-wholesaler-retailer chains it has no horizontal interaction at any one of these levels.

different choices of channel (including direct selling to retailers). So do wholesalers. Retailers may use either manufacturers or wholesalers as sources of supply. And, significantly, there is competition at every level and, indeed, between levels as well as between systems, making new mutations and recombinations a frequent phenomenon, and indeed enabling one to speak of the entire industry simulated as in some respects constituting a "super-system." Without this feature competitive considerations, changing power relationships and loyalties and similar concepts crucial to full-blown systems simulation could simply not emerge.[37]

The INTOP Distribution Systems Simulation may be played by a maximum of 72 teams.[38] Component elements are manufacturers, wholesalers, retailers, wholesaler-owned retail outlets (optional) and consumers. As usual, end consumer markets are simulated by computerized demand functions. A maximum of 24 companies may engage in manufacturing. All manufacturers are chartered in Area 2, which is now reduced to representing an accounting "storage bin" for such companies. This makes it feasible to set shipping costs, inventory and sales expediting charges in a manner suitable to the dimensions and scale of operation of manufacturing companies.

Distributor and retailer teams, of which there may be a maximum of 48 collectively (a proportion of distributors to retailers in the range of one to three to perhaps one to five seems reasonable), may be active in Area 1 and Area 3. If there are relatively few teams participating, they may be confined to Area 1. The game may be made domestic in the sense that the demand functions and market potentials for the two areas are made identical, and shipments between the two are prevented. In this manner one may demonstrate to participants how a differentiation in such parameters as inventory costs, shipping charges (intra-area transfer between wholesalers and retailers) and interest rates may shift the balance of power between manufacturer-dealer systems as well as between the component elements of such systems. Parameters may, for instance, be set to favor, subtly, independent distributors in one area, while the direct manufacturer-retailer relationship is made more economical in the other.

If the administrator so prefers, it is fully possible to retain the international features of the game, including product shipments between the two marketing areas. Should he wish to base the simulation

---

[37] The Greenlaw-Herron-Rawdon "system" simulation would seem largely confined to a demonstration of inventory swings in three-level distribution chains, and of techniques to control such swings. For a sophisticated distribution system simulation not based on gaming, see Frederick E. Balderston and Austin C. Hoggatt, *Simulation of* *Market Processes* (1962).

[38] If yet another dimension is to be introduced, i.e., the possibility of wholesalers or retailers integrating "backwards" to comprise captive manufacturing, a maximum of 24 teams are possible. The reason, as suggested in the text, is that manufacturing is confined to one "area."

on the parameters used in INTOP Standard runs as far as possible, he needs to consider whether he wants marketing to take place in the relatively similar U.S. and EEC or in one of these areas and Brazil. Where the U.S.-EEC combination is preferred, manufacturing should be relocated to Area 3 for accounting purposes.

To facilitate differentiation in the characteristics of component elements at various levels of a system and to demonstrate more effectively these differences to participants it is advisable to make X and Y refer to the same product by setting cross-elasticity of demand very high. X may refer to a wholesaler-marketed brand, Y to a manufacturer-owned brand. A limitation is that X can only be made in X plants, and Y only in Y plants. Presumably, the characteristics of X and Y plants should be made identical. If a manufacturer wants to sell directly to retailers (i.e., sponsor his own Y brand), he may be obliged to spend $50,000 or $100,000 per decision period on advertising (in "Area 2" — the fact that this will have no direct effect on demand matters not) and perhaps also to establish a captive selling organization (again in "Area 2").[39] No such costs are incurred if he sells X to distributors. Inventory charges at the manufacturing level may be made high on a unit basis, but with modest rate of acceleration. The shipping charge for brand Y should be stiff: by selling directly to retailers Ys are only shipped once, while Xs are transshipped via distributors. Also, in selling directly the time lag between manufacturer and retailer is limited to one quarter, while a lag of two quarters is necessary in going via wholesalers.

Shifting our attention to the area (or areas) in which wholesalers and retailers are located, we find that wholesalers will have obtained their X and retailers their Y (if any) by inter-company transactions (INTOP Decision Card No. 3) from the manufacturers. Retailers will have obtained their X (if any) from wholesalers in the same area (or from the other area, if the simulation is international). As warehousing is a classical wholesaler function, inventory charges for X should be made low, and they should not begin to accelerate except at quite high levels.[40] Conversely, retailers are not suited to carry big inventories — hence Y inventory charges should be high both on a unit and accelerated basis. Intra-area shipping rates for X should be low enough to permit distributors a viable existence.[41] Wholesale companies may sell independently of retail teams (making for interesting bargaining

---

39   As the captive sales organization expenditure will be in the nature of a fixed cost, one might consider making advertising a variable one, such as one dollar per unit of Y sold each quarter.

40   The fact that X inventory charges necessarily will be equally low at the retail level (or even lower, due to the absence of acceleration supercharges at this level) is not dysfunctional, as in real life the wholesaler may well defray part of inventory carrying costs of retailers.

41   Unless there is a special reason to encourage trade among retailers, shipping charges for Y in Area 1 (and 3, if used) should be set high.

relationships) by establishing their own chain-type retail outlets.[42] If manufacturers have been obliged to conduct pre-selling type of advertising, the minimal effective amount of advertising may be set lower for Y than for X.

Initial specialized roles in the system should be assigned. Manufacturers may be allocated two X factories ready to produce at the beginning of the game and one quarter's supply of inventory. Their cash resources should be small. Retailers should also have X inventory on hand for the first quarter and a modest cash allocation. Clearly, their aggregate resource allocation will be a good deal smaller than that of manufacturers. Wholesalers should have X inventory enough to supply a requisite number of retailers for a quarter. Considering the traditional financing function of wholesalers, they should also be given an ample allocation of cash.[43] In this manner a distributor may effectively reassert himself as the coordinating influence in at least one major vertical system from producer to consumer, while in other systems he may find he will have to dance to the tune of the manufacturer. Standing relationships of various kinds should be encouraged, but not forced upon participants. If manufacturers wish to begin making their own Y brands they will have to build Y factories first — weighing any advantages involved in such a measure against the appreciable fixed-cost economies of a third X plant.

The introduction of seasonal variations as well as business fluctuations will help to focus the attention of participants on "distribution pipeline management," but may take some of their attention away from economically more basic problems of coexistence as systems components. As usual, the administrator must keep in mind the purpose for which he is running the simulation. To provide for new perspectives, teams may be rotated between system levels at mid-game.

The use (or non-use) of the home office part of the INTOP Standard program and of a monitor company may be governed by considerations similar to those discussed in Section 4E above.[44] While INTOP was indeed designed to permit a Distribution Systems Simulation of the kind outlined here, such a simulation has not yet been staged at the time of writing. When it is, it will clearly be necessary to undertake an extensive revision of the *Player's Manual* used in standard runs of the game.

---

[42] We prevail upon the regional sales office parameters in INTOP Standard. Indeed, if so desired the same privilege can be extended to retailers, although this seems to be an unnecessary complication. It does, however, have the merit of showing up the differential advantage of having both a manufacturer (Y) and a distributor (X) brand. By contrast, common economies for X and Y could easily be eliminated in the case of conventional C & A unit costs (i.e., costs corresponding to agency fees in INTOP Standard).

[43] This will enable the wholesalers to give loans (with whatever tying clauses they are able to negotiate) to manufacturers and retailers. They may also use their financial leverage to pay manufacturers cash, while allowing retailers to follow the accounts payable delay routine built into the model.

[44] Cf. *supra*, 286.

6. INTOP-INDUSTRIAL—
An Exercise in Flexibility

HAVING DISCUSSED various avenues of simplification and re-combination of INTOP modules we will bring this volume to a close by a brief account of the most complex simulation staged thus far without any change in the computer program. This system, labeled INTOP-INDUSTRIAL, was developed for an industrial marketing management course at Chicago. Involving an industrial component as well as an end consumer product incorporating the component, INTOP-INDUS-TRIAL is especially appropriate to educational programs directed towards the problems of internationally diversified, industrially integrated concerns. The simulation may, however, also be reoriented to the domestic scene.

Multiple scheduling, inventory, make-or-buy, subcontractor relations and intra-corporate coordination problems constitute the major new dimensions in this simulation. If both components and end products are to be made, is it preferable to specialize company divisions by components manufacture and assembly (such as the Fisher Body and Chevrolet Divisions in General Motors), or should each division rather be a self-contained unit serving a given geographical area? What rules should govern intra-company transfers of goods? What are some of the determinants of relative bargaining power when companies of varying size and degree of integration deal with each other? These are some of the issues management encounters in industrial marketing and intra-corporate economics.

Some of the subtlest problem situations in the simulation — as in real business life — occur at the crossroads of the domestic and international areas. For instance, under what conditions should components be made in one country to be assembled in the other? For our assembly plant in Europe, should we subcontract component products locally, import components from our U.S. plants or perhaps duplicate component-making facilities in the EEC? Will an industrializing country, such as Brazil, look with greater favor on local assembly of final products or on local components manufacture? Under what circumstances is the assignment of patent licenses preferable to other modes of overseas operations, such as selling through local distributors or establishing our own sales organization?

To stimulate the imagination of participants they are instructed to think of product X as a fractional horsepower motor and of product Y as a vacuum cleaner. Companies specializing as component motor manufacturers are assured of a reasonable degree of independent bargaining power by the fact that there is a relatively small but faithful market for the motors, consisting largely of hobbyists and do-it-yourself fans. Clearly, substantial interaction may take place between the overall X and Y markets due to X's dual character of an end consumer good and a necessary component of Y.

Vacuum cleaners are built "from the motor up"; companies are informed that it is not economically feasible to build Y except with X as the starting point. Hence there is no such thing as "unfinished vacuum cleaners" in the game. This automatically presents the teams with a major scheduling problem. If a company intends to build a certain number of vacuum cleaners in a given area in a given quarter Q_t, a corresponding number of motors must be either available in ending inventory of the preceding quarter Q_{t-1},[45] or in shipment during Q_t from another company (located in the same or any other area) or from a captive motor plant in another area. The notion is that motor shipments from other companies or areas have been scheduled well enough in advance to arrive in time for use in cleaner assembly during the current quarter.

To allow motors to be available in time for assembly into vacuum cleaners in the first quarter of production in cleaner plants, the construction period for motor plants is shortened by one quarter. When X and Y plants owned by a single company are located in the same area, the X plant is presumed to be under the control of a common area (or Y) manager. Hence, motors are always priced at direct manufacturing cost in such a case, as far as the official output data are concerned. (If this is not agreeable, the company is free to keep separate books based on whatever transfer prices it finds suitable.) When X and Y plants owned by a company are located in different areas, it is presumed that the X manager is autonomous, and the company must set up its own norms for intra-corporate transfers. These two presumptions help to enrich the game and at the same time permit the use of INTOP Standard income statement formats without any modification.[46]

A maximum of 24 companies may play INTOP-INDUSTRIAL. What might otherwise be the twenty-fifth company must be reserved for administrative use. As there is no way to physically merge X and Y units, this "company" serves as the "dump" for motor units built into vacuum cleaners (these motors would otherwise continue to be shown in X inventory). As in INTOP Standard, considerable emphasis is placed on product innovation. Each product may have up to four patented improvements. Manufacture of vacuum cleaners of a given level of improvement requires the incorporation of motors of at least the corresponding grade. To make a given number of cleaner Y_3 it is necessary to use an equal number of X_3 or X_4 motors.[47] At the same time, the customary limitation of maximum two grades per product in any given area inventory at any given time is maintained. In combination, these two features present teams with another challenge in the scheduling and coordination of their manufacturing and marketing efforts.

45   It matters not whether the motors were manufactured locally or purchased from the outside in Q_{t-1}.

46   Nor is there any need for changing other decision or output forms.

47   The game administrator or computer liaison man should be prepared to set aside about five minutes per team per decision period to arrange for the elimination of motors built into cleaners from company inventories and to control that motor grades are at least as high as corresponding cleaner grades (where this is not the case, cleaners are simply down-graded).

Sample player's manual and administrative instructions for INTOP-INDUSTRIAL are available from Thorelli.

Appendices

*Note: All other standard forms used in INTOP are also reproduced in this work as follows:
  Administrator forms reproduced in Chapter 5:
    Master Control Card
    Administrator's Wonder Card, standard
  Administrator forms reproduced in Computer Liaison Instruction, Appendix V:
    Wonder Card for Cash and Retained Earnings Adjustment
    Form for Marketing Research Items 17 and 18

Dictionary of Program Parameters

and State Variables

THIS "Dictionary" lists names of all INTOP program parameters and company state variables in any given period of history in the simulation. Thus, it gives a convenient overview of the major elements in the model. The prime practical significance of the Dictionary is that with the administrator's "Wonder Card" it constitutes a vehicle of *change* which is simple, versatile and powerful at once. The administration of change ranging from basic model transformations to a trivial adjustment of a given account of an individual company in a certain period of a particular run of the simulation is discussed in Chapter 5, with supplementary comments in the Computer Liaison Instruction.

For obvious discretionary reasons it was considered inappropriate to include as well a listing of actual parameter values in INTOP Standard. The administrator will automatically get a printout of these values when the FORTRAN program is compiled on his computer. In addition, two output sheets giving all current values of the 450 parameters (as well as their symbols and English names) constitute a part of the administrator's output each period during a given run.

The first part of the Dictionary gives the program parameters; the second part, the state variables. Within each part the items are divided according to conventional management functional areas (marketing, finance, etc.) as indicated in the symbols column.

Some comments regarding the column headings:

(1) The first letter of a given symbol indicates program parameters (P), company state variables (V) or company decisions (D). The second letter indicates management functional areas as follows:

A = accounting
F = finance
M = manufacturing
R = research and development or marketing research
S = marketing

We emphasize once more that the symbols are those actually employed in the FORTRAN computer program.

(2) Explanation of the symbols in the subscript column:

$A =$ area
$C =$ company (state variables and decisions only)
$F =$ factory
$G =$ grade (X_1, Y_2, etc.)
$M =$ model (standard–deluxe)
$P =$ product

The subscripts indicate the several contexts in which analogous parameters, state variables and decisions occur, as a majority of them recur in more than one module of the program. A single program parameter heading will typically refer to *six* individual parameters representing as many product-area variations. This is most readily apparent on the output of current parameter values which constitutes a part of the administrator's output each period.

A single state variable or decision heading, such as VM06 Production Amount, may actually identify up to 900 variations (2 models, 3 factories, 2 products, 3 areas, 25 companies).

The symbol and subscript(s) are a necessary and sufficient means of identifying on a Wonder Card any individual parameter(s) or state variable(s) embraced by a given heading, even though it (they) may share a common name with many other parameters or state variables. (Being uniquely defined home-office parameters require no subscript.) Cf. discussion of Wonder Cards in Chapter 5.

(3) The names of program parameters, state variables and decisions follow closely the format used on standard output and decision forms wherever applicable. Note that there are also a number of state variables which do not appear on company output forms (e.g., VS11 Effective Price). The current values of such state variables constitute parts of the administrator's special output each period.

(4) The accounts column for state variables is of interest primarily to game designers. It is of significance to administrators of the simulation mainly as a check on the balancing of accounts. Explanation of symbols employed:

$A =$ asset
$L =$ liability

(A) and (L) refer to assets and liabilities in an intermediary sense, i.e., the values are not retained from one period to the next.

*   denotes state variables not in the nature of assets or liabilities in either a formal or an intermediary sense.

(5) The comments column offers some "quick and easy" explanations. For a more detailed discussion the reader is referred to Chapters 2, 3 and 5.

Dictionary of Complete INTOP Program

(1) SYMBOL	(2) SUBSCRIPT	(3) NAME	(4) ACCT.	(5) COMMENTS
		Marketing Parameters		
PS01	P, A	Base Quantity in Sales Function		For *each* of standard and deluxe models.
PS02	P, A	Base Price in Sales Function		
PS03	P, A	Base Advertising in Sales Function		
PS04	P, A	Exponential Weight Price		PS04, PS05 see "Time and Change" Section of Chapter 3.
PS05	P, A	Exponential Weight Advertising		X_0 and Y_0 are usually set equal to 1.
PS06	G, P	Grade Differentials in Sales Function		The impact of a given elasticity value will differ somewhat depending on the relative number of companies active in the corresponding product-area market and on whether redistribution of demand due to stock-outs is involved, cf. Chapter 3.
PS07	P, A	Elasticity–Price Industry Both Models		
PS08	P, A	Elasticity–Price Industry One Model		
PS09	P, A	Elasticity–Price Firm Both Models		
PS10	P, A	Elasticity–Price Firm One Model		
PS11	P, A	Elasticity–Grade Ind. Both Models		
PS12	P, A	Elasticity–Grade Ind. One Model		
PS13	P, A	Elasticity–Grade Firm Both Models		
PS14	P, A	Elasticity–Grade Firm One Model		
PS15	P, A	Elasticity–Redist. Ind. Both Models		Redistribution elasticities are generally set equal to price elasticities in INTOP Standard.
PS16	P, A	Elasticity–Redist. Ind. One Model		
PS17	P, A	Elasticity–Redist. Firm Both Models		
PS18	P, A	Elasticity–Redist. Firm One Model		
PS19	P, A	Elasticity–Advert. Ind. Both Models		
PS20	P, A	Elasticity–Advert. Firm One Model		
PS21	P, A	Elasticity–Other Product Ind.		
PS22	P, A	Elasticity–Other Product Firm		
PS23	P, A	Economic Index Elasticity		Set at 1 in INTOP Standard.
PS24	P, A	Economic Index		

Dictionary of Complete INTOP Program (Continued)

(1) SYMBOL	(2) SUBSCRIPT	(3) NAME	(4) ACCT.	(5) COMMENTS
PS25	P, A	C & A, Captive, Cost/Unit		C & A = Commercial and Administrative Cost.
PS26	P, A	C & A, Agency, Cost/Unit Combined		
PS27	P, A	C & A, Agency, Cost/Unit Isolated		
PS28	A	C & A, Captive, Cost/Office		
PS29	A	C & A, Captive, Cost/Open–Close		
PS30	P, A	Sales Expediting, Cost/Unit		Penalty in addition to manufacturing cost.
PS31	P, A	Inventory Charges, Linear Term		
PS32	P, A	Inventory Charges, Square Term		
PS33	P, A	Shipping Cost from Area 1		Shipping "from" a given area "to" the same area refers to intra-area shipments between companies.
PS34	P, A	Shipping Cost from Area 2		
PS35	P, A	Shipping Cost from Area 3		
		Manufacturing Parameters		
PM01	P, A	Fixed Factory Cost for Non-Zero Prod.		Applies only if fixed cost is "inventoried." For a detailed discussion of the manufacturing cost function see Chapter 3. Practicable ranges for certain parameters in INTOP Standard are indicated in Chapter 5.
PM02	P, A	Maximum Cost Per Unit		
PM03	P, A	Minimum Cost Per Unit		
PM04	P, A	Cost Multiple – One Model		
PM05	P, A	Optimum Level – One Model		
PM06	P, A	Cost Multiple – Total		
PM07	P, A	Optimum Level – Total		
PM08	P, A	Cost Multiple, One Model Level Change		Cost of any change in amount produced from last period. If no prod. last period cost is 0.
PM09	P, A	Cost Multiple, Total Prod. Level Change		

Code	Class	Description	Notes
PM10	P, A	Exponential Wt. Methods Expense	Cf. PS04.
PM11	P, A	Area Grade Differential Multiple	Set at 1 in INTOP Standard.
PM12	P, A	Obsolescence Cost in Mfg.	A "0" would mean instantaneous construction.
PM13	P, A	Factory Construction Time	
PM14	P, A	Methods – Maximum Cost Reduction	
PM15	P, A	Meth. Exp. Giving Half Max. Reduction	
PM16	G, P	Grade Cost Differentials	X_0 and Y_0 are usually set equal to 1.
PM17	P, A	Factory Acquisition Cost	
PM18	P, A	Maximum Factory Capacity	
PM19	F, P, A	Factory Overhead Cost	Note differences between individual plants.
PM20	P, A	Depreciation Rate	
		New Product and Market Research Parameters	
PR01	P	Expon. Wt. Research Expenditure	PR01, PR02: cf. PS04.
PR02	P	Expon. Wt. Research Probability	
PR03	P	Minimum Useful Research Expenditure	
PR04	P	Add. Expenditure Yielding Prob. ½	Makes R & D deterministic.
PR05	P	Threshold Probability	
PR06	P, A	Total Ind. Advert. Exp. Last Period	PR06-PR11 refer to actual dollar values. They are needed to calculate the running averages identified by PR17, PR20 and PR25.
PR07	P, A	Total Ind. Advert. Exp. This Period	
PR08	P, A	Total Ind. Methods Exp. Last Period	
PR09	P, A	Total Ind. Methods Exp. This Period	
PR10	P	Total Ind. R & D Exp. Last Period	
PR11	P	Total Ind. R & D Exp. This Period	
PR12	P	Gazette Subscription Fee Per Year	PR12-PR29 indicates the *prices* of standard and marketing research items as given in
PR13	P	All Consumer Sales by Company	

Dictionary of Complete INTOP Program (Continued)

(1) SYMBOL	(2) SUBSCRIPT	(3) NAME	(4) ACCT.	(5) COMMENTS
PR14		Total Industry Consumer Sales		the Schedule of Costs, etc., in the *Player's Manual.* The actual market research data for PR13-27 appear on the administrator's Market Research 2 output sheet each period. Companies may order 3 (possibly 6) items per period.
PR15		Number of Companies Advertising		
PR16		Current Industry Advertising Expense		
PR17		Average Industry Advertising Expense		
PR18		No. of Companies with Methods Expense		
PR19		Current Industry Methods Expense		
PR20		Average Industry Methods Expense		
PR21		Number of Producing Plants		
PR22		Number of Companies in Consumer Sales		
PR23		Number of Companies in R & D		
PR24		Current Industry R & D Expense		
PR25		Average Industry R & D Expense		
PR26		No. of Companies in Marketing Research		
PR27		Current Industry Marketing Research		
PR28		Test Mkt. for Any One Product & Grade		For PR28 and PR29 (Market Research Items 17 and 18) see Computer Liaison Instruction.
PR29		Consultant's Estimate of Variable Cost		
		Financial Parameters		
PF01	A	Capital Transfer Tax – Area to Home		Use decimal fractions (.05 is 5%, etc.).

Code		Description	Notes
PF02	A	Fraction A/R 2 to A/R 1	Use decimal fractions for PF02-PF05.
PF03	A	Fraction A/R 1 to Cash	
PF04	A	Fraction A/P 2 to A/P 1	
PF05	A	Fraction A/P 1 to Cash	
PF06	A	Interest Rate – Savings	
PF07	A	Interest Rate – Borrowing	
PF08	A	Interest Rate – Supplier Credit Low	
PF09	A	Switch-over Amount Supplier Credit	
PF10	A	Interest Rate – Supplier Credit High	
PF11	A	Income Tax Rate	
PF12	A	Fraction Tax Loss Carry Forward	
PF13	A	Fraction Area Bank Loan Limit	Limit is this fraction of working capital.
PF14	A	Capital Transfer Tax – Home to Area	Use decimal fractions (.05 is 5%, etc.).
PF15		Income Tax Rate	PF15-PF26 all relate to the Home Office.
PF16		Interest Rate – Savings	
PF17		Interest Rate – Supplier Credit Low	
PF18		Switch-over Amount Supplier Credit	
PF19		Interest Rate – Supplier Credit High	
PF20		Minimum Cash Balance	
PF21		Fraction Tax Loss Carry Forward	
PF22		Exponential Weight Dividends	PF22, PF23: cf. PS04.
PF23		Exponential Weight Earnings	
PF24		Min. Div./Earn. Ratio Stk. Mkt. Conf.	
PF25		Max. Div./Earn. Ratio Stk. Mkt. Conf.	
PF26		Stk. Mkt., Max. Frac. Div. Returned	

Marketing State Variables

Code		Description	Notes
VS01	M, P, A, C	Industrial Sales Units	*
VS02	M, P, A, C	Intra-Company Sales Units	*

Dictionary of Complete INTOP Program (Continued)

(1) SYMBOL	(2) SUBSCRIPT	(3) NAME	(4) ACCT.	(5) COMMENTS
VS03	M, P, A, C	Consumer Sales Units	*	
VS04	M, P, A, C	Industrial Sales Revenue	(L)	
VS05	M, P, A, C	Intra-Company Sales Revenue	(L)	
VS06	M, P, A, C	Consumer Sales Revenue	(L)	
VS07	M, P, A, C	Price in Consumer Sales	*	
VS08	P, A, C	Shipping Expense	(A)	
VS09	P, A, C	Advertising Expense	(A)	
VS10	P, A, C	Sales Expediting Expense	(A)	
VS11	M, P, A, C	Effective Price	*	Cf. PS04.
VS12	P, A, C	Effective Advertising	*	Cf. PS05.
VS13	P, A, C	Marketing Effectiveness Index	*	Natural log., see Comp. Liais. Instr.
VS14	A, C	The Number of Regional Sales Offices	*	
VS15	A, C	Change in No. Regional Sales Offices	*	
VS16	P, A, C	Commercial and Administrative Expense	(A)	
VS17	M, P, A, C	Inventory Units	*	
VS18	M, P, A, C	Inventory Grade	*	
VS19	M, P, A, C	Ave. Inventory Cost, Beginn. of Per.	*	VS19 is used in the calculation of VS20.
VS20	M, P, A, C	Cost of Goods Sold	(A)	
VS21	P, A, C	Inventory Expense	(A)	
VS22	M, P, A, C	Inventory Value	A	
VS23	M, P, A, C	Industrial Purchases Units	*	
VS24	M, P, A, C	Intra-Company Purchases Units	*	
VS25	M, P, A, C	Industrial Purchases Cost	(A)	

VS26	M, P, A, C	Intra-Company Purchases Cost	(A)	
VS27	M, P, A, C	Redistribution Variable, Z	*	
		Manufacturing State Variables		
VM01	P, A, C	No. of Factories Allowable	*	Maximum is 3 plants per area and product.
VM02	P, A, C	No. of Factories Constructed This Period	*	
VM03	P, A, C	Effective Methods Expense	*	Cf. PM10.
VM04	P, A, C	Methods Expense	(A)	
VM05	M, P, A, C	Production Grade	*	
VM06	M, F, P, A, C	Production Amount	*	
VM07	M, F, P, A, C	Previous Production Amount	*	
VM08	P, A, C	Depreciation and Fixed Factory Cost	(A)	Fixed cost part used in direct costing only.
VM09	M, F, P, A, C	Manufacturing Cost	(A)	
VM10	F, P, A, C	Factory Age	*	
VM11	F, P, A, C	Net Plant and Equipment Value	A	
VM12	F, P, A, C	Factory Acquisition Cost	*	
		New Product and Market Research State Variables		
VR01	P, C	Maximum Producible Grade	*	
VR02	P, C	Licensing Income	(L)	
VR03	P, C	Licensing Expense	(A)	
VR04	P, C	Probability of Receiving Patent	*	
VR05	P, C	R & D Expense	(A)	
VR06	P, C	Effective Research Expense	*	Cf. PR02.
VR07	C	Market Research Expense	(A)	Cf. PR01.

Dictionary of Complete INTOP Program (Continued)

(1) SYMBOL	(2) SUBSCRIPT	(3) NAME	(4) ACCT.	(5) COMMENTS
		Financial State Variables		
		Operating Areas		
VF01	A, C	A/R 1	A	
VF02	A, C	A/R 2	A	
VF03	A, C	A/P 1	L	
VF04	A, C	A/P 2	L	
VF05	A, C	Cash	A	
VF06	A, C	Home Office Control	L	
VF07	A, C	Tax Loss Carry–Forward	*	
VF08	A, C	Supplier Credit	L	
VF09	A, C	Capital Transfer Tax	(A)	
VF10	A, C	Bank Loan Borrowing Limit	*	
VF11	A, C	Government Securities	A	
VF12	A, C	Area Bank Loan	L	
VF13	A, C	Interest Income	(L)	
VF14	A, C	Interest Expense	(A)	
VF15	A, C	Income Tax	(A)	
		Home Office		
VF16	C	Cash	A	
VF17	C	Loans Payable	L	Inter-Company and Home Office bank loans outstanding.
VF18	C	Interest Paid	(A)	Interest on loans specified in VF17.
VF19	C	Investment Inter-Company	A	

Code	Source	Description	Type	Cf.
VF20	C	Interest Received	(L)	
VF21	C	Government Securities	A	
VF22	C	Interest on Securities	(L)	
VF23	C	Subsidiary Control	A	
VF24	C	Supplier Credit	L	
VF25	C	Common Stock	L	
VF26	C	Income Tax	(A)	
VF27	C	Capital Transfer Tax	(A)	
VF28	C	Paid-In-Capital	L	
VF29	C	Effective Dividends	*	
VF30	C	Effective Earnings	*	
VF31	C	Dividends Paid	(A)	
VF32	C	Cumulative Dividends Paid	*	Cf. PF22.
VF33	C	Tax Loss Carry-Forward	*	Cf. PF23.

Accounting State Variables
Income Statement — Area

Code	Source	Description	Type
VA01	M, P, A, C	Gross Margin	(L)
VA02	P, A, C	Total Gross Margin	(L)
VA03	P, A, C	Total Operating Expense	(A)
VA04	P, A, C	Net Operating Earnings	(L)
VA05	A, C	Total Net Operating Earnings	(L)
VA06	A, C	Gross Earnings	(L)
VA07	A, C	Net Earnings	(L)

Balance Sheet — Area

Code	Source	Description	Type
VA08	A, C	Total Inventory Value	(A)
VA09	A, C	Total Current Assets	(A)
VA10	A, C	Total Net Plant and Equipment	(A)
VA11	A, C	Total Assets	(A)

Dictionary of Complete INTOP Program (Continued)

(1) SYMBOL	(2) SUBSCRIPT	(3) NAME	(4) ACCT.	(5) COMMENTS
VA12	A, C	Total Current Liabilities	(L)	
VA13	A, C	Retained Earnings	L	
VA14	A, C	Total Equity	(L)	
VA15	A, C	Total Liability and Equity	(L)	
		Income Statement — Home		
VA16	C	Total Nonoperating Income	(L)	
VA17	C	Total Nonoperating Expense	(A)	
VA18	C	Gross Earnings	(L)	
VA19	C	Net Earnings	(L)	
VA20	C	Addition of Retained Earnings	(L)	
		Balance Sheet — Home		
VA21	C	Total Current Assets	(A)	
VA22	C	Total Assets	(A)	
VA23	C	Total Liabilities	(L)	
VA24	C	Retained Earnings	L	
VA25	C	Total Equity	(L)	
VA26	C	Total Liability and Equity	(L)	
		Income Statement — Consolidated		
VA27	M, C	Consumer Sales	L	The consolidated income and balance sheet data specified by VA27–VA68 appear each period on the administrator's indus-
VA28	M, C	Intra-Company Sales	L	
VA29	M, C	Industrial Sales	L	

try-wide tabulation in PART 1 of the output. These data do not recur in the state variable output in PART 2. As these data are not retained from one period to the next (being derived each period simply by adding across the company Balance Sheet and Income Statement) it is not practicable to change them by Wonder Cards. These state variables would, however, be of significance in any major re-design of the program.

Code		Description	
VA30	M, C	Cost of Goods Sold	A
VA31	M, C	Gross Margin	L
VA32	C	Total Gross Margin	L
VA33	C	C & A Expense	A
VA34	C	Advertising Expense	A
VA35	C	Shipping Expense	A
VA36	C	Inventory Expense	A
VA37	C	Expediting Expense	A
VA38	C	Methods Expense	A
VA39	C	Depreciation and Fixed Expense	A
VA40	C	Total Operating Expense	A
VA41	C	Net Earnings from Operations	L
VA42	C	Total Net Operating Earnings	L
VA43	C	Miscellaneous Interest	L
VA44	C	Total Nonoperating Income	L
VA45	C	Total Interest	L
VA46	C	Total Nonoperating Expense	A
VA47	C	Gross Earnings	A
VA48	C	Income Tax	L
VA49	C	Capital Transfer Tax	A
VA50	C	Net Earnings	A
VA51	C	Addition to Retained Earnings	L

Balance Sheet — Consolidated

Code		Description	
VA52	C	Cash	A
VA53	C	A/R 1	A
VA54	C	A/R 2	A
VA55	C	Total Inventory Value	A
VA56	C	Government Securities	A
VA57	C	Total Current Assets	A

Dictionary of Complete INTOP Program (Continued)

(1) SYMBOL	(2) SUBSCRIPT	(3) NAME	(4) ACCT.	(5) COMMENTS
VA58	C	Total Net Plant and Equipment	A	
VA59	C	Total Assets	A	
VA60	C	A/P 1	L	
VA61	C	A/P 2	L	
VA62	C	Supplier Credit	L	
VA63	C	Area Bank Loans	L	
VA64	C	Total Current Liability	L	
VA65	C	Total Liability	L	
VA66	C	Retained Earnings	L	
VA67	C	Total Equity	L	These accounts are used to keep the books in balance when the Income Statement and Balance Sheet are created. The printed values should be approx. 0. If they are not, this is generally an indication that a Wonder Card has been misused.
VA68	C	Total Liability and Equity	L	
VA69	A, C	Asset Balance – Area	A	
VA70	A, C	Liability Balance – Area	L	
VA71	C	Asset Balance – Home	A	
VA72	C	Liability Balance – Home	L	
		Decisions Made This Period Operating Areas		
DM02	P, A, C	Number of New Plants Built		DM02–DF11 appear on the Operations Decision Form (No. 1). Decisions may not be changed by Wonder Card: these symbols are primarily of programmer interest. Decision forms and corresponding
DM04	P, A, C	Methods Improvement Expense		
DM05	M, P, A, C	Grade of Units Produced		
DM06	M, F, P, A, C	Units Produced		

Code	Category	Description	Notes
DS07	M, P, A, C	Price in Consumer Sales	punch cards for *all* periods should always be saved during a run, in case of malfunction at any stage. After the run is over they may be discarded, as DM02–DR13 (with the Wonder Card and Inter-Company Transactions registers) provide a permanent record of all decisions made during the run.
DS09	P, A, C	Advertising Expense	
DS15	A, C	Reg. Offices Open (+)/Close (−)	
DF06	A, C	Cash from (+)/to (−) Home	
DF11	A, C	Borrow (+)/Invest (−)	

Home Office

Code	Category	Description	Notes
DF21	C	Securities Invested	DF21–DR13 appear on the Home Office Decision Form (No. 2).
DF31	C	Dividend Expense	
DR05	P, C	R & D Expense	Ordinarily only three items may be ordered. However, the program will handle up to six items per company and period. DR11–DR13 would then have column numbers 43-48 on the Home Office form.
DR07	C	Consulting Market Research Expense	
DR08	C	Item 1 Market Research	
DR09	C	Item 2 Market Research	
DR10	C	Item 3 Market Research	
DR11	C	Item 4 Market Research	
DR12	C	Item 5 Market Research	
DR13	C	Item 6 Market Research	

Appendix II

Standard FORTRAN Output of Company Financial and Marketing Research Data

COMPANY   8   INTOP - UNIVERSITY OF CHICAGO   PERIOD 12

BALANCE SHEET

	AREA 1	AREA 2	AREA 3	HOME OFFICE	CONSOLIDATED
ASSETS					
CASH	-0.	203935.		75018.	278953.
A/R FIRST QUARTER	2582989.	939986.		751998.	4274972.
A/R SECOND QUARTER	0.	1095000.		577759.	1672759.
INVENTORY STANDARD X	214411.	228452.	151442.		
DELUXE X	433535.	336250.	223961.		
STANDARD Y	1130981.	525265.	257965.		
DELUXE Y	0.	568803.	0.		
TOTAL	1778927.	1658770.	633367.	0.	4071065.
SECURITIES	0.	0.	0.	1800000.	1800000.
TOTAL CURRENT ASSETS	4361916.	3897691.	1963124.	1875018.	12097748.
NET PLANT AND EQUIP.	2280000.	2950000.	1155000.	0.	6385000.
INVESTMENT INTERCOMP.				4614999.	0.
SUBSIDIARY CONTROL				0.	0.
TOTAL ASSETS	6641916.	6847691.	3118124.	6490017.	18482748.
LIABILITIES					
A/P FIRST QUARTER	1459888.	1075361.	426289.		2961539.
A/P SECOND QUARTER	0.	497631.	252493.		750124.
SUPPLIER CREDIT	137977.	0.	141589.	-0.	279566.
AREA BANK LOANS	0.	0.	0.	0.	0.
TOTAL CURRENT LIABILITY	1597865.	1572992.	820371.	-0.	3991228.
LOANS PAYABLE			0.	0.	0.
TOTAL LIABILITIES	1597865.	1572992.	820371.	0.	3991228.
STOCKHOLDER EQUITY					
COMMON STOCK AT PAR				10000000.	10000000.
PAID IN CAPITAL				161937.	161937.
RETAINED EARNINGS	2199051.	3969698.	1832753.	-3671919.	4329584.
HOME OFFICE CONTROL	2845000.	1305000.	465000.		
TOTAL EQUITY	5044051.	5274698.	2297753.	6490018.	14491521.
TOTAL LIAB. AND EQUITY	6641916.	6847691.	3118124.	6490018.	18482750.

COMPANY 8 INTOP - UNIVERSITY OF CHICAGO PERIOD 12

INCOME STATEMENT	AREA 1		AREA 2		AREA 3		HOME OFFICE	CONSOLIDATED
	PRODUCT X	PRODUCT Y	PRODUCT X	PRODUCT Y	PRODUCT X	PRODUCT Y		
STANDARD SALES								
CONSUMER	1008000.	1566204.	0.	0.	392044.	496000.		3462248.
INTRA-COMPANY	0.	0.	0.	0.	0.	0.		0.
INDUSTRIAL	0.	0.	1050000.	1200000.	0.	0.		2250000.
LESS-COST OF GOODS	505382.	1069521.	409144.	508075.	147997.	252166.		2892285.
GROSS MARGIN	502618.	496683.	640856.	691925.	244047.	243834.		2819964.
DELUXE SALES								
CONSUMER	596777.	1134000.	0.	0.	556353.	0.		2287129.
INTRA-COMPANY	0.	0.	0.	0.	0.	0.		0.
INDUSTRIAL	0.	0.	0.	1400000.	0.	0.		1400000.
LESS-COST OF GOODS	310761.	622687.	0.	547965.	229861.	0.		1711275.
GROSS MARGIN	286016.	511313.	0.	852035.	326492.	0.		1975855.
TOTAL GROSS MARGIN	788634.	1007996.	640856.	1543960.	570539.	243834.		4795819.
OPERATING EXPENSES								
COMMER. AND ADMIN.	105669.	147368.	0.	0.	59212.	33810.		346058.
ADVERTISING	80000.	95000.	0.	0.	40000.	24000.		239000.
SHIPPING	0.	0.	30000.	100000.	0.	0.		130000.
INVENTORY	2651.	0.	0.	0.	255.	0.		2907.
SALES EXPEDITING	0.	0.	0.	0.	0.	0.		0.
METHODS IMPROVEMENT	40000.	60000.	30000.	50000.	40000.	32000.		252000.
DEPRECIATION AND FIXED	215000.	190000.	165000.	250000.	125000.	70000.		1015000.
NET OPERATING EXPENSE	443320.	492368.	225000.	400000.	264467.	159810.		1984965.
NET EARNINGS FROM OPER.	345314.	515627.	415856.	1143960.	306072.	84024.		2810854.
TOTAL NET OPER. EARNINGS		860941.		1559817.		390096.		2810854.
NON-OPERATING INCOME								
INTEREST INTERCO. LOANS								
LICENSES-X							0.	
LICENSES-Y							0.	
MISC. INTEREST		0.		0.			30600.	
TOTAL NON-OPER. INCOME		0.		0.			30600.	30600.
NON-OPERATING EXPENSE								
MARKET RESEARCH							4000.	4000.
LICENSES-X							0.	0.
LICENSES-Y							72000.	72000.
R AND D NEW PRODUCT X							0.	0.
R AND D NEW PRODUCT Y							0.	0.
TOTAL INTEREST		7810.				8014.	0.	15824.
TOTAL NON-OPER. EXPENSE		7810.				8014.	76000.	91824.
GROSS EARNINGS		853131.		1559817.		382082.	-45400.	2749629.
LESS-TAXES		425433.		618027.		114624.	0.	1158085.
LESS-CAPITAL TRANS. TAX		0.		0.		0.	0.	0.
NET EARNINGS		427698.		941789.		267457.	-45400.	1591544.
LESS-DIVIDENDS							500000.	500000.
TO RETAINED EARNINGS		427698.		941789.		267457.	-545400.	1091544.

COMPANY 8 INTOP – UNIVERSITY OF CHICAGO

ANCILLARY DATA	AREA 1 PRODUCT X	AREA 1 PRODUCT Y	AREA 2 PRODUCT X	AREA 2 PRODUCT Y	AREA 3 PRODUCT X	AREA 3 PRODUCT Y
STANDARD SALES UNITS						
CONSUMER	36000.	31324.	0.	0.	10317.	8000.
INTRA-COMPANY	0.	0.	0.	0.	0.	0.
INDUSTRIAL	0.	0.	30000.	25000.	0.	0.
DELUXE SALES UNITS						
CONSUMER	17051.	18000.	0.	0.	10699.	0.
INTRA-COMPANY	0.	0.	0.	0.	0.	0.
INDUSTRIAL	0.	0.	0.	25000.	0.	0.
MFG. COST ANALYSIS						
PL(1) STANDARD COST	214411.	0.	228452.	525265.	149307.	257965.
UNITS	18000.	-0.	15000.	25000.	10000.	8000.
DELUXE COST	0.	1130981.	0.	0.	0.	0.
UNITS	-0.	32000.	-0.	-0.	-0.	-0.
PL(2) STANDARD COST	-0.	0.	-0.	-0.	-0.	-0.
UNITS	378700.	0.	336250.	568803.	223961.	0.
DELUXE COST	18000.	-0.	15000.	25000.	10000.	0.
UNITS	0.	0.	0.	0.	0.	0.
PL(3) STANDARD COST	0.	0.	0.	0.	0.	0.
UNITS	-0.	-0.	-0.	-0.	-0.	-0.
DELUXE COST	-0.	-0.	-0.	-0.	-0.	-0.
UNITS	1.	-0.	1.	1.	0.	1.
STANDARD GRADE	1.	-0.	2.	3.	1.	3.
DELUXE GRADE	3.	4.	2.	3.	1.	-0.
INTRA-CO. PURCHASES						
STANDARD COST	0.	0.	0.	0.	0.	0.
UNITS	0.	0.	0.	0.	0.	0.
DELUXE COST	0.	0.	0.	0.	0.	0.
UNITS	0.	0.	0.	0.	0.	0.
INDUSTRIAL PURCHASES						
STANDARD COST	0.	0.	0.	0.	0.	0.
UNITS	0.	0.	0.	0.	0.	0.
DELUXE COST	0.	0.	0.	0.	0.	0.
UNITS	0.	0.	0.	0.	0.	0.
ENDING INVENTORY						
STANDARD UNITS	18000.	32000.	15000.	25000.	10149.	8000.
GRADE	1.	4.	1.	1.	0.	0.
DELUXE UNITS	21009.	0.	15000.	25000.	10000.	0.
GRADE	3.	3.	2.	3.	1.	0.
NO. REG. SALES OFFICES	5.		0.		5.	
MAX. GRADE OF IMPROVEMENT	3.	4.				

COMPANY   8   INTOP - UNIVERSITY OF CHICAGO   PERIOD 12

MARKET RESEARCH 1

	AREA 1				AREA 2				AREA 3			
	PRODUCT X		PRODUCT Y		PRODUCT X		PRODUCT Y		PRODUCT X		PRODUCT Y	
PRICES POSTED THIS QRT.	STD.	DEL.	STD.	DEL.	STD.	DEL.	STD.	DEL.	STD.	DEL.	STD.	DEL.
COMPANY NUMBER 1	39.	52.	-0.	-0.	45.	55.	51.	-0.	45.	-0.	-0.	-0.
COMPANY NUMBER 2	32.	-0.	55.	80.	44.	-0.	57.	84.	36.	-0.	-0.	-0.
COMPANY NUMBER 3	-0.	-0.	55.	80.	-0.	-0.	57.	77.	-0.	-0.	-0.	-0.
COMPANY NUMBER 4	48.	-0.	65.	-0.	52.	-0.	72.	-0.	-0.	-0.	-0.	-0.
COMPANY NUMBER 5	-0.	-0.	-0.	-0.	59.	-0.	49.	59.	36.	-0.	54.	69.
COMPANY NUMBER 6	40.	45.	55.	-0.	-0.	-0.	-0.	80.	-0.	-0.	-0.	-0.
COMPANY NUMBER 7	-0.	-0.	-0.	-0.	-0.	-0.	57.	80.	-0.	-0.	-0.	-0.
COMPANY NUMBER 8	28.	35.	50.	63.	-0.	-0.	-0.	-0.	38.	52.	62.	-0.
COMPANY NUMBER 9	-0.	-0.	-0.	55.	-0.	-0.	-0.	-0.	39.	52.	64.	-0.
COMPANY NUMBER 10	-0.	-0.	45.	-0.	-0.	-0.	48.	-0.	-0.	-0.	-0.	-0.
COMPANY NUMBER 11	47.	65.	60.	-0.	43.	48.	50.	61.	38.	50.	60.	-0.
COMPANY NUMBER 12	35.	40.	62.	-0.	44.	-0.	74.	-0.	45.	70.	66.	-0.
COMPANY NUMBER 13	-0.	-0.	45.	-0.	50.	-0.	60.	-0.	50.	-0.	-0.	-0.
COMPANY NUMBER 14	50.	73.	-0.	-0.	31.	58.	45.	54.	40.	-0.	55.	-0.
COMPANY NUMBER 15	28.	50.	62.	75.	48.	59.	-0.	-0.	-0.	-0.	-0.	-0.
COMPANY NUMBER 16	-0.	-0.	65.	-0.	-0.	-0.	-0.	-0.	66.	-0.	60.	-0.
COMPANY NUMBER 17	-0.	-0.	-0.	-0.	-0.	-0.	-0.	-0.	-0.	-0.	-0.	-0.
GRADES MFG. FOR NEXT QRT.												
COMPANY NUMBER 1	1.	-0.	-0.	-0.	1.	-0.	1.	-0.	-0.	-0.	-0.	-0.
COMPANY NUMBER 2	0.	-0.	-0.	4.	-0.	-0.	1.	4.	0.	-0.	-0.	-0.
COMPANY NUMBER 3	-0.	-0.	1.	4.	-0.	-0.	1.	-0.	-0.	-0.	-0.	-0.
COMPANY NUMBER 4	2.	-0.	3.	-0.	2.	4.	3.	3.	-0.	-0.	0.	3.
COMPANY NUMBER 5	-0.	4.	-0.	-0.	-0.	4.	1.	3.	-0.	-0.	-0.	-0.
COMPANY NUMBER 6	1.	-0.	-0.	4.	-0.	-0.	-0.	4.	0.	2.	-0.	-0.
COMPANY NUMBER 7	-0.	-0.	-0.	-0.	-0.	-0.	3.	3.	-0.	-0.	-0.	-0.
COMPANY NUMBER 8	1.	3.	-0.	-0.	1.	2.	1.	-0.	0.	1.	0.	-0.
COMPANY NUMBER 9	-0.	-0.	-0.	-0.	-0.	1.	-0.	-0.	1.	1.	1.	-0.
COMPANY NUMBER 10	-0.	-0.	0.	-0.	-0.	-0.	1.	3.	1.	-0.	-0.	-0.
COMPANY NUMBER 11	-0.	-0.	-0.	-0.	1.	-0.	1.	-0.	-0.	2.	-0.	-0.
COMPANY NUMBER 12	-0.	-0.	-0.	-0.	-0.	2.	0.	-0.	0.	-0.	1.	-0.
COMPANY NUMBER 13	1.	2.	-0.	-0.	2.	1.	0.	1.	1.	-0.	0.	3.
COMPANY NUMBER 14	-0.	-0.	3.	4.	1.	2.	0.	1.	1.	-0.	-0.	-0.
COMPANY NUMBER 15	2.	4.	3.	-0.	1.	2.	3.	-0.	-0.	2.	0.	-0.
COMPANY NUMBER 16	1.	2.	3.	-0.	1.	2.	-0.	-0.	2.	-0.	1.	-0.
COMPANY NUMBER 17	-0.	-0.	-0.	-0.	-0.	-0.	-0.	-0.	-0.	-0.	-0.	-0.

NOTE. -0 DENOTES NO PRODUCTION. 0 DENOTES THAT ZERO IS THE GRADE BEING MANUFACTURED

Appendix III

Selected Special Outputs
for the Administrator

A. Consolidated Balance Sheet and Income Statement

B. Inter-Company and Special Transactions Register

C. Administrator's Output of Market Research 2

INTOP - UNIVERSITY OF CHICAGO

PERIOD 12

A. CONSOLIDATED BALANCE SHEET

COMPANY	CO. 1	CO. 2	CO. 3	CO. 4	CO. 5	CO. 6	CO. 7	CO. 8	CO. 9	CO.10	CO.11	CO.12	CO.13
ASSETS													
CASH	791.	2454.	2029.	907.	1951.	524.	1573.	279.	469.	506.	1973.	1362.	1437.
A/R FIRST QUARTER	2869.	3413.	3616.	4189.	1832.	3140.	1421.	4275.	909.	3247.	2746.	2027.	4737.
A/R SECOND QUARTER	1406.	1267.	1127.	1069.	1828.	252.	1341.	1673.	659.	758.	2278.	1143.	1225.
INVENTORY STANDARD X													
DELUXE X													
STANDARD Y													
DELUXE Y													
TOTAL	3440.	4522.	4145.	9020.	3712.	4805.	2121.	4071.	1693.	3066.	3107.	11032.	4028.
SECURITIES	3000.	900.	0.	0.	4000.	700.	7500.	1800.	4800.	2750.	3600.	900.	0.
TOTAL CURRENT ASSETS	11506.	12556.	10917.	15185.	13323.	9421.	13955.	12098.	8530.	10327.	13703.	16464.	11427.
NET PLANT AND EQUIP.	5795.	8200.	3600.	6300.	5930.	8415.	4375.	6385.	1890.	4920.	4850.	0.	12600.
INVESTMENT INTERCOMP.	0.	0.	0.	0.	0.	0.	0.	0.	0.	0.	0.	0.	0.
SUBSIDIARY CONTROL													
TOTAL ASSETS	17301.	20756.	14517.	21485.	19253.	17836.	18330.	18483.	10420.	15247.	18553.	16464.	24027.
LIABILITIES													
A/P FIRST QUARTER	1741.	3224.	3088.	3630.	1826.	3273.	1422.	2962.	605.	2281.	2147.	3598.	3276.
A/P SECOND QUARTER	384.	455.	564.	603.	1194.	109.	540.	750.	444.	340.	965.	1341.	485.
SUPPLIER CREDIT	403.	-0.	95.	3326.	170.	37.	301.	280.	0.	73.	117.	374.	2.
AREA BANK LOANS	0.	0.	0.	0.	0.	0.	0.	0.	0.	0.	0.	0.	1500.
TOTAL CURRENT LIABILITY	2528.	3679.	3747.	7559.	3190.	3419.	2263.	3991.	1048.	2694.	3230.	5313.	5263.
LOANS PAYABLE	0.	0.	0.	0.	0.	2000.	0.	0.	0.	0.	0.	0.	2500.
TOTAL LIABILITIES	2528.	3679.	3747.	7559.	3190.	5419.	2263.	3991.	1048.	2694.	3230.	5313.	7763.
STOCKHOLDER EQUITY													
COMMON STOCK AT PAR	10000.	10000.	10000.	10000.	10000.	10000.	10000.	10000.	10000.	10000.	10000.	10000.	10000.
PAID IN CAPITAL	167.	1241.	0.	1545.	1178.	497.	1125.	162.	265.	810.	1670.	989.	443.
RETAINED EARNINGS	3945.	5836.	769.	2381.	4885.	1920.	4942.	4330.	-894.	1743.	3654.	161.	5821.
HOME OFFICE CONTROL													
TOTAL EQUITY	14113.	17077.	10769.	13926.	16063.	12417.	16067.	14492.	9371.	12553.	15324.	11151.	16264.
TOTAL LIAB. AND EQUITY	16641.	20756.	14517.	21485.	19253.	17836.	18330.	18483.	10420.	15247.	18553.	16464.	24027.

INTOP – UNIVERSITY OF CHICAGO

PERIOD 12

A. CONSOLIDATED INCOME STATEMENT

COMPANY	CO. 1	CO. 2	CO. 3	CO. 4	CO. 5	CO. 6	CO. 7	CO. 8	CO. 9	CO.10	CO.11	CO.12	CO.13
STANDARD SALES													
CONSUMER	4049.	4148.	3611.	8853.	2307.	3660.	1388.	3462.	1019.	3740.	4710.	5034.	7196.
INTRA-COMPANY	0.	0.	125.	0.	0.	840.	0.	0.	0.	0.	784.	0.	0.
INDUSTRIAL	330.	0.	0.	0.	0.	0.	1320.	2250.	0.	0.	0.	0.	1200.
LESS-COST OF GOODS	1706.	1801.	1702.	4439.	1084.	2047.	1245.	2892.	700.	1656.	2404.	3861.	3190.
GROSS MARGIN	2673.	2347.	2033.	4414.	1223.	2452.	1463.	2820.	319.	2084.	3090.	1172.	5207.
DELUXE SALES													
CONSUMER	1558.	3615.	3683.	0.	3255.	1174.	1760.	2287.	628.	3001.	2510.	82.	1312.
INTRA-COMPANY	0.	0.	175.	0.	0.	0.	0.	0.	0.	0.	0.	0.	0.
INDUSTRIAL	960.	0.	600.	0.	0.	0.	0.	1400.	0.	0.	0.	0.	0.
LESS-COST OF GOODS	1140.	1214.	1979.	0.	1318.	430.	479.	1711.	313.	1403.	1184.	60.	533.
GROSS MARGIN	1379.	2401.	2479.	0.	1937.	744.	1281.	1976.	315.	1599.	1326.	22.	780.
TOTAL GROSS MARGIN	4051.	4748.	4512.	4414.	3160.	3196.	2745.	4796.	634.	3683.	4416.	1194.	5986.
OPERATING EXPENSES													
COMMER. AND ADMIN.	349.	428.	613.	579.	280.	272.	181.	346.	142.	738.	630.	380.	488.
ADVERTISING	150.	288.	350.	900.	345.	300.	290.	239.	225.	75.	122.	430.	850.
SHIPPING	30.	0.	140.	0.	0.	126.	60.	130.	0.	180.	180.	0.	60.
INVENTORY	178.	63.	28.	389.	21.	114.	108.	3.	02.	23.	28.	266.	13.
SALES EXPEDITING	0.	0.	0.	0.	0.	0.	0.	0.	0.	0.	0.	0.	0.
METHODS IMPROVEMENT	80.	140.	150.	140.	120.	100.	150.	252.	40.	45.	96.	0.	231.
DEPRECIATION AND FIXED	700.	900.	580.	890.	725.	550.	460.	1015.	295.	700.	625.	0.	1270.
NET OPERATING EXPENSE	1487.	1820.	1861.	2898.	1490.	1463.	1250.	1985.	764.	1581.	1681.	1077.	2912.
NET EARNINGS FROM OPER.	2565.	2929.	2651.	1516.	1670.	1733.	1495.	2811.	-131.	2102.	2735.	118.	3075.
TOTAL NET OPER. EARNINGS	2565.	2929.	2651.	1516.	1670.	1733.	1495.	2811.	-131.	2102.	2735.	118.	3075.
NON-OPERATING INCOME													
INTEREST INTERCO. LOANS	0.	0.	0.	0.	0.	0.	0.	0.	0.	0.	0.	0.	0.
LICENSES-X	0.	0.	0.	0.	0.	0.	36.	0.	0.	0.	0.	0.	0.
LICENSES-Y	0.	0.	0.	0.	0.	0.	60.	0.	0.	0.	0.	0.	0.
MISC. INTEREST	51.	15.	0.	0.	68.	12.	127.	31.	76.	47.	61.	15.	0.
TOTAL NON-OPER. INCOME	51.	15.	0.	0.	68.	12.	223.	31.	76.	47.	61.	15.	0.
NON-OPERATING EXPENSE													
MARKET RESEARCH	0.	60.	12.	0.	12.	0.	0.	4.	0.	0.	18.	0.	60.
LICENSES-X	0.	0.	0.	0.	40.	36.	0.	0.	0.	0.	0.	0.	0.
LICENSES-Y	0.	0.	0.	0.	0.	60.	0.	0.	0.	0.	0.	0.	0.
R AND D NEW PRODUCT X	0.	0.	0.	0.	0.	0.	0.	72.	0.	0.	0.	0.	90.
R AND D NEW PRODUCT Y	0.	0.	5.	246.	10.	82.	17.	16.	0.	3.	0.	0.	0.
TOTAL INTEREST	23.	60.	5.	246.	62.	178.	17.	92.	-55.	3.	7.	28.	133.
TOTAL NON-OPER. EXPENSE	23.	60.	17.	246.	62.	178.	17.	92.	-55.	3.	25.	28.	283.
GROSS EARNINGS	2593.	2884.	2633.	1270.	1676.	1567.	1702.	2750.	41.	2146.	2772.	105.	2791.
LESS-TAXES	1133.	1289.	1289.	615.	705.	887.	902.	1158.	909.	1151.	147.	1356.	
LESS-CAPITAL TRANS. TAX	0.	0.	0.	0.	0.	0.	0.	0.	-96.	0.	0.	0.	0.
NET EARNINGS	1460.	1595.	1344.	655.	971.	680.	799.	1592.	-96.	1236.	1621.	-42.	1436.
LESS-DIVIDENDS	100.	500.	0.	750.	300.	200.	600.	500.	125.	300.	450.	200.	150.
TO RETAINED EARNINGS	1360.	1095.	1344.	-95.	671.	480.	199.	1092.	-221.	936.	1171.	-242.	1286.

B. INTER-COMPANY AND SPECIAL TRANSACTIONS REGISTER

SPECIAL TRANSACTIONS OF TYPES 1, 2, AND 3

1. BANK LOANS
2. INTERCOMPANY LOANS
3. LICENSING

TYPE	FROM	TO	LOAN	INTEREST	LICENSE	PRODUCT(1=X,2=Y)	GRADE	
1	-0	1	-2000000.	-0.	-0.	0	0	OK
1	-0	6	-0.	80000.	-0.	0	0	OK
3	15	5	-0.	-0.	40000.	1	4	OK
3	7	6	-0.	-0.	60000.	2	4	OK
3	15	8	-0.	-0.	36000.	1	4	OK
1	-0	13	-0.	83000.	-0.	2	0	OK

INTERCOMPANY SALES

FROM		TO		UNITS	PRICE	PRODUCT	MODEL	GRADE	REVENUE	COST	SHIPPING	
1	1	12	1	20000.	48.	1	2	2	960000.	474948.	20000.	OK
1	1	6	1	10000.	33.	1	2	1	330000.	164469.	10000.	OK
17	1	2	2	10000.	27.	1	1	0	270000.	350000.	30000.	OK
3	1	6	1	10000.	60.	2	2	4	600000.	351354.	20000.	OK
7	2	12	2	10000.	46.	2	1	1	460000.	229039.	20000.	OK
7	2	5	2	20000.	43.	2	1	1	860000.	458078.	40000.	OK
17	2	12	1	10000.	50.	2	1	1	500000.	600000.	60000.	OK
8	2	12	2	25000.	48.	2	1	1	1200000.	508075.	50000.	OK
8	2	12	2	25000.	56.	2	2	3	1400000.	547965.	50000.	OK
8	2	12	2	30000.	35.	1	1	1	1050000.	409144.	30000.	OK
17	1	12	3	5000.	54.	2	1	0	270000.	275000.	60000.	OK
13	1	12	1	30000.	40.	2	1	1	1200000.	574493.	60000.	OK
15	1	12	1	10000.	68.	1	2	4	680000.	291309.	10000.	OK

INTRACOMPANY SALES

FROM		TO		UNITS	PRICE	PRODUCT	MODEL	GRADE	REVENUE	COST	SHIPPING	
3	2	3	3	5000.	25.	2	1	4	125000.	115770.	60000.	OK
3	2	3	3	5000.	35.	2	2	4	175000.	140734.	60000.	OK
6	2	6	1	21000.	40.	2	1	1	840000.	358736.	126000.	OK
11	2	11	3	10000.	40.	2	1	1	400000.	186459.	120000.	OK
11	2	11	3	12000.	32.	1	1	1	384000.	150308.	60000.	OK
15	1	15	3	20000.	22.	1	1	2	440000.	350764.	100000.	OK
15	1	15	3	15000.	44.	2	2	4	660000.	470755.	180000.	OK
15	1	15	3	10000.	41.	2	1	3	410000.	282453.	120000.	OK
15	1	15	3	16000.	34.	1	2	4	544000.	466095.	80000.	OK

This output is from the same run and quarter as other output samples in the Appendix. Thus we find Co. 8 license payment and inter-company sales recorded. In the register of inter-company and intra-company sales the first column under "From" and "To" indicates company number, the second indicates area number.

COMPANY 0

INTOP 2 UNIVERSITY OF CHICAGO PERIOD 12

C. MARKET RESEARCH 2

	AREA 1				AREA 2				AREA 3			
	PRODUCT X		PRODUCT Y		PRODUCT X		PRODUCT Y		PRODUCT X		PRODUCT Y	
	STD.	DEL.	STD.	DEL.	STD.	DEL.	STD.	DEL.	STD.	DEL.	STD.	DEL.
SALES THIS QUARTER(000)												
COMPANY NUMBER 1	12.0	13.3	0.	0.	16.0	15.8	42.0	0.	16.0	0.	0.	0.
COMPANY NUMBER 2	15.1	0.	24.1	23.5	4.2	0.	29.9	20.6	12.4	0.	0.	0.
COMPANY NUMBER 3	0.	0.	35.0	23.9	0.	0.	29.6	23.0	0.	0.	0.	0.
COMPANY NUMBER 4	28.5	0.	60.3	0.	28.4	0.	29.0	0.	0.	0.	0.	0.
COMPANY NUMBER 5	0.	26.1	51.0	0.	3.1	0.	22.0	45.8	8.0	0.	14.0	8.0
COMPANY NUMBER 6	21.4	0.	0.	0.	0.	0.	24.4	0.	0.	0.	0.	0.
COMPANY NUMBER 7	0.	0.	0.	0.	0.	0.	0.	22.0	0.	0.	0.	0.
COMPANY NUMBER 8	36.0	17.1	31.3	18.0	0.	0.	0.	0.	10.3	10.7	8.0	0.
COMPANY NUMBER 9	0.	0.	0.	0.	0.	0.	52.6	0.	9.7	12.1	10.0	0.
COMPANY NUMBER 10	0.	0.	27.0	54.6	22.0	13.0	41.2	20.0	10.0	13.3	7.0	0.
COMPANY NUMBER 11	0.	0.	15.0	0.	27.0	0.	25.0	0.	3.7	1.2	5.0	0.
COMPANY NUMBER 12	18.7	0.	10.0	0.	31.7	0.	24.4	0.	15.5	0.	0.	0.
COMPANY NUMBER 13	20.1	32.8	59.3	0.	20.3	12.0	43.0	37.3	4.2	0.	8.0	0.
COMPANY NUMBER 14	0.	0.	0.	0.	0.	0.	0.	0.	0.	0.	0.	0.
COMPANY NUMBER 15	21.0	10.0	20.0	43.5	12.0	0.	0.	0.	2.9	0.	7.0	0.
COMPANY NUMBER 16	18.8	18.3	29.0	0.	0.	11.9	0.	0.	0.	0.	0.	0.
COMPANY NUMBER 17	0.	0.	0.	0.	0.	0.	0.	0.	0.	0.	0.	0.
TOTAL SALES(000)	191.5	117.5	362.0	163.5	164.8	52.7	363.2	168.7	92.8	37.3	59.0	8.0
	STD.	DEL.	STD.	DEL.	STD.	DEL.	STD.	DEL.	STD.	DEL.	STD.	DEL.
	191.5	117.5	362.0	163.5	164.8	52.7	363.2	168.7	92.8	37.3	59.0	8.0
NO. OF COS. ADVERTISING	9		10		10		10		10		6	
TOT. IND. ADV..CURRENT	970.		1610.		742.		1589.		470.		163.	
TOT. IND. ADV..3QAVG	995.		1137.		688.		1520.		382.		131.	
NO.OF COS. IN METH.IMP.	8		8		8		12		8		5	
TOT.IND.METH.IMP..CURR.	284.		430.		219.		524.		225.		86.	
TOT.IND.METH.IMP..3QAVG	277.		347.		215.		510.		194.		76.	
NO. OF PRODUCING PLANTS	18		20		19		25		15		7	
NO.COS. IN CONS. SALES	9	6	11	5	9	4	11	6	10	4	7	1
NO. OF COS. IN R AND D	2		1									
TOT.IND. R AND D. CURR.	140.		100.									
IND. R AND D. 3Q AVG.	207.		283.									
NO.OF COS. IN MKT. RES.	8											
TOT.IND. MKT.RES..CURR.	250.											

Standard Decision Forms and Standing Contract Forms

A. Standard Decision Forms

IMPORTANT:
USE PENCIL
NOT INK!

DON'T FORGET COMPANY AND PERIOD NUMBERS IN ALL AREAS

Region	FINANCE		MARKETING		MANUFACTURING		
	BORROW (O) OR INVEST (−) (000)	CASH FROM (O) OR TO (−) HOME (000)	OPENED (O) CLOSED (−) REG. OFFICES	ADVERTISING (000)	PRICE FOR GRADES SOLD	PRODUCTION (000)	

PRODUCTION (000) columns: X PLANT 1, Y PLANT 4, X PLANT 2, Y PLANT 5, X PLANT 3, Y PLANT 6; GRADE PROD. (0-4); MODEL STD / DEL

UNITED STATES
- FINANCE: Borrow/Invest O| 36 ; 66 − − 69 ; Cash O| 35 ; 62 − − 65
- MARKETING: Opened/Closed O| 34 ; NO. 61 ; Advertising 31 − 33 ; 58 − 60
- PRICE FOR GRADES SOLD: 19 20 ; 29 30 ; 47 48 ; 56 57
- Production STD: GRADE 12, X PLANT 1: 13 14, X PLANT 2: 15 16, X PLANT 3: 17 18
- Production STD Y: Y PLANT 4: 41 42, Y PLANT 5: 43 44, Y PLANT 6: 45 46
- Production DEL: GRADE 22, 23 24, 25 26, 27 28
- Production DEL Y: 50 51, 52 53, 54 55
- METHODS IMPROVEMENT (000): 9 10 ; 38 39
- NO. OF NEW PLANTS: 8 ; 37
- PRODUCT X ; Y
- Co. # 9 1 2 3 ; 1 4 ; 2 7 ; Period # 5 6

EEC
- FINANCE: Borrow/Invest O| 36 ; 66 − − 69 ; Cash O| 35 ; 62 − − 65
- MARKETING: Opened/Closed O| 34 ; NO. 61 ; Advertising 31 − 33 ; 58 − 60
- PRICE FOR GRADES SOLD: 19 20 ; 29 30 ; 47 48 ; 56 57
- Production STD: GRADE 12, 13 14, 15 16, 17 18
- Production STD Y: 41 42, 43 44, 45 46
- Production DEL: GRADE 22, 23 24, 25 26, 27 28
- Production DEL Y: 50 51, 52 53, 54 55
- METHODS IMPROVEMENT (000): 9 10 ; 38 39
- NO. OF NEW PLANTS: 8 ; 37
- PRODUCT X ; Y
- Co. # 9 1 2 3 ; 2 4 ; 2 7 ; Period # 5 6

BRAZIL
- FINANCE: Borrow/Invest O| 36 ; 66 − − 69 ; Cash O| 35 ; 62 − − 65
- MARKETING: Opened/Closed O| 34 ; NO. 61 ; Advertising 31 − 33 ; 58 − 60
- PRICE FOR GRADES SOLD: 19 20 ; 29 30 ; 47 48 ; 56 57
- Production STD: GRADE 12, 13 14, 15 16, 17 18
- Production STD Y: 41 42, 43 44, 45 46
- Production DEL: GRADE 22, 23 24, 25 26, 27 28
- Production DEL Y: 50 51, 52 53, 54 55
- METHODS IMPROVEMENT (000): 9 10 ; 38 39
- NO. OF NEW PLANTS: 8 ; 37
- PRODUCT X ; Y
- Co. # 9 1 2 3 ; 3 4 ; 2 7 ; Period # 5 6

HOME OFFICE—INTOP DECISION CARD NO. 2

Use pencil, not ink!

Item	Decision	Card Column
	9	1
Company #	☐☐	2-3
	4	4
Period #	☐☐	5-6

FINANCE:

Government Securities	(000's) ☐☐☐☐☐	12-16
Dividends	(000's) ☐☐☐☐	17-20

RESEARCH AND DEVELOPMENT:

R & D for product X	(000's) ☐☐☐	22-24
R & D for product Y	(000's) ☐☐☐	26-28

MARKETING RESEARCH AND GAZETTE:

Special consulting services (state *amount* payable for *this item only*, in thousands of $)	☐☐☐	34-36
Maximum of three selections among marketing research items nos. 1-18 (specify *item numbers*)	☐☐ ☐☐ ☐☐ 37 38 39 40 41 42	

If item 17 or 18 was selected, specify product and grade (e.g., X_3, Y_2)_____

                                                                    (no punch!)

Notes: 1. Transfer of funds from Home Office to an Area goes on the Area Card.
       2. Home Office Bank Loans (see administrator) go on Card No. 3.

Period # _____

INTER-COMPANY AND SPECIAL TRANSACTIONS—INTOP DECISION CARD NO. 3

Use pencil, not ink!

<u>Item</u>	<u>Decision</u>	
Transaction Type (see list at bottom of page)		☐ 1
Lender, Licensor or Seller	Co. #	☐☐ 2 3
Area from which goods are transferred, if any	Area #	☐ 4
Borrower, Licensee or Buyer	Co. #	☐☐ 5 6
Area to which goods are transferred, if any	Area #	☐ 7

Lender Licensor Seller

FINANCE (inter-company and and Home Office bank loans):

Amount of Loan (o) or Repayment (–)   <u>0</u> ☐ 13   (000's)   ☐☐☐☐ 14 – – 17

Amount of Interest   (000's)   ☐☐☐☐ 18 – – 21

RESEARCH AND DEVELOPMENT (licenses):

License Payment   (000's)   ☐☐☐☐ 25 – – 28

For X (1 if yes)   ☐ 29

For Y (1 if yes)   ☐ 30

Product Grade (1-4)   ☐ 31

MARKETING (inter-company and intra-company sales):

X Transfer (1 if yes)   ☐ 37

Y Transfer (1 if yes)   ☐ 38

Std. Transfer (1 if yes)   (see *seller's* inventory)   ☐ 39

Del. Transfer (1 if yes)   ☐ 40

Units Transferred (thousands)   (000's)   ☐☐ 42 43

Unit Price ($) (Also in intra-company sales!)   ($)   ☐☐ 45 46

Borrower Licensee Buyer

Transaction Type

1	Home Office Bank Loan (see Administrator)
2	Intercompany Loan
3	Licensing
4	Industrial (inter-company) Sales
5	Intra-Company Sales

REMEMBER: *Only one transaction (or a single transfer) on each of these cards!*

B. Standing Contract Forms

INTOP BANK LOAN CONTRACT

Borrower Company   _____

Principal $_____

Period, quarters   _____

Interest 3% per quarter, i.e., $_____

The entire principal will be paid in the last quarter of the loan, i.e., in

Quarter   _____

This is a long-term contract − prepayment is not acceptable.

Other regulations:

Liechtenstein, in the _____th quarter

_____   _____
President, Borrowing Co.   For Chase-A-Martini Bank

Note: *Failure to submit quarterly interest payment by means of DECISION CARD 3*
may result in foreclosure of the loan or penalty payments.

INTOP INTER-COMPANY LOAN CONTRACT

Lending Company _____

Borrowing Company _____

Principal $_____

Period, quarters _____

The money will be available immediately.

Interest _____ % of principal per quarter, to be paid each quarter for the duration of the loan $_____ (unless prepayment is made).*

The entire principal will be paid in the last quarter of the loan, i.e., in Quarter _____. Unless otherwise specified below, prepayment is acceptable. In such a case, interest shall only be paid on outstanding principal.*

Other regulations:

Note: It is understood that in case of default on the loan, the lender shall be given a license on any patents *developed* by the borrower, in addition to any funds allotted to the lender in the bankruptcy proceedings.

Liechtenstein, in the _____th quarter

_____   _____
President, Lending Co.   President, Borrowing Co.

*If prepayment is not acceptable cross out irrelevant parts of contract text and add a clause under "Other regulations," such as "No prepayments."

INTOP STANDING SUPPLIER CONTRACT

Supplying Company _____ (seller)

Buying Company   _____

Period of supply   _____ quarters (must be *at least two* under a
                                                          Standing Contract)

Product   _____

Grade   _____

Units of the product to be shipped each quarter: _____ (000 units)

Price per unit $_____

Shipments (and payments) will begin in the   _____ th quarter.

The goods will be shipped *from* Area No.   _____

The goods will be shipped *to* Area No.   _____

Other regulations:

*Note: Payment will be made from area to which products are shipped to area
from which they are shipped.*
If this contract is broken prematurely by unilateral action, the defaulting
party agrees to pay damages of 20% of the aggregate then outstanding
value of the contract, the value to be determined by multiplying quantity
and price specified above with the number of quarters in default.

Liechtenstein, in the _____ th quarter

_____   _____
President, Supplier   President, Buyer

INTOP PATENT LICENSE AGREEMENT

License-granting Company _____

License-taking Company   _____

Product   _____

Grade Licensed   _____

License Period: _____   forever ⎫ (Indicate what is
                                                          ⎬ applicable; note
                                                  number of ⎨ minimum of *two*
                                                  quarters ⎭ quarters)

Territorial coverage: _____   worldwide ⎫ (Indicate what is
                                                           ⎬ applicable)
                                                  U.S., EEC, ⎨
                                                  Brazil ⎭

Payment in lump sum_____

Quarterly royalty_____per units produced*   ⎫ (Indicate what is
                                                       ⎬ applicable)
Guaranteed minimum royalty____per quarter*   ⎭

The highest grade of this product already possessed by the licensee is
_____.

Other regulations:

                              Liechtenstein, in the _____th quarter

_____   _____
President, Licensor Company   President, Licensee Company

*Note: Patent License Agreements automatically become invalid if and when
       the Licensee obtains a higher grade of the product.
       Royalty per unit must be rounded off to nearest half-dollar.
       All royalty payments begin in the quarter after that in which contract is
       signed. Combinations of lump-sum payments and royalty are, of course,
       possible.

INTOP SPECIALIZATION AGREEMENT — RESEARCH

1. Company No._____(hereafter Co. A) hereby rents from Company No._____(hereafter Co. B) its research laboratories for product X
   product Y
   both products

2. The lease shall run forever _____
   for_____quarters

3. Co. A agrees to spend a *minimum* of $_____per quarter on research in the Co. B labs.

4. Until further notice, the amount invested on research in the B labs shall be $ _____ for X and $_____for Y per quarter. Co. B agrees to incur this expense on the Home Office Card. Co. A will transfer an identical amount to Co. B each quarter on an Inter-Company Transaction Card. (Technically, this is a Number 2 transaction – an inter-company loan of facilities from B to A – and payments should be made in the form of "interest" from A to B.) Co. A will notify Co. B of any change in quarterly R & D expense (which shall never be less than specified in point three above).

5. Co. B shall have the right to make use of any patents developed in the B labs (it will in effect be able to market such products one quarter ahead of Co. A). Co. B is *not* allowed to sublicense such patents.

6. Co. A for the duration of the agreement shall otherwise have the exclusive disposition of such patents, and is authorized to license the patents to himself and other companies in Co. B's name. If at any time it is more convenient to Co. A to have license payments from third parties made to Co. B than to himself, Co. B agrees to transfer these amounts to Co. A (or set them off against Co. A research expense, as agreed).

7. Co. B shall have the right to use any patent cross-licensed to his lab from Co. A against a royalty of $_____ per unit produced each quarter.
   without any fee _____.
   Whenever a patent of higher grade shall be developed in the B labs such payments shall terminate.

8. Other provisions:

                                                    Liechtenstein in the _____th Quarter

President, Co. No._____(Co. A)   President, Co. No._____ (Co. B)

Appendix V

Standard Operating Instructions

A. Computer Liaison

Computer Liaison

I. *Purpose and Duties*

The purpose of the computer liaison function is to coordinate the processing of the decision sheets and the flow of information which is the vital nerve of the simulation. Essential duties include *editing and assembling the decision forms, proofreading the key-punched decision cards and preparing for the run on the computer*. Computer Liaison is a key responsibility, requiring a comprehensive knowledge of the rules to facilitate the discovery of errors on the decision cards. Improper editing of the decision cards may cause unnecessary disappointments among the teams. To prevent this, careful attention must be given to the details of the decision cards.

From the administrative viewpoint, Computer Liaison is the link between cause and effect. Computer Liaison must at all times work closely with the game administrator. Throughout the run of the simulation the administrator may decide to introduce *environmental changes* affecting the behavior of the teams. Two types of environmental changes are possible. Production restrictions, import quotas and capital transfer prohibitions suggest a few of the changes that can be enforced very easily via the decision forms.[1] In such cases the given environmental changes are simply checked against the appropriate boxes on the forms submitted by the companies. For instance, a strike in the vacuum cleaner industry in the U.S. is made effective simply by checking that all Y production boxes for the U.S. are empty on the Operations Cards. Infractions of the rules may result in a cash fine or a public rebuke to the erring company. In all instances the company's decisions must be altered to conform with the current rule.

The second type of environmental change requires the use of Wonder Cards.[2] Parameter changes concerning manufacturing costs, advertising elasticities, interest charges and other parts of the computer program require the introduction of Wonder Cards into the system. (The mechanics involved in using Wonder Cards are discussed in Chapter 5, Section 2 of this book and Section IV of this Instruction.) Environmental changes requiring the use of Wonder Cards are typically long run in character. Environmental changes relating to the decision forms are generally short run in nature, usually affecting only one or two quarters of operations; hence there is no need to alter the basic game parameters.

Checking the decision cards — without however "doctoring" them — is especially important in the beginning of the game. Numerous

[1] In the same category is the Brazilian securities deposit requirement for new plants during the first three quarters of INTOP Standard runs.
[2] It will be assumed in the following that the reader is thoroughly familiar with the INTOP *Player's Manual* as well as with Chapter 4 and at least the first two sections of Chapter 5 of this book.

errors may be made before teams develop an understanding for the routine involved. Common errors include attempts to produce higher grades than 0 before any product improvements have been obtained, making production decisions before plant construction has been completed, posting prices before there is any inventory to sell. Some errors, such as the first two of the three just cited, are also checked by the computer. Others, such as the posting of fictitious prices, are not.[3] In all cases the teams should be informed of their mistakes which may be based upon misconceptions of the rules.

Finally, *a monitor company* may be operated as part of the computer liaison function. The advantages of having a monitor company are several; the main one is that such a company permits administrative intervention without having to resort to Wonder Cards for all types of transactions. Thus, the monitor company should be given the maximum grade of product improvements, permitting the game administrator to license these improvements as a management consulting service. By building the maximum number of plants for each product in each area, the monitor company can produce all grades of each product from the beginning of the game. This permits selling to other companies or entering an underdeveloped consumer market if the administrator wishes to do so. The monitor company may also engage in governmental purchasing if excess inventory exists in an area. In addition, the monitor company may be used to test various parameter changes on an experimental basis.[4]

---

[3] It is true that a price posted in the absence of inventory will not be reprinted on the Market Research 1 output sheet, where it would clearly serve to confuse other teams. However, such prices are still undesirable in that they affect the "effective price" in the subsequent period of the company posting them. This is no calamity, but may give the team in question a certain advantage or disadvantage in that period. If so desired, Computer Liaison may redress the balance by manipulating effective price — Dictionary Symbol VS11 — or the marketing effectiveness index — VS13 — of the company by a Wonder Card in the following period.

[4] Assuming that there are n teams participating (n is 24 or less), the monitor company should be given number $n + 1$.

Monitor's special resources are created by Wonder Cards (see Chapter 5 of the book and Section IV of this instruction). It is suggested that Wonder Cards 4 or 4A be made out to provide monitor with forty million dollars in home office cash and that standard Wonder Card 4 be used to equip monitor with product improvements X_4 and Y_4 (state variable VR01) from the outset. (These cards may be submitted with quarter 1 [Q1] decision cards.)

In Q1 it is recommended that monitor transfer nine million dollars in cash to all areas on the regular Operations Form No. 1. While there is no real need to submit any Home Office forms, it may be well to submit one in Q1, indicating one or two orders for Market Research Item 2, as companies may be interested in buying at a reduced price slightly obsolete data of that item. If no Home Office forms are submitted later this order will be repeated automatically each quarter.

In addition, the non-existent inventory in Q1 should be artificially upgraded, so that inventory grades (VS18) will be as follows:

	U.S.	EEC	Brazil
Standard	X_0, Y_0	X_1, Y_1	X_3, Y_3
Deluxe	X_1, Y_1	X_2, Y_2	X_4, Y_4

Two standard Wonder Cards (one for each product) are needed for this purpose, as indicated by the figure, "Wonder Card Processing Logic" in Chapter 5 of this book. Note that the inventory grades on each card will appear as

II. *Preparing for a First Run or a New Run. Identification of a Run. Changing Number of Companies. Continuous Runs.*

A. PREPARING FOR A FIRST RUN OR A NEW RUN

Before staging an actual run of the simulation a test run should be made. The test run serves the following purposes:

1. During the test run the program will be compiled in the form of a deck of binary cards later to be used in identical form in each period of the actual run.

2. Minor local computer equipment variations may make modifications in the procedures suggested in this instruction desirable. Such matters, if any, should be straightened out before the actual run.

3. As in all other efforts involving the cooperation of several persons, administrative routines need to be worked out. It will make a better impression on participants in the simulation if these matters have been worked out beforehand in a mock run rather than on an *ad hoc* basis during the actual run — especially in cases when time is scarce.

Virtually all that is needed for the test run is the INTOP program tape and the local computer equipment. To make the test run as much like a real run as possible while saving local time and effort, a five-period set of decisions for several companies has been inserted at the end of the program tape. If output of the regular format and without obvious flaws in the data reported from this mock run is obtained at the end of the test, the test has been successful and everything is technically prepared for the real run.

The test run procedure is as follows:

1. Mount the program tape on the local IBM 1401 for tape-to-card conversion. The output obtained will be a complete deck of cards of the INTOP FORTRAN II, Version 2 language problem and the set of cards representing the five-period test decisions.

---

six items under heading New Items.

The two Wonder Cards specifying monitor inventory grades should be submitted every quarter. This will guarantee that grades sold will be those specified if and when any sales take place (whether by expediting or from actual inventory). Note, however, that on the Ancillary Data sheet of the monitor company output the grades may be different if there is no standard inventory (as the last thing the computer does is to turn deluxe into standard if standard inventory is 0).

As products may be shipped by monitor from any area to any buyer area, and as any amount of goods may be shipped in inter-company transactions (sales expediting), monitor may be used to supply any grade of product at any time from Q1 on, if so desired. The fact that its computer output may look a bit scatter-brainish may not matter as the data are likely to come only before the eyes of administrative personnel.

If so desired, monitor may of course also build plants and produce for inventory. (This may minimize sales expediting, but may generate quite high inventory charges — "neat" monitor output is hard to obtain!) To prevent companies ordering Market Research Item 10 — number of plants currently producing — from being misled, teams should be notified when monitor plants are producing for stockpiling purposes.

2. Add in front of the card deck an Identification (ID) card of the type employed at the local computer installation.

3. Using the deck of ID, program and test decision cards as input, undertake a monitor run on the main computer. In this run the FORTRAN program will be compiled into machine language, and in addition the computer will automatically process the five-period test decisions. All output to be printed will appear on the monitor output tape. Card output data (machine-language program and history for period 5 of the test run) will appear either on the monitor output tape or on another tape, depending on the convention of the local installation. (For loading scheme see p. 351.)

4. The output tape(s) will then be processed on the 1401 to get final output.

Without further human intervention output should emerge in the following order:

a. a printed listing of the entire FORTRAN program;

b. a complete card deck of the INTOP program in machine language;

c. standard outputs of the five-period test decisions (all five periods in one sequence); and

d. punch-card history for period 5 of the test run. These cards should be thrown away as soon as the true-to-type nature of the printed output of the five-period test decisions has been ascertained.[5] A cross-company Consolidated Balance Sheet and Income Statement for period 4 of the test run is included in the INTOP FORTRAN User's Package to facilitate the examination of your test run output.

5. Go back to the FORTRAN program deck of cards. This deck contains a number of "monitor control cards." These are, in the following order:

Execute Card (★ in Col. 1, XEQ in Cols. 7-9)

★ Chain (1, 2)	
★ Chain (2, 2)	These cards indicate links in
★ Chain (3, 2)	the program and are inserted
★ Chain (4, 2)	at various intervals among
★ Chain (5, 2)	the program cards.
★ Chain (6, 2)	
★ Data (last card in deck)	

---

[5] Note that the test run makes no pretense of being a model run in the sense of setting a high standard of play. On the contrary, all decisions for all companies and all periods were made out in advance, without any attempt of pursuing systematic strategies. In particular, financial scheduling was largely disregarded, and a number of decisions were made for automatic re-implementation in several periods (hence the fictitious pricing decisions in period 2, for instance).

Four companies participated in all five periods. To illustrate the technique of adding companies, a fifth company was added in period 4. It was given $20,000,000 in cash and common stock, the full number of "plants allowable" (VM01) — although only two plants for each product in each area were built — and X_4 and Y_4 patents, as evidenced on period 4 Wonder Card output. Company 5 might thus be thought of as a monitor company.

Produce duplicates of these monitor control cards and insert them in the deck of local machine-language program cards at exactly the same positions as they have in the FORTRAN program deck.[6] *The deck of machine-language cards is now ready to be used in identical form each period of the actual run of the simulation.*

The procedure just outlined is, of course, a one-time phenomenon at each computer installation. Once the FORTRAN program has been compiled in machine-language card form the identical deck of program cards may be used over again in new runs of the simulation indefinitely.

At the beginning of any given run Computer Liaison may wish to set aside a company for monitor purposes. If monitor is to have any other characteristics than those initially given all other companies (as suggested above), these characteristics should be given the monitor company by Wonder Card in period 1.[7]

It is advisable always to make a *duplicate copy of the machine language program (including control cards)*. Should the program cards ever get into disarray, a duplicate deck of program cards is an invaluable asset.[8]

Finally, it may be added that the program-compiling and test run is a fairly demanding one. It will require some *fifty minutes of 7090 processing time,* and about *one hour of 1401* output printing and tape-to-card converting time. The printed output of program listings and full histories of the five-period test run amounts in the aggregate to some 30,000 lines.[9]

B. IDENTIFICATION OF A RUN. CHANGING NUMBER OF COMPANIES

A given run of INTOP must be given an identification on the Master Control Card. Rules for the use and changing of identification of INTOP runs are given in Chapter 5. Naturally, the identification used on the Master Control Card — which is for administrator and Computer Liaison use only — need not be the same as that used on the identification (ID) card placed ahead of all INTOP cards to identify the run to the management of the local computer installation.

[6] This is better than simply transplanting the FORTRAN monitor control cards, which would make the FORTRAN deck unworkable in case of future need.

[7] While it is possible to add a monitor company at any time during the simulation, experience indicates the value of including it from the outset.

[8] Cf. *infra*, 353.

[9] If a user wishes to avoid the sizable equipment use involved in compiling the program on his own installation he may obtain a card program on special request. This program will have been compiled at Chicago, but there is unfortunately no guarantee that it will work in unmodified form on the equipment configuration at the user's installation, even if that also happens to be an IBM 7090–1401 Tape combination. However, where the possible saving of computer time is extremely important, the potential user may first wish to try a card program test run. If it fails he may either give up the idea of using the simulation or proceed to compiling from the program tape.

The changing of number of companies in the course of a run is also discussed in Chapter 5. Only two matters of detail need be added here. If it is desired to add one or several companies with characteristics similar to those automatically given INTOP Standard teams at the beginning of a run three Wonder Cards are called for:

1. Home Office Cash (VF16):   add $10,000,000
2. Common Stock (VF25):   add $10,000,000
3. Number of Factories Allowable (VM01):   add 3 for each product and area

New companies may, of course, be given any other characteristics desired. Keep in mind, however, that "Number of Factories Allowable" will always be 0 for both products and all areas for a company entering the game *after* period 1 unless a Wonder Card is used to specify the maximum allowable number.[10]

If a company other than that which happens to have the highest number[11] is to be eliminated from a run, steps must be taken to prevent its last set of Operations (Decision Card 1) and Home Office (Card 2) decisions from becoming automatically re-implemented in all future periods. All Computer Liaison needs to do is to fill out a Form 1 and a Form 2 with company number and period number *only* in all areas and Home Office in the *first* period after the company's dropping out.

There is usually no need to "clean up" the records of the drop-out company. When cross-company Consolidated Financial Statements are distributed other teams may simply be instructed to disregard the figures indicated for the drop-out team. Should a complete clean-out of the record be desired one must proceed as follows:

1. Eliminate all plants (see last section of this instruction).
2. Dispose of all inventory (transfer it to monitor company or eliminate by Wonder Card).
3. Eliminate all sales offices (by Form 2 or Wonder Card).
4. Wait one period for time-lag effects.
5. Eliminate any remaining numbers other than 0 by Wonder Card.

C. CONTINUOUS RUNS

Only one remark needs to be added to the discussion of continuous runs (involving the simultaneous processing of several periods) in Chapter 5. The output from *all* periods involved will emerge in one continuous block at the end of all computer processing. For this reason, the number of copies required of both sets of reports should be set to 0 on the Master Control Card for all the periods processed except the last one.

---

10 The output formats place an upper limit of three plants per product and area, i.e., a total of eighteen plants per company.

11 In this case all that is needed to eliminate the company is simply to reduce the "Number of Companies This Period" item on the Master Control Card by one.

III. *Editing and Sorting of Decision Forms.*
Proofreading Punched Cards. Register of
Decision Cards

A. EDITING

Editing the decision sheets involves the following routine procedure
for all forms:

1. Amplify decisions with blue pencil when necessary to increase
readability.

2. Check that numbers using fewer digits than the number of
spaces are located furthest to the right in the box. This is especially
important regarding company number and period number. (Forgetting
their primary school training, some people tend to put tens in the units
column and vice versa.)

3. Check that all team decision forms contain the company
number and period number, keeping in mind point 4 below.[12]

4. Note that if decisions *have* been made, any neglected company number and/or period number should be filled in if it is deter-
minable. (Do *not* add in company or period number in areas where no
decisions have been made on Card 1, as the team may wish to have
prior decisions automatically re-implemented.)

5. Check that there are *no letters* in any of the boxes. (A common error is filling in X_0, Y_2, etc. in the grade box on area forms. This
box should contain only the grade number, not the product.)

6. Check that no signs appear in other than sign boxes, as this
may stop the computer.[13] Note also that any *minus* sign inserted by
inadvertence, i.e., a minus sign not followed by any quantitative decision, should be eliminated.

7. Remember to check for any infractions of the environmental
changes and make the necessary adjustments on the forms.

Operations Card 1. When editing Operations Card 1, Computer Liaison may wish to assist the key-punch operator by crossing
over any *area* sector on the form in which there are *no decisions and
no designation of company number and period number*.[14] However,
he should *not* cross out area sectors which *do* have a company number
and period number. If no other boxes are marked, the computer will

---

[12] If Computer Liaison is present at
the decision-making session, this check
should be made as the forms are handed in.

[13] If Computer Liaison is present at
the decision-making session he should
check that sign boxes have been filled
in whenever teams have indicated a
corresponding quantitative decision. If
not, companies may properly face the
consequence of their negligence, as the
computer will read a 0 (generally interpreted as a +) in the sign box.

[14] An alternative is simply to instruct
the operator not to punch Card 1 for
areas in which there is no company or
period designation. This will save the
operator some work, but is not *functionally* necessary. Whether a card is
included or not, any prior decisions
which the company may have made in
the area will be automatically re-implemented.

read zero in all of them. For example: In period 1, Company 3 builds 1 X plant in the EEC (Area 2). In period 2, the second quarter of plant construction, Company 3 needs to submit an Operations form indicating the company number and period number in Area 2. If no form was submitted for Area 2, the computer would repeat the decision for period 1 and begin construction of a second X plant in the EEC.

Companies will be grateful to a charitable Computer Liaison if the following points are also observed:

1. Whenever a *price* is given in a deluxe box, but no standard price is set, a charitable Computer Liaison may go back to the Ancillary Data Sheet of the previous quarter output of the company in question to check whether one or two grades are in inventory. If two grades are in inventory, it may be assumed that the company wished to keep the standard goods in inventory, and no change should be made. If there is only one grade in inventory, it is *always* standard goods, and the price should be moved from the deluxe to the standard box. The company should be informed, and fined or rebuked.

2. If a *production* decision has been made which substantially exceeds the maximal capacity of the plant in question, it is likely that the team actually intended to split the decision on several plants but recorded only the total production figure. A generous Computer Liaison may check on the number of company plants in existence, and split the total production evenly over both or all three plants. A fine or rebuke is again in order.

Home Office Card 2. Confusion may arise concerning Market Research on the Home Office Card. Box 34–36 is to be used only for *special* consulting services. The *amount payable* for such services should be entered in the box in terms of thousands of dollars. Boxes 37–38, 39–40 and 41–42 are for Marketing Research Items number 1 through 18. (See Marketing Research Detailed in Chapter 2.) These boxes should contain the *item number* but *not* the cost of the items. It is necessary to check that no company has entered in the special consulting services box the total expense for Market Research items ordered in boxes 37 through 42.[15] The computer automatically makes the necessary charges.

If *Market Research Item 17 or 18* is ordered, the company must indicate the product and grade for which the information is desired. Computer Liaison will fill out the necessary forms for Items 17 and 18 as well as keep statistics of which companies order Items 17 and 18 by quarter, product and grade. Remember to check with the administrator whether these two items may be given out *at* the same game session in which they are ordered, or whether the information will be

---

[15] The Home Office Card should be checked for *Gazette* subscriptions in quarters 3, 7, 11, etc. Especially in quarter 3 teams are apt to write in 40 instead of 1 and mix the boxes. The correct entry is 1 in box 38 and no more. The administrator may decide to make continued *Gazette* subscription obligatory.

MARKET RESEARCH AND CONSULTING SERVICES

ITEM NO. 17 – *Test Marketing of Any One Product Grade*

Company _____   Quarter _____

Other circumstances being equal (competitive action, business climate, etc.) you should be able to increase your price of Grade _____ by _____ to_____% in relation to _____0 and still be able to sell the same quantity as you would of the lowest grade. (Or, conversely, you should be able to increase your quantity sold by a corresponding percentage at unchanged price.)

ITEM NO. 18 – *Consultant's Opinion on Increase in Variable Manufacturing Cost for Any One Product Grade*

Company _____   Quarter _____

Other circumstances being equal (rate of capacity utilization, age of plant, etc.) you may expect that your variable manufacturing cost for Grade _____ in relation to _____0 would be from_____ to _____% higher.

delivered only with the regular output *after* the session. The INTOP FORTRAN User's Package contains standard forms for Market Research 17 and 18 as well as the relevant statistical data. A sample form is reproduced on p. 338.[16] The statistics are percentage figures stated in relation to X_0 and Y_0. Purchase of these items will indicate which grade improvements for X and Y are duds.[17]

Inter-company and Special Transactions Card 3. It is *essential* that the proper transaction type be indicated in box 1 on the Inter-company and Special Transactions Card. If it has been omitted the transaction type may be derived from the data on the form. In addition, transactions type 1 through 4 should bear the appropriate signatures before being approved for processing. All Card 3 special transactions types 1 through 4 should be checked against the standing contract file.[18] Indication should be made on each contract that the proper Card 3 has been received. The contracts file needs to be kept current. Expired contracts may be given to the game administrator.

On *Home Office Bank Loans, Transaction Type 1*, boxes 2 and 3 will remain empty. The borrower's company number will appear in boxes 5 and 6. It is necessary to indicate the proper sign in box 13, showing whether the loan is being received (0) or repaid (−). When interest payments are being made, box 13 must remain *empty*, unless payment on the principal is also made. A sign appears in box 13 *only* when principal of the loan is being received or paid.

Licensing, Transaction Type 3, necessitates filling out license sheets for junior grades of the product. For example, assume that Company 1 licenses Y_3 to Company 5. Also assume that the highest grade possessed by Company 5 is Y_1. Under these circumstances one of the companies will submit a Transaction Type 3 licensing Y_3. It is then necessary for Computer Liaison to fill out another Transaction Type 3 licensing Y_2 from Company 1 to Company 5. The program allows product improvements 1 through 4 to be received in consecutive order only. Thus to receive Y_4, one must have previously received through licensing or research and development Y_1, Y_2 and Y_3. Also the license payment must *always* indicate the *product* and *grade* for which the payment is being made, whether the actual transfer of the license was made in the current or in a previous quarter.

Inter-company and Intra-company Sales, Transaction Types 4 and 5. Occasionally companies will fail to specify *area* numbers. These may sometimes be ascertained by checking standing contracts or Ancillary Data output sheets, in which case Computer Liaison may insert the numbers. If the numbers cannot be ascertained without ambiguity

---

16 The requisite data are given in Item 9 of the FORTRAN User's Package.

17 Note that a company may order Item 17 or 18 for up to three grades in a given quarter, as it is perfectly possi-

ble to insert the same item number in several Marketing Research boxes.

18 Standing contracts are those with a validity of more than one quarter, cf. below.

(or if the administrator feels that the companies have to live with their own mistakes), the form in question may as well be withheld, as incomplete forms of this type will be rejected by the computer.

A fairly common mistake is neglecting to specify the *product and/or model* (standard or deluxe) involved in a sales transaction. Analogous rules apply. If no *price* is stated, no correction should be made — transfers are perfectly feasible at a price of 0. If no *quantity* is stated, the form may as well be withheld, unless a glance at a standing contract makes the insertion of the correct number feasible.

Standing Contracts. "Standing Contracts" is the technical term for all inter-company and home office bank loan transactions which span over more than one quarter. All patent license agreements fall in this category, as the *Player's Manual* specifies a minimum period of two quarters for the validity of such agreements.

Computer Liaison maintains a file of standing contracts. Standard forms are provided for inter-company loans and home office bank loans, standing supplier contracts, and patent licenses and R & D specialization arrangements.[19] Of these types of arrangements, that involving R & D specialization has not been frequently used in INTOP Standard runs.

When two teams have made a long-range agreement Computer Liaison checks that the standing contract form has been properly filled out and signed, *and* that an inter-company transactions form (Decision Form No. 3) has been made out to effectuate the part of the total contract scheduled to be executed during the current quarter. It is believed that the instructions given on the forms are detailed and explicit enough to obviate the need for further comment. Let us merely re-emphasize that when a patent license agreement has been made it devolves upon Computer Liaison to make out requisite Decision Forms No. 3 to give the licensee the grades of the product licensed not already possessed by him and lower than the grade transferred by the Decision Card No. 3 filled out by the companies themselves.[20]

When a patent license expires,[21] Computer Liaison must check the prior quarter's output to determine if the licensee has obtained an improvement higher than that covered by the license. If a higher grade improvement has been received, the expiration of the license requires no further attention. However, when a license expires and the licensee has no superior improvement, one must check what the licensee's maximum grade of improvement was in the *last quarter before* the agreement was negotiated.[22] A Wonder Card is then filled out to reduce

---

[19] The forms are reproduced in Appendix IV of this book. Moreover, a set of sample forms is included in the User's Package (exception: the R & D specialization form is only reproduced in the book).

[20] Cf. 339 above.

[21] Note again that the *Player's Manual* prescribes a minimum license period of two quarters.

[22] This is indicated on the standing contract form through which the license was obtained.

the company's maximum grade of improvement to its earlier level.

Each quarter Computer Liaison should make a note on each standing contract form in his file as to whether the parties are complying with the agreement. A simple "Q10" written in a corner of the form may be used to indicate that the contract was complied with in quarter 10. The raw material for this examination of compliance is furnished by the Decision Cards No. 3 submitted by all teams in the quarter. After computer processing these data show up on the output in the form of a register of Inter-Company and Special Transactions. In cases where a patent license agreement has been made exclusive either with regard to licensee or territorial applicability (the latter has occurred very rarely in the past) Computer Liaison should check that the parties abide by the arrangement.[23]

The file of standing contracts serves a dual purpose. It enables the administrator to keep tabs on contract performance and to assist in the enforcement of contracts when a party defaults for no good reason. It also provides a set of useful records for a review and evaluation of the entire run and of individual company participation therein.

B. SORTING DECISION FORMS FOR KEY-PUNCHING

The computer will accept decision forms (including Wonder Cards) in any order (or disorder). *Hence there is no functional necessity of sorting decision forms before key-punching.* However, it is generally *desirable* to do so, as this will facilitate *proofreading* punch cards against the original forms (cf. under C below).

The decision sheets should be collected, put in ascending order and grouped by Operations Form 1, Home Office Form 2, Special Transactions Form 3 and Wonder Cards Form 4. The following procedure is used for arranging the sheets:

1. Form 1 is sorted according to ascending company order. (Card column 2-3)

2. Form 2 is sorted on the same principle of ascending company number. (Card column 2-3)

3. Form 3 is sorted in ascending order first on column 1, then column 2-3 and finally column 4. (Sole exception: Bank loans where one jumps from column 1 to column 5-6 to find a number.)

    a. Sort according to transaction type in ascending order.

    b. Transaction Type 1 sort according to borrower company number in ascending order.

    c. Transaction Types 2 through 5 sort according to *company* number (column 2-3) and within companies according to area number (column 4), all in ascending order.

4. Form 4 is sorted in ascending order according to columns 1 through 7.

[23] If an agreement contains provisions questionable from an antitrust or other public policy viewpoint this fact should be brought to the attention of the administrator.

WARNING: *All decision forms and Wonder Cards must have a digit in column 1.* A "blank" in column 1 is a signal to the computer to stop.

After the decision sheets are sorted they are delivered to be key-punched. Key-punching should be done on cards with 80 (*not* 60 or 72) columns printed on the top line. To facilitate proofreading, the cards should be printed while being key-punched, so that the punched numbers appear on the top edge.

C. PROOFREADING THE CARDS

After the decision sheets have been key-punched on cards, they must be proofread to check the accuracy of the key-punching, and as a final check that the original sheets have been filled out correctly by the players. The suggested method is for two people to compare *verbally* the sheets with the punched cards.[24] Computer Liaison should read aloud the column number and the contents of that column written on the *original decision sheets.* A second person ascertains that the correct number and column were punched on the card. When errors are found new cards must be punched to replace the incorrect card. *Special care should be taken in proofreading Wonder Cards and the Master Control Card(s).*

Common Errors on Company Decision Cards. When checking the punched cards against the company decision sheets one should check for the following common errors:

1. Column 1 never contains an 8.
2. Columns 2 and 3 must contain a number between 1 and 25 (or the highest company number in the game), except that Transaction Type 1 (Bank Loans) are blank in these digits.
3. Column 4 on *Operations and Home Office* cards must contain a number between 1 and 4 inclusive.
4. Either column 29 or column 30 on *Transaction Type 3* (Licensing) must contain a 1, but not both.
5. Either column 37 or 38 and column 39 or 40 on *Transaction Type 4 and 5* (inventory shipments) must contain a 1. Thus there are only four possibilities:

Column	37	38	39	40
Card #1	1	0	1	0
Card #2	1	0	0	1
Card #3	0	1	1	0
Card #4	0	1	0	1

These columns must be filled in correctly or the card will be rejected during the run.

24 The proofreading is further facilitated if a printout of the cards has been obtained from the card printer.

6. The letter O has been punched instead of the digit 0.[25]

7. Common errors occur in punching numbers in the wrong columns because all columns are not read consecutively on all cards, e.g., on Transaction Types 4 and 5 columns 41 and 44 are blank and not indicated on the sheets; column 25 on the Home Office Card is not used; and columns 11 and 21 are not used on Operations Form 1.

NOTE AGAIN: All decision and Wonder Cards *must* have a digit in column 1.

D. REGISTER OF DECISION CARDS. SAVING DECISION CARDS

At the very end of the output of each period appears a complete register of all Decision Cards 1 and 2 accepted by the computer, in the form they were accepted. Rejected cards of these types, if any, are registered immediately before the Wonder Cards at the very beginning of the output. Any human error from the time a company made (or neglected to make) a decision to computer processing may thus be traced, and a correction may be made in a subsequent period, if warranted.

Inter-Company and Special Transactions (Decision Cards 3) are listed in a special register following on the Wonder Card output. The cards *formally* in order are indicated by an "OK." Cards not acceptable to the computer are indicated by the word "REJECT."

The special register of Wonder Card changes similarly distinguishes between formally acceptable and unacceptable cards.

The registers of decision and Wonder Cards furnish a valuable record of game history, in addition to the fact that they resolve any doubt as to the nature of the information fed into the computer. Nevertheless, the original decision forms submitted by the companies should be preserved at least until the teams have had a chance to comment on any real or alleged errors.

The punched decision and Wonder Cards of each period should be saved to the end of the last period of a simulation run. Should the punch card history in any period ever get into disarray, and output tape is no longer available to reproduce it, a new history may be created by rerunning all previous periods in continuous processing.[26]

IV. *Wonder Cards*

Wonder Cards Form 4 are the administrator's special instrument of control over the simulation. Use of the Wonder Card permits changing any one of the parameters of the INTOP model or adjusting the historical data ("state variables") of any company in a particular run of the simulation. Three different types of Wonder Cards exist:

25 This mistake would rarely occur on other than Wonder Cards. Note that in such Dictionary symbols as PS03, VM08 the 0 is a digit. If the letter O is punched in its place this will stop the computer.

26 Cf. *infra*, 354.

Form 4   The Standard Wonder Card — may *always* be used.
Form 4A   Special Wonder Card for adjustment of Home Office
            Cash and Retained Earnings accounts of a given com-
            pany.
Form 4B   Special Wonder Card for adjustment of Area Cash and
            Retained Earnings accounts of a given company.

A. STANDARD WONDER CARDS

The Standard Wonder Card is discussed at length in Chapter 5 of this
book. At the level of detail the following comments may be added:

1. If *decimal* numbers are to be used under the *Multiple for Old
Item* and *New Items* headings, it does not matter in what columns
within the respective boxes provided the numbers are written, as the
decimal point — whenever placed in these columns — will uniquely
specify the magnitude of the number to the computer.

2. If no decimal is indicated, i.e., the number is an *integer*,
the number should *always be written as far to the right as possible* in
the box of columns provided. (Should this rule be neglected, the number read by the computer will be one or several powers of 10 too large.)
Note that all numbers must be written out *in extenso* on Wonder
Cards; these cards do *not* deal in thousands, as is sometimes the case
with the decision forms used by the teams.[27]

3. If a number takes up less than all the columns provided in a
box, there is no need to insert zeros in front of it. As a general rule,
the computer will read zeros in any column left blank.

4. If several of the numbers having a common Dictionary symbol are to be changed *differentially* by replacement or addition (subtraction), a maximum of six consecutive items may be involved. The
meaning of "consecutive" is spelled out in Chapter 5. If an intervening
item is *not* to be changed, the number representing the item must
still be spelled out in full *as if* the item were to be changed, in order to
preserve "consecutiveness."[28] In each case when more than one item is
to be changed, it is necessary to define *Final Item* as well as *Initial
Item.*[29] Should the number of items specified by the initial and final
item designations be smaller than the number of items indicated in
columns 27–80, *the computer will only process the items specified in
columns 8–21*. Should the items specified in columns 8–21 be greater
than six, the entire card will be rejected.

5. The range of size of individual numbers on the Wonder Card
is great enough to serve virtually any change which may sensibly be
made by replacement or addition (subtraction). The only numbers

---

[27] In working with Wonder Cards and
Master Control Cards it is important
that the differentiation of the letter O
and the digit 0 be observed. In the parameter symbol PS03 the 0 is a digit;
should the letter O be punched this will
stop the 7090 — a costly and irritating
event.

[28] Should the box be left empty by
mistake the number will be changed to
zero.

[29] Hence it is *not* enough simply to
give the new numbers in columns
27–80.

beyond this range in the entire INTOP Standard framework are *certain coefficients in the manufacturing cost function*, i.e., PM04, PM06 and PM08, and the *squared term coefficient in the inventory cost function*, PS32. If the administrator wishes to change these particular items, multiplication, or a multicard combination of replacement and multiplication, should always be used due to the extraordinarily small values involved. If only minor change is involved, it may be readily accomplished by multiplication by an appropriate decimal number.

If major change is contemplated the standard value(s) should first be replaced by means of a Wonder Card carrying the number(s) desired in seven decimals (the maximum permissible on the card as the decimal point will take one column). A second Wonder Card is then used (and this may be done in the same period as that in which the first card is fed into the program) to multiply the number(s) with the appropriate power of (−10) in the *Multiple for Old Item* box. The smallest multiple possible is .0001. If necessary, the operation may be repeated on one or several Wonder Cards in the same period.[30]

B. ECONOMIC INDEX CHANGES BY WONDER CARD

In INTOP Standard the six economic indices (one for each product and market, Dictionary symbol PS24) are changed every period of a run.[31] This is easily accomplished, as indicated by the example on pp. 346–47. *The illustration is a replica of the card you should fill out in quarter 4* (i.e., the first period of sales), *if the economic index figures suggested for INTOP Standard are to be used.* As may be derived from the Wonder Card discussion in Chapter 5 of this book, the items on the card are listed (and processed) in the order

Area 1	Product X
Area 2	Product X
Area 3	Product X
Area 1	Product Y
Area 2	Product Y
Area 3	Product Y

Finally, it should be observed that for computer purposes an index number of 100 is represented by 1.00. An index of 123 should be 1.23 on the form, one of 92 should be .92. This is important: *misplacing the decimal point will make the market a corresponding power of 10 larger or smaller than intended.*

30 Note that the administrator's register of Wonder Cards in PART 1 of the output carries only five decimals. Smaller numbers will appear as 0. However, the implementation of these extra-small numbers may be verified on the reprint of all current parameter values which appears at the very beginning of PART 2 of the output of the period.

31 Suggested economic index values for each period are given in Item No. 9, "Table of Sample Economic Index Numbers and Marketing Research Items 17 and 18 Values in INTOP Standard," in the INTOP User's Package.

FIG. 4I   ADMINISTRATOR'S WONDER CARD

INTOP DECISION CARD NO. 4

Heading Code: (6 for Parameters; 7 for State Variables)   [6] 1

Time Period Number   [ ] [4]
                       2   3

Dictionary Symbol (note: applies to all items changed)   [ ] [2] [4] [ ]
                                                           4   5   6   7

Type of Item Changed

Initial Item (or single item)

Grade Index: (0, 1, 2, 3, or 4, use for PM16 & PS06 only)   [ ] 8

Model: (1 is standard; 2 is deluxe)   [ ] 9

Factory: (1, 2 or 3)   [ ] 10

Product: (1 is X; 2 is Y)   [1] 11

Area: (1 is U.S.; 2 is EEC; 3 is Brazil)   [1] 12

Company: (1, 2, . . . , 25) *State Variables Only*   [ ] [ ]
                                                        13 14

Multiple for Old Item: (If replacement or addition/subtraction is intended, write 0 for replace and 1 for addition/subtraction in col. 26)

Final Item, If Consecutive Changes

Grade: [ ] 15

Model: [ ] 16

Factory: [ ] 17

Product: [2] 18

Area: [3] 19

Company: [ ] [ ]   [ ] [ ]   [0]
            20 21   22 24   26

FIG. 41   ADMINISTRATOR'S WONDER CARD   (Continued)

New Items: (In sign box 0 if addition; — if subtraction)

	Sign		Value			
First Item Number	0 (27)	1 (29)	.	0 (31)	8 (33)	(35)
Second Item Number	0 (36)	1 (38)	.	0 (40)	9 (42)	(44)
Third Item Number	0 (45)	1 (47)	.	0 (49)	8 (51)	(53)
Fourth Item Number	0 (54)	1 (56)	.	0 (58)	0 (60)	(62)
Fifth Item Number	0 (63)	(65)	.	9 (67)	5 (69)	(71)
Sixth Item Number	0 (72)	1 (74)	.	0 (76)	6 (78)	(80)

Any column left blank will be interpreted as zero. All numbers are integers unless a decimal point is indicated.

Notes: (1) Under *Multiple for Old Item* all items designated in cols. 8-21 are multiplied by the same constant value. (2) Under *New Items*, if only the *first item number* is filled in, the changes will be interpreted as *replacing, adding or subtracting* this single constant value to *all items included* between the type designations in cols. 8-21. (3) Also under *New Items*, replacement or addition/subtraction of *different* numbers may be performed on a maximum of *six consecutive items* having a common dictionary symbol. Specify the items in cols. 8-21.

This two-page display of the standard Wonder Card is not ideal for reproduction. Sample mimeographed and/or printed Wonder Card forms are included in the INTOP Users Package delivered with the program tape.

C. CASH ADJUSTMENT IN HOME AND AREA BY SPECIAL
   WONDER CARDS

In almost any run of the simulation, adjustments of the cash account
in one of the geographical areas or in the Home Office (and, for balance, in the corresponding retained earnings account) is by far the
most common use of Wonder Cards. This may be done for many
reasons: to mete out damages or rewards, to compensate teams for
lost profit opportunity due to past mistakes in their use of decision
forms (when occasionally the administrator may feel that it would
be unduly harsh to make the teams take the consequences of their own
mistakes), to arrange for inter-company cash transfers not related to
sales, licenses, or loans[32] and so forth. The special Wonder Cards Nos.
4A and 4B are designed to routinize completely cash adjustments.[33]
Wonder Card 4A pertains to Home Office and 4B to the areas. Of these,
Wonder Card No. 4B is reproduced on p. 349. Sample of both cards are
included in the User's Package. To illustrate the way in which these
cards are used, the card reproduced here has been filled out to institute
a subtraction of cash from Company 7 in the EEC (Area 2) in quarter
5 in the amount of $25,000. As is apparent from its format this form
will actually result in two punch cards, of which the second handles
the subtraction from retained earnings necessary to maintain a balance of accounts. The Home Office Card is used in a completely analogous fashion, with the exception that there is no area number to
fill in.

v. *Master Control Card*

The Master Control Card is discussed at length in the first
section of Chapter 5 of this book. Computer Liaison should keep in
mind that items f and g on the card (pertaining to the number of
copies of the first and second sets of reports) are *not* automatically
implemented by the computer. The machine will print out only a *single*
copy of PART 1 and PART 2 of the reports without human intervention. Any additional copies required should be marked in items f and
g. The Computer Operator must then be told to check these instructions in each quarter and print the requisite number of copies (keeping
in mind the desirability of using multi-part paper).[34]

In consecutive runs, i.e., when several periods are processed simultaneously, the number of copies indicated in f and g should be 0
in all except the last period. As the output of all simultaneously processed periods will appear in one continuous block on the output tape,
the number of copies desired should only be indicated on the Control
Card for the last period. Indeed, in consecutive runs it may be advis-

---

[32] Inter-company cash transfers may
also be handled in other ways, see Section X below.
[33] Two standard cards could, of
course, also be used — one for the cash
and one for the retained earnings account.
[34] Cf. *infra*, 352.

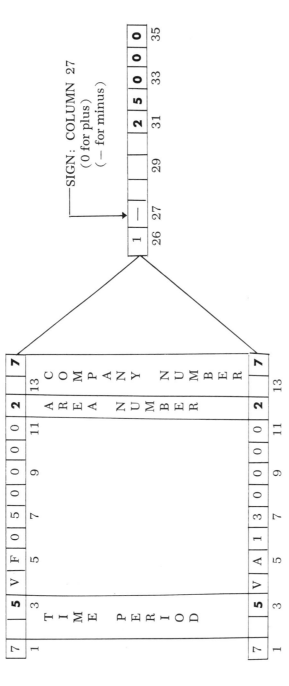

ADMINISTRATOR'S WONDER CARD NO. 4B

AREA CASH AND RETAINED EARNINGS

(Additions or Subtractions)

Card No. 1

SIGN: COLUMN 27
(0 for plus)
(– for minus)

Card No. 2

Note for key-punching: These are two separate cards with Columns 26–35 to be punched identically on both cards, please!

Comments:

1. Do not forget sign in Column 27.

2. Write the cash item you wish to add or subtract as far to the right in Columns 28–35 as possible. The number must be written out in extenso (thousands are not abbreviated).

3. If the number occupies less than Columns 28–35 there is no need to add zeros in front of it.

able to amplify the output printing instruction orally or by separate message.

VI. *Data Delivered to the Computer Operator Each Period*

The data delivered to the Computer Operator as input for each period of a run of INTOP Standard using punch cards for all data is specified in detail in the first section of Chapter 5 of this book. Section II of the instruction described the compilation of the INTOP program on machine language cards — this deck of program cards is used in identical form each period. Section III described the editing and sorting of decision forms and Wonder Cards as well as the key-punching and proofreading of the punch cards on which the data on decision forms and Wonder Cards are recorded. Remember the insertion of identification, control and blank cards at positions specified.

In the *first* period of an INTOP Standard run history will be automatically created — there is no input of history cards. Do not forget to use History Option No. 4 on the Master Control Card.

In subsequent periods punch card history is used in most INTOP Standard runs.[35] Remember to check that the first and last cards of the history carry the three big V's.[36]

In some cases it may be preferable to use *history tape input and output.* In this situation ID, control and blank cards plus the program and decision cards are delivered to the computer in the same order as usual. In addition, the history tape created as output in period $t-1$ is now part of the input of period t. As indicated on the Master Control Card the history tape should be mounted on Tape Unit 9 (A5). The input tape obtained from program and decision cards is the FORTRAN monitor input tape. The Master Control Card input and output options No. 2 should be used. The history tape from period $t-1$ should be saved until the orderly output of period t has been obtained and verified by Computer Liaison. The new history tape produced in period t emerges on Tape Unit 10 (B4), as indicated on the Master Control Card. It should be retained for use as input in period $t+1$.

Finally, we re-emphasize that *the INTOP FORTRAN program is written for automatic, uninterrupted processing. This means that there are no stops for operator's instructions in the program.* Should Computer Liaison find it desirable to insert special instructions of some kind in the program this may be done in the regular FORTRAN manner by "★ PAUSE" cards preceded by the "★" cards on which the instructions are contained.[37] Similarly, the Computer Operator (of the 1401) at each installation must be instructed to check for the number

---

[35] Special rules for consecutive runs are given in Chapter 5.

[36] To avoid one possible source of a mechanical hang-up of the computer, it may be advisable to check the readability of the card history. This may be done by using the 1401 to print out a copy of the data on the card history.

[37] For a possible example in *tape history* operations, see *infra*, 352, note 42.

of copies required of the first and second sets of reports on the first page of output after the loading map.[38] Alternatively, Computer Liaison may convey his desire as to number of output copies by other means. The point is simply, that in the absence of special instructions to the contrary, Computer Liaison cannot expect to get more than the single copy of all outputs which is produced automatically.

VII. *Computer Operator's Guide*[39]

Once the INTOP program has been compiled in the machine language of your installation (as described in Section II above) INTOP runs may be handled according to standard operating procedure. Whenever possible INTOP should be the *first* job in a monitor run, to permit easy printing of multiple copies of the output.

When all-card input is used, the input tape should first be made. For loading purposes it should be noted that like other FORTRAN II programs the INTOP simulation in principle requires eight tapes. INTOP is a chain job; the six links are all stored on Tape Unit 2. Tape Units 3 and 4 are used for intermediate storage. The loading scheme is as follows:

Physical Tape Designation	Logical Tape Designation, No.
Chain links	2
Intermediary tapes	3 and 4
Input tape	5
Output tape	6
FORTRAN System tape	1
Channel A5	9*
Channel B5	10*

*Used for history tape input (9) and/or output (10) only — not for punch card history.

The library routines of your installation will establish the correspondence between this arrangement and your particular equipment configuration.

Ordinarily, all output will appear on a single output tape (Logical Tape No. 6). That tape will then produce both printed output and punch card history. Occasionally the part of the output embraced by the Master Control Card designation for punch card history will first be recorded on a separate tape, i.e., the installation separates output which is to be printed and output to be converted into cards, and records the latter type of output on a special tape. That tape then has to be converted into punch cards.

As for the printed output, one full copy is, of course, automatically produced during the computer processing operation. Ordinarily,

[38] The instructions on the Master Control Card emerge on this page. Note that the Computer Operator never sees the Master Control Card itself.

[39] This is a sample guide only, and should be adjusted to local conditions.

however, additional copies are required. Unless the Computer Operator has been given other special instructions, he should check the *instructions as to number of output copies required printed on the first page of the output after the loading map.* These instructions are in two parts, "first set of reports" and "second set of reports." Of these, the "second set of reports" comprises all the printed output as it originally came off the computer. It is marked with "End of PART 2" all over the last page. As the computer automatically has produced one copy of these reports it is only necessary to print the number of copies requested *minus one.* (Remember to press the stop button after the "End of PART 2" page has been reached, or the machine may switch to make an additional punch card history.)

To print the requisite number of copies of the *first* set of reports, rewind the tape to the beginning and print output until the page marked all over with *"End of PART 1"* appears.[40] Stop the printing here. If multi-part paper is being used — highly advisable — divide the number of copies requested by the number of copies obtained in each print-out to find the necessary number of repeat printings.

In some installations history tape *input and output* is used rather than punch card history. In this case, Channel A5 is used for the history input, while the history output tape will be produced on Channel B5. The latter channel should be loaded with a blank tape. Generally, the loading scheme is that indicated earlier.[41] If so appraised by Computer Liaison, watch for PAUSE and printout of written instructions.[42]

Computer Liaison should be notified as soon as the output is ready. All cards *and tapes* must be saved and disposed of according to Computer Liaison Instruction.

VIII. *Difficulties in Computer Processing and Their Sources*

The general principle of the INTOP program is that "the show must go on." Thus, minor deficiencies in input are simply by-passed, and once begun, processing is programmed to be carried to its conclusion independently of human intervention. As usual, this does not mean that the skill of the operator is immaterial. No computer equip-

---

[40] Computer Liaison may find it advisable to tear a copy of the "End of PART 1" and "End of PART 2" sheets from the output of the test run to serve as a guide for the Computer Operator.

[41] Cf. *supra,* 351.

[42] In history tape runs, Computer Liaison may consider routinizing the instruction procedure by inserting after the "★ XEQ" card three new cards as follows:

> ★ MOUNT INTOP HISTORY INPUT ON TAPE A5

> ★ READY BLANK ON TAPE B5. LABEL "INTOP HISTORY OUTPUT" AND SAVE

> ★ PAUSE

The text part of the cards goes in columns 7–72. The ★ sign is a signal to the computer to print out the message. The PAUSE card is a signal to the Computer Operator to read the printed message; in the meanwhile the computer is stopped until the Operator starts it again.

ment is mechanically foolproof, and occasionally when the computer will stop due to unacceptable deficiencies in input a skilled operator will find a way of circumventing the difficulty. A considerable number of flawless runs lends strength to the belief that computer stoppage will not likely be due to any inherent weakness in the INTOP program itself.

Generally, computer stoppage will be due to one of three major sets of causes: (1) history or program input cards are in disorder, (2) mechanical difficulties with the equipment or (3) deficient or "illegal" data on the Master Control Card or a particular company Decision Card or Wonder Card.

The computer must always be expected to stop if a history or program card has been allowed to get lost. If a history card is lost it is necessary to make a new set of history cards by running the output tape of the preceding period through the tape-to-card converter. If history cards are in disarray rather than lost, the computer may or may not stop. If it does not stop there may or may not be irregularities on the printed output. Should the computer stop or irregularities appear on the output which may be suspected as due to disarray among the history cards, it is generally wise to rerun the period with a new deck of history cards obtained from the output tape of the preceding period.[43]

If a *program* card is lost, the situation in INTOP is no brighter than when this occurs in any other computer operation. It is precisely for this eventuality that we recommend that a *duplicate* set of program cards be maintained at each computer installation where the simulation is in use. The cards in the incomplete deck may be disposed of, and the duplicate deck should be used to run the program. As soon as the processing of the particular period in which this occurs has been completed, a new copy should be taken from the duplicate cards as a reserve against future contingencies. Should the program cards be in disarray it is possible to reorder them by checking them off against the duplicate set (by using the identification designations in columns 73–80). Generally, however, the time involved in such a procedure is worth a good deal more than using the duplicate program and then reduplicating it. This, therefore, should be normal procedure.

To recompile the program (as in Section II above) when a card is lost or in disorder is an emergency solution due to the considerable computer time and expense involved. Clearly, every person laying his hands on INTOP cards should be mindful that keeping their order intact is crucial.[44]

It should be evident from this discussion that *the only incurable calamity which may occur in INTOP computer operations is an acute*

[43] Unfortunately, the machine cannot always be counted on to inform the operator of the cause of a malfunction.

[44] Sole exception: the order in which decision and Wonder Cards are fed into the machine within a given period is inconsequential.

disarray of history input cards with no record of the past permitting the compilation of a new card history. For this reason it is wise to save the output tape (or the special output tape for punch card history, as the case may be) from period $t-1$ right up until the final output of period t has been verified. If something goes wrong in period t processing, a new card history may be produced from the tape. Alternatively (or in addition), one may save *all* punched decision and Wonder Cards from the very first period of a run of the simulation to the very last one. If anything goes wrong in an intervening period t, the card history from period $t-1$ may always be reproduced by rerunning the simulation by consecutive processing from the first period to, and including, period $t-1$, with the history option for punch card output in that last period of the rerun.[45]

Mechanical malfunctioning is unfortunately not unheard of either in IBM or in Univac equipment. Card-reading is somewhat of a weak spot — the experience of the writers includes cases of the machine reading data from a blank card as well as reading a punched card as if it were blank. Either of these mistakes may cause stoppage or garbled output as *a blank card in the INTOP FORTRAN program is a signal to the computer to stop reading in data.* Occasionally cards may get "jammed" into disarray. Should the machine stop for these or other mechanical malfunctioning reasons it is sometimes possible to continue the run after removing a faulty card and, if possible, substituting a correct one. On other occasions it will be necessary to rerun the period from the start, with or without finding and correcting the malfunction. It has happened to INTOP, as to a good many other complex computer programs, that computer processing was successful on a second trial after an initial failure, even though no particular corrective action intervened.

The following "illegal" characteristics of input cards will generally (in some cases, invariably) stop the computer:

a. Master Control Card

1.   If in the *first* period of the simulation there is no identification on the Master Control Card, or if in *subsequent* periods the identification is not identical with that of the first period.[46]

2.   If the periods following the first one are not numbered in successive order (t, $t+1$, $t+2$, $t+3$, etc.)[47]

3.   If the "number of companies this time" is set at less than 2.

4.   If other than legitimate and, in consecutive processing of several periods, mutually consistent numerical designations of history input and/or output options have been indicated.

[45] Note that new Master Control Cards are needed, specifying "history in" for all periods between the first one and period $t-1$.

[46] Rules for changing identification are given in Chapter 5 of this book.

[47] In INTOP Standard the first period should be set to 1. Rules for setting other first period numbers (including 0), or changing period numbers during a run, are given in Chapter 5.

5. If letters or signs appear in any other columns than those reserved for identification.

6. If column 1 is left *blank* – hence an identification should be chosen which includes a letter or number in column 1.

b. Company Decision Cards (1, 2 and 3) and Wonder Cards

1. If *letters and signs* (other than the minus sign in the special columns reserved for it) occur on any Company or Wonder Card. Sole exception: the two letters used in Dictionary symbol identification on Wonder Cards.[48]

2. If a *minus sign* occurs in any other columns than those explicitly reserved for it.

3. If a decimal number occurs in the company number and period number boxes.

4. If there is a *blank* in column 1 (as this is a signal for the computer to stop).

A good number of mistakenly, although not "illegally," marked cards will simply be rejected and by-passed by the computer, in order that processing of correct data not be held up. Examples: inter-company transactions with companies with fictitiously high numbers or without company (or area, product, etc.) designations when such designations are necessary for the orderly implementation of the trans-action; Wonder Cards with more than six consecutive items specified between "initial item" and "final item" or without any Dictionary sym-bol or with an incorrect symbol (note: if the symbol by mistake carries more than two letters the computer will stop).

Now and then it is likely to happen that output is *qualitatively* displeasing, even though computer processing took place in regular order. This will be due to neglected, negligent or mistaken decisions on Company Decision Cards or Wonder Cards. *Such "mistakes" can never be corrected after the run.* This points up the importance of editing and proofing and systematic treatment of all cards *before* processing. Given a "sloppy" output, Computer Liaison is faced with two alternatives: either to incur the cost of a complete reprocessing of the period with the "mistakes" eliminated *or* to make as reasonable an adjustment as possible in a subsequent period by means of Wonder Cards and/or inter-company transactions of the monitor company.

It is never possible to guard against, or even to specify, all con-ceivable contingencies. In the final analysis there is no adequate sub-stitute for extreme care in the handling of tapes and cards, and, above all, good judgment and a willingness to cooperate on the part of all concerned.

---

[48] It is vital that the distinction be-tween the letter O and the digit 0 be observed. In such Dictionary symbols as PS03, VM08 the 0 is a digit. Should the letter O be punched this will stop the computer.

IX. *Statistics*

As indicated in Section III, Computer Liaison maintains a statistical record of Market Research Items 17 and 18 ordered by company, quarter, product and grade.[49] If companies are given an option on delivery of the information *before* or *after* current period decisions are made the record should indicate the option chosen.

If plant disposal and renewal will be a feature of the run[50] (check with administrator) Computer Liaison should keep a record of such disposals by company, quarter, area and product.

The Consolidated Income Statements and Balance Sheets for *all* companies which constitute part of the administrator's output each period furnish a wonderful history of any given run of the simulation. In addition, statistical raw materials abound in the printout of state variables and the record of company decisions in the history output. All that is needed to get industry-wide data on such vital matters as inventory, number of plants, number of sales offices, production in the current period, new plants built and some 500 other variables is simply to add up a few columns in which the data are given by company.[51] Such information is ideal for the *Gazette,* for oral comments by the administrator or for management audit at the end of the simulation. The facility of obtaining all kinds of position and performance data is especially vital when the simulation is used for research purposes.

X. *Cash Transfer Between Companies*

Most cash transfers between companies occur in connection with inter-company sales, loans and licensing transactions. The cash transfer is then automatically implemented with other elements of the transaction.

Occasionally, teams may want to transfer cash between themselves in other than the standardized ways. If Computer Liaison wishes to accommodate such desires, cash transfers of a more unorthodox kind may be arranged in several forms:

1. Two Wonder Cards 4A, subtracting from the paying company's home office cash and retained earnings accounts, and adding to the receiving company's corresponding accounts.

2. Two Wonder Cards 4B, subtracting from the paying company's cash and retained earnings accounts in *any* area, and adding to the receiving company's corresponding accounts in *any* area.

3. A combination of 1 and 2, involving payment from Co. A Home Office to Co. B Area 1, 2 or 3 – or vice versa.

[49] The decision variables output of market research items ordered (DR08–DR10) will indicate only company and Market Research item numbers.

[50] Cf. INTOP Memo 4 in Appendix VI-A and technical instructions for plant disposal and renewal, Section XII below.

[51] The model Secretary Instruction contains suggestions for a few statistical series to be continuously updated.

4. Most easily – but least elegantly – a transfer of cash may be arranged in the form of payment of interest on a fictitious inter-company loan. Decision Form 3, Transaction Type 2 is used. The receiving company is listed as "lender" and the paying company as "borrower," and the amount to be paid is entered as "interest." (No sign in box 13, please.) This transfer will be between the two Home Offices.

We may note that a *distributor* company is likely to be especially grateful if the opportunity for cash transfer to supplier areas by means of Wonder Card is offered them. As in real life, distributor companies in INTOP tend to be strong on cash, while cash is often at a premium among producer firms. A mutual advantage may be gained by *cash* payments for goods. To by-pass the A/R and A/P routines of the two companies, the *goods* shipment should be entered at zero (0) price on a regular Decision Form 3, Transaction Type 4.

XI. *Sales Advantage*
(See Chapter 4 of this book for administrator's procedures.)

Each company may receive at the discretion of the administrator a sales advantage (or disadvantage) in consumer selling, which may apply discriminately to any or all areas and products in the simulation. This sales advantage (or "marketing-effectiveness factor") can be expressed as a decimal fraction of the normal sales quantity where the normal sales quantity is taken to be one. For example, the administrator may increase consumer sales to 1.2 (a 20 per cent increase) for product X in the EEC or decrease consumer sales to 0.9 (a 10 per cent decrease) for product Y in Brazil, etc. The administrator must supply Computer Liaison with three facts: the amount of the sales advantage (or disadvantage) as a decimal fraction, the product(s) and area(s) and company to which it will apply and the number of periods for which it will be in effect.

To give a sales advantage to a particular company, Computer Liaison must fill out a Wonder Card indicating each area and product to which the sales advantage is applicable. This Wonder Card will change a "state variable" on the history which will automatically adjust the company's consumer sales. The location of the six sales advantages on the history is given in Table A in terms of the product and area type designations. (Cf. the INTOP Dictionary.)

TABLE A[52]

		Area 1 (P, A)	Area 2 (P, A)	Area 3 (P, A)
VS13	Sales Advantage, Product X	(1, 1)	(1, 2)	(1, 3)
	Sales Advantage, Product Y	(2, 1)	(2, 2)	(2, 3)

[52] As with all state variables, a company number must also be supplied with each Wonder Card change.

The actual fractional increase (or decrease), however, cannot be entered directly into these locations. Computer Liaison must convert these fractions into their *natural logarithms* in order for them to be acceptable into the consumer sales function. This can be done by referring to published tables of natural logarithms or by using some of the selected values in Table B. Since the logarithm of one (the normal sales quantity) is zero, the numbers in the history automatically created by the program tape in the first quarter of an INTOP Standard run are zero.[53]

TABLE B

Fraction of Consumer Sales	Natural Logarithm of the Fraction
0.8	− 0.222
0.9	− 0.105
1.0	0
1.1	+ 0.096
1.2	+ 0.183

For every sales advantage change Computer Liaison fills out a Wonder Card using the information from Table A to determine the proper identification (columns 1–21). Normally replacement (a zero in column 26) is used. The actual number or numbers (columns 27–80 on the Wonder Card) should be written in with the decimal point punched in the column field and the sign in the appropriate box (columns 27, 36, 45, 54, 63 or 72). Note that if other values are used from published tables, the numbers entered are natural logarithms to the base e, not logarithms to the base 10.

Once the sales advantage is given to a company, it remains in effect until it is removed from the history. Therefore, *after the sales advantage is no longer desired, Computer Liaison must make out another Wonder Card which sets the value to zero.* Simply fill out a Wonder Card for the same identification (columns 1–21) but with zeros in columns 22–80.

XII.   *Plant Disposal by Wonder Card*
(See INTOP Memo 4 for player's procedures.)

Any company may sell a plant at any time during the simulation. The company must inform Computer Liaison of the area in which the plant will be sold, the number of the plant (1, 2 and 3 of the X plants or 1, 2 and 3 of the Y plants) and the quarter in which the sale will take place. Conditions in replacing old plants with new ones are set forth in INTOP Memo 4. In the case of renewal of a plant Decision Form 1 should be filled out for new construction in the usual manner, regardless of what number plant was sold. The usual construction periods will apply.

[53] It follows that for product-area combinations where no adjustment is to be made the corresponding "New Item" box may simply be left empty. Standard rules for "consecutive" items apply.

Computer Liaison will have to adjust the history by making out six Wonder Cards for each plant disposed of. The first card will increase CASH in the given area by the salvage value (see schedule in Memo 4). The second card will set NET PLANT AND EQUIPMENT to zero for the particular plant eliminated. The third card will adjust RETAINED EARNINGS so that the capital gain or loss will be reflected on the balance sheet. The change in RETAINED EARNINGS equals the increase to CASH minus the value of the NET PLANT AND EQUIPMENT account. Typically the adjustment to RETAINED EARNINGS will be negative since a capital loss will result from the plant sale. The fourth card will set the PLANT AGE to zero. The fifth card will set the ACQUISITION COST for the particular plant to zero. The sixth card will increase the number of ALLOWABLE PLANTS by one. This variable tells the computer the maximum number of plants that may be constructed at any given time. It may never exceed three.

To make the calculations for the six Wonder Cards, certain information must be gathered from the history. Computer Liaison will obtain this information from the history immediately preceding the quarter in which the plant disposal will be made. Five items must be obtained. They are given in Table C[54] with their appropriate type designations for the factory, product and area affected. (Cf. the INTOP Dictionary.) This table will suffice for any plant disposal desired.

As an illustration, the five items that are needed for a disposal of the second X plant in Area 1 are marked with an (*). Correspondingly the (*) in Area 2 would be needed for disposing of the first Y plant. Items numbered (6) and (7) are not used in the calculations but will be the amounts changed by the third and first Wonder Cards.

Assume that the area and the plant number are given, then the following calculations must be made using the five items obtained from the history. Let the five items as numbered in Table C be:

(1) t_c = The PLANT CONSTRUCTION TIME (always 3 quarters in INTOP Standard)

(2) U = The number of ALLOWABLE PLANTS

(3) t_a = The AGE OF THE PLANT since the decision to build

(4) C = The ACQUISITION COST OF THE PLANT

(5) N = The value of NET PLANT AND EQUIPMENT

The First Wonder Card. Computer Liaison pays a certain amount of cash to the company selling a plant depending upon the age of the plant sold. If the sale is made according to INTOP Memo 4, 66 per cent of the original plant cost C is paid during the construction of the plant; if the plant has produced for one quarter, 64 per cent of C is paid; if two quarters of production have elapsed, 62 per cent of C is paid. For each subsequent quarter for which the plant has produced there is a further deduction of 2 per cent.

This schedule of payments for buying a plant can be generalized into a mathematical expression, which varies with the age of the plant sold.

Let:

S = the amount of cash paid for the plant (or the salvage value)

R = the rate of salvage paid during construction as a decimal fraction

L = the rate of salvage lost for each quarter of subsequent production as a decimal fraction

Then:

$$S = [R - L(t_a - t_c)] [C] \qquad \text{where } t_a \geqq t_c$$

If the plant is still being constructed, then,

$$S = (R) (C) \qquad \text{where } t_a < t_c$$

Using the schedule of salvage rates in INTOP Memo 4 as an example, we have:

$$R = .66 \text{ and } L = .02$$

so that the expression can be simplified to:

$$S = [.66 - (.02) (t_a - t_c)] [C] \qquad \text{where } t_a \geqq t_c$$
$$S = (.66) (C) \qquad \text{where } t_a < t_c$$

The first Wonder Card will *add to area* CASH for the particular company the salvage value S just calculated. Table C gives the Dictionary symbol and the type designations of the cash account to be added to.

The Second Wonder Card. The present net value of the plant to be disposed of must be eliminated from the balance sheet of the selling company. This net value, which is called N, is the number contained in the NET PLANT AND EQUIPMENT account for the particular factory, product and area of the selling company. The second Wonder Card will *set the value N of* NET PLANT AND EQUIPMENT *to zero*. Table C indicates the symbol and type designations on the history of the Net Plant and Equipment value to be eliminated.

The Third Wonder Card. The capital loss or gain from a plant disposal will be reflected in the retained earnings account of the company. If E is the amount of this loss or gain in asset valuation, then:

$$E = S - N$$

There will be a net loss (E being negative) if N is greater than S; a net gain (E being positive) if S is greater than N; if S equals N there is no change in RETAINED EARNINGS and no Wonder Card is needed because E is zero.

This third Wonder Card maintains the accounting identity on the balance sheet (total assets equals total liabilities) *by adding E to (or subtracting E from)* RETAINED EARNINGS. Table C gives the symbol and type designations of the RETAINED EARNINGS account on the history.

   The Fourth Wonder Card. This Wonder Card change sets the current PLANT AGE t_a *equal to zero* for the particular plant eliminated. Table C indicates the symbol and type designations on the history of each individual plant age.

   The Fifth Wonder Card. This Wonder Card sets the initial PLANT ACQUISITION COST C *equal to zero* for the particular plant disposed of. Table C gives the symbol and type designations for this Wonder Card change.

TABLE C

DATA NECESSARY FOR PLANT DISPOSAL CHANGES†

			Area 1 (P, A)	Area 2 (P, A)	Area 3 (P, A)
1.	PM13	Plant Construction Time X	$(1, 1)^*$	$(1, 2)$	$(1, 3)$
		Plant Construction Time Y	$(2, 1)$	$(2, 2)^*$	$(2, 3)$
2.	VM01	Number of Allowable Plants X	$(1, 1)^*$	$(1, 2)$	$(1, 3)$
		Number of Allowable Plants Y	$(2, 1)$	$(2, 2)^*$	$(2, 3)$

			(F, P, A)	(F, P, A)	(F, P, A)
3.	VM10	Plant Age 1 of X	$(1, 1, 1)$	$(1, 1, 2)$	$(1, 1, 3)$
		Plant Age 2 of X	$(2, 1, 1)^*$	$(2, 1, 2)$	$(2, 1, 3)$
		Plant Age 3 of X	$(3, 1, 1)$	$(3, 1, 2)$	$(3, 1, 3)$
		Plant Age 1 of Y	$(1, 2, 1)$	$(1, 2, 2)^*$	$(1, 2, 3)$
		Plant Age 2 of Y	$(2, 2, 1)$	$(2, 2, 2)$	$(2, 2, 3)$
		Plant Age 3 of Y	$(3, 2, 1)$	$(3, 2, 2)$	$(3, 2, 3)$
4.	VM12	Plant Acquisition Cost 1 of X	$(1, 1, 1)$	$(1, 1, 2)$	$(1, 1, 3)$
		Plant Acquisition Cost 2 of X	$(2, 1, 1)^*$	$(2, 1, 2)$	$(2, 1, 3)$
		Plant Acquisition Cost 3 of X	$(3, 1, 1)$	$(3, 1, 2)$	$(3, 1, 3)$
		Plant Acquisition Cost 1 of Y	$(1, 2, 1)$	$(1, 2, 2)^*$	$(1, 2, 3)$
		Plant Acquisition Cost 2 of Y	$(2, 2, 1)$	$(2, 2, 2)$	$(2, 2, 3)$
		Plant Acquisition Cost 3 of Y	$(3, 2, 1)$	$(3, 2, 2)$	$(3, 2, 3)$
5.	VM11	Net Plant and Equipment 1 of X	$(1, 1, 1)$	$(1, 1, 2)$	$(1, 1, 3)$
		Net Plant and Equipment 2 of X	$(2, 1, 1)^*$	$(2, 1, 2)$	$(2, 1, 3)$
		Net Plant and Equipment 3 of X	$(3, 1, 1)$	$(3, 1, 2)$	$(3, 1, 3)$
		Net Plant and Equipment 1 of Y	$(1, 2, 1)$	$(1, 2, 2)^*$	$(1, 2, 3)$
		Net Plant and Equipment 2 of Y	$(2, 2, 1)$	$(2, 2, 2)$	$(2, 2, 3)$
		Net Plant and Equipment 3 of Y	$(3, 2, 1)$	$(3, 2, 2)$	$(3, 2, 3)$

			(A)	(A)	(A)
6.	VA13	Retained Earnings	(1)	(2)	(3)
7.	VF05	Cash	(1)	(2)	(3)

   †The (*) denotes examples of data needed for removing Plant No. 2 of product X in Area 1 and Plant No. 1 of product Y in Area 2 (cf. 359). In the standard version of INTOP items 1 and 4 may also be found in the Schedule of Costs, etc. "State variables" require a company number on each Wonder Card change in addition to the type designations given here (i.e., Items 2, 3, 4, 5, 6 and 7 above).

The Sixth Wonder Card. All that needs to be done further is to adjust the number of ALLOWABLE PLANTS U. Since we have disposed of one plant by the previous five Wonder Cards, we must *increase the number of* ALLOWABLE PLANTS *by one*. We may either add one to this account or enter the correct number by Wonder Cards with replacement.

$$U_t = U_{t-1} + 1$$

Thus, if the value is now zero we replace it by one; if it is one, it becomes two; and if it is two, it becomes three. The number of ALLOWABLE PLANTS can never be greater than three.

Care should be taken that Computer Liaison and the company officials agree upon which numbered plant should be eliminated. *The company must be reminded not to use the Decision Form box from which they have just sold their plant until any new plant they may be building there is ready.* The expense of such a mistake could be disastrous.

B. Editor of the *Gazette*

General Instructions for Each Issue

As an introduction you should read relevant parts of Chapter 4 of this book.

1. Prepare "standing features." See A] below.

2. Check with administrator for student contributions and administrator items.

3. Check your copy of current output for pertinent data.

4. Check statistics compiled by Secretary for items which may be of interest.

5. Check list of content suggestions below.

6. Check old volumes and sample issues of the *Gazette* (if available) for further suggestions.

7. Consult your own mind and write.

8. Determine layout, observing points below.

9. Hand manuscript in for typing and processing.

10. Make sure that the masters are proofed — especially statistics and numbers.

11. The first issue of the *Gazette* should be numbered identically with the quarter in which it is distributed (ordinarily quarter 4), and the numbers of subsequent issues should also be made to coincide with quarters. (This may require numbering an issue 6–7, 9–11, etc., if several sets of decisions are to be made in one session.)

Contents

---

[1] Some observations to keep in mind (and occasionally insert) in commenting on the index series:

The postwar lesson about different timing and amplitude of business cycles in different parts of the world.

Point up relative skill of forecasters in continuing to ride a trend in the various areas.

Point up their relative inability to predict turning-points in the cycle, although international comparisons ought to help.

Rationalize past mistakes in forecasts (when big enough) and also at times boast about your accuracy.

The more volatile an economy, the harder to predict.

The really skilled international manager of the future will ride the crest of the boom around the world.

6. From Market Research 2 you may give some inkling of *trends* (but *not* actual data!) in total industry methods improvement, advertising, R & D, marketing research.
7. New standing contracts (see standing contracts file, use data with discretion).
8. Import-export statistics by area & product (from transactions output).
9. Fictitious prices – quoting a price when you have no inventory to sell – are misleading and risk the goodwill of customers. (General Reminder)
10. Notes from the *Player's Manual* on elasticities, plant obsolescence, methods improvement, paid-in-capital, etc.
11. "Hold on to your *Gazette* – some chiselers are still not subscribing."
12. Needle companies about obtaining special consulting services from Arthur DeBig (administrator).
13. If Monitor is producing, advise companies that plant statistics in MR2 may be misleading in overstating number of plants producing for current sales.
14. Number of regional sales offices by company and area.
15. Any time a company wants to amend or revise its business philosophy and objectives, this is fine. But do hand in an account of the change to the administrator. (Reminder)
16. Fictional interview with the secretary of WFAM.
17. Actual interview with representatives of participating companies.

c] COMPANY GOSSIP

Note: Knowing that they are being evaluated, teams will often hand in very detailed plans and other data in which they have an obvious proprietary interest. These must not be reproduced indiscriminately. Use your discretion – when in doubt check with administrator.

1. Report record-high sales volume when some company has it.
2. A ship was seen in Rotterdam's new Europort loading cleaners for Co. _____ in Brazil.
3. Rumors, rumors (about plans, plants, contracts, improvements, dividends, profits, etc.). Be sure to include some half-truths now and then.
4. Gossip on advertising appropriations by individual companies.
5. P. R. Society of America Award for best annual report.
6. American Marketing Association medal "Marketing Plan of the Year," etc.
7. National Science Foundation Awards for product improvements in Q1, Q2 and any later quarters when teams derive improvements which cannot be exploited immediately (check with administrator).

8. A regional sales manager in Co. _____ decided he had enough and is going into business for himself. (Note: this must be paralleled by manipulation of Operations Card – see administrator.)

9. Quotes from company plans and reports – *important,* but use discretion.

D] ADDITIONAL POINTERS FOR PARTICULAR ISSUES

(We are assuming that the first issue is numbered 4, appearing before Q4 decisions are made.)

Issue No. 4

1. Company numbers (and names, if any), names of executives and their titles.
2. Availability of Market Research 2, Items 17 and 18 – immediately or with a lag. (Check with administrator.)
3. Number of plants by product, area and company, plus totals for areas and products.

Issue No. 5

Extracts from company objectives.

Issues No. 7, 11

Remind companies about subscription renewal – or you may be out of your editor job!
Whenever management has been rotated, companies have reorganized, submitted revised objectives, plans, merged, etc., this should be adequately reported.

E] LAYOUT

1. Business Climate (including Economic Indices)
2. CHASE-A-MARTINI
3. Environmental Changes
4. DeBig items, if any
5. Industry Inventory Situation
6. Dividends (Paid-In-Capital)
7. Statistics and inside dope
8. Extracts from annual reports, business plans, etc.
9. Advertisements
10. Gossip
11. Contributions from companies, press releases, letters to the editor, etc.
12. LIVE BETTER ELECTRICALLY.
13. Contributions to the *Gazette* are always welcome! They may even be published.

C. Secretary

1. *Functions.* The Secretary assists in the administration of INTOP by proofreading punched cards, by processing computer outputs, by producing the *Gazette,* by recording current statistics in the simulation and by maintaining necessary forms and other supplies. These functions are outlined below. She cooperates with the administrator, Computer Liaison and *Gazette* Editor, and may be assigned additional duties by them from time to time.

2. *Proofreading Punched Cards.* Each decision period in the simulation (called a "quarter") the decision forms filled in by the companies will be key-punched. The punched cards will be proofread by the Secretary, working with Computer Liaison, before the cards are put on tape for the computer.

3. *Processing Computer Outputs*

(*a*) As soon as you have found out that a given quarter has been run off on the computer you should proceed to process the output.

(*b*) Tear off the perforated strip at the right-hand side of all output sheets.

(*c*) Use machine to separate output copies from each other, and dump carbon paper (unless non-carbon-requiring output paper is used).

(*d*) Save complete strips of all output (PART 1 and PART 2) for the administrator and if so instructed Computer Liaison and the *Gazette* Editor.

(*e*) All remaining copies of output will comprise PART 1 only. For each copy tear off that part of the strip which comes before the sheet labeled "Company 1 Balance Sheet" from the rest of the output. Save that first part of the strip for the administrator or discard it, if so instructed.

(*f*) Proceed to separate the various company outputs from each other. Company 1 should have that part of the strip which comes before "Company 2 Balance Sheet," Company 2 should have the part which then remains before "Company 3 Balance Sheet," and so on. Each company will always get Balance Sheet, Income Statement, Ancillary Data and Market Research 1 output. Most, but usually not all, of them will have a Market Research 2 Sheet as well. In some quarters there will also be a Consolidated Balance Sheet and a Consolidated Income Statement included in each company output. Hence the minimum number of output sheets for a company is 4, and the maximum is 7.

(*g*) Save one copy of the company output for the administrator. The other copies will be distributed to the teams.

4. *Production of the Gazette*

(*a*) After carrying game statistics up to date as indicated in 5 below, ask Editor if he needs any of the statistical data for the *Gazette.*

(*b*) After receiving manuscript from Editor type and proofread mimeograph masters.

(*c*) Mimeograph and collate *Gazette* in requisite numbers of copies.

5. *Statistics*. The Secretary maintains and updates a series of statistical data about company and industry performance quarter by quarter:

(*a*) Retained Earnings and Paid-in-Capital

Quarter	Company 1		Company 2		
	R.E.	Paid-in	R.E.	Paid-in	
1					
2					etc.
		etc.			

(*b*) Total Assets. This table may either be made separately in the same fashion as that above, or asset data may be incorporated with the table as follows:

Quarter	Company 1			Company 2			
	R.E.	Paid-in	Total Assets	R.E.	Paid-in	Total Assets	
1							
2							etc.
		etc.					

Retained Earnings, Paid-in-Capital and Total Assets data are all taken from the quarterly Consolidated Balance Sheet for all companies in the industry. This appears close to the beginning of the administrator's output (PART 1).

(*c*) Plant Construction, Disposal and Replacement, by company, product, area and quarter. This is a practical format:

Company	X (radios)			Y (cleaners)		
	U.S.	EEC	Brazil	U.S.	EEC	Brazil
1	$B_1\ B_1\ B_5$				$B_2\ B_3$	
2		$B_1\ D_8\ B_9$	$B_3\ D_9$			
		etc.			etc.	

B_3 refers to a plant built in quarter 3.
D_8 refers to a plant disposed of in quarter 8.

In the example above, Company 1 built two X plants in the United States in quarter 1 and an additional one in quarter 5. Company 2 built an X plant in the EEC in quarter 1 which was sold in quarter 8 and replaced by another X plant in quarter 9.

Plant construction data may be obtained from Decision Form 1, Operations (or from the administrator's output of state variables in PART 2, under the heading "DM02 Number of Plants Built"). Check with the administrator if plant disposal and replacement will be a feature of the simulation; if not the table will be confined to new plant construction each quarter. If disposal and replacement may occur during the game, the Secretary may obtain the data needed from Computer Liaison.

(d) Total Industry Inventory, in thousands of units, by company, product, area and quarter. Suggested format:

Quarter	X (radios)			Y (cleaners)		
	U.S.	EEC	Brazil	U.S.	EEC	Brazil
1						
2						
		etc.			etc.	

Industry inventory data are obtained by adding up individual company data appearing under "VS17 Inventory Units" on the administrator's output of state variables. Note that there are two tables with that heading in PART 2 of the output, one for standard and one for deluxe product. Whenever a company has both standard and deluxe units of a product in inventory, the two numbers should simply be added to each other (for this table no distinction between standard and deluxe is made).

6. *Supplies.* Before the simulation begins, folders should be prepared for each company. Each folder should contain the following materials: 20 copies each of Decision Forms Nos. 1, 2 and 3, three carbon papers, a few paper clips, a few copies each of Sample Worksheet for Demand Studies, accounting and/or statistical worksheets and graph paper.

Each folder cover should have a designated space for indication of company number and the names of the president and other members of the team.

The Secretary maintains a central stock of INTOP supplies. Additional decision cards, standing contract forms, Wonder Cards and other similar materials should be mimeographed as needed.

Appendix VI

Ancillary Documentation for Discretionary Use

A. Explanatory Memos
INTOP Memo I

EARLIEST POSSIBLE DECISION SEQUENCE

QUARTER 1

Areas	*Home Office*
Cash transfer to areas Investment in areas Plant construction	Investment in Government securities R & D Market Research [Note: while most items are of little interest before Q4 you should consider test marketing and cost estimates (Items 17 and 18).]

QUARTER 2: No Change

Additional decisions possible in QUARTER 3

Production Methods Improvement Advertising [Note that the part of advertising's effectiveness which is immediate will be wasted in Q3.] Borrowing in areas where current assets exceed current liabilities Establishment of captive sales organization if and where prospective consumer sales seem to warrant it	Subscription to *Gazette* for Q4–7

Additional decisions possible in QUARTER 4

Pricing for consumer market All types of inter-company sales and intra-company transfers	Dividends (not sensible until your operations have at least once shown a profit on a con- solidated quarterly income statement)

Home Office may negotiate *inter-company loans* any time, and *licensing* as soon as any company has a product improvement.

Chase-A-Martini Bank will announce when it is open for business (i.e., home office bank loans).

NOTE: In deciding on your plant investments keep in mind that you will have to finance production for one quarter before you can expect any income from sales.

INTOP MEMO 2

COMMON ECONOMIES

This list of common economies is intended as a memory aid in your planning only; no attempt at quantification is made. The list does not purport to be exhaustive. Considerable information as to the relative magnitude of such common economies may be derived from the *Player's Manual* and the Schedule of Cost, etc. As in real life, to capitalize upon one set of common economies often means passing up others.

Most common economies are in fact limited to *one* company. For instance, ordinarily it would not be optimal to have the sales organization of a company in a given area distribute more than the output of about 3 X plants and 3 Y plants (whether the products were made by the company or brought from outside). Similarly, after a certain level of R & D expense has been reached, incremental R & D expense has a very low yield. If you want to specialize in a function, product or market beyond the "normal" confines of one company, the thing to do is to contract with other companies to prevail on their facilities — rent their labs, have them distribute part of your goods, etc.

GLOBAL ECONOMIES

R & D. Patent improvements from your own labs are always valid in all areas.

COMMON ECONOMIES FOR X AND Y IN A GIVEN AREA

Agency fees

Captive sales organization overhead

> NOTE: Inventory charges are an example of *diseconomies,* in that these charges accelerate as the combined number of units of X and Y in area inventory grows.

COMMON ECONOMIES FOR STANDARD AND DELUXE OF X (OR OF Y) IN A GIVEN AREA

Plant overhead. Both qualities may be made in one plant; note that

this entails certain diseconomies at the same time.
Advertising
Certain consumer preference for buying from suppliers of both stand-
ard and deluxe models.

COMMON ECONOMIES IN PRODUCTION

Plant overhead may be minimized by concentrating plant construction for a given product to as few areas as possible.
The effect of methods improvement may be maximized in the same
way.

As a general rule there is a premium on stable and even growth.
There are usually diseconomies flowing from erratic behavior. Of
course, the profits from a daring move will sometimes be even greater!

INTOP MEMO 3

ECONOMIC INDEX

Clearly, general economic indicators are of little *immediate* relevance in Quarters 1–3, as no radios or cleaners can be sold in consumer markets during the first three quarters of operation.

Sales in Quarter 4 may be smaller than general economic indicators might suggest, as companies encounter customary new product
introduction resistance, and as no company at this early stage of the
game is likely to have a full line of standard and deluxe products.

Generally speaking, postwar experience of business cycles has
been that both *timing* and *amplitude* describe international variations.
Raw-materials producing, less industrialized countries are first and
most violently affected (influenced primarily by changes in the rate
of advance buying by American industry). The United States follows
next in the time sequence as well as with regard to amplitude of the
fluctuations. The EEC is last affected, and also evidences the mildest
fluctuations. Superimposed on the short-term cycles is the general
growth trend of the economy, which at least for purposes of INTOP
is highest in Brazil and lowest in the United States.

In all countries the growth trend is also appreciably higher for
radios than for cleaners. The difference between radio and cleaner
growth rates is again greatest in Brazil and smallest in the United
States. Separate indices will be published in the *Gazette* for X and Y.
Generally the Y-index (cleaners) well reflects the state of the economy
in general, while transistor radios have a stronger momentum of
growth. However, the direction and varying of fluctuations is broadly
the same in the two industries (barring unforeseen environmental
events).

Some of these developments are suggested by the Y and X indices
for the two-year period before the beginning of radio and cleaner sales
to the consumer market.

	Y Index (cleaners and business in general)			X Index (transistor radios)		
	U.S.	EEC	Brazil	U.S.	EEC	Brazil
4 Qs before INTOP	97	96	105	101	98	108
3 Qs before INTOP	103	98	112	106	100	115
2 Qs before INTOP	107	100	111	109	103	111
1 Qs before INTOP	103	102	106	104	103	107
Q0	100	100	100	100	100	100
Q1	95	97	88	101	98	106
Q2	90	95	92	103	100	107
Q3	95	93	98	106	101	110
Forecast of quarter 4	99	95	104	110	105	115

The base of the series is quarter 0.

P. S. It may be a good idea for the executive responsible for forecasting in your company to draw a continuous diagram of economic trends.

INTOP MEMO 4

PLANT DISPOSAL

A given plant can be sold at any time, subject to the conditions below. Buyers are always assumed to be engaged outside the X and Y industries (hence no sales of plants between INTOP companies). Buyers are represented by the administrator.

There is a lag of one quarter involved in plant disposal, as it takes some time to find a customer, settle on terms, make legal arrangements, etc.

> While under construction a plant may be sold for 66 per cent of original investment.
> In 1st Quarter of production a plant may be sold for 64 per cent of original investment.
> In 2nd Quarter of production a plant may be sold for 62 per cent of original investment.
> In 3rd Quarter of production a plant may be sold for 60 per cent of original investment, and so on (a sliding scale of 2 per cent per quarter).

Unless you have an oversupply of inventories plant disposal should be scheduled in such a manner that you are sure of an uninterrupted production flow. This is not difficult as long as you have only one or two plants making a given product in an area, and you want to replace only one plant at a time.

Assume, for instance, that you want to replace a plant in Q8. Here is a schedule of your moves:

> Q6 Build a new plant.
> Q7 New plant under construction. Notify administrator – who will dispose of old plant in Q8.
> Q8 Produce in new plant. Old plant eliminated – disposal price paid into your area cash account.

If you have *three* X plants or three Y plants in a given area this arrangement is not possible, as the new plant must be built on the site of one of the old ones. Hence you should make arrangements with an outside supplier (or transship goods from your subsidiary in another area) to cover your product needs during the two quarters in which the new plant is under construction.

Please make sure to find out the number of your new plant from the administrator! If you place your production decision in the wrong Plant Number box on Form 1 you will get 0 production.

INTOP MEMO 5

MERGERS

While at least formally retaining their corporate identities, two companies may merge subject to the conditions specified below. (The administrator may also oblige a company to merge. Further, you will usually not be permitted to merge during the first year or two of operations.)

The advantages which may stem from a merger are of three main types: certain common economies, certain tax benefits and increased flexibility. *Common economies* may be derived as regards both fixed cost of production and methods improvement (by consolidating all X plants in an area to one of the companies, and all Y plants in the area to one or the other of the two), and in some cases, captive distribution costs. If sales are handled by only one of the companies, advertising expenditure may also be consolidated (if advertising is carried on by both companies there will be no common economies in this area).

Note, however, that there are definite limits to the common economies available, as indicated by INTOP Memo 2. In R & D for instance, centralization to one lab instead of dividing an equal total amount on two labs, will generally result in a smaller aggregate probability of product improvement.

Further, centralization of marketing, to one of two (or more) merged companies may also lead to diseconomies. The savings obtained in the C & A and advertising areas *may* be more than outweighed by smaller aggregate sales than if both companies were marketing. (This is no more remarkable than the fact that GE probably sells more appliances by using two brands – GE and Hotpoint – than if all GE-made appliances were distributed in the same way and with the same name.) *If* you do want to consolidate all sales effort of a product in an area to *one* company, please keep in mind that extra-large volume operations presumably demand a low-price (and, possibly, high-promotion) type of policy. (To put it more bluntly: if your particular price-advertising-quality combination warrants sales of 20,000 units, this is what you will sell whether you have 20,000 or 100,000 units in inventory. If you have *two* sales organizations using the same combination of marketing variables the aggregate sales will be a great deal more than 20,000 units, although they will rarely be twice that high.)

The *tax advantage* may be considerable if one of the companies prior to the merger had accumulated a considerable deficit, while the other had been profitable. Under the liberal rules of INTOP the combined concern will get a tax refund of 50% of the cumulative deficit of the former company, as long as such 50% do not exceed the accumulated taxes paid by the latter company. (Where this is the case, the refund will be scaled down proportionately.) In addition, minor tax advantages may be secured on a continuous basis after the merger is completed. For instance, if one of the companies is making a profit while the other one is making a loss, the latter company can grant the former one a loan from which the interest proceeds may be charged off against the loss.

Increased flexibility manifests itself in several ways. As the returns to R & D expense for a single company increase at a decelerating rate (after reaching beyond a certain minimum level), a combined concern interested in R & D may wish to decentralize its laboratories to both of the merged companies, thereby in effect increasing its chances of a product improvement for a given level of expense. Inventory charges accelerate with the growth of stock in a given area — hence under some circumstances it may be desirable to decentralize inventory as well. In some respects a merger also permits greater room for *deliberate experimentation*. If one of the companies handles two grades of X in an area, for instance, the other company may handle two other grades in the same area (or handle the same grades with a different set of marketing policies). In this way the combined concern is able to get around the two-qualities-per-product-per-area limitation. Finally, from an organization viewpoint it may be noted that X and Y may be held completely separate in one and the same area for accounting purposes if one of the companies specializes on X and the other one on Y. In this manner a division of responsibilities between an X and a Y manager is facilitated in cases where such a division seems desirable.

RULES GOVERNING MERGERS

A merger can be effectuated only by one company (hereafter Co. A) buying out the other (hereafter Co. B). The purchase price is a matter of negotiation between the companies. Of this sum, *two-thirds* shall be transferred to Co. B Home Office during the quarter in which the merger takes place, while *one-third* is paid out directly to the stockholders of Co. B (represented by the administrator). If the Chase-A-Martini Bank approves of the merger it may grant Co. A a loan covering up to 50 per cent of the purchase price.

As in corporate marriages in real life the status of Co. B may vary all the way from equal partnership to insignificance. This is again a matter of bargaining. A minimum requirement is that the corporate shell of Co. B remain at least *pro forma*, as *it is necessary to continue to hand in decision forms for both companies*. However, cash, products, product improvements, etc., may be freely transferred — in either direction, for that matter.

Note that sales expediting is *not* allowed between the merged companies.

A contract of merger setting forth as a minimum the purchase price, any tax refund expected, the quarter in which the merger is to take place, and signed by the presidents of both companies must be delivered to the administrator.

INCENTIVES TO MERGE

It may be assumed that the buying company (A) is aware of the advantages to be derived from a merger. There are also incentives for Co. B, however. Any tax credit due will be paid out to Co. B, as will 2/3 of the purchase price. Management of Co. B is free to negotiate for the retention of these funds in the Co. They may also stipulate that Co. B management, as a group, or individual members thereof, be retained in their positions. The future division of decision-making powers and responsibilities may also be negotiated. It should be borne in mind that any rights not explicitly retained by Co. B will be transferred to the president of Co. A as a result of the merger.

B. The *Gazette*
sample

the intop...

GAZETTE

Organ of the World Federation of Appliance Manufacturers

GAME: WINTER 1962   No. 7-8

        Editor: Gerald Zaltman

MOTTO: ELECTRO-LUX ET VERITAS

BUSINESS CLIMATE

Economic advances predicted for Brazil in quarters 6 and 7 failed to occur. The changes and causes were so abrupt and clandestine that only now the latter factors are observable. Consequently, forecasts for quarters 8 and 9 are for conditions even less favorable than existing at present. However, we are quite confident that quarter 8 will represent the low point and the Brazilian economy will quickly regain its former levels. The U.S. seems to be experiencing difficulties reflecting in part the sudden reversals in Brazil and in part the electrical workers' strike threat. Given these factors plus the prediction of Harvard economists that the U.S. will experience vigorous growth in the quarters immediately beyond our forecast, we dare not suggest that quarter 9 will represent a turning point as in Brazil. There may even be a further movement downward. The E.E.C. shows no real signs of the troubles plaguing other areas (however, note X index). We have mentioned in the past the apparent slowness (lag) of the E.E.C. to respond to any change in the world business environment. It would be wise to keep this in mind should the current reverses in the other areas prove more pervasive than at present. Here's how the figures are stacked.

GENERAL ECONOMIC INDEX

Qtr.	U.S.	E.E.C.	Brazil	Nature of Data
5	108	99	120	Actual
6	114	104	115	"
7	110	110	106	"
8	106	115	100	Forecast
9	104	118	105	"

The preceding index is most reflective of the economy as a whole and the X index for only a segment. There is, however, an interesting contrast between them particularly in Brazil and the E.E.C. Our optimism in Brazil is in large part due to the opening of a new radio station which may increase demand for X. We also expect an increase in the effectiveness of advertising there! Here are the figures.

X ECONOMIC INDEX

Qtr.	U.S.	E.E.C.	Brazil	Nature of Data
5	111	106	125	Actual
6	120	107	121	"
7	117	112	129	"
8	118	123	133	Forecast
9	112	120	140	"

CHAS-ING NEWS

Chase-A-Martini has released up to date revisions concerning the standard Home Office Credit line with the Bank. Present rates are 10% of Home Office equity (net equity less prior existing loans), down 5% from the previous rate, or 15 times Paid-In-Capital, up from 10. The greater of the two figures will be used as the base for your loan. Also, a reminder that Chase standard loans are for four quarters.

the intop...
                    gazette

WINTER 1962   No. 7-8

FORTRESS EUROPA?

The following whispers are floating around Europe. (1) There will be a slowdown in Y plants in quarter 10 if no new labor contract. (2) There may be a revaluation of E.E.C. currencies in the offing. The governments emphatically deny it--per usual. (3) The Gazette may hereafter be published from the Prison Beneath The Hague.

INDUSTRY INVENTORIES AT END OF Q6

	US	EEC	BRAZIL
X	203	235	95
Y	265	180	68

Thousands of units, as usual.

EAST-WEST TRADE

The Russians, apparently in another divisive move against Western solidarity, are offering to buy 40,000 economy model X_0 from E.E.C. radio manufacturers. They (the radios, that is) are for shipment to Crimean seaside resorts where they are going like hotcakes among the newly-arrived bourgeoisie.

Like the shrewd capitalists they are when it please them the Imperialski Radiogonow Combinatnik--the import trust, to you--will make up their minds on the competitive bids. These will have to be submitted by February 6 at 9 P.M. at the latest to the Administratorski. Delivery and payment Quarter 9. Partisan treatment guaranteed.

American newspapers are pretty upset about the whole thing, but being as it is with the torrid inventory situation in the European X industry the State Department doesn't feel it can bring pressure to bear. One European manufacturer was heard to say,

"I think I'll submit a bid--rather than have some other blackguard get it." Other E.E.C. firms were talking about submitting joint bids. This is okay with the Russians, who, however want one firm formally responsible as coordinator in such a case.

U. S. LABOR SETTLEMENT

Hot news item: After strenuous bargaining, X manufacturers in the States will be relieved to learn that a settlement was reached with Mr. Carey. The industry wage and fringe benefit package will now be increased enough to evidence itself in a $1 increase in variable manufacturing cost from Quarter 8 on for X_0 in the U.S., and proportionately more for higher grades of X. Mr. Carey agreed to sign up for two years--also not to strike Y plants in the U.S. during that time.

The industry owes a vote of thanks to EDWARD POWERS, its designated representative, without whose gallant effort the settlement would more likely than not have been much more onerous.

TO WHOM IT MAY CONCERN

To interested investors:

Company 11 hereby declares a stock dividend of 10%; all holders of company 11 stock have 10% more stock as of beginning of quarter 8.

Company #9 announces an attractive profit opportunity:

License for X_2 available in E.E.C. Contact R. W. Prensner, President, F16-0300 during business hours for details.

the intop...
                              gazette

SNOOPER SYNOPSIS

Companies 1 and 8 did not subscribe to the Gazette--the chislers! They forget that once a WFAM member you are always one.

Cash dividends in Quarter 6 were paid by Companies 7 ($125,000) and 4. The former for the first time, the latter for the second.

Company #7 charge $99 for X deluxe in Brazil. We are glad to see such consistency between thought and action. Unfortunately none sold at this price.

The following is the ranking of all companies according to consolidated equity positions: Co. 1-8; Co. 2-5; Co. 3-2; Co. 4-1; Co. 5-9; Co. 6-13; Co. 7-3; Co. 8-12; Co. 9-14; Co. 10-6; Co. 11-7; Co. 12-10; Co. 13-4; Co. 14-11.

There was approximately a 4 million dollar gap between the first and last companies.

Company 9 received Grade 3 improvement in Product X in Quarter 7. It was, however, an expensive improvement. Approximately 25,000 units of X were knocked down from X_1 to X_0. Where's the long-range planning?

TEENAGE TRANSISTOR CRAZE IN EEC

Teenagers in Europe are going berserk for transistor radios this season. Basking in bikinis on the Riviera, or twisting at Sweet-Sixteen parties--wherever a teenager a transistor.

While EEC manufacturers naturally expect to benefit from this boom there is moderation in their voices. Actually, X inventories in the EEC at the end of Quarter 7 are at a record high of 200 thousand, while the industry rarely sells more than 80-100 thousand in any one quarter (including deluxe). So considerable inventory as well as production trimming is still in order. And that goes for Co. 6 as well, by the way! In fact, the general inventory situation for all areas in relation to sales is such that we wonder whether or not companies are producing as avocations rather than vocations.

WHO's WHO

Co. 6   Pres. - Mr. Rohn
        V.P. Marketing - Mr. Bauder
        V.P. Production - Mr. Mahon
        V.P. Finance - Mr. Peterson
        V.P. R&D - Mrs. Husen

Co. 7   Pres. - Mr. Gennuso
        V.P. Finance - Mr. Kapple
        V.P. U.S. & Brazil - Mr. Pomeran
        V.P. E.E.C. - Mr. Gray

Co. 8   E.E.C. (Comptroller) - Mr. Nadel
        E.E.C. Marketing - Mr. Wish
        U.S. Marketing - Mr. Foley & Metz
        Long-Range Planning - Mr. Hahn
        Pres. - Mr. Forwalter

Co. 9   Pres. - Mr. Prensner
        V.P. Finance - Mr. Severance
        V.P. Marketing - Mr. Van Meter
            and R&D
        V.P. E.E.C. - Mr. Warzynski
        V.P. U.S. - Mr. Wilson

Co.10   Pres. - Mr. Rezabeck
            R&D
        V.P. Marketing-Mr. J.S. Magruder
        V.P. Manufacturing - Mr. Lipsey
        V.P. Finance - Mr. Young

Co.11   Pres. - Mr. Gatter
        V.P. Long-Range Planning-
            Mr. Albrecht
        V.P. Finance - Mr. Hendrickson
        V.P. Marketing - Mr. J. Magruder
        Sales Manager- Mr. Murphy

Co.12   Pres. - Mr. Lowell
        Exec. V.P. - Mr. Sprung
        V.P. Marketing - Mr. Ryan
        V.P. Finance - Mr. Wolf
        V.P. Prod. - Mr. Myer-Oertel

C. Business Philosophy and Goals
sample

Co. 6 — *Tempo Electric, Winter 1962*

We wish to establish a corporation to both produce and market electrical appliances. We want to both produce and market so that we can exert greater control over both areas of operation.

At the outset, we will be involved with one product — *portable transistor radios*. We chose "transistors" because they represent a healthy rate of growth. This is a reflection, as well as an integral part, of our overall goal of growth.

We're purposely "holding back" to one product in one area (EEC) at the outset, so that we'll have resources available to move into areas that have little or no activity. Throughout the growth of our company, we shall most probably add more electrical appliance products to our line. In fact, we may later decide to diversify into other product areas to assure greater stability of growth. If we make such a decision, one possible route of expansion could be through the acquisition of other companies. However, this decision is most probably several years in the future.

We should maintain *both standard and deluxe* product classes. The latter can be a reflection of the product quality which is to become part of our image. The former may possibly be an important factor in private label business or in the area of discount outlets, as well as in filling out our line. Moreover, the standard product class will help satisfy the demand of the "teen" market. Both private label business and the use of discount outlets are decisions that have yet to be made. We're aware that dangers exist in both areas.

For example, in the private label area we must be ever alert to the effect this type of business might have on our branded product class. In this respect, were we to produce private label products, we may decide to market them in an area(s) physically (geographically) separate from the area(s) in which we sell our branded items.

We want to have both standard and deluxe products. Also, today's growth depends to a great extent on innovation. The company will maintain a *modest R & D program* — spurring its innovative activities *primarily* by licenses from others. Only if licensing conditions turn out to be unreasonable will the company devote a major part of its managerial talent and other resources to a large-scale captive R & D program. We feel this philosophy is wise because we believe that there will be an industry-wide scramble in R & D, making patent licenses available at modest rates.

In the early stages, we will produce and market in *the EEC* for reasons listed elsewhere. As we grow, we may possibly move into other geographical areas. We want to be flexible enough so that we can vary the products and even the mode of operation in these new areas, if we so desire.

We want to be a growth company characterized by flexibility. We're not interested in a wild, risky type of growth. Rather, we want a continuous, stable climb upward. In other words, we don't believe "growth" and "conservative" are antithetical. As a point of fact, we believe that a certain element of conservatism is necessary for a mature, stable, long-lasting increase in sales, profits, assets — as well as the other factors which represent growth.

An offshoot of our goal of stable growth is our desire for a healthy balance between paying dividends and "ploughing back." As soon as we make profits on a regular basis we will pay out 30 per cent of earnings to gain the confidence of the stock market.

Why the EEC?

1. The EEC is a "moderate" area in relation to the following factors: capacity, acquisition cost, fixed cost, interest rates, Commercial and Administrative Expense, growth rate, business cycle swings, price elasticity, advertising sensitivity, tax rates.
2. One reason for entering the EEC is really a reason for *not* entering Brazil. The deposit of $1.5 million per plant would have required a total deposit of $4.5 million for our three plants.
3. By entering the EEC, we shall be physically, economically and politically close to the Home Office. This may possibly preclude, for example, "restrictions on the remittance of profits abroad."
4. GNP is growing at a more rapid rate in the EEC than in the U.S.
5. The EEC has the lowest fixed cost to capacity ratio.
6. Common economies stemming from joint administration of several plants is greater in the EEC.
7. The EEC has the most favorable cash-accounts receivable ratio.

D. Position Description
sample

MARKETING MANAGER

THE MARKETING MANAGER is responsible for completing all the marketing decisions required by *Form 1*. On routine quarterly decisions he receives advice from the Analyst, and his final decisions are subject to the review of the President. On major decisions involving the firm's marketing policy or grossly affecting the operations of some other department, he receives instructions from the President and his decisions are subject to the review of the President.

The Marketing Manager is chairman of the Product Planning Committee advising the President on innovation management. There are no restraints on the Marketing Manager's contacts with the Finance Manager or the Product X and Product Y Managers, but he exercises no control over them.

A prime obligation of the Marketing Manager is the preparation of *long-range marketing plans*, which must be laid in such a manner as to promote and reflect the overall business plans of the Company. An important element of the long-range marketing plan is the functional budget. Once confirmed, it gives the framework for such expense allocations as the Marketing Manager finds necessary.

Operating Decisions

1. Analyze market conditions based on current market research report.
2. Suggest to Analyst additional information needed, e.g., by way of Market Research 2.
3. Obtain estimates of the financial constraints from Finance and production constraints from Production.
4. Adjust policies in the various operating areas to respond to competition. When necessary, we meet high sales promotion expenditures by competitors with low prices and low price with increased quality.
5. Revise sales estimates, and make new forecast with Analyst.
6. Clear completed decisions with the President when required.

Bases of Performance Evaluation

1. Successful achievement of Company sales volume and market share goals.
2. Jointly responsible with Production Manager for holding company-wide inventory costs below $200,000 any given quarter.
3. Minimization in C & A cost — responsible for proper channel selection and dimensioning.
4. Keep inter-company transactions profitable.
5. Contribution to Company long-range planning effort.

Job Description — Analyst — Sample

Work closely with the department heads and the Product Planning Committee in:

1. Analyzing long-run financing alternatives.
2. Developing financial sales and cost analysis techniques.
3. Maintaining surveillance of the Brazilian scene — whenever government policies seem reasonable down there we will go in.
4. Coordinating flow of information from marketing and production to finance.
5. Recommend Market Research 2 and consulting services, subject to review by President.

BASES OF PERFORMANCE EVALUATION

Performance of your staff functions will be continuously reviewed by the President – after hearing the department heads – on these criteria:

1. Availability, timeliness, accuracy and relevance of data for decision-making and the Company's long-range planning effort.
2. Usefulness of forms and worksheets developed.*

E. Management Audit Report
sample

(Illustration from INTOP run at the International Center for the Advancement of Management Education, Graduate School of Business, Stanford University, Fall 1962).

We have carefully examined the books of accounts, records, documents and objectives of the company as presented before us for audit up to the quarter ending 12 and submit herewith our report on the aims, objectives, organization and the overall performance of the company along with our comments and recommendations. In evaluating the success or otherwise of the company we have consistently applied with complete objectivity the best of the available criteria of management audit.

The report consists of three sections. Section I gives the summary of our findings along with the detailed and critical comments on various operations and managerial decisions of the company; Section II comprises our principal recommendations and the final section is devoted to a general evaluation of the company's action potential.

SECTION I. *Summary of Findings*

1. *Objectives and Performance:* Most reluctantly we have to state that the company's policies and performance were not always in conformity with its well defined objectives and goals. From the performance of the company it is apparent that there is remarkable discrepancy between its objectives as set at the time of its incorporation and its subsequent decisions over the period under audit. Some such discrepancies have been found in regard to the following matters:

   (*a*) The company's objectives state, "We are also cognizant of our obligations to the investors in the company and consider it an obligation to earn a reasonable rate of return on their investments to maintain a stable dividend, and to aim for a progressive appreciation in capital value." In practice, the management of the company failed to fulfill their commitments to the stockholders by pursuing the payment of a low rate of dividend and thus probably failed to gain the confidence of the capital market as is evidenced from the low amount of paid-in-capital.

---

* To derive full benefit from the simulation, it is imperative that each participant study and digest the *Player's Manual*. It is, of course, especially useful that each manager master all Manual information pertinent to his area. This may well be included in each job description.

(b) The management of the company had committed them-selves "fully and from the very start to a continuing program of product development and methods improvement." It was found that the company did not do much to honor this com-mitment as the company, in spite of wasteful expenditure of a large sum of money, could serve their consumers with only Y_2 and X_0. In an era of high technological improvement followed by competitive market the competitors of the com-pany were able to get as high grades as X_4 and Y_4, so the low grade products of the company can not speak highly of the efficiency of the management and also can not ensure the management of a good response from the market in the near future.

(c) The company's promise to consumers as made in the objec-tives is also very high-sounding. It states, ". . . of passing on to the consumers the major part of the benefits from technological improvements and production efficiencies that may be achieved." The irony of the fate of the consumers is that instead of passing on to the consumers the benefits, the heavy burden of the management inefficiency on technolog-ical improvements were passed on to the consumers by high price policy no matter whether the products warranted it or not.

(d) We are struck by a glaring lapse in the objectives of the company. In the modern business world, no management can ignore the great task of human relations. But the man-agement of the company made no commitments in the ob-jectives to their employees and also their past activities and plans for future failed to define their personnel policies and to make provisions for employee welfare activities. We won-der how long their employees can be neglected in these days of labor consciousness.

2. *Organization and Division of Responsibilities:* The company does not seem to have given sufficient thought to its organization struc-ture and also the matter of division of responsibilities, not to speak of job descriptions. To our knowledge the company has no organi-zation chart, though the company has a large amount of assets to administer.

3. *Plans and Their Formulation:* It was found that the management made and approved plans for their future actions. But the merit of such endeavor is totally lost if no room is left for comparing its performance with plans. So while realizing the importance of plans, the nature and quality of the plans followed by the man-agement left much to be desired. Plans were not fully quantified, targets were not set and hence they remained delightfully vague. Almost exclusive exploitation of product Y and tardy growth of product X is a glaring example of the management's lack of initia-tive in product diversification, although it was smartly stated in the objectives that "the company had promised to divert resources to the production of transistor radios (X)." In practice this was done haltingly and in a 'hand-to-mouth' manner. There is also not

much evidence to show that the company adopted a long-range view of its operations. Hence its plans do not display enough imagination and vision of the management.

4. *Financial Management:* The management displayed admirable skill for financial expansion both by retention of earnings and loans, thus ending in quarter 12 with a large amount of retained earnings and widened base of assets. But to our mind building up of high retained earnings and large amount of assets by depriving the stockholders of dividends and the consumers of quality by ill-planned inadequate spending on R & D, and also by neglecting the welfare of the employees, cannot speak very highly of the management. Instead they would have achieved remarkable success if they would have released a portion of the assets for the above purposes.

   The short-term financial policy of the company is not fully understandable to us. It seems that the management has neglected the value of cash budgets for a corporation. In quarter 11, in Area 2, the company had $1,230,386 in cash and in Area 1, a bank loan of $721,860. Similarly in quarter 12 the company obtained huge supplier credit although it had enormous cash in hand at the home office. However, we like to put on record our appreciation of the management's efficiency in the *overall* management of finance.

5. *Production Management:* Sufficient information is not available. However, the actual performance of the company shows that the management's attitude toward plant utilization was sound and capable of contributing to the success of the enterprise. The management decision to produce Y at maximum capacity in both areas 1 and 2 for achieving advantage of the economic trends deserves appreciation.

6. *Price Policy:* By and large the price policy took good advantage of the economic trends. However, some of the decisions it seems were in conflict with the company's objective of "not emerging in price-competition." We are constrained to suppose that the desire to maximize profits lured the management to pursue a rather erratic price policy — sometimes designed to take advantage through price competition and sometimes withholding from consumers benefits which could have been legitimately passed on to them.

7. *House-keeping and Decision-making Machinery:* The company's housekeeping has been of a fairly high order. The management has also made good use of some of the managerial tools of analyzing data for decision-making. The graphs and charts as shown to us are commendable.

8. *Marketing and Sales Management:* The company seems to have made good use of market research. However, the management's failure in regard to product X_2 provides a surprising lapse and indicates lack of awareness of the market situation which had shown in the past that product X_2 was a dud. The sales management was fairly satisfactory but the advertising policy was somewhat mechanical and unimaginative.

9. *Research and Development:* Contrary to its declared aims the management seems to have neglected R & D. Such neglect, in spite of its financial success, is disappointing.

SECTION II. *Recommendations*

(a) Plans should be formulated more specifically. The objectives should be constantly kept in mind in making plans. Plans are to be broken down so as to assign responsibilities at all levels of management. Targets are to be fixed in advance and be possible of adjustment if environment warrants. A comparison of performance with plans for determining and disposing of variance is highly important in planned management.

(b) The management should prepare cash budget and funds flow statements so as to avoid loans not warranted by the financial condition of the company.

(c) Attention should be paid to the long-run benefits of the company by building high action potential through research on product and process improvements and market research.

(d) More attention should be paid to diversification of activities. Development of product X and improvement of product Y are essentially needed for the future benefits of the company.

SECTION III. *Conclusions*

We are of the opinion that with the existing philosophy of the management the company's future potentialities can not be rated as A-1. If short-term profit maximization is regarded as the only goal, the company's performance has been good. But such a goal exposes the narrow horizon and limited outlook of the management. If the company is to serve itself and the economy as a whole, it will have to shift towards a well thought out and enlightened philosophy of management and then alone it can have a prolonged success.

F. Worksheet for Demand Studies
sample

(All figures in 000's except price)

Product _____ Area _____

A. STANDARD MODEL

Variables	Quarter____			Quarter____			Quarter____			Quarter____		
	Grade	*Forecasted*	*Actual*	*Grade*	*Forecasted*	*Actual*	*Grade*	*Forecasted*	*Actual*	*Grade*	*Forecasted*	*Actual*
Inventory ending												
Sales, units												
Price												
Advertising*												

B. DELUXE MODEL

Variables	Quarter____			Quarter____			Quarter____			Quarter____		
	Grade	*Forecasted*	*Actual*	*Grade*	*Forecasted*	*Actual*	*Grade*	*Forecasted*	*Actual*	*Grade*	*Forecasted*	*Actual*
Inventory ending												
Sales, units												
Price												
Advertising												

* Common economies for advertising for standard and deluxe products are 100 per cent. To gauge its effect on sales the full amount should be stated in both standard and deluxe tables.

The empty line may be used for any data you wish. Competitive intelligence, such as industry price and advertising trends, your market share, etc., may be considered.

A Note on Organization
Simulation by Gaming[*]

Use in Organization Planning and Simulation

The most powerful reason for using simulation in organization planning is that it frequently may be a great deal cheaper both in direct costs and indirectly in human relations and lost time costs than experimental tinkering with the real organization itself. Where this is the case, simulation is likely to become increasingly used, provided there is any reason to believe that tenable conclusions can be reached. It would seem that on the latter point we may be moderately optimistic. Organized behavior systems seem to be governed largely by three major sets of interacting variables:

    a. The personalities involved
    b. The goals and structure of the organization
    c. The environment in which the organization operates

As to personality types the military for many years have been using games to study the behavior of more or less risk-minded commanders in varying organizational and environmental circumstances. It should be equally feasible to use other criteria, such as production-centered vs. employee-oriented leaders. At the present time we have little knowledge of how the game experience itself will affect the behavior of the players. It would seem advisable for the time being not to use the people who will themselves be affected by the organization planning effort in the simulation, at least not in the positions they may expect to take up in real life.[1] Other personalities with somewhat similar characteristics to the real-life personnel available may be used. It is, of course, also possible to hold the personality variable "constant" in some degree by a randomized composition of teams.

The goals of the organization would presumably be stated by management in advance of the simulation exercise, and thus be a parameter rather than a variable in the exercise. As organization structure is likely to comprise the set of variables of prime import in game simulation of decision-making systems, we shall discuss this area separately in the last few pages of the paper.

Whether the environment in which the organization operates should be a given or a variable in organization simulation would again

[*] This is an excerpt from an essay written by Hans B. Thorelli entitled "Game Simulation of Administrative Systems" which appeared in *Marketing and the Computer* (1963, pp. 334–48), edited by Wroe Alderson and S. J. Shapiro. Permission to quote these sections was granted by Prentice-Hall, Inc., Englewood Cliffs, New Jersey.

[1] It is another matter that management games may be used educationally to "break in" personnel into an organizational scheme which already has the official stamp of approval by top management.

be dependent on the purpose in mind. If the environment is known in salient respects and the intention is to try out alternate types of organization, the thing to do is to set the parameters of the game model in such a way as to reflect principal features of the environment. If the organization is more or less given, at least initially, and the intention is to examine ways in which it might most effectively cope with environmental change, a great degree of variability in the market variables in the course of the simulation exercise is clearly desirable. Again, it may be stated with considerable confidence that INTOP offers great possibilities in the area of environmental change – from many to few competitors, from homogeneous to highly differentiated markets, from relative stability to violent change, etc. Its modular design also facilitates its use in trying to simulate a *particular* real-life market with some effectiveness, although this would involve more work. Generally speaking, the author feels that the simulation of particular environments with appreciable degrees of faithfulness and detail usually will require models of such complexity and specificity that one might prefer to abstain from the game feature as such.

Proceeding, then, to the core area of organization simulation, we shall discuss the aspects mentioned initially in this paper, namely problems of structure, centralization vs. decentralization, and communications.

Simulation of Structuring Approaches

A crucial problem in marketing-oriented diversified companies is whether to structure primarily by customer groups, products, geographical areas, or management functions at the various levels of organization. Assuming that field-level organization is oriented toward customer categories, balanced performance usually requires emphasis on one of the other structuring approaches at the level or levels immediately below the executive officer. INTOP was explicitly designed with this type of organizational problem in mind. Areas, products, and management functions are all labels on sets of variables in the game vital and complex enough to stimulate experimentation with different types of structure. As indicated by the operating statements reproduced earlier, data outputs (as well as decision inputs) are arranged in such a way that far-reaching divisionalization based on profit responsibility by area or products is possible. As many successful businesses have a functional top management organization, such a structure must have other, compensating advantages. These may be most clearly apparent in a fairly centralized operation based on division of labor according to professional specialties of the management group.

At this point, it may be worthwhile to recount briefly an informal experiment in the structure area undertaken with a cohort of some seventy Chicago area middle managers during the Spring of 1961.[1] The men were randomly distributed over 14 different INTOP company teams. Believing the game was played for educational purposes exclu-

[1] These men were going through the final semester of the two-year Executive Program run by the Graduate School of Business at the University of Chicago.

sively, they were unaware of participating in an experiment. It was merely pointed out to them that the complexity of the game, and the relatively brief decision periods, was apt to require an efficient division of labor within each team. Their attention was drawn to a passage in the Player's Manual emphasizing that game data would be continuously presented in a manner making divisionalization based on profit responsibility by area or product possible, and that functional organization has other, compensating advantages. The executives were encouraged to take up positions in the company teams other than those corresponding to their own real-life jobs, and most of them did.

Focusing the discussion on the level of line executives reporting directly to the President, we find that although a majority of companies (8 of 14) were in both the product X and the product Y businesses none of them went in for a product-oriented top management structure. Five companies started out with area managers, while the other nine adopted a functional setup. At mid-game, all companies were required to rotate managerial positions in order to broaden the experience of participants. They were also asked to reconsider in this connection their division of labor. All five area-oriented companies retained their structure. Interestingly, however, no less than six of the nine functionally organized groups switched to area management. Four of these expanded into one or two new areas around the time of management reorganization.[1] Three firms had functional administration throughout. Of these, two were engaged in only one product business each, and all three at the beginning of the game were active only in one area (in the latter part all three conducted multi-area operations). Not a single company changed from area to functional organization.

It should be emphasized that most area organizations included some type of functional officer on the first line level, or in a parallel staff position, most commonly a controller. Where personnel resources permitted, companies were prone to add a level of product or functional managers below the area manager in the most important area, rather than to add staff specialists at the corporate level. This example is suggestive of organizational change to meet changing environmental conditions, or of a re-interpretation of existing conditions.

One of the chief merits of organization simulation by gaming is that it rapidly and tangibly will make the planner aware of many of the problems likely to arise under different administrative schemes. A good example is the introduction of corporate "services," i.e., functional specialists with staff authority only in relation to principal line managers but with varying degrees of line authority over corresponding line or functional specialists below these managers. INTOP would seem well qualified to simulate such situations.

[1] In a written review of operations at the end of the game the President of one of these companies stated that "the original company organization was structured functionally and therefore had a President, Chief Financial Officer and Production, Marketing and R & D Specialists. It was soon found that the peculiarities of each market were such that we could better operate with area decentralization. We now have a President, Chief Financial Officer and three Area Managers, each completely responsible for all operations in his area."

Simulation of Centralization vs. Decentralization (Delegation)

Strongly suggestive evidence concerning the efficacy of varying degrees of centralization and decentralization (the term used in the sense of delegation of authority *per se* rather than geographical or other divisionalization of operations) in a given type of environment should be obtained by game simulation. Given sufficient time and resources for the experiment, a game of the INTOP type could also be used to get at least preliminary answers to such vexing problems as whether centralization or decentralization of authority should be emphasized in a highly competitive or rapidly changing market.

One aspect of authority delegation of particular interest in the simulation of marketing organization concerns the effects of given policy constraints in various areas of decision making. Management may wish to know how far authority to set prices (or deviate from posted prices) should (or can) be delegated; where in the organization authority to negotiate contracts with the outside for sales, licensing, purchasing, loans, etc., should be vested; whether there should be provisions for pre- or post-audit in such instances, etc. In many real-life situations, a given manager at a subordinate level may have general authority in his sphere of activity but still be subject to a number of specific exceptions of withheld authority in matters such as those just illustrated.

A group of policy constraint and authority allocation problems for whose simulation INTOP is especially well suited are in the area of intra-corporate marketing. In shipments from the U.S. to the EEC (or from one product division to another), what rules should govern transfer pricing? If division manager B feels division manager A is charging him too much or otherwise is uncooperative, should B be allowed to buy from sources outside the company, or even go into the making of A's product himself? If B develops new patents, must he give his inside customer A an exclusive right to use them for a certain time, or can he decide to license the innovations to outsiders at once? If area managers are measured on profit performance and the Brazilian manager finds he can export to the U.S. market profitably, shall he be allowed to do so over the protests of the U.S. area manager? By what decision-making machinery should these various types of questions be resolved? These are the types of problems INTOP teams are often grappling with, and they have a suitably realistic background.

Communications

One would expect that organization planning would consider problems of communication mostly in connection with problems of structure and/or authority allocation. The operational question for the simulation exercise then becomes, What are the information needs at various points in the organization, and by what communications processes shall they be met? Players in INTOP soon observe, just like real-life decision makers, that over-communication may be as much of a problem as under-communication and scarcity of data; the processing and routing of vital data should indeed be part of organization planning. Communications systems may be tried out by simulation both for general efficiency and to examine the need for special committees or management meetings for cross-communications.

The realism of simulation efforts in organization planning generally and with regard to communications in particular, may be enhanced appreciably by limiting the amount of face-to-face communications within company management groups to somewhat realistic proportions. This may involve locating the members of a team in different rooms, and placing a limit – or cost – on the amount, type, or duration of direct communication within the group. In some cases it might even be realistic to place the members of a team ostensibly located, say, in the EEC in a room with the EEC managers from all other companies. In this manner the fact that managers tend to generate a dual loyalty to their own local operating environment in addition to their loyalty to the company itself may be built into the simulation.

Select Bibliography

For easy reference this select bibliography is divided into three sections, one pertaining to bibliographical sources, one to general literature on gaming and simulation and one to references to specific simulations in game form. The first two volumes listed under bibliographical sources are also listed under the general literature heading. They are both good introductions to the field of business simulation by gaming.

A general principle of selection has been emphasis on recent literature; for additional references prior to 1960 the reader is referred to the bibliographical source references. In the second section references to simulation in the general sense have been included only when they seemed pertinent to gaming. The third section is confined to published materials regarding specific games. A very large number of games exist for which no such literature is readily available. Again, the Greenlaw-Herron-Rawdon and Kibbee-Craft-Nanus volumes contain valuable directories of numerous simulation exercises, including some of their characteristics and relevant publications and/or resource persons.

I. *Bibliographical Sources*

Greenlaw, Paul S., Herron, Lowell W., and Rawdon, Richard H. *Business Simulation in Industrial and University Education.* Englewood Cliffs, N. J.: Prentice-Hall, 1962.

Kibbee, Joel M., Craft, Clifford J., and Nanus, Burt. *Management Games: A New Technique for Executive Development.* New York: Reinhold, 1961.

Malcolm, D. G. "A Bibliography on the Use of Simulation in Management Analysis," *Operations Research,* VIII (March, 1960), 176–77.

Shubik, Martin. "Bibliography on Simulation, Gaming, Artificial Intelligence and Allied Topics," American Statistical Association *Journal,* LV (December, 1960), 736–51.

2. *General Literature on Gaming and Simulation*
A. BOOKS AND MONOGRAPHS

Acer, John W. *Business Games: A Simulation Technique.* Iowa City: Bureau of Labor and Management, State University of Iowa, 1960.

American Management Association, General Management Division. *Simulation and Gaming: A Symposium.* AMA Management Report No. 55. New York: American Management Association, 1961.

Bleicher, K. *Unternehmungsspiele; Simulationsmodelle für unternehmerische Entscheidungen.* Baden-Baden: Verlag für Unternehmenführung, 1962.

Bonini, Charles P. *Simulation of Information and Decision Systems in the Firm.* Englewood Cliffs, N. J.: Prentice-Hall, 1963.

Churchill, Neil C., Miller, M. H., and Trueblood, R. M. *Auditing and Business Games.* Homewood, Ill.: Irwin (announced for publication).

Dill, William R., Jackson, James R., and Sweeney, James W. (eds.). *Proceedings of the Conference on Business Games as Teaching Devices Sponsored by the Ford Foundation and School of Business Administration, Tulane University, April 26-28, 1961.* New Orleans, La.: Tulane University, 1961.

Fessler, M. E., Saunders, C. B., and Steele, J. D. (eds.). *Proceedings of the National Symposium on Management Games, December 12-13, 1958.* Lawrence, Kan.: Center for Research in Business, University of Kansas, May, 1959.

Greenberger, M. "Computer Simulation of the United States Social Economy" (unpublished Ph.D. thesis, Harvard University, Cambridge, Mass., December, 1957).

Greenlaw, Paul S., Herron, Lowell W., and Rawdon, Richard H. *Business Simulation in Industrial and University Education.* Englewood Cliffs, N. J.: Prentice-Hall, 1962.

Guetzkow, Harold. *Simulation in Social Science; Readings.* Englewood Cliffs, N. J.: Prentice-Hall, 1962.

Guetzkow, Harold, Alger, Chadwick F., Brody, Richard A., Noel, Robert C., and Snyder, Richard C. *Simulation in International Relations: Developments for Research and Teaching.* Englewood Cliffs, N. J.: Prentice-Hall, 1963.

International University Contact for Management Education. *Management Games.* Summary Report. Delft, The Netherlands, 1963.

Kaufmann, A., Faure, R., and LeBauff, A. *Les Jeux d'entreprises.* Paris: Presses universitaires de France, 1960.

Kennedy, John L., Durkin, James E., and Kling, Frederick R., Department of Psychology, Princeton University. *Growing Synthetic Organisms in Synthetic Environments.* Mimeographed address at the 1960 Meeting of the Eastern Psychological Association, n.d.

Kibbee, Joel M., Craft, Clifford J., and Nanus, Burt. *Management Games:*

A New Technique for Executive Development. New York: Reinhold, 1961.

Litwin, G. L. and Ciarlo, J. A. *Achievement Motivation and Risk-Taking in a Business Setting.* New York: Relations Services, The General Electric Company, n.d.

Malcolm, Donald G. (ed.). *Report on Systems Simulation Symposium Co-Sponsored by AIIE, ORSA and TIMS, New York, May, 1958.* Baltimore: Waverly Press, 1958.

Orcutt, Guy H., *et al. Microanalysis of Socioeconomic Systems; A Simulation Study.* New York: Harper, 1961.

Plattner, J. W. and Herron, L. W. *Simulation: Its Use in Employee Selection and Training.* AMA Personnel Division, Management Bulletin No. 20. New York: American Management Association, 1962.

Proceedings of the Conference on Business Games as Teaching Devices Sponsored by the Ford Foundation and the School of Business Administration, Tulane University. See Dill, William R.

Rawdon, Richard. *Learning Management Skills from Stimulation* [sic] *Gaming.* Ann Arbor, Mich.: Bureau of Industrial Relations, The University of Michigan, December, 1960.

B. ARTICLES

Allen, V. B. "The Business Game — A New Dimension in Management Development," *Proceedings* of the Second Conference of the Computing and Data Processing Society of Canada, 1960, 332–37.

Anon. "Putting Executives in a Goldfish Bowl; with closed-circuit TV and group analysis, top men at RCA are observed as they react to simulated problems," *Business Week* (September 23, 1961), 162–64+.

Bastable, C. W. "Business Games, Models, and Accounting," *Journal of Accountancy,* CIX (March, 1960), 56–60.

Bechberger, G. W., *et al.* "These Men Are Playing Maintenance Management Games," *Factory,* CXIX (February, 1961), 80–83.

Bloomfield, Lincoln P. "Political Gaming," *U. S. Naval Institute Proceedings,* LXXXVI (September, 1960), 57–64.

Christian, William. "Don't Bet on Business Games," *Business Automation,* July, 1961, 22–25.

Clark, D. F. and Ackoff, R. L. "A Report on Some Organizational Experiments," *Operations Research,* VII (May, 1959), 279–93.

Cohen, Bernard C. "Political Gaming in the Classroom," *Journal of Politics,* XXIV (May, 1962), 367–81.

Cohen, Kalman J. and Rhenman, Eric. "The Role of Management Games in Education and Research," *Management Science,* VII (January, 1961), 131–66.

Collett, M. M. "Simulation as a Management Development Tool," *Personnel Administration,* XXV (March, 1962), 48–51.

Dill, William R. "What Management Games Do Best," *Business Horizons,* IV (Fall, 1961), 55–64.

Dill, William R., Hoffman, W., Leavitt, H. J., and O'Mara, T. "Some Educational and Research Results of a Complex Management Game," *California Management Review,* III (1961), 38–51.

Geisler, Murray A. and Steger, Wilbur A. "How to Plan for Management in

New Systems," *Harvard Business Review*, XL (September-October, 1962), 103–10.

Goldhamer, Herbert and Speier, Hans. "Some Observations on Political Gaming," *World Politics*, XII (October, 1959), 71–83.

Gray, J., *et al.* "Business Game for the Introductory Course in Accounting," *Accounting Review*, XXXVIII (April, 1963), 336–46.

Greene, J. R. "Business Gaming for Marketing Decisions," *Journal of Marketing*, XXV (July, 1960), 21–25.

Greenlaw, Paul S. "Designing Parametric Equations for Business Games," Academy of Management *Journal*, VI (June, 1963), 150–59.

Greenlaw, Paul S. and Kight, Stanford S. "The *Human Factor* in Business Games," *Business Horizons*, III (Fall, 1960), 55–61.

Haines, George H. "The Rote Marketer," *Behavioral Science*, VI (October, 1961), 357–65.

Haines, G., Heider, F., and Remington, D. "The Computer as a Small-Group Member," *Administrative Science Quarterly*, VI (December, 1961), 360–74.

Howard, W. D. "The Computer Simulation of a Colonial Socio-Economic System," *Proceedings* of the Western Joint Computer Conference, XIX (1961), 613–22.

Jacobson, L. and McGovern, P. J. "Computer Simulation of a National Economy," *Computers and Automation*, XI (August, 1962), 14–16.

Kinkade, Robert G. and Kidd, J. S. "The Use of an Operational Game as a Method of Task Familiarization," *Journal of Applied Psychology*, XLVI (February, 1962), 1–5.

Lockner, M. R. "Toward a General Simulation Capability," *Proceedings* of the Joint Computer Conference, Spring, 1962, 1–14.

McKenney, J. L. "Evaluations of a Business Game in an MBA Curriculum," *Journal of Business*, XXXV (July, 1962), 278–86.

McRaith, J. F. and Goeldner, Charles R. "A Survey of Marketing Games," *Journal of Marketing*, XXVI (July, 1962), 69–72.

Massy, William F., King, Peter S., and Fogg, C. Davis. "The Place of a Business Game in the Marketing Curriculum," *Industrial Management Review*, II (May, 1961), 43–58.

Megginson, Leon C. "Business Game as a Pedagogical Technique," *Southwestern Social Science Quarterly*, XL (1959), 33–40.

Nicholson, B. "Sales Management [Magazine] Plays the Game [at Burroughs Corporation]," *Sales Management*, LXXXVIII (January 19, 1962), 43–47.

Orcutt, Guy H., *et al.* "Simulation: A Symposium," *American Economic Review*, L (December, 1960), 893–932.

Pool, Ithiel de S., and Abelson, Robert. "Simulmatics Project," *Public Opinion Quarterly*, XXV (Summer, 1961), 167–83.

Sisson, R. L. "Games: Use in Operations Research and Management Science," *Systems and Procedures*, XII (May, 1961), 32–36.

Smit, O. G. "Simulation Exercises," *De Onderneming*, X, 20:723–25.

Smith, R. M. "Management Games: Toy or Trend," *Office Management and American Business*, XXI (September, 1960), 15–18+.

Sprouls, R. C. "The Role of Computer Simulation in Accounting Education," *Accounting Review*, XXXVII (July, 1962), 515–20.

Stanley, John D. "Management Games: Education or Entertainment?"

Personnel Journal, XLI (January, 1962), 15–17, 23.

Stern, M. E. "Catalytic Power of Business-Decision Gaming in Teaching Management Science," *Computers and Automation*, XI (November, 1962), 12–14+.

Thorelli, Hans B. "Review of 'Don't Bet on Business Games,' Business Automation July 1961, pp. 22–25, 66," *Computing Reviews*, November-December, 1961, 201.

———. "Simulate to Stimulate in International Marketing," *Proceedings* of the American Marketing Association, December, 1963.

Watkins, H. R. "Business Games in Business," *Operations Research Quarterly*, X (December, 1959), 228–44.

Webster, F. M. "Why Management Games?" *Data Processing*, III (August, 1961), 9–13.

Wegmueller, W. "Simulation de gestion a l'aide d'un calculateur électronique," *Revue économique et sociale*, XIX (October, 1961), 4:342.

Williams, E. H. "Business Games: Their Use for the Training of Managers," *Personnel Management*, XLIII (December, 1961), 239–44.

Zimmerman, R. E. "A Criterion for Realism in War Games," *Operations Research*, IX (November-December, 1961), 903–04.

3. *Published Materials on Specific Games*
A. BOOKS, MONOGRAPHS, MANUALS

Andlinger-Thorelli Marketing Management Game. Graduate School of Business, University of Chicago, 1961. (Mimeographed.) Introduces price as a variable in the original Andlinger game as described in G. R. Andlinger, "Business Games – Play One," *Harvard Business Review*, XXXVI (March-April, 1958), 115–25.

Anton, Hector. *The "A" Game General Information and Rules of Play*. Berkeley: School of Business Administration, University of California, October 23, 1962. (Mimeographed.)

Balderston, Frederick E. and Hoggatt, Austin C. *Simulation of Market Processes*. Berkeley: Institute of Business and Economic Research, University of California, 1962.

Bass, Bernard M. *Experimenting with Simulated Manufacturing Organizations*. Technical Report 27, Behavior in Groups Contract N70NR35609. Washington, D.C.: Group Psychology Branch, Office of Naval Research, March, 1961.

Benson, Oliver. *A Computer Simulation of International Politics*. Paper presented for the Midwest Conference of Political Scientists, Columbia, Mo., May 12, 1961.

Cohen, Kalman J., Dill, William R., Kuehn, A. A., and Winters, P. R. *The Carnegie Tech Management Game*. Homewood, Ill.: Irwin (announced for publication).

Dale, Alfred G., May, Francis B., Clark, Charles T., Lymberopoulos, P. John. *The Small-Business Executive Decision Simulation*. Three sections: I: Administrator's Manual, II: Background Report, III: Operating Manual. Austin, Tex.: Bureau of Business Research, The University of Texas, 1963. For Small Business Administration.

Day, Ralph L. *Marketing in Action: A Dynamic Business Decision Game*.

Homewood, Ill.: Irwin, 1962.

Forbes, John L. and Greene, Jay R. *The Top-Level Educational Planning Game: An Academic Management Decision-Making Aid for Institutions of Higher Learning.* Tempe, Ariz.: Arizona State University, 1961.

Greene, J. R. and Sisson, R. L. *Dynamic Management Decision Games, Including Seven Noncomputer Games.* London: Chapman and Hall, 1959.

Herron, Lowell W. *Executive Action Simulation.* Englewood Cliffs, N. J.: Prentice-Hall, 1960.

The European Institute of Business Administration (INSEAD). *INSEAD Marketing Business Game.* Fontainebleau, France: INSEAD, 1963.

Levitan, Richard and Shubik, Martin. *A Business Game for Teaching and Research Purposes.* Part I: General Description of the Game. IBM Co., July 17, 1962.

Linsup Game. Linen Supply Association of America, 22 West Monroe Street, Chicago 3, Ill. (Mimeographed.)

Manchester Executive Development Associates (MEDA). *Integrated Marketing and Production Decision-Making Exercise.* Manchester, England: Department of Industrial Administration of Manchester College of Science and Technology, March, 1963.

Martin, E. Wain. *Management Decision Simulation.* Homewood, Ill.: Irwin, 1961.

Murty, Varanasy S. *Management Game.* Bombay: Bombay University Press, 1960.

Olivetti-Bull. *Modello dinamico di gestione aziendale, descrizione del modello ITALIA 104.* Olivetti-Bull, n.d. (Mimeographed.)

Omre's Non-Computer Business Game. Oslo, Norway: Oddvar Omre, Eiksv. 45A, Röa, Oslo, January 15, 1960. (Mimeographed.)

Project SOBIG. *Player's Manual, Project SOBIG Stock Market Game.* Princeton, N. J.: Princeton University, Spring, 1961. (Mimeographed.)

Säljinstitutets Företagsledningsspel. Stockholm: Säljinstitutet, 1961. (Mimeographed.)

Thorelli, Hans B., Graves, Robert L., and Howells, Lloyd T. *The International Operations Simulation (INTOP) Player's Manual.* New York: Free Press of Glencoe, 1963.

Thorelli, Hans B. *See* also Andlinger.

Vance, Stanley. *Management Decision Simulation – A Noncomputer Business Game.* New York: McGraw-Hill, 1960.

Wagner, Harvey M. and Haldi, John. *Simulated Economic Models: A Laboratory Guide to Market Behavior.* Homewood, Ill.: Irwin (announced for publication).

Wagner, Helmut. *Planspiel III und Planspiel V.* Münster, Germany: Institut für industrielle Unternehmensforschung an der Universität Münster, 1963. (Mimeographed.)

B. ARTICLES

Agersnap, Torben and Johnsen, Erik. "Oekonomispil – et nyt redskab for forskning og undervisning i virksomhedsledelse," *Erhvervsoekon. Tidskrift* 1: 1–15, 1958.

Anon. "Students Become the Plant 'Managers,'" *Journal of College Placement*, February, 1962. The Procter and Gamble Company MATRIX Game.

———. "Teaching Computer to Dissect a Business," [Leviathan project will simulate operations of a corporation or any large group] *Business Week,* May 5, 1962, 60–62.

———. "Tycoon – A *Statist* Business Game," *The Statist,* CLXXVIII (December 21, 1962), 836–38.

Bloomfield, Lincoln P. and Padelford, N. J. "Three Experiments in Political Gaming," *American Political Science Review, LIII* (December, 1959), 1105–15.

Cohen, Kalman J., *et al.* "The Carnegie Tech Management Game," *Journal of Business,* XXXIII (October, 1960), 303–21.

Corbin, Arnold and Blagowidow, George. "A Decision Exercise in Inventory Management," *Stores,* March, 1963, 9–13.

Davison, W. Phillips. "A Public Opinion Game," *Public Opinion Quarterly,* XXV (Summer, 1961), 210–20.

Dennick, William H. and Olanie, Francis X., Jr. "The Bank Management Game," *Bankers Monthly,* LXXVII (September 15, 1960), 56–60.

Drury, J. "A Business Management Game," *Computer Bulletin,* VI (September, 1962), 57–60.

Hansen, Knud. "The Reinsurance Game – A Tool for Education and Research," *Journal of Insurance,* XXVIII (June, 1961), 2:11–18.

Hawkes, R. "Computer Simulates Executives' Problems [Lockheed's Aerospace Business Environment Simulator]," *Aviation Week,* LXXVI (June 18, 1962), 87+.

Hoggatt, Austin C. "An Experimental Business Game," *Behavioral Science,* IV (July, 1959), 192–203.

Kehl, William B. "Techniques in Constructing a Market Simulator" in *Marketing: A Maturing Discipline,* edited by Martin L. Bell, Chicago, American Marketing Association, 1961, 75–84. Description of the Pitt-Amstan Simulator.

Kennedy, M. "A Business Game for Accountants," *Journal of Accountancy,* CXIII (March, 1962), 219–22.

King, Peter S., *et al.* "The M.I.T. Marketing Game," in *Marketing: A Maturing Discipline,* edited by Martin L. Bell, Chicago, American Marketing Association, 1961, 85–102.

Litterer, Joseph A. "A Simulation of Organizational Behavior," Academy of Management *Journal,* V (April, 1962), 24–35.

McGuiness, John S. "A Managerial Game for an Insurance Company," *Operations Research,* VIII (March, 1960), 196–209.

Saxhaug, Asbjörn. "Företagsspelet – en träning för företagsledningen," *Affärsekonomi* 1:82–94, 1962. Swedish version of the Compagnie Machines Bull game UMPD 104.

Stanford Research Institute, "The Tribulations of Hawkeye – A Study in Planning," *Journal of the Stanford Research Institute,* V, Entire Issue, 4th Quarter, 1961.

Thompson, Donald L. "Next Sales Meeting – Try a Game," *Journal of Marketing,* XXVII (January, 1963), 71–74.

Thorelli, Hans B. "An International Business Operations Game," *Data Processing,* IV (October, 1962), 22–27.

Thorelli, Hans B., Graves, Robert L., and Howells, Lloyd T. "The International Operations Simulation at the University of Chicago," *Journal of Business,* XXXV (July, 1962), 287–97.

Williams, W. J. "Business Management Exercise," *Management International,* 3:127–44, 1962.

INDEX

THE READER should find the overall Table of Contents (pp. xii-xviii) and the special tables of contents of the Appendices (pp. 293-94) and of the Computer Liaison Instruction (p. 329) of much value as an index source. The *Player's Manual* has its own index. While this general index should be helpful no pretense is made for full coverage of even the items listed therein.

Bargaining, emphasis on, 275; negotia-
tion, 46; research in, by gaming, 7.
Bias of designers, in general, 13f; in
INTOP, 35ff, 44ff.
Binary cards, 332; program, 210f.
Boeing's Operation Interlock, 28.
Brand loyalty, 63n, 65.
See also Cross elasticity of prod-
ucts; Redistribution.
Brazil (Area 3), background data, 62ff.
Briefing, 32n, 150.
Business cycles, 68, 371; Economic
Index Wonder Card, 345; *Gazette*
sample, 377.
Business planning, see Planning.
Business policy course, 186ff.

Capacity, see Plant.
Capital, beginning, 57, 149, 191, 209,
243, 249; costs of, 66; finance game,
280ff.
Capital transfer tax, 39, 192; income
statement item, 312.
Captive sales organization, see Sales
offices.
Carnegie Institute of Technology game,
10, 13, 16f, 20, 26, 30, 178n.
Case method, and games compared,
26ff; INTOP as a case, 200.
Cash, adjustment by Wonder Card,
348; budgeting, 109.
Cash balance, minimum in Home Office, 59; parameter selection, 268.
Cash-flow analysis, 158, 164n, 179.
Cash transfer, between areas, 57n; between companies, 356; between
Home Office and areas, 50, 57.
Change, changing model parameters,
166, 230ff; changing number of
teams, 216ff; changing period num-
bers, 218; changing state variables,
221ff; changing time, 217; differ-
ential, 224; instruments of, 219ff;
multiple, 224.
See also Business cycles; Cost;
Dictionary; Environmental de-
velopments; Wonder Cards.
Channels of distribution, 54ff, 97ff,
201; system simulation, 287ff.
Chase-A-Martini, 159.
See also Bank loans.
Collusion, see Antitrust.
Commercial and Administrative ex-
pense, 65f, 76, 97ff, 255f.
Committee management, 163.
Common economies, 40ff, 49, 52, 153,
370.
Common stock, 150, 249, 281.
Companies, see Teams.
Competition, in consumer market, 89ff;
intra-team, 154; between teams, 146.
Competitive intelligence, 34, 70, 174,
178.

Compilation of FORTRAN program,
332ff.
Comprehension of model evaluated,
180.
Computerized game, value of, 11f.
Computer equipment, requirements,
144f, 215f.
Computer Liaison, 167f, 329-62.
Computer operations, 167, 207ff, 332ff,
351ff.
Computer processing, 116ff, 226.
Computer program, 116ff, 207ff; avail-
ability, 144.
Consecutive processing, see Processing.
Consolidated balance sheets, 213, 307f,
356; reproduced, 316.
See also Balance sheet.
Consolidated financial statements, 215.
Consolidated income statement, 213,
306f, 356; reproduced, 317.
See also Income statement.
Constraints, on parameter change,
240ff; resource, 142.
Consulting services, 73, 159n, 160.
Consumer market model, 92.
Consumer prices, see Price.
Consumer sales statistics, 71, 78.
Continuous play, 22, 152.
Continuous processing, see Processing.
Contract, see Standing contracts.
Control; administrative, 171.
Cost, analysis, 179; in changing rate
of output, 102f; in changing sales
offices, 98; of INTOP run, 145.
Costs, in INTOP model, 74ff.
See also Manufacturing costs.
Courses, 181ff.
See also Ch. 6.
Critique session, 23f, 202ff.
Cross elasticity of products, 90, 92, 145,
262, 273.
Currency revaluation, 192f.

Damages, 195.
Data, evaluating comprehension, 180;
processing routines, 179.
See also Information.
Dataphone system, 23.
"Debriefing," see Critique session.
Decision forms, 208; reproduced, 321-
23.
Decision-making, group, 29, 35, 146,
172, 202f.
Decision periods, changing period numbers, 218; number of, 18, 21, 42;
telescoping initial periods, 154; telescoping periods, 217.
Decision rules, definition, 231; in extending time span of decisions, 176.
Decisions, deliberate, 164; fine for late
decisions, 157; time available, 21,
176.

Market dynamics, 43.

Market potential, adjustment easy, 148; automatically adjusted in certain cases, 145, 209, 217; in INTOP, 62ff, 74f; selection, 252; use of monitor, 166.

Marketing, cost, 97; management, 53; research in, by gaming, 5; simulation, 279f, 287ff; tasks, 118, 122ff.

Marketing effectiveness index, 195, 221, 357.

Marketing management course, 183ff.

Marketing manager, sample job description, 380ff.

Marketing research, 60f, 70ff, 132f, 160, 162, 201, 259; list of services, 78f; Market Research Item 17-18, 337ff; Market Research output 1, 314; Market Research output 2, 319; number of items per period, 242.

Master control card, 117, 210ff, 218, 348; reproduced, 212.

Mathematical models, see Ch. 3.

MATRIX game, 7n, 11n.

Measurement, see Evaluation.

Memos, No. 1 Earliest Possible Decision Sequence, 369; No. 2 Common Economies, 370; No. 3 Economic Indices, 371; No. 4 Plant Disposal, 372; No. 5 Mergers, 373.

Mergers, 147, 160f, 373.

Methods improvement, 51, 104, 106, 243, 257.

MIT marketing game, 11, 20.

Models, 35ff.
   See also Ch. 3.

Monitor company, 166, 191, 331.

Multi-period processing, 212.

Multiple changes by Wonder Card, 224f.

Multi-product simulation, 284.

Mutual evaluation, within and among teams, 202ff.

National Science Foundation award, 156.

Negotiation, see Bargaining.

Nichemanship, 41.

Non-interactive simulations, 11, 275ff.

Non-optimal decisions, 115.

Number of, periods, see Decision periods; teams, see Teams.

Objectives, see Goals.

Observation of teams, 180.

Obsolescence, 104, 263; of goods, 53; of plants, 51.

Operating expense, see Commercial and Administrative expense; Production; Inventory; Interest rates; Transfer cost.

Operating statements reproduced, balance sheet, 311; income statement, 312.

Operations card, 321.

Optimal plant capacity, 115, 260.

Oral presentation, 32n, 150.

Order of tasks, 121ff.

Organization, committee management, 163; division of labor, 153; organization and policy courses, 186ff; research by gaming, 5ff, 271ff; simulation by gaming, 387ff; of teams in INTOP, 36f, 48, 151ff, 172.

Orienting participants, 150f.

Output, 172; computer, 207ff, 211; copies, 169, 213; printing, 216.

Outside experts, use of, 150, 194.

Paid-in-capital, 107, 195.
   See also Stock market confidence.

Parameters, 116; area and product variations, 232; change, 166; choice and change, 230ff; current parameter values, 209n; elimination of, 265; program, 225; range of values, 230ff.

Participants, see Teams.

Patent licenses, 49, 61f, 77; procedures in processing, 339; sample form reproduced, 327.

Patents, see Patent licenses; Research and Development.

Performance, 7, 25f, 31, 195ff.
   See also Evaluation.

Periods of decision-making, see Decision periods.

Personnel, needed in INTOP, 143; testing, 7n.

Pitt-Amstan Simulator, 8, 22, 28.

Planning, evaluating, 198, 204; long-range 20, 29, 34, 159, 176; use of games in, 8.

Plant, acquisition, 51, 74, 250; capacity, 66, 74; construction period, 50, 87; disposal, 51, 160f, 358ff, 372; number of, 51, 241; overhead, 100; renewal, 160f.
   See also Depreciation; Limit on grades; Methods improvement; Obsolescence.

Player's Manual, 69, 181, 209, 230.
   See also entire Ch. 2.

Plugboards, 178n.

Policy, experimentation simulation, 275f.
   See also Business policy course.

Position descriptions, 204; sample, 380f.

Predetermined objectives, 149.

President, role of, 153, 186.

Price, elasticities, 82, 84, 90, 262; limit on price, 53, 243, 251f; posted when no inventory, 331n; role in economic model, 89ff; sensitivity to price, 64;